The C/Unix
Programmer's Guide

Jason W. Bacon

This book was typeset using *Another Programmer's Editor* (APE) and LaTeX 2.09 running under *FreeBSD* 2.1.7 on a 486-based PC. All figures were produced using `xfig` or `xwd`, converted to *Postscript* using `fig2dev` or *Netpbm*, and incorporated into the LaTeX document using `psfig`. (Later editions will most likely use LaTeX2e and `includegraphics`.) The DVI output was converted to *Postscript* using `dvips`. The cover was produced and exported to *Postscript* using `xfig`. All major program examples were tested under *FreeBSD* 2.1.7. Some programs were also tested under SCO OpenServer 5.0.4, Slackware Linux 3.2, and Sun Sparc Solaris 2.6.

Library of Congress Catalog Card Number: 99-72453

ISBN 0-9670596-0-7

http://www.execpc.com/acadix
acadix@execpc.com

Acknowledgments

Special thanks to the following people for their efforts and editorial feedback...

Dina M. Bacon

John Keenan III

Phil Marden

Vesna Vukotic

Chris Weerts

Contents

List of Figures

List of Tables

Chapter 1

Introduction

1.1 How to Proceed

My primary objective in writing this text is to provide the reader with enough knowledge and insight to become a confident, self sufficient, and well-rounded Unix programmer. I hope that each section provides more than enough information to help you reach a clear, basic understanding of the subject at hand. At the same time, I have taken care to avoid presenting too much detail in any one area, so that the reading will always remain fresh and engaging.

Unix is well known for its detailed (and often cryptic) on-line manuals, commonly called **man pages**. While the man pages provide a wealth of detailed information on virtually every aspect of Unix, they tend to be *very* difficult to learn new subjects from, mainly because they are written as references rather than tutorials. This text is intended to serve as a starting point for investigations into many common areas of Unix programming. After reading the appropriate sections in this text, you will be much better prepared to understand and utilize the vast information available in the on-line manuals. This text will provide you with all the information you need to tackle many complex Unix programming tasks, and if you ever need more, you will likely be able to find it in the man pages.

The book is organized primarily as a tutorial on using C in the Unix environment, with each chapter building on the essentials of the previous chapter. I have made every attempt to keep each chapter as pure and focused as possible, so that the chapters may be covered in a different order than presented, and so that the book will also serve as a well-organized reference for experienced users.

Each chapter consists of some or all of the following components:

- What to read first

  For most chapters, except the first few, some prior knowledge must be assumed. At the beginning of each chapter is a brief explanation of what you should know before diving in. This will hopefully ensure the chapters are read in a logical order, if not the order in which they are presented.

- Essentials

  The early sections of each chapter cover the essential topics for beginning C programmers. If you're in a hurry to get through, you can just read the *essentials* sections and come back to the more advanced sections later. This will allow you to quickly gain an overall understanding without getting bogged down in too many details.

- Performance

  C and Unix are both known for their unparalleled performance. As such, performance issues are integrated throughout the text. Wherever applicable, a discussion is included of factors that affect performance. General tips are provided for maximizing speed and minimizing resource usage.

- Portability

  Portability is another major advantage provided by C and Unix. As with performance, portability issues are integrated throughout the text, and presented alongside each topic. Many programmers achieve portability by paraphrasing sections of code for each system they port to. The tips provided here are aimed at showing you how to avoid this trap, and produce code that will run on any Unix system without redundancy or alterations.

- Advanced topics

  Sections marked as *advanced* cover more intricate details of C programming. The advanced topics are an important part of C programming, and should be covered by every reader eventually. However, novice C programmers may prefer to skip them initially in favor of moving on to more fundamentals in the next chapter.

There are many facts about languages, hardware, and technique, that are important for programmers to know. My goal in writing this text is to provide insight and understanding, rather than just facts and formulas. Rather than leave potentially distracting loose ends in the readers' minds, I prefer to explain the underlying concepts to a reasonable level.

For example, it is important to know that computer number systems have range and accuracy limitations. Awareness of this fact is crucial to good programming, and knowing the cause of these limitations increases awareness. Therefore, I have provided a brief explanation of how to determine range and accuracy of binary number systems.

In order to get the most out of your reading, I strongly recommend typing in and running the examples given, or better yet, similar short programs of your own design. Simply reading on without taking some time to practice what you've learned will leave your knowledge of the subject vague and ineffective.

Proficiency at any task comes from the *time spent* doing it. The familiar Chinese term "Kung Fu" (sometimes spelled "Gung Fu") is often translated as simply "time spent". To those who practice it, Kung Fu represents the lifelong accumulation of skill, strength, and character gained from hard work, practice, and attention to detail. Take some time to solidify your understanding of each fundamental so that you *get it right before moving on* to more advanced material. In the long run, a little time spent practicing will save you a great deal of time in reviewing.

1.2 Why use C?

C is currently the world's most widely used programming language. C is available for virtually every computer and every operating system.

C was originally designed as a high-level systems programming language, which could be used as a substitute for assembly language. The design goals of C were to create a portable language that would produce machine code that is nearly as fast as assembly language, and would allow programmers to do virtually *anything*. The design was so successful, that about 90% of the original Unix operating system was written in C, the other 10% being assembly language. Most other high level languages are much more restrictive, which is why earlier operating systems had to be written in assembly language. Soon after its creation, C became popular with application programmers, due in large part to its elegance, portability, and efficiency.

Since C allows the programmer a great deal of freedom, C programming requires plenty of self-discipline. Like any powerful tool, C can cause some problems when misused. If, however, you're serious about programming, and your goal is to write lightening-fast, highly portable programs, then C is one of the most important languages to know.

As mentioned earlier, there are many reasons for the popularity of C. A few of the key features of C are discussed below.

1.2.1 C is Fast

The job of a compiler is to translate high-level language programs to machine language. C compilers tend to produce tighter (smaller) and faster machine code than other high-level languages. This is because C is less abstract than many other high-level languages, i.e. C is designed to work with hardware features, rather than hide them. In fact, it is sometimes referred to as a **high-level assembler**. This is not to say that C resembles assembly language: it doesn't even begin to. However, it does provide many of the features that are otherwise only available in assembly language.

Generally, the efficiency of languages can be ranked as follows:

1. Assembly language (unbeatably fast, but not portable)

2. C

3. Other simple compiled languages (Pascal, FORTRAN)

4. Complex compiled languages (C++, PL/1[1])

5. Byte-interpreted languages (BASIC, JAVA, PERL)[2]

6. Raw interpreted languages (Shell scripts)

On today's hardware, a program written in just about any language may seem fast enough to get the job done, especially if you test it on a state-of-the-art personal workstation. There are some important things to consider, however. For instance, your users may simply be running the program on slower computers with less memory and disk resources. In addition, your software may be run on systems under heavy load. It's common for Unix workstations to support hundreds of simultaneous users. If your software uses more CPU time, memory, or disk resources than necessary, it might not be noticeable on your development platform, but could have serious consequences on a more heavily used system.

There are many new tools and languages available that make programming easier, especially special-purpose programming, such as database management, WEB site design, etc. Some use a layered approach to hide the low-level details of programming. With each layer, however, comes a loss of performance.

Interpreted languages such as JAVA, BASIC, and Perl can be tens or hundreds of times slower than C for some programs, and will use substantially more memory. The reason is simply that interpreted languages require an interpreter to run the program. Interpreters, being roughly equivalent to compilers, are complex programs which tend to be slow and use a lot of memory.

Inevitably, programmers are going to take advantage of today's faster computers by programming at a higher level, using slower interpreted languages such as JAVA or PERL. These are perfectly acceptable languages for light-duty computing, or for infrequently used programs, and can save the programmer a significant amount of work.

If, however, a program is computationally intensive, or will be run by many users simultaneously on the same system, C becomes a very attractive choice.

---

[1]PL/1 (Programming Language 1), is a general purpose high-level language used on IBM mainframes, which supports many of the features of FORTRAN, COBOL, and Pascal.

[2]Byte-interpreted languages have their keywords and other components compressed to one-byte codes before the program is run, so that the interpreter can identify them more quickly. Byte code dramatically improves program speed for interpreted languages, but is still many times slower than a compiled program.

1.2.2   C is powerful

It has been said that C is the only programming language the world needs. This is true in that any programming job *can* be done in C. C is commonly used to write an enormous variety of programs such as editors, compilers, CAD (Computer Aided Design) systems, database managers, games, and even entire operating systems such as Unix.

Of course, there are cases where writing a C program is not the easiest, or the best solution. Specialized tasks such as database queries are more easily written in SQL[3], for example.

Also, certain parts of operating systems are more conveniently or efficiently written in assembly language.

1.2.3   C is portable

The C language is widely available for all kinds of hardware and operating systems. Many programs written in C can be easily recompiled on other operating systems, although it is occasionally difficult to port programs between vastly different operating systems, such as Unix and *DOS* (Disk Operating System) or *MVS* (Multiple Virtual System, IBM's mainframe operating system).

Most important to this discussion is the fact that C is nearly 100% portable across Unix platforms. C programs written on a personal computer running Unix can very easily be recompiled on RISC (Reduced Instruction Set Computer) workstations or mainframes running their own brands of Unix. This has become even more true with the recent adoption of standards such as IEEE (Institute of Electrical and Electronic Engineers) POSIX (Portable Operating System Interface) and X/OPEN (X Windows Open Standard). Older versions of Unix also tend to adhere to standards such as BSD (Berkeley Systems Distribution) or SYS V (System 5).

By using C and Unix together, you will never be dependent on one specific hardware or software vendor, as is often the case with other platforms such as *Windows* or *MVS*. Unix runs on practically any type of hardware, and C is available for *all* brands of Unix.

---

[3]SQL (Structured Query Language) is a special purpose language for specifying database operations

1.2.4   C is small and flexible

The C language itself is quite minimal compared with other high-level languages. This makes it relatively easy to produce a C compiler for new hardware platforms. The C compiler recognizes only about 30 keywords, compared to more than 500 for some of the largest languages, such as PL/1.

The reason C is so small is because most of its functionality is in its libraries – sets of pre-compiled functions (subprograms) stored in archives. The orignal designer of C, Dennis Ritchie of AT&T, carefully avoided including any feature in the language itself if it could be provided by other means.

1.2.5   C is Popular

C is the most commonly used programming language of the past two decades. Whether or not this is a good reason to use C is a matter of philosophy. Nevertheless, it motivates everyone in the industry to continue using the language. Millions of programs have been written in C, and even if a better language existed for the job, it would take an enormous investment of time and money to rewrite them. Therefore, the popularity of C is likely to continue long into the future.

As a case in point, it's worth noting that virtually *all* GNU software is written in C. In fact, the GNU coding standards, which can be found at *http://www.gnu.org*, specifically urge contributing programmers to write all *new* GNU software in C, and provide a long list of reasons for doing so.

1.2.6   C vs. other languages

C is referred to as a **procedural** language. This means a C program describes a procedure for solving a problem, much like a recipe explains how to make a stir-fry. Other examples of procedural languages include Pascal, FORTRAN, and PL/1.

Object oriented programming, or OOP, focuses more on the structure of the *data*, rather than the structure of the algorithm. The idea is to encourage a more in-depth analysis of the problem, which will result in better organized, and more reusable code. C++, Small-talk, and JAVA are all examples of languages with object oriented support.

So how does one choose between C and C++? First, you should be aware that C++ is a *superset* of C. This means that a C++ compiler recognizes all of the constructs of

Language	Executable	Stripped executable	Memory use
C	3811	2436	820k
C++	18033	5364	1052k

Table 1.1: Size of C and C++ Executables

C, and more. Most of the added constructs support the object oriented programming style.

However, C++ does not *enforce* the object oriented style. This fact has contributed to the success of the language, since it allows existing, non object-oriented C code to be compiled with a C++ compiler. Unfortunately, it also creates loopholes that allow new C++ code to be written with little or no adherence to good OO programming practices. If you choose to use C++ for it's object oriented features, it's entirely up to you to maintain good object oriented practices when you code. Just choosing an OO language doesn't make you an OO programmer.

Furthermore, C++ programs tend to be significantly larger than equivalent C programs, due to the inclusion of bulky class constructs used in C++. They are also often noticeably slower, due to a more complex machine code format, and other factors. Table 1.1 shows the differences between the C and C++ versions of a small C program compiled and run on *Linux*. Note that the two executables were produced from the exact same source code, one through `gcc` (the GNU C compiler) and the other through `g++` (the GNU C++ compiler). The differences between C and C++ will vary, depending on the compilers used, and are not always this dramatic. However, C++ executables will generally be noticeably larger than their C counterpart, especially where C++ class libraries are used heavily.

Most importantly, unlike C, C++ is a *highly complex language*, with many features that even experienced programmers have some difficulty learning.

On the other hand, the object-oriented features of C++, if used properly, can be a helpful guide to produce more maintainable code, which will reduce maintenance time down the road. This is a highly valuable feature, since programmer time is by far the most costly factor in program development.

The approach I recommend is to learn C first, and then tackle C++ when you're better prepared for it's complexities. This way, you'll be dealing with a much simpler language as a beginner, and will gain important experience with procedural programming. Note that object oriented programming is an *extension* to procedural programming, rather than an *alternative*. Using C++ as your first programming language will mean learning both procedural and OO techniques, as well as a highly complicated language syntax. All of this can cause quite a bit of confusion, even to the most talented beginners. Learning to program is hard enough already, so starting with a simple language is a wise move that can make the experience much more enjoyable.

1.3 Why use Unix?

The Unix operating system was carefully designed from its conception, to take full advantage of hardware features, allowing all types of terminals, multiple concurrent processes, multiple users, and so on.

Most other operating systems, on the other hand, were initially designed to meet a particular need, and gradually had new features pasted on in order to keep up with their competitors. This latter approach has in most cases led to poorly integrated systems, with some rather obvious design flaws.

DOS, for example, was designed to run on a small personal computer, often with as little as 128 kilobytes of memory and only a single floppy disk for long term storage. As part of it's original design, *DOS* imposed an inherent 640 kilobyte memory limitation on user programs. This early design flaw has caused enormous expense in attempts to expand the capabilities of *DOS*-based PC's. Techniques such as expanded memory and extended memory have allowed recent versions to utilize the greater memory capacity of 286, 386, 486 and Pentium processors. These techniques temporarily switch the CPU into **protected mode** in order to access memory beyond the 1 megabyte boundary. The normal mode used by *DOS*, called **real mode**, is limited to 1 megabyte since the CPU generates 20 bit addresses in this mode. The *DOS* operating system further reduces available memory to 640 kilobytes, and reserves the upper 384 kilobytes for operating system use. Using expanded and extended memory can reduce program performance by a factor of 3 or more, compared to the same program running within the 640k boundary. All this mode switching takes time, and makes memory management very complicated.

MVS, the popular IBM mainframe operating system, was designed to work with punch cards, and creating more user-friendly interfaces has proven very difficult. The IBM 3270 terminals now used with *MVS* are essentially electronic punch-card emulators, sending and receiving 1920 character (80 × 24) screen images. Truly interactive operation (e.g. response to individual keystrokes) is virtually unheard of in the *MVS* environment. *MVS* also has a 16 megabyte memory limit similar to the

640k limit of *DOS*. As with *DOS*, recent versions of *MVS* have found a way around this limitation, but remnants of the 16 megabyte limit are still noticeable.

The designers of Unix were able to produce a simple, elegant, and seamless system by learning from nearly two decades of experiences in system design that began in the 1950's. Unix was developed at AT&T Bell Laboratories around 1970, and since then has served as a model for operating system study. Unix has dominated academic and scientific computing for a long time. Unix is gradually gaining popularity in the business world as well, as older, more expensive, multiuser systems such as *MVS* and *VMS* (Virtual Memory System) are gradually phased out. The phenomenal advances in microcomputer technology are largely responsible for this trend. A typical desktop PC today can outperform the large, expensive mainframes and minicomputers of the 1970's for a tiny fraction of the cost. Most businesses are going through a "down-sizing" phase, replacing their mainframes and minicomputers with PC's or RISC workstations. Many of the newer operating systems, such as *DOS*, *OS/2*, and *Windows* are essentially subsets of Unix. Their appearance and functionality closely mimic features of Unix, but they lack many important features such as multiuser support and platform independence.

To date, no operating system has proven more powerful or elegant. We will discuss a few of the major features here for comparison.

1.3.1   Portability

One of the most important Unix design decisions was to focus on *source code* compatibility, rather than *binary* (machine code) compatibility. Two systems that are source compatible can share programs, even if they use entirely different hardware. The only requirement is that the programs need to be compiled separately on each system, which is usually a trivial matter. Binary compatible systems will run the same programs without recompiling, but must use the same type of hardware. Maintaining binary compatibility over long periods of time requires hardware manufacturers to design their new hardware to mimic existing hardware, and prevents them from implementing many new and possibly beneficial innovations.

Unix is currently the *only* operating system which runs on many different types of computers. This fact alone provides Unix with an enormous economic advantage. Software developers can write new programs on PC's running Unix, and very easily port them to other Unix platforms, such as RISC workstations, mainframes and supercomputers running their own brand of Unix. Even as hardware manufacturers come and go, your existing Unix programs can live on with very few changes. In

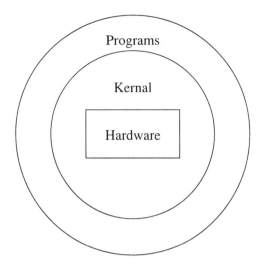

Figure 1.1: The Unix kernel encapsulates hardware

addition, there are many different companies that sell and support their own versions of Unix, so you'll never be entirely dependent on one vendor.

The key to portability is in the Unix **kernel**. The Unix kernel hides, or **encapsulates** the hardware, and in doing so, blocks ordinary programs from directly accessing it. (Figure 1.1) Any time a Unix program needs use to a hardware resource, it must send a request to the kernel. The details of kernel design are beyond the scope of this book, but are discussed in many assembly language or operating systems texts. [14, 15]

The Unix kernel ensures portability by providing a *standard* program interface for all types of hardware. Programs written in high-level languages for Unix are almost completely oblivious to the type of hardware they will run on. If you want to upgrade from a PC running Unix to a *Sun Sparc* workstation, you will *not* need to rewrite all your software. The programs will need to be recompiled (ported) to the *Sun Sparc* machine language, but the C source code will require little change, if any. Unix programs that took years to develop can usually be ported to entirely different hardware platforms in a matter of hours.

For example, a Unix program that needs to receive input must use the `read()` function. The `read()` function provides a *standard* interface to the Unix kernel, and is an example of a **system call**. The `read()` function is called exactly the same way on every Unix system, regardless of what type of computer is running it or what type of input device is being used. Many details of how the `read()` function works are defined by the **POSIX** (Portable Operating System Interface base on Unix) standard.

In contrast, the *DOS* and *Windows* kernels do not entirely encapsulate the hardware. (Figure 1.2) As a result, porting *DOS* or *Windows* software to another system usually involves rewriting major portions of it. This includes the so-called "well-behaved" programs, which allow *DOS* or *Windows* to perform all their hardware control. Even though well-behaved programs don't access specific hardware directly, they are written with *DOS* or *Windows* system calls, and these systems only run on PC compatibles. To complicate matters further, there are many different compilers available for *DOS* and Windows, and they are not compatible with each other. Programs written in Borland C, for example, will generally not compile under Microsoft C, or Watcom C.

Other operating systems have similar restrictions. Even other protected mode operating systems such as *OS/2* and *Windows NT* will only run on one or two different platforms, and the interfaces they provide to programs are very different from each other. It is often very difficult to port software from *OS/2* to *Windows NT*, from *MVS* to *OS/2*, etc.

Writing programs for Unix is one way to guarantee that they'll still be usable when the next generation of hardware arrives.

1.3.2   Stability

The encapsulating kernel also provides a level of stability that cannot be approached by any other means. By controlling all hardware resources, the kernel prevents flawed and malicious programs from bringing down the system, or causing problems for other programs. Since programs *must* ask the kernel to perform all hardware operations for them, it isn't possible for one Unix program to interfere with the operation of others. Programs that attempt to do so, whether accidentally or maliciously, are terminated by the kernel. Such terminations are usually accompanied by the creation of a **core dump** file, which the programmer can use to instantly track down the problem in the offending program.

It is fairly common for Unix systems to run for more than a year at a time without experiencing a system crash. This is because problems that occur with Unix tend to reside at the surface, rather than at the foundation. You can compare problems with your operating system to problems with your house. If you own a well-built house that needs a paint job, you're in pretty good shape, even though your neighbors can't stand the sight of it at the moment. On the other hand, if your house if beautiful

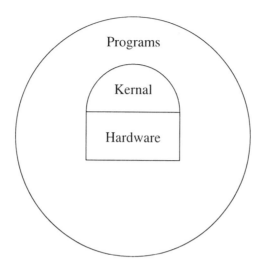

Figure 1.2: Model of the *DOS* kernel

on the outside, but the foundation is weak and unstable, there isn't much you can do besides tear it down and rebuild it from scratch. If you choose your operating systems based on the "paint job", you'll eventually pay the price in aggrevation. With a little knowledge of how operating systems work internally, you'll be better prepared to choose an operating system that will serve you well for the long term.

In contrast, the *DOS* kernel provides hardware control services, but it *does not* prevent programs from taking control of hardware directly. In fact, many *DOS* programs do bypass the operating system and control hardware on their own, often because the *DOS* kernel simply doesn't offer the services they need. (Figure 1.2) For instance, DOS has no interrupt-driven serial port drivers, so programs must include their own, or utilize a special library of functions which is purchased separately from DOS. Many *DOS* program bugs go unnoticed, since the kernel doesn't mediate between the programs and hardware. The results are generally unpredictable. *DOS* programs can and often do corrupt areas of memory occupied by the kernel or other software, causing severe problems and even system lock ups.

Programs that access hardware only through the *DOS* kernel, and never directly, are deemed "well-behaved". Well-behaved *DOS* programs generally create fewer problems if the *DOS* configuration is changed. They are also more likely to run properly on *DOS* emulators, which are available for *Windows, OS/2* and many Unix systems.

The *Windows* kernel provides much improved services, but also does not completely encapsulate the hardware. As a result, certain program bugs under *Windows* can cause system failures.

1.3.3   Power, performance, and Scalability

As mentioned earlier, Unix was designed from its conception to get the most out of any hardware. There are a wide variety of Unix brands available for Intel PC's, and they tend to outperform other PC operating systems by a wide margin. Figure 21.1 (page 453) shows the results of a simple benchmark test comparing Unix and *Windows* on the same machine.

On a larger scale, since Unix is portable, you won't outgrow Unix even as you outgrow your hardware. Unix runs the SAME software on anything from an Intel PC to a Cray supercomputer or mainframe. The cost of porting your code from *SCO Unix* on a PC to *Amdahl UTS* on a 3090 mainframe is a tiny fraction of what it would cost to port all your *Windows* software to a new platform. Even if Unix is more than you need right now, the costs of converting your entire software base to a new OS later should be a motivating factor in selecting Unix from the start.

For example, adding host capabilities (e.g. the ability to use the system from a remote location) to a *Windows* PC is impractical at best. While it is possible with the right software (such as *PC Anywhere*), *Windows* simply lacks many of the features to make it practical to use on a regular basis. *Windows* is designed to be a single user system, with no security features in a normal installation. Thus, any additions made to allow remote access must be accompanied by the addition of some sort of security package. Furthermore, accessing a PC remotely with *PC Anywhere* *requires* a relatively fast network connection (don't even try it with a modem). You must also use a similar PC as the remote terminal, and *PC Anywhere* must be installed on *both* machines. A true host operating system, such as Unix, allows users to access it using virtually any type of terminal hardware with a network or modem connection, and *no* special software needs to be installed on either end.

As another example, creating a `make`[4] facility under *MVS* is essentially impossible, since *MVS* doesn't record the modification times of its data sets (files). Such time stamps are essential in order for `make` to function properly.

Fortunately, the designers of Unix were aware of the problems caused by such limitations, and went to great lengths to ensure that Unix would not present any similar problems.

---

[4]Make is a standard programming tool on Unix systems which allows programs to be updated automatically after any source files have been altered.

1.3.4 Multitasking

Another benefit of Unix is it's *true* multitasking features. In true multitasking, the computer runs several programs essentially at the same time, by letting them take turns using hardware resources such as the CPU, memory, and disk.[5] None of the programs are placed on hold indefinitely, and all will progress toward completion. Hence, while you edit a letter, and the word processor is waiting for you to press a key, the computer can also perform a file transfer, process your latest payroll, or solve your matrix equations. The computer will spend some of it's time on each of the programs until they are all completed. Instead of sitting idle while you think about what to type next, the CPU can be kept busy running other programs for you or someone else. Operating systems with true multitasking include Unix, *MVS*, *VMS*, *CMS*, *OS/2* and *Windows NT*, to name a few.

DOS is an example of a single-task operating system, because it can only run one program at a time. It isn't capable of running other programs while it waits for you to type the next character of a letter. *Windows 3.1* and *Windows 95* have multitasking capabilities which are somewhat limited, partly due to their compatibility with *DOS*.

1.3.5 Multiuser support

Unix also allows multiple users to work on the same computer simultaneously, provided each person has their own *terminal*. Terminal types vary from simple ASCII terminals costing about \$100 to sophisticated Xwindow servers with *Windows* and graphic capabilities, at a thousand dollars or more. Given the power of today's desktop computers, it is possible for hundreds of users to work on a single PC running Unix. Another advantage is that users can share data without the need for complicated and expensive local area networks.

Other multiuser operating systems tend to be restricted to big, expensive mainframes or minicomputers. *MVS* (Multiple Virtual System) is the primary operating system for the IBM 360 family of mainframe computers. *VMS* (Virtual Memory System) is a multiuser OS for Digital Equipment Corporation's VAX computers. It's probably worth noting that Unix is also available for both the 360 family and the VAX. *Amdahl UTS* is a Unix clone for the IBM 360 series, and *DEC Ultrix* and *BSD* (Berkeley Systems Division) are commonly used on VAX computers.

---

[5]A typical modern Unix system runs each active program for 1/100th of a second before rotating control to the next one in line.

OS/2 and *Windows NT* both offer true multitasking, but only support a single user. Therefore, each user must have their own computer with a registered copy of the operating system, which can get very expensive. If users want to share data, they will need to exchange floppy disks or tapes, or set up a local area network.

1.3.6   Simplicity and Elegance

We'll close this sales pitch with a discussion of one of the most revered features of Unix – simplicity. The design of Unix was based largely on an earlier system called Multics. Multics was the result of an early attempt to design a complete, seamlessly integrated system. Unfortunately, Multics turned out to be far too large to run on most computers of the time. The designers of Unix learned from both the successes and failures of Multics, and managed to design a greatly simplified model of the system, which was eventually implemented as Unix. Initially, Unix was small enough to run on 16-bit DEC PDP (Programmed Data Processor) minicomputers.

Since then, Unix has grown tremendously, but the basic elegance of it's design has remained. Each problem posed by operating system design was solved in the simplest and most generalized way possible. In many cases, the design philosophy is not obvious, but upon examination you'll tend to see that it *is* extremely flexible and efficient. Many features from basic file security and encryption, to hard and soft links, may seem strange at first, but ingenious once you understand them.

More than any other operating system in existence, Unix is free of arbitrary limitations and contingencies that might complicate your job as a programmer. For example, *DOS* limits programs to 640 kilobytes of memory, and also imposes limits on the size of a disk partition. The solutions to these problems came in the form of *additional* OS features, like extended memory, expanded memory, and extended partitions, all of which are a nuisance to the programmer and user alike. Unix systems, in contrast, have few software-imposed limits, and the few limits that do exist are usually well beyond the capabilities of current hardware. For example, most current versions of Unix allow partitions, and even individual files, to be many times the size of a typical hard disk. As you gain experience with Unix, you'll see many examples of its elegance, and hopefully learn to follow its clean and simple problem solving approach.

Part I

Introduction to Computers and Unix

Chapter 2

Binary Information Systems

2.1 Why do I need to know this stuff?

A firm understanding of computer hardware is essential to becoming a good programmer, regardless of the language being used. By understanding the computer's behavior, you will be better equipped to program it.

The goal here is not to teach digital design, but simply to de-mystify computer hardware enough to provide a foundation for learning solid programming skills. Without this foundation, many of the programming concepts presented may leave you wondering what's happening behind the scenes. On the other hand, a solid understanding of the underlying hardware will help you become comfortable with new concepts more quickly and easily. While an in-depth knowledge of binary is not necessary for most types of high-level programming, it is helpful to just about everyone who programs.

2.2 Representing Information in Binary

All of the information inside a computer, stored on a disk, or passing across a network is represented in **binary**. Binary is the general name for any system that represents information as patterns of 0's and 1's.

Binary really isn't much different from the traditional ways we represent information. Our Arabic numbers are simply patterns of 10 decimal digits, and our English words are patterns of the 26 letters from the alphabet. Each has a simple set of rules that state how digits are combined to represent numbers, or letters to form words. The binary alphabet consists of only the two symbols 0 and 1. In this respect, binary is the simplest way possible to represent information.

The reason for using binary has to do with hardware cost. The fewer symbols we use to represent a piece of information, the easier it is to build digital electronic circuits that can work with it. For example, a decimal digital circuit would have to be capable of accurately maintaining ten different voltage levels to represent the digits 0 through 9. Binary digital circuits, on the other hand, need only two states, representing 0 and 1. Typically, a 0 is represented by the absence of voltage or current, and 1 is represented by a positive voltage such as 5V for TTL (Transistor-Transistor Logic) or 12V for MOS (Metal Oxide Semiconductor).

It's a good idea for any programmer to learn more about binary and computer hardware by taking courses in digital logic, machine language, and computer architecture. (See [9] and [10]) We will discuss some bare essentials here to help build a basic understanding of hardware. It isn't necessary to know all the nuances of your computer's inner workings, but a firm grasp of how the main components work will do wonders for your programming skills.

2.2.1   The Usual Jargon

A few terms are necessary for discussing binary. A **bit** is a binary digit, i.e. a 0 or 1. A **byte** is a package of 8 bits. A **word** is a package of bits whose size depends on the type of computer, and refers to the largest number of bits that the computer can process at once. A 32 bit computer, for example, has a 32 bit word. Hence, a 32 bit computer is inherently faster than a 16 bit computer with similar features, since the 16 bit computer would need to perform two operations to compute a single 32 bit result. A **long word** is a somewhat standardized term that usually refers to 32 bits. Similarly, a **short word** is generally agreed to be 16 bits. Both of these terms are used by the C language. A rather uncommon term that might pop up on occasion is the **nybble**, which represent 4 bits. Most computers can't process data packets smaller than a byte, so nybbles aren't generally important to programmers.

2.2.2   Binary Number Systems

Binary number systems are very similar to the decimal systems we work with every day. The only difference is that binary systems use a base of 2, whereas decimal uses a base of 10.

The abstract number systems we use can represent numbers from negative infinity to positive infinity. Computers, however, are finite machines and therefore have some limitations.

There are two common types of number systems used by computers:

Fixed point numbers are a limited variation of our familiar Arabic numeral system. It's called fixed point because the system has a fixed number of whole digits and a fixed number of fractional digits, so that the decimal point (or binary point) is always in the same location.

For example, a 4 digit fixed point decimal number with 2 fractional digits would always have the form ##.##. The value .01 would appear as 00.01, and 57 would appear as 57.00. A number like 472 could not be represented in this system, because it requires three digits to the left of the decimal point.

An **integer** system is a fixed point system with no fractional digits. You may recall learning about integers in first or second grade math, where you learned to add and subtract whole numbers. Integer arithmetic is generally discarded in favor of more flexible real numbers by the third or fourth grade.

However, integers are commonly used in computer systems due to the difficulty in handling real numbers efficiently. For this reason, you'll need to re-familiarize yourself with integer arithmetic if you're new to programming.

Floating point number systems use a storage technique resembling scientific notation. They can represent a subset of the real number set $\Re$, as well as very large integers which are beyond the range of typical integer systems. Floating point systems are limited in that they cannot represent numbers that require more than a fixed number of significant digits, typically 7 or 16 significant decimal digits. Unlike fixed point, however, floating point systems can represent virtually any number that can be specified within a certain number of digits, regardless of how many digits are whole or fractional. In essence, the decimal point (or binary point) can "float" to any position necessary. Many computers, including most PC's until very recently, didn't have any hardware for dealing with floating point numbers — a testament to the complexity and expense involved in implementing them. Modern PC's and workstations generally have hardware support for floating point numbers up to 64, 80, or 128 bits.

Floating point systems suffer from efficiency and precision problems, and should only be used in cases where integers will not suffice. Because they are stored in a more complex format resembling scientific notation, floating point addition and multiplication require several steps to complete, and take several times longer than the same integer operation. Floating point systems also have difficulty representing decimal fractions, and often introduce errors during calculations. This is discussed in more detail in section 2.2.6.

Most modern computers offer both integer and floating point systems. A third system, called Binary Coded Decimal (BCD), is seldom supported by computer hardware, but is popular in business applications where decimal values are heavily used. It has the advantage of being more accurate than floating point when dealing with decimal fractions such as 1/10 and 1/100, which often appear in dollar amounts. The C language does not support BCD directly, so it will not be discussed further in this book. To learn more about BCD, consult a textbook on COBOL, PL/1, or digital hardware design.

2.2.3   Fixed Point and Binary Integers

What makes patterns of digits represent numbers? How do we know what $16,234.05$ means?

The answer lies in the definition of the Arabic numeral system. Our everyday system is the decimal, or base 10 system. We can specify base ten explicitly by placing a subscript on the number, as in $16,234.05_{10}$. To determine the number represented by a sequence of digits, each digit is multiplied by a power of ten, and the products are added:

$$16,234.05_{10} = 1 \times 10^4 + 6 \times 10^3 + 2 \times 10^2 + 3 \times 10^1 + 4 \times 10^0 + 0 \times 10^{-1} + 5 \times 10^{-2}$$

The digit immediately left of the decimal point has exponent 0 by convention. Exponents increase to the left, and decrease to the right.

We use decimal (base ten) numbers for a simple reason; most humans (not including my barber) have ten fingers.

Binary fixed point systems use the same approach, but use base 2 instead, because digital circuits are easier to design this way.

For example:

$$10011.01_2 = 1 \times 2^4 + 0 \times 2^3 + 0 \times 2^2 + 1 \times 2^1 + 1 \times 2^0 + 0 \times 2^{-1} + 1 \times 2^{-2}$$

Bits	Range
8	0 to $2^8 - 1$ (255)
16	0 to $2^{16} - 1$ (65535)
32	0 to $2^{32} - 1$ (4,294,967,295)
64	0 to $2^{64} - 1$ (1.84 x 10^{19})

Table 2.1: Common unsigned integer ranges

Performing the arithmetic, we find that

$$10011.01_2 = 19.25_{10}$$

Since the binary digits are always 0 or 1, and it's kind of silly to multiply by 0 or 1, we generally take a shortcut when figuring out the decimal values of binary numbers, and just write down the value of each '1' bit, as follows:

$$10011.01_2 = 2^4 + 2^1 + 2^0 + 2^{-2}$$

The rightmost bit in a number always has the lowest exponent, so it is called the **least significant bit**, or LSB. The leftmost bit is similarly called the **most significant bit**, or MSB. Bits toward the right are generally referred to as **lower bits**, and bits to the left are **higher bits**.

Computer fixed point systems are almost always integers, and come in fixed sizes, generally 8, 16, 32, or 64 bits. Given a limited number of digits, we cannot represent any integer. The largest possible four digit decimal integer, for example, is 9999_{10}. Similarly, the largest possible eight bit integer is 11111111_2, which equals 255_{10}. In general, the range of a binary integer system with N bits is from 0 to $2^N - 1$. This can be determined by adding up all the powers of 2, which grows tiresome pretty quickly, or by recognizing that any binary number of the form $111 \cdots 11$ is equal to $1000 \cdots 00 - 1$, much like 999 equals 1000 - 1. A binary number like 1000 is easily recognized as 2^3, since there is only one digit to calculate, hence 111_2 is the same as $1000_2 - 1$, or $2^3 - 1$.

Table 2.1 outlines the ranges of several popular binary integer sizes.

Each type of computer has it's own word size, which reflects the maximum number of bits it can process with one instruction. For example, an 8 bit computer can only process 8 bit values, while a 32 bit computer can handle up to 32 bits at once. Most of the home computers of the early 1980's had 8 bit CPUs. For example, the Apple II and Commodore 64 both use the Motorola 6502 8 bit microprocessor. The Texas Instruments TI-99 uses the 16 bit TMS 9900 microprocessor. The original PC and PC-XT use the 16 bit 8086 or 8088. The PC-AT uses a 16 bit 80286. Most currently operating PCs use an 80386, 80486 or Pentium, all of which are 32 bit microprocessors. The Apple Macintosh has always used a 32 bit microprocessor of the Motorola 68000 family. Still more powerful are the Unix workstations like the DEC Alpha, which uses a 64 bit RISC (Reduced Instruction Set Computer) chip.

2.2.4   Binary Arithmetic

Binary arithmetic works much like decimal arithmetic, but in fact is much easier. The addition and multiplication tables of decimal are rather long and it takes time to memorize them. In binary, we have only 0 and 1 to add, subtract, multiply or divide.

In adding, $0+0 = 0$, $0+1 = 1$, and $1+1 = 10_2$, which requires us to carry the 1 into the next digit.

When computers add integers, there is one addition catch — the number of digits in the sum is limited to the same number of digits in the terms being added. This means there will be situations where the true sum cannot be contained, and an error condition will result.

Example:

Add $1001_2 + 1011_2$.

		Decimal
	1 11	
	1001	9
+	1011	11
	1 0100	20

The true sum of 20_{10} (10100_2) cannot be contained in 4 bits (recall the range of a 4 bit binary integer is 0 to $2^4 - 1$, which is 15). The fifth bit is lost from the result, and the computer will give an answer of 0100_2, or 4_{10}. We call this an **overflow**, since there were too many bits in the result to fit in the 4 bit "container".

The carry out will be detected by the CPU, however, so that a larger numbers can be handled by using multiple instructions. The carry bit is actually stored in a register called the **carry flag**. Using the carry flag, a 16 bit computer can add two 32 bit integers using two 16 bit additions. A normal add instruction is used for the low bits, followed by an **add with carry** for the high bits, which adds two values along with the contents of the carry flag. This is an example of **multiple precision arithmetic**. It was commonly used in older 8 bit and 16 bit microcomputers, but in today's world of 32 bit processors, multiple precision integer arithmetic is primarily used only in specialized scientific applications.

2.2.5 Signed Integers

So far, we have only discussed **unsigned** integers. To represent negative integers in binary, there are several **signed integer** formats available. Since all information must be in the form of 1's and 0's, we must use one of the bits to represent the sign. In most systems, a sign bit of 1 means negative, and 0 means non-negative.

The format most commonly used for storing integer values is called 2's complement.

A positive value in 2's complement looks the same as it would in unsigned format, provided that it can be done within the specified number of bits. For a 2's complement number to be positive, the *leftmost bit must be 0*. For example, the 8 bit 2's complement representation of $+12_{10}$ is 00001100. $+12$ cannot be represented in 4 bit 2's complement, since 1100 would represent a negative number in 2's complement.

To negate a 2's complement value, we complement all the bits, and then add 1. This technique eliminates redundant forms of the value 0, and simplifies hardware design. For more information, consult a textbook on digital logic or computer architecture.

Example:

Represent $+6$ and -6 in 4 bit 2's complement.

Since the number $+6$ is positive, we simply represent it as an unsigned value.

$$+6_{10} = 0110_2$$

To represent -6, we would first find $+6$ and negate it according to 2's complement rules.

$$-6_{10} = -(0110_2) = 1001_2 + 1 = 1010_2$$

Note that when we negate 1010_2, we get $0101 + 1$, which brings us back to the original value of 0110_2.

Example:

Negate 0000_2, 4 bit 2's complement.

$$-(0000_2) = 1111 + 1 = 0000_2$$

The result is actually 10000, but since we are working with a 4 bit system, the 5th bit (carry out) is discarded. Thus, 2's complement has only one way to represent the number 0.

When using signed integers, the positive range for a given number of bits is cut in half, since half the binary patterns are used to represent negative numbers.

No matter what format is used with N bits, there are exactly 2^N different patterns of 1's and 0's possible. There cannot be more than 2^N *different* values represented.

With 2's complement, half the patterns represent negative numbers, and the other half are used for positive numbers and zero. The range for any N bit 2's complement system is therefore -2^{N-1} to $+2^{N-1} - 1$. Table 2.2 summarizes the range of several 2's complement systems.

Note that the range of a 32 bit integer is rather inadequate for many purposes. Even 64 bit integers, where available, fall short of the range needed for some frequently used values such as Avogadro's number, 6×10^{23}. Larger numbers, as well as non-integer values, are better handled by floating point systems, which are discussed in section 2.2.6.

The real advantage of 2's complement is in the simplicity of arithmetic operations. To add any two values in 2's complement, *we treat them as unsigned binary values*. This reduces hardware cost, because we can use the same circuit to add both signed and unsigned values.

Bits	Range	Decimal
8	-2^7 to $+2^7 - 1$	-128 to +127
16	-2^{15} to $+2^{15} - 1$	-32768 to +32767
32	-2^{31} to $+2^{31} - 1$	-2,147,483,648 to +2,147,483,647
64	-2^{63} to $+2^{63} - 1$	± 9.2 x 10^{18}

Table 2.2: Signed integer range for 2's complement

Example:

Add 0010 and 1011 in binary. Check the result in both unsigned and 2's complement formats.

Binary	Unsigned	Signed
0010	2	+2
1011	11	-5
1101	13	-3

We can see that the value 1101_2 represents 13 if taken as unsigned, and -3 if taken as 2's complement, which verifies that the bitwise adding process works for both systems.

Detecting an overflow works differently in signed arithmetic. When adding a positive to a negative, overflow is not possible since the sum will always have a smaller magnitude than one of the terms being added.

When adding two numbers of the same sign, an overflow is indicated by the result having the incorrect sign. For example:

Example:

An overflow in 2's complement.

```
     0111
+    0100
     ────
     1011
```

We can see immediately that adding two positives gave a negative result, which obviously cannot be correct. If we check using decimal arithmetic, we see that adding +7 and +4 gave a result of -5, instead of +11 as expected. We can see why this occurred by calculating the range of a 4 bit 2's complement system, which turns out to be from -8 to +7.

2.2.6   Floating Point

Floating point systems vary somewhat among computers, although the IEEE (The Institute of Electrical and Electronic Engineers) floating point standard is rapidly taking hold on newer systems.

Floating point systems are similar to scientific notation, which consists of a **mantissa**, **exponent**, and **radix**. The value of a scientific notation number is:

$$mantissa \times radix^{exponent}$$

The radix used in scientific notation is 10, while computer floating point systems typically use a radix of 2.

For example, the decimal number .0000328 could be represented with a mantissa and exponent as $.0000328 \times 10^0$, or 328×10^{-7}. There are an infinite number of ways to vary the mantissa and exponent. To standardize the way numbers are represented, both scientific notation and floating point numbers are **normalized**. The "normal" form for a scientific notation value has one non-zero digit to the left of the decimal point, so that $1 \leq mantissa < 10$. Hence, the normalized form of .0000328 is:

$$3.28 \times 10^{-5}$$

Floating point systems use a similar approach. The most important difference between floating point and scientific notation is that scientific notation can use an unlimited number of digits in the mantissa and exponent.

Floating point systems use a fixed number of bits for both mantissa and exponent, so they have a limited range and precision.

The IEEE floating point standard defines both 32 bit and 64 bit forms. We will discuss only the 32 bit form. The 64 bit form is essentially the same, but uses a wider exponent and mantissa.

The general form is

S	E	M

S is a single bit which represents the sign of the mantissa, and hence, the sign of the number. S is 0 for a positive number, and 1 for a negative.

E is eight bits long, and *indirectly* represents the exponent. E is an **excess-127** value, meaning that it is 127 more than the value it represents. In other words, the true exponent is actually E-127. This excess notation, also known as biased notation, is just one more way to represent signed integers. The excess value is always positive, so it can be stored and manipulated as an unsigned value.

Note that a 0 in the leftmost bit indicates a *negative* value in excess notation.

M is 23 bits long, and represents the *fractional part* of the normalized mantissa. The normalized mantissa is a 24 bit binary value of the form 1.M. The digit to the left of the binary point is always 1, so it need not be stored in the computer's memory. This **implied bit** gives us one extra bit of precision for free. When performing calculations, the computer's floating point hardware or software will include the 1 automatically.

The radix in IEEE floating point is 2.

The actual value of an IEEE number is then:

$$\pm 1.M \times 2^{E-127}$$

Example:

Represent the value +6.25 in 32 bit IEEE format.

Solution:

1. Convert the value to binary fixed point.[1]
   $+6.25_{10} = 110.01_2 (\times 2^0)$

2. Normalize
   $110.01_2 \times 2^0 = 1.1101_2 \times 2^2$

   By shifting the binary point 2 places to the left, we decrease the value of the mantissa by 2^2. (Much like moving a decimal point

---

[1]Check: $110.01 = 1 \times 2^2 + 1 \times 2^1 + 0 \times 2^0 + 0 \times 2^{-1} + 1 \times 2^{-2} = 6.25_{10}$

left multiplies by a power of 10) We therefore must increase the exponent by 2 to compensate.

3. Store the normalized value in IEEE format

$$E = 2 + 127 = 129 = 128 + 1 = 2^7 + 2^0 = 10000001_2$$

$$M = 11010000000000000000000$$

Since the value is positive, S = 0.

The final result is:

0	10000001	11010000000000000000000

2.2.7   Floating Point Range and Precision

With floating point systems, determining the range is not quite as simple as it is with integers. However, the process is straightforward and logical. With integers, the only values of interest are the largest positive and smallest negative values we can represent. All the integer values in between can also be represented.

With floating point, there are five points of interest:

- The *largest positive* value

- The *smallest positive* value

- The *largest negative* value

- The *smallest negative* value

- The *precision*, or maximum number of significant digits

Range is determined by all three components — the mantissa, exponent, and radix. Each of these components is a fixed point value, which you should know how to handle at this point. If not, back up and read section 2.2.3 before moving on.

The largest positive value, for example, is found by selecting the largest positive mantissa and the largest positive exponent. The radix is fixed for a given system, so we don't have any choice in this aspect.

Example:

Find the largest positive value possible with IEEE 32 bit floating point.

The largest mantissa is

$$1.11111111111111111111_2 = 1.999999881$$

The largest possible value of E is

$$11111111_2 = 255$$

making the largest possible exponent 255-127 = 128.

The largest positive value is therefore

$$1.999999881 \times 2^{128} = 6.805646 \times 10^{38}$$

To find the smallest positive value, we take the lowest positive mantissa, and the *smallest negative* exponent. Note that the smaller of negative two values is the negative value with the *largest* magnitude. For example, -10 is smaller than -2.

Example:

Find the smallest positive value representable in 32 bit IEEE floating point.

The smallest possible positive mantissa is +1.0.

The smallest negative exponent possible is -127.

Hence, the smallest value possible is

$$1.0 \times 2^{-127} = 5.877471 \times 10^{-39}$$

The smallest and largest negative values are analogous to the smallest and largest positive values. We simply need to change the sign bit of the values in the examples above.

The precision of a floating point system is determined by the mantissa alone, as is the case in scientific notation.

For example, the value

$$3.5006 \times 10^3$$

has five significant digits. Changing the radix or exponent will increase or decrease the magnitude of the number by adding leading or trailing zeros, but the resulting value will still have the same number of significant digits.

The 32 bit IEEE system has twenty three stored mantissa bits plus one implied bit, giving it an precision of twenty four bits. Generally, we would like to express precision in terms of *decimal* digits, not binary digits. Expressing the features of your programs in binary may frighten off potential customers, or get you fired if your boss isn't from cyberspace. The number of decimal digits is found by the formula:

$$\log_{10}(2^{\text{bits}})$$

This formula is unlikely to produce a whole number. For example, $\log_{10}(2^{24}) = 7.224719896$. The actual maximum number of significant digits will be 7 or 8, depending on the value.

2.2.8   Other Number Systems

Binary has the advantage of being the simplest possible way to represent information. The disadvantage is that we need a large number of bits to represent even small values.

Fewer digits are needed in decimal, but it is difficult to convert between binary and decimal. For this reason, **octal** (base 8) and **hexadecimal** (base 16) are commonly used in place of binary. These systems work exactly like decimal and binary, for example:

$$377_8 = 3 \times 8^2 + 7 \times 8^1 + 7 \times 8^0 = 255_{10}$$

$$25_{16} = 2 \times 16^1 + 5 \times 16^0 = 37_{10}$$

Hexadecimal, hex for short, has become the popular choice, because most computers now handle data in 8, 16, 32, or 64 bit packets. These word sizes represent exactly 2, 4, 8, or 16 hexadecimal digits. Hex digits are the same as decimal up to 9, but we need to represent numbers from 10_{10} to 15_{10} with a single digit as well. The letters A - F are used for this purpose.

Decimal	Binary	Octal
0	000	0
1	001	1
2	010	2
3	011	3
4	100	4
5	101	5
6	110	6
7	111	7

Table 2.3: Binary $\Leftrightarrow$ Octal conversions

The greatest advantage of octal and hexadecimal stems from the fact that binary can be easily converted to or from another base which is a power of 2. This can be mathematically proven, but I'll spare us both the agony. Each octal digit represents exactly 3 bits, and each hexadecimal digit represents 4. A base 4 digit would represent 2 bits, but this isn't much of an advantage.

By knowing the binary equivalent of each octal or hexadecimal digit, we can convert numbers of all sizes. Table 2.3 shows the binary equivalent of each octal digit. Table 2.4 shows the binary equivalent for each hexadecimal digit.

To convert from octal to binary, we simply replace each octal digit by it's 3 bit binary value.

$$733_8 = 111011011_2$$

To convert from hexadecimal to binary, we replace each hexadecimal digit with it's 4 bit binary equivalent.

$$FF05_{16} = 1111111100000101_2$$

To go from binary to hexadecimal, we begin at the far right, grabbing 4 bits at a time and converting them to a hexadecimal digit.

$$10110_2 = 16_{16}$$

Similarly, to convert from binary to octal, start at the right, and convert each group of three bits to an octal digit.

Decimal	Binary	Hexadecimal
0	0000	0
1	0001	1
2	0010	2
3	0011	3
4	0100	4
5	0101	5
6	0110	6
7	0111	7
8	1000	8
9	1001	9
10	1010	A
11	1011	B
12	1100	C
13	1101	D
14	1110	E
15	1111	F

Table 2.4: Binary ⇔ Hexadecimal Conversions

Pitfall: Getting the Right Bits

When converting from binary to octal or hexadecimal, it is important *not* to begin grouping bits at the left. Doing so may result in too few bits being used for the least significant digit. This would be the equivalent of adding trailing zeros, or inserting zeros, either of which alters the value of the number. For example, converting 10110_2 to octal, we take the rightmost three bits, 110, and then the leftmost two bits are properly interpreted:

$$\underbrace{10}\ \underbrace{110}$$

Hence the correct conversion is 26_8. If we begin from the left, taking 101, and then 10, we would get 52_8:

$$\underbrace{101}\ \underbrace{10}$$

Note that the valid octal digits are 0 through 7. For any base N, the valid digits are 0 through N-1.

2.2.9 Character Representations

In modern computers, characters are stored as 8 bit binary codes. The American Standard Code for Information Interchange, or ASCII, is the standard used by most types of computers. The ASCII standard allows different types of computers to communicate with each other over networks, or to read each other's data from disks or tapes, provided the data contains only ASCII characters. Files written in raw binary, rather than ASCII codes, may or may not be readable to different types of computers.

The assignment of 8 bit ASCII codes to each character is somewhat arbitrary, but follows some logical patterns. The ASCII set is divided into three general areas:

- Control Characters

  Codes 00000000 – 00011111 (0 – 31 decimal) and code 01111111 (127 decimal) are the **control characters**. They are used to control output devices like printers and terminals. For example, the carriage return character, ASCII character 13_{10}, causes the print head of a printer or cursor on a terminal to return to the left margin.

- Printable Characters

  Codes 00100000 – 01111110 (32 – 126 decimal) are the printable, or graphic characters. Each one of these codes is associated with a typographic character commonly found on a typewriter.

  When a terminal (or printer) receives a printable character, it will print the associated image and advance to the next position on the screen (or page).

  These codes are also sent by a terminal when the key is pressed.

- Extended ASCII

  The original ASCII set was a 7 bit code, so it ended at character 127. Since most computers now work with bytes as the smallest unit of data, the code was extended to 8 bits. The extended codes, 10000000 – 11111111 (128 – 255 decimal) are not standardized, however, and may be used for different purposes on different computers or terminals.

  The IBM PC defines additional graphic characters to handle foreign languages, and represent special symbols, like smiley faces and outlines for text windows. In addition, the **International Standards Organization**, or **ISO**, defines several extended character sets based on the ASCII standard, which provide various non-English characters such as ñ and ö.

Note that ASCII codes are *not* numbers, but are often represented as decimal numbers for convenience, simply because numbers are easier for people to remember and recognize than 8 bit binary patterns. Table 2.5 lists the standard 7 bit ASCII codes.

IBM mainframe computers also use another code based on the BCD system, called EBCDIC (Extended Binary-Coded Decimal Interchange Code). These computers are rapidly being replaced by smaller workstations which use ASCII and ISO character sets, so EBCDIC is essentially obsolete.

00 nul	01 soh	02 stx	03 etx	04 eot	05 enq	06 ack	07 bel
08 bs	09 ht	10 nl	11 vt	12 np	13 cr	14 so	15 si
16 dle	17 dc1	18 dc2	19 dc3	20 dc4	21 nak	22 syn	23 etb
24 can	25 em	26 sub	27 esc	28 fs	29 gs	30 rs	31 us
32 sp	33 !	34 "	35 #	36 $	37 %	38 &	39 '
40 (	41)	42 *	43 +	44 ,	45 -	46 .	47 /
48 0	49 1	50 2	51 3	52 4	53 5	54 6	55 7
56 8	57 9	58 :	59 ;	60 <	61 =	62 >	63 ?
64 @	65 A	66 B	67 C	68 D	69 E	70 F	71 G
72 H	73 I	74 J	75 K	76 L	77 M	78 N	79 O
80 P	81 Q	82 R	83 S	84 T	85 U	86 V	87 W
88 X	89 Y	90 Z	91 [	92 \	93]	94 ^	95 _
96 `	97 a	98 b	99 c	100 d	101 e	102 f	103 g
104 h	105 i	106 j	107 k	108 l	109 m	110 n	111 o
112 p	113 q	114 r	115 s	116 t	117 u	118 v	119 w
120 x	121 y	122 z	123 {	124		125 }	126 ~	127 del

Table 2.5: The 7 bit ASCII character set

Chapter 3

Hardware and Software

Before you begin...

You should be familiar with the material on binary informations systems presented in chapter 2.

3.1 What Makes Computers Tick?

Computers perform their work by running **programs**. A program is a highly detailed sequence of instructions that guides the computer in performing some sort of (hopefully) useful work.

For instance, a word processor is a program used by writers to create documents. A scientist might use a spreadsheet program to analyze data. Everyone who uses a computer must have programs to make the computer perform the work they want done.

3.2 The Main Components

Modern computers have three major components:

- The central processing unit (CPU)

- Electronic memory

- Input/output (I/O) devices and mass storage

Although I/O devices and mass storage have distinct purposes, as we will see shortly, they appear very similar from the programmer's perspective, and are often considered part of the same group.

3.2.1   The Central Processing Unit: CPU

The CPU interprets the instructions in a program, and directs the operation of the other components in order to execute the instruction. In other words, it's the job of the CPU to **run** the programs. Most computers have only one CPU, which directs the operation of all the other components according to the program's instructions. Some special purpose computers may have several or even several thousand CPUs, so that they can process many pieces of data simultaneously, or **in parallel**.

The CPU can only interpret a limited set of simple instructions, called **machine instructions**. Machine instructions are, like all other information inside the computer, represented in binary. Each type of CPU uses a different set of machine instructions, or **machine language**.

For example, an Intel Pentium^{tm} processor uses a different machine language than a *Sun Sparc*. The Pentium is a member of the Intel i86 family of processors. The first was the 8086. The 8088 is a low-cost modification of the 8086 which uses the exact same machine language, but uses an 8 bit external bus[1], instead of the 16 bit bus used by the 8086. The effect is a cheaper, but slightly slower processor. The 80186 and 80188 are faster versions of the 8086 and 8088 with a few additional instructions added to the machine language. The 80286 is an extension of the 80186. The 80286 understands all the same instructions as the 80186, plus several new ones. It is also much faster, has a greater memory capacity, and supports multitasking, so that it can run operating systems like Unix and OS/2 effectively. A machine instruction on the 8086, 80186 or 80286 can handle up to 16 bits at a time. Therefore, they are called 16 bit processors.[2] The 80386 is a 32-bit version of the 80286. This makes it much easier to work with large numbers and large amounts of data in memory. The 80486 and Pentium are the most recent evolutionary steps beyond the 80386.

---

[1] The external bus is used to access memory and input/output devices.

[2] The 8088 is technically a 16 bit *internal*, 8 bit *external* processor.

They represent significant increases in speed over the 80386, but are very similar in terms of their instruction sets.

Machine instructions are typically very primitive. A single instruction might add two numbers, compare two numbers, input a single character, or jump to another location in the program, for example. Consequently, it takes a large number of instructions to accomplish what we might consider simple tasks. For example, to print a number like 456.01 on your screen may require a sequence of hundreds of instructions. First, the computer must convert the number from its internal binary form to a string of ASCII characters. Then, each character must be sent out to the terminal one at a time.

A CPU today is generally classified into one of two categories, RISC (Reduced Instruction Set Computer) or CISC (Complex Instruction Set Computer). The difference, in a nutshell, is that RISC processors have far fewer instructions in their language, and the instructions are more primitive. A typical RISC machine language consists of only a few dozen unique instructions, while a CISC CPU may have hundreds. Examples of RISC CPU's include the *DEC MIPS*, *DEC Alpha*, *Sun Sparc*, *IBM RS-6000*, and *Apple Power-PC*. CISC processors include the *Intel i86* family, *DEC VAX*, *IBM 360*, and *Motorola 68000*. The idea behind RISC design is to make the CPU simple, and very fast. A program in RISC machine language may require two to three times more instructions than the CISC equivalent, but individual RISC instructions execute much faster, because the hardware needed to implement them is so much simpler. Furthermore, most programming is now done in high-level languages, rather than assembly language, and it is difficult to create a high level language compiler smart enough to utilize all the instructions of a CISC CPU. As a result, RISC processors tend to perform somewhat better.

3.2.2 Electronic Memory: RAM and ROM

When you run a program, the instructions are loaded from the disk into electronic memory, along with the data the program needs. Electronic memory is a fairly large storage space which can be accessed very quickly. A typical memory holds millions of pieces of information, and takes between 10 and 100 nanoseconds to access any one of them. By contrast, accessing data on a typical hard disk takes about 10 milliseconds, about a million times longer than electronic memory.

There are two types of electronic memory, called Random Access Memory (RAM), and Read Only Memory (ROM). The term **random access** implies that any one of the memory cells can be accessed immediately, without having to search for it. For example, records and compact disks are somewhat randomly accessible. You can go directly to the beginning of your favorite song any time you like. In contrast, a cassette or 8-track tape is a **sequential** device. In order to listen to the third song on the tape, you have to get past the first two by playing them or using fast forward.

The term RAM is somewhat of a misnomer, since ROM is also randomly accessible. RAM really refers to memory which can be both read and written to, so Read-Write Memory (RWM) is a more accurate term. Nevertheless, the term RAM is so entrenched in literature, it is not likely to disappear any time soon.

RAM, or RWM uses electricity to store it's information. The electric impulses in RAM can be changed as needed to store different information. Hence, RAM is referred to as **volatile** memory, since it's contents are lost when the power is cut off. ROM, on the other hand, has it's contents physically fixed, and does not need a supply of electricity to maintain them. ROM is **non-volatile**, meaning that it will not lose it's information when the computer is turned off. Electricity *is* needed to read the contents of ROM, but not to maintain them.

Every computer must have at least a small amount of ROM containing instructions that get the computer started when it's turned on. This ROM-based program may run the computer indefinitely, or more often, will load other programs from disk which will then take over.

3.2.3   Input/Output Devices

I/O devices are what we in the living world use to communicate with computers. An input device is anything the computer uses to receive information from users, and an output device is anything it uses to present information to users.

Typical input devices include keyboards, mice, scanners, light pens, touch sensitive screens, microphones, and track-balls.

Typical output devices include monitors, printers, brail pads, and speakers.

3.2.4   Mass Storage Devices

Mass storage devices include disks and tapes. They typically hold much larger quantities of information than electronic memory, but are much slower.

An important feature of disks and tapes, is that they offer non-volatile storage, so they can store information while the computer is turned off. Mass storage devices

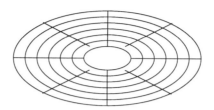

Figure 3.1: Model of a disk surface

are therefore used for long-term storage of programs and data.

Tapes store information linearly along the length of the tape. Disks store information in concentric circles called **tracks**, and disk drives contain a moving read/write head which can be positioned over any of the tracks. In addition, each track is divided into several smaller blocks called **sectors**. (Figure 3.1)

There are two popular types of disk storage, **magnetic** and **optical**. While both are non-volatile, the information on magnetic disks can be erased or overwritten, while optical disks contain permanent information, which is literally burned into the surface by a laser.[3]

Hard disks and floppy disks use a magnetic storage method, which simply polarizes a small area of the magnetic disk surface, usually an ultra-thin coating of an iron-oxide material.

---

[3]Technically, the reflective bits on an optical disk can still be burned to change their value, and only the burned bits are irreversible. However, making practical use of this fact would be an incredibly difficult and pointless technical venture.

3.3   Programs and Programming Languages

3.3.1   Machine Language

A program is a *detailed sequence of instructions* which computers follow to complete a task.

Programs that are executed by the CPU directly are in a binary code called **machine language**. Programs written in languages other than machine language must either be translated to machine language by a compiler or assembler, or run by an interpreter, which itself must be in machine language form. No matter what type of program is running, the CPU is always executing machine language instructions behind the scenes.

The binary code of each machine instruction specifies the operation to be performed and operands to perform it on. For example, a simple machine instruction could have the following format:

| Operation code | Operand 1 | Operand 2 |

A hypothetical machine instruction to add the contents of register 5 and register 6 might look like this:

| 00000001 | 0101 | 0110 |

The 00000001 specifies the add operation, and the operands are binary numbers specifying registers 5 and 6.

3.3.2   Assembly Language

Machine language is not much fun to read and work with. After a long day of punching in 1's and 0's, most machine language programmers showed various signs of stress, such as irritability, nervous twitches, or a craving for haggis.

To make things a bit easier, **assembly language** was created. An assembly language is a *symbolic* form of a machine language. An assembly language generally consists of the exact same set of instructions as it's corresponding machine language, but they are represented in a more readable form than binary. Some assembly languages have **pseudo instructions**, which may translate to more than one machine instruction, but are still very simplistic in nature.

For example, the add instruction above might be represented in assembly language as

```
ADD R5,R6
```

Most would agree that the symbolic form is more appealing. However, since the CPU understands only machine language, assembly language programs must be converted to machine language by a program called an **assembler**. The assembler is a simple program which translates one instruction at a time from its symbolic text form to the binary equivalent. The output of the assembler is a machine language program, ready to be run.

Although assembly language is much easier to use than machine language, it still suffers from two major drawbacks. Both stem from the fact that assembly language really *is* machine language written in a different form.

- Assembly instructions are very primitive, so assembly language programs tend to be very long.

- Each type of CPU uses a different machine language, so programs written in assembly language are not portable. If you trade your PC in for a DEC workstation, you will have to rewrite all your assembly language code from scratch.

Example:

To compute the function $y = a + b \cdot c/d - 5$ using VAX assembly language, we would use the following sequence:

```
mulf3    b,c,r0
divf2    d,r0
addf2    a,r0
subf3    r0,5,y
```

Note that the VAX has an exceptionally powerful instruction set. The same statement on other machines, particularly RISC machines, would require a much longer sequence of instructions. One reason for this is that most RISC instructions cannot access memory, but must have their operands loaded into registers first.

For example, the DEC MIPS is a RISC processor (with some similarity to the VAX). The equivalent MIPS program would look something like this:

```
ld.f    b,r0
ld.f    c,r1
mul.f   r0,r1,r2
ld.f    d,r0
div.f   r2,r0,r2
ld.f    a,r0
add.f   r2,r0,r2
ld.f    5,r0
sub.f   r2,r0,r2
st.f    r2,y
```

Assembly language is rarely used any more. Nevertheless, it is well worthwhile to learn how to program in assembly language. For one thing, no high-level language compiler can produce better code than a good assembly language programmer, and it is sometimes advantageous to write small portions of a program in assembly in order to maximize performance. In addition, some special purpose routines such as device drivers are more easily and effectively written in assembly language.

Even if you don't plan to use it in the future, learning how to program in assembly language will improve your understanding of how computers work and make you a better programmer in all languages.

3.3.3   High Level Languages

Given the problems of assembly language with programming effort and portability, a team at IBM lead by John Backus set out to create a new kind of language which is portable, and much easier to use. The result of their years of effort was the first FORTRAN (FORmula TRANslator) compiler. FORTRAN was designed to use simple, English-like statements and algebraic expressions to perform typical input, output, and computational tasks. FORTRAN is an example of an **imperative** language, meaning that programs consist of imperatives, or commands to the computer. **Functional** languages provide an alternative which does not consist of commands. Functional languages consist only of expressions, and are typically used in theoretical computer science research.

The name "FORTRAN" is derived from the fact that it can recognize algebraic formulas and translate them to the appropriate sequence of machine instructions. For example, the expression $y = a + bc/d - 5$, (which we did before using VAX assembly language) can be computed with the following FORTRAN statement:

```
y = a + b * c / d - 5
```

The FORTRAN statement very closely resembles the actual mathematical expression. The only difference is in that FORTRAN uses a '*' to explicitly denote multiplication. The differences between high-level languages and ordinary mathematical expressions are generally a matter of what can be typed on a typical keyboard.

FORTRAN was originally designed for scientific computing. Since then, many other high-level languages have been created, most of which very similar to FORTRAN in their basic design, but provide more high-level features and more freedom in formatting. Examples include Pascal, Ada, BASIC, COBOL, PL/1, C, C++, and JAVA, to name a few.

3.4 The Programming Process

Programs are hypothetical "machines" that implement computational recipes called **algorithms**. As you may know, or soon will learn, computer science is not as much about programming languages as it is about *problem solving* techniques.

The most difficult part of solving a problem is designing a solution detailed enough to be called an algorithm. Once the algorithm is designed, writing the program is primarily a matter of translating the algorithm into a given programming language, and then spending some time perfecting, or debugging the program.

A **top-down design** is an outline to follow in writing the program. It's essentially the same as writing an outline for a term paper, or any other project. Following an outline organizes your view of the "big picture", and helps you avoid wasting time on programming that doesn't lead anywhere. We call it a top-down design because you begin with a rough, high-level description, and gradually work your way down into more detailed lower levels. We start with a single statement of the problem, and break it into *a few* smaller steps. Then break each smaller step into *a* *few* still smaller steps, until you feel the outline is detailed enough to translate into a program. The overall process is called **stepwise refinement**.

Top-down designs are generally written in **pseudo-code** form, which is simply a series of plain English statements or phrases that look somewhat like a program. The rigid organization overcomes the ambiguity of ordinary spoken English, but the pseudo code is still much less detailed and easier to read than a program.

Example:

Outline the process of solving a quadratic equation.

We begin with a general statement of the problem:

Solve a quadratic equation $Ax^2 + Bx + C = 0$ using the quadratic formula:

$$x = \frac{-b \pm \sqrt{b^2 - 4ac}}{2a}$$

For the first refinement, we break it into four steps:

1. Solve a quadratic equation $Ax^2 + Bx + C = 0$ using the quadratic formula:
$$x = \frac{-b \pm \sqrt{b^2 - 4ac}}{2a}$$

   (a) Input the coefficients of the equation, A, B, and C
   (b) Compute the discriminant: $b^2 - 4ac$
   (c) If the discriminant is not negative, compute the solutions.
   (d) If the discriminant is negative, print an error message.

Steps (a), (b), and (d) are trivial to program, but (c) can be further refined as follows:

1. Solve a quadratic equation $Ax^2 + Bx + C = 0$ using the quadratic formula:
$$x = \frac{-b \pm \sqrt{b^2 - 4ac}}{2a}$$

   (a) Get the coefficients of the equation, A, B, and C
   (b) Compute the discriminant: $b^2 - 4ac$
   (c) If the discriminant is not negative, compute the solutions.

       i. Compute $2a$

      ii. Compute $\sqrt{discriminant}$

    iii. Compute first solution: $\frac{-b+\sqrt{discriminant}}{2a}$

    iv. Compute second solution: $\frac{-b-\sqrt{discriminant}}{2a}$

  (d) If the discriminant is negative, print an error message.

Top-down designs are best sketched out in a notebook, far away from the distractions of a computer terminal. If you find yourself thinking deep thoughts in front of a terminal, you probably haven't planned the program well enough, and will need to go back and refine your top-down design. Once finished, have the outline by your side, as you write the program by simply converting the pseudo code into the chosen language. You may even want to type the top-down design into the program file as comments before you begin writing the code. This will make it easier to view the outline as you fill in the code.

Another form of plan is the **flow chart**, which graphically depicts the sequence of events, or flow, of the algorithm. Flowcharts can be very helpful in visualizing complex tasks that are difficult to describe in words. A flowchart for the quadratic equation problem is shown in figure 3.2.

An algorithm is independent of the programming language ultimately used to write the program. In fact, you shouldn't give a thought to which language you'll use until *after* the algorithms are designed. The reason is simple: some languages are better suited for implementing certain algorithms than others. For example, SQL is a good language for many database manipulation algorithms, and FORTRAN is well suited for scientific computations, especially if exponents or complex numbers are involved. C is a good general purpose language, especially where high performance is needed, but it isn't the easiest language to use for *every* situation.

Planning is also important in determining whether or not a program is needed at all. After designing the necessary algorithms for solving a problem, you may decide that a program isn't necessary. For example, a thesaurus program would be fairly easy to implement, and potentially useful to many people. However, it might not be worth implementing, since it wouldn't be much easier to use than a printed thesaurus, which anyone can buy for a few dollars.

You might also determine from your planning that writing a program would simply be too difficult. For example, NASA is still struggling to design unmanned space vehicles, because the algorithms required to operate a vehicle in space require more

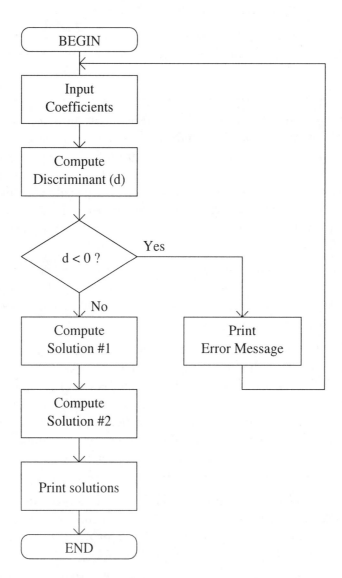

Figure 3.2: Flow chart for solving a quadratic equation

intelligence than today's technology can offer. Programs can easily be written to handle the day to day operation, but dealing with unforeseen problems will probably require human intervention. At this point, it's still necessary to send a crew along on complex missions.

Unfortunately, many programmers neglect to take the time to design an algorithm first, and instead begin the coding process too soon. This is often because each programmer has a favorite language, which they would prefer to use for everything they do. To be an effective programmer, however, you'll need to learn several different languages commonly used for the types of programming you do, so that you can choose the best one for the job, and minimize your own programming effort.

The best way to go about a programming task is outlined in the **software life cycle**:

1. Problem specification: Make sure you have a clear idea of what the program is supposed to do. In the academic environment, this is usually done for you by your instructor. In the workplace, it usually involves repeated, lengthy discussions with the people who will use the program.

2. Solution: Design any algorithms necessary to solve the problem. This is the creative phase of software development, where you develop a thorough outline of your program in the form of top-down designs and/or flowcharts.

3. Language selection: Choose a language which will make the program easy to implement, and efficient. Talk to other programmers who are familiar with languages that you *don't* know. They might be able to suggest a language that is much more appropriate than any that you know. For a large project, it might be worth your while to learn a new language, instead of struggling with the wrong one. You could easily end up saving time this way, and you'll improve your resumé in any case.

4. Coding: Translate the algorithms into the selected language, testing the partially completed program frequently as you progress. A common mistake is to write too much new code at once, without compiling and testing. This creates debugging nightmares, and often ends in a lot of wasted time. Write a dozen or so new lines of code, and then compile the program and test it if possible. This way, you'll never be overwhelmed with too many problems at once.

5. Testing: Once the program is essentially finished, it should go through an extensive testing phase before being released to customers. **Alpha testing** is

done by the programmer, or other employees where the program was written. **Beta testing** is done by typical users in the real world for whatever length of time is necessary to work out the remaining bugs. Beta testing is important, because real users will make different kinds of mistakes with a program than the programmers who wrote it. You can never be confident about a program's usability until it has been tested by real users.

6. Production: After the software has been beta tested and the known bugs are worked out, it's time to make a release version available to potential customers. This will involve some form of advertising, production of installation media and manuals, taking orders, and shipping.

7. Support and enhancement: After the product is in use, you'll want to stay in contact with your customers to provide assistance, and receive feedback which may lead to improvements in the software, and improved sales in the future.

If you are working in an academic environment, try to practice all aspects of the software life cycle, even though most of the programs you write for class assignments will never be marketed. Feedback from your instructor (often in the form of a grade) can serve as final customer feedback. You can practice beta testing, production, and support by having other students test your software and provide feedback, preferably students who would normally make use of the software, and haven't written similar software themselves. You can then make enhancements and provide your "customers" with upgrades.

You may find that some of your peers are reluctant to provide critical feedback, for fear of offending you. This is a common challenge in testing software, especially in the alpha testing phase, which is another reason that beta testing is so important. Real customers will be much more objective, and less sensitive to your ego, so they are more likely to point out and problems they encounter with your programs.

Chapter 4

Unix Overview

Before you begin...

You should be familiar with the material on basics of computer hardware presented in chapter 3.

4.1   What is an Operating System?

An operating system is a software package which helps you operate your computer. Operating systems are frequently referred to as programs, but this is a bit of a misnomer. An operating system is actually a large suite of programs and subprograms which perform a variety of tasks such as basic hardware control, input and output (I/O), communication, and word processing.

Operating systems vary so dramatically in their features that it's difficult to agree on a detailed definition of what an operating system is. However, all operating systems share a few general components, so we'll focus on those.

- The **kernel** is a set of highly technical subprograms which directly operate and manage computer hardware. (See figure 1.1, page 11.) Ordinary programs call kernel subprograms when they need to perform I/O, or any other operation that requires access to hardware other than the CPU and memory. Calls to kernel subprograms are known as **system calls**. Well-designed operating systems do not allow ordinary programs to access hardware directly, since conflicts could occur between programs that try to use the same hardware at the same time. Having all hardware access handled by the kernel keeps things in order.

Device drivers are groups of routines in the kernel which perform the actual input and output operations by talking to I/O devices such as the keyboard, mouse, and printer. In a multitasking operating system, the kernel also has routines responsible for dividing CPU time among many running programs, called **processes**.

- The **bootstrap** program is a simple program which starts up an operating system. The bootstrap's job is to load the kernel into memory, and start up the necessary programs to allow users to access the computer.

- A **user interface** is a program which allows people to interact with the computer. Most operating systems provide more than one user interface. All user interfaces fall into one of two general categories: **command-driven** and **menu-driven**. These two types are discussed in more detail in section 4.2.1.

- **Utility programs** are tools provided to perform common tasks, such as creating and manipulating files, communicating with other users, printing documents, and so on. Utility programs and their associated data files (fonts, configuration files, etc) comprise the bulk of most modern operating systems.

In a **protected mode operating system**, such as Unix, the kernel has complete control of all hardware resources. Ordinary programs that need to allocate memory or perform I/O operations must ask the kernel to do it for them.

In addition, most protected mode operating systems support **virtual memory**, which uses hard disk space to extend the apparent size of the computer's RAM. In the virtual memory environment, programs generate **virtual addresses**, which the memory unit translates to either a **physical address** (RAM address), or to a disk address in the **swap space**, which may be either a special disk partition or an ordinary file. If the virtual address maps to a physical address in RAM, the entire operation is handled by hardware, so that it has minimal impact on performance. If a virtual address maps to the swap space, then the operating system assists in loading the data from disk. Virtual memory actually allows the computer to run programs that require more memory than the computer has in the form of RAM, although much more slowly than it would if it had enough RAM available. Virtual memory also allows portions of a program that aren't being used to be swapped out to disk, freeing up memory for other programs.

DOS, in contrast, is a **real mode operating system**. Ordinary programs running in the *DOS* environment can take complete control of hardware, and access memory using physical addresses directly. Hence, programs are limited by the amount of real memory available, and the entire program must be stored in RAM while it runs. Under *DOS*, the maximum amount of memory directly available to any program is about 600 kilobytes. It is possible for *DOS* programs running on an 80286 or higher CPU to access more than this, but only using special (and time consuming) techniques such as extended memory and expanded memory, which temporarily switch the CPU into protected mode.

Real mode operating systems were common on smaller microcomputers prior to and including the IBM PC, but are rapidly being replaced by protected mode systems.

Microsoft Windows is an extension to *DOS*, which provides a graphical user interface, and adds protected mode features and multitasking, with some limitations. The *Windows* environment has retained some real mode features for compatibility with older *DOS* programs, but it has been gradually evolving into a protected mode system. Because of the fundamental differences between real and protected modes, it is difficult to maintain complete compatibility between *DOS* and *Windows.*

Windows 95 is a step closer to true protected mode operation, but still maintains compatibility with *DOS* real mode programs. When buying software for *Windows 95*, it's best to look for the "Made for Windows 95" label. This label signifies that the program was compiled to run in *Windows 95* protected mode. Programs written for *DOS* or *Windows* 3.x will run under *Windows 95*, but will place limit its performance and ability to run multiple programs at the same time.

One of the more trendy features of protected mode operating systems is **DOS emulation**, which allows them to run many *DOS* programs simultaneously. *DOS* emulation has some severe limitations, however, because the emulators cannot mimic every detail of a PC's hardware. You'll achieve much better performance and fewer headaches if you stick to software designed for the OS you are using. If you want to run *DOS* programs, it's best to run them under *DOS*, rather than under an emulator.

As a final note, be aware that there are differences among operating systems in how multitasking is achieved. Most modern systems are based on the standard preemptive model, while some are based on **threads**. Unix is based on the standard preemptive model, but many modern Unix systems also offer multi-threading

support. The differences between multitasking models is the topic for an advanced
course in systems programming or operating systems, which is beyond the scope
of this book. We'll be content just to say that the standard preemptive model is
a proven, reliable, and efficient method, and serves most purposes well. Threads
offer an alternative that can simplify programming and improve performance of
cooperating processes, i.e. processes that need to share data extensively.

4.2   The Unix Operating System

Unix is a powerful multiuser, *true* multitasking operating system, with an enormous
amount of utility software included. One of the great benefits of Unix is the fact
that it includes so many tools that would have to be purchased separately for other
operating systems.

To fully understand all that Unix has to offer would require years of study. We'll
focus on the essentials of writing programs in the Unix environment, and leave the
rest to the Unix textbooks.

4.2.1   Logging In

Since Unix is a multiuser operating system, each user must **log in** to the system to
begin using it, and **log out** when finished. The login procedure allows the system to
identify the user for security purposes. Each user can have their own files, some of
which may contain love letters, top-secret bean dip recipes, or other information that
other users aren't supposed to see. Unix makes it easy to either protect information
from other users, or share it with them.

To log into a Unix system, you must provide a **login name** and a **password**.

The login name is used to identify each individual user on the system. Hence, if there
are two users on the system named Bonafacio Bonini, then each will be assigned a
different login name so that they can be distinguished from one another.

The password is used to verify the identity of each user when they log in, and to
perform other operations that require verification. It is very important that you keep
your password a secret, especially if your Unix system is attached to the Internet.
Even if you aren't concerned about others getting into your files, hackers who gain
access to your account may use it to hack into more secure sites. The end result is
the hacker gets away with a crime, while you (at least temporarily) get blamed for it.
This may sound a bit James Bond, but it happens every day. The best precaution

is to follow a few simple rules about maintaining your password. The only way a hacker can get into your account is by finding out your password. Although it's hard to guess your password, it is easy to verify whether a guess is correct. The following rules will help prevent this from occurring:

- Passwords should be at least 8 characters long. The longer the password, the harder it is to guess. Many systems will only use the first 8 characters, but allow passwords to be longer if desired.

- Never tell anyone your password, especially over the phone. Anyone who has the authority to access your account will be able to do so *without* knowing your password, so if someone asks you for it, be suspicious.

- Never write your password on anything, be it a notebook or bar napkin. Odds are, someone will find it.

- Use a variety of character types in the password. A password that is all lower case letters is easy to guess using a fast computer. A mix of upper and lower case is harder. Throw in some digits and punctuation symbols, and it becomes next to impossible.

- Never use a real word or anything close to it. A hacker with even a slow computer can simply try every word in the dictionary in a few seconds.

After turning on your terminal and possibly jumping through a few hoops on your local system, you will be prompted for your login name and password. You must provide each one to get into the system. You may also need to specify your terminal type.

The whole sequence will look something like this:

login: <u>Enter your login name here</u>

password: <u>Enter your password here</u>

TERM = (unknown) <u>Enter your terminal type here</u>

The terminal type is a very important piece of information for many Unix programs. Each type of terminal has it's own set of **magic sequences**, sequences of characters that the computer sends to the terminal to control the screen, or are sent when keys are pressed. If you don't specify the correct terminal type, the computer and terminal won't be able to communicate with each other properly. Some terminals, such as the DEC vt100, are capable of identifying themselves. The Unix `qterm` command will ask a terminal to identify itself, and then interpret the response. See the manual page (discussed in section 4.5) on qterm for details.

Once you complete the login procedure, you are ready to work in the Unix environment. There are two main types of user environments available for any operating system:

- Command Interpreters, or **shells**, are programs which accept typed commands from the user and execute them.

- Menu-based systems display choices on the screen, which the user selects by pressing a single key or mouse button.

The advantage of the command-driven shell environment over a menu is that the user has immediate access to *all* the available commands on the system. The disadvantage is that the user has to memorize potentially complex commands, or frequently refer to documentation in order to use the system.

Some common shells include `command.com` in *DOS*, and **Bourne shell** (`sh`), **C shell** (`csh`), **T-shell** (`tcsh`), **Korn shell** (`ksh`) and **Bourne-again shell** (`bash`) to name a few for Unix. A natural extension of a command interpreter is a **script language**, which can be used to write programs that execute multiple commands in a controlled sequence, rather than just accepting one command at a time from the user. All Unix shells support script languages, as does command.com under *DOS*. Shell scripts are discussed in section 4.11.

The advantage of a menu-driven system is that the user does not have to memorize anything. Instead, the available choices are always displayed on the screen for the user to select from. This type of system is much easier for a novice to use. With a well designed menu system, new users will require little or no training.

The down side is, only a limited number of choices can be displayed on the screen at once. In order to improve functionality, a menu system must be divided into a series of cumbersome sub-menus, which can bog down and annoy an experienced user. This is why many menu systems include **hot keys**, special keys the experienced user can use to bypass the menus.

Generally speaking, menu systems are best for simple programs, novice users, and programs that aren't used frequently, and thus aren't worth memorizing. Command-driven systems are best for providing a high-powered, productive environment for experts who use a system on a daily basis, and for whom it is worthwhile to expend some effort learning the commands.

A **Graphical User Interface**, or **GUI** (pronounced goo-ey), is a popular type of menu based environment, where commands are displayed as pictures called **icons** as well as text. The main difference between a GUI and a text menu system is in how the menu items are selected. A mouse is typically used in GUI environments, instead of the keyboard, which is more typical for text menus.

Examples of GUI systems include *Windows* for *DOS*, *Presentation Manager* for *OS/2*, and *Motif* for Unix.

X Windows is often mistakenly referred to as a GUI, but is actually a graphical *program* interface for Unix which is used to implement Motif and other GUI Unix applications.

4.3   The Unix File-system

A disk in a Unix system typically contains thousands of programs, documents, and other data. All information on disk is stored in **files**.

Some operating systems have several different types of files which may be split into fixed or variable length **records**. For example, 80 byte records are typical for text files that contain human-readable documents, since most printers and terminal screens are 80 columns wide. Such systems typically allow the user to choose any record length up to some system-imposed limit.

A Unix file, on the other hand, is simply a chain of characters (letters, digits, punctuation, etc.), which is given a unique name to identify it among all the other files on the disk. Any structure within a Unix file is determined solely by the file's contents. Only a program designed to work with the file will understand the structure within it: as far as Unix is concerned, it's just another string of characters on the disk. One important result is that there are no limitations to what kind of record structure an application can create within a Unix file. In addition, by leaving the file's internal structure up to the application, the Unix file system is greatly simplified, as are many Unix commands. This results in better overall performance and less waste.

Unix disks are usually divided into several separate **partitions**, each containing a separate **file-system**. Each file-system is organized into **directories**, so that the

files can be more easily located.[1] The organization of a disk is analogous to that of
a typical file cabinet. Both a disk and a file cabinet are used to organize documents
so that they may be easily retrieved later on.

The inner workings of the Unix file-system are covered in chapter 24. For now, we
will cover the Unix filesystem from the user's perspective.

4.3.1   Partitions

A disk is usually divided into two or more fixed sized **partitions**. Disk partitioning
is only done by the system administrator, but a little knowledge is helpful to any
user, so we'll cover the basics here.

Partitions are analogous to the drawers of a file cabinet. In a *DOS* or *Windows*
system, the C: and D: logical drives usually represent separate partitions on the
same disk.

In Unix, there are no logical drives. Instead, all of the file-systems are combined
into a single directory structure by **mounting** one file-system under another.[2] Each
Unix system has a **root** file-system, under which all other file-systems are mounted.
As a result, the partitioning of disks under Unix is essentially invisible to the average
user.

In fact, even partitions on other machines can be mounted across a network connection into the local directory structure using the Unix **NFS (Network File System)**
facilities. This makes it exceptionally easy to share data between two computers
that both run Unix, since users can directly access files without even knowing which
computer they are stored on. NFS differs from *DOS* or *Windows* file servers such as
Novell, in that NFS is a **distributed file system**, rather than a centralized one.
Each Unix system in an NFS network can act as both a NFS server and a NFS
client, whereas a machine running Novell is typically dedicated as a server for the
rest of the machines, which act exclusively as clients.

You might be wondering why partitions are necessary at all. Dividing a large disk
into smaller partitions generally improves performance, since the system has less to
search through when looking for files.

Using separate partitions also protects important files in case a particular filesystem
becomes corrupted, due to sudden power-loss or some other catastrophic event. If

---

[1]Some operating systems, such as *MVS*, have no directory structure at all. This can make files
very difficult to find if you forget the filename.

[2]This is analogous to using the `join` command under *DOS* or *Windows*.

something goes wrong while a file is being updated, the filesystem containing that file may be damaged, but other filesystems will not be affected. If you have only one file system, and it becomes damaged, it may not be possible to restart the system, and you may have to re-install the entire operating system!

Finally, PC systems have a long track record of imposing arbitrary limits on disk and partition size. Older *DOS* systems limited the primary partition to 32 megabytes, making it necessary to divide larger disks into a primary and extended partition.

More recent PC's imposed a 1024 cylinder limit within the BIOS. Larger disks must have their boot partition contained within the first 1024 cylinders in order to work properly. This limitation required anyone using an **IDE** (**Integrated Drive Electronics**) disk to purchase a new **EIDE** disk adapter and/or BIOS, which could support more than 1024 cylinders using **Logical Block Address Mode**. In **LBA** mode, a large disk with more than 1024 cylinders appears to the BIOS as one with fewer cylinders and more sectors per cylinder. The BIOS is thus tricked into believing the disk has fewer than 1024 cylinders, and provides requests which must be translated by the adapter. This is not an attractive solution, since it overcomes a design flaw by adding more hardware, rather than eliminating the root of the problem.

SCSI (**Small Computer Standard Interface**, pronounced "scuzzy") disk systems don't have the same design limitations as IDE and EIDE, since they are essentially independent of the PC BIOS.[3] The SCSI interface is used by all types of small computers from PC's to workstations to minicomputers, and works with many types of devices such as hard disks, CD-ROMS, and tape drives. System performance is generally much better than IDE/EIDE systems as well, because SCSI controllers are somewhat smarter and thus require less attention from the CPU. Another important advantage of SCSI is the ability to connect up to 7 devices to a single SCSI adapter, as opposed to 2 for each IDE/EIDE adapter. If you are considering building your own PC system, going with a SCSI interface could make your life much easier.

4.3.2   Directories

Each Unix partition contains a **file-system**, which is organized into **directories**. A directory within a file-system is conceptually analogous to a folder within a drawer of a file cabinet. A folder in a file cabinet typically contains many documents, and may also contain more folders. Similarly, a directory in a Unix (or *DOS*) system

---

[3]In fact, when you install a SCSI disk in a PC, the BIOS configuration should be set to "no disk installed".

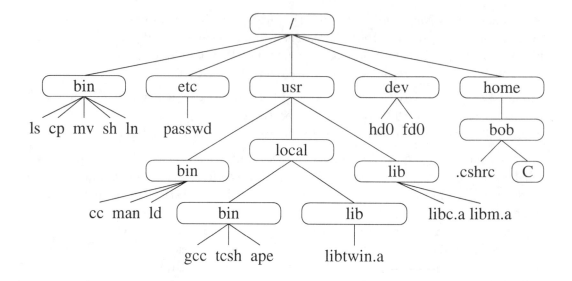

Figure 4.1: Unix Directory Tree

may contain many **files**, and also may contain **subdirectories**, which in turn may hold more files and subdirectories. In fact, many people prefer to use the terms **folder** and **document** in place of directory and file.

The Unix directory structure is a hierarchical structure, which can be imagined as an upside-down tree, with branches spreading downward and outward from the **root** directory at the apex. Figure 4.1 shows a portion of a Unix directory tree. Each box represents a directory, and each name without a box around it is a file.

There are two ways of specifying a directory or filename in Unix. All Unix commands will accept filenames in either format.

- A **full pathname** describes the entire path leading from the root directory to the directory or file. For example, the full pathname of Bob's .cshrc is */home/bob/.cshrc*. To view Bob's .cshrc file, you could type the following:

      tcsh 1: more /home/bob/.chsrc

- A **relative pathname** states the path starting from the **current working directory**. Relative pathnames save us a lot of typing, especially when the full pathname of the current working directory has a long name. Every Unix process has its own current working directory. Immediately after you log into the system, your shell's current working directory is set to your **home** directory. For example, Bob's home directory in figure 4.1 is */home/bob*.

When you specify a pathname that doesn't begin with a '/', Unix will append it to the current working directory name to construct the full pathname. For example, if Bob just logged in, then the current working directory for his shell is */home/bob*. If he wants to view his .cshrc file from here, he can use a relative pathname as follows:

```
tcsh 1: more .cshrc
```

The current working directory for the shell can be changed using the `chdir` command, often abbreviated `cd`. Simply type `cd` followed by the full or relative pathname of the desired working directory.

Typing `cd` with no arguments sets the working directory back to your home directory. Thus, if you ever get lost in the Unix directory tree, you can always get home by just typing `cd`.

The `pwd` command will display the shell's current working directory.

The following sequence of Unix commands demonstrates how directories and pathnames work:

```
tcsh 1: more /etc/passwd
root:*:0:0:Charlie &:/root:/bin/sh
...

tcsh 2: cd /etc
tcsh 3: pwd
/etc
tcsh 4: more passwd
root:*:0:0:Charlie &:/root:/bin/sh
...

tcsh 5: cd
tcsh 6: pwd
/home/bob
```

User	Group	World
rwx	rwx	rwx

Figure 4.2: File Permission Bits

Many of the the directories shown in figure 4.1 are standard among Unix platforms. For example, most standard Unix commands are kept in the directories */bin* and */usr/bin*. Non-standard programs, typically added on to the system, are usually stored in */usr/local/bin*, and less frequently in */usr/contrib/bin*. The */etc* directory contains the password file, and many other administrative tools. The */dev* directory contains **device drivers**, special filenames that don't refer to actual disk files, but can be used to access input and output devices like terminals, mice, and printers, as if they were ordinary files.

4.3.3   File Modes and Permissions

Permissions

Each file and directory in a Unix filesystem has a set of **permissions** associated with it. The permissions determine who can access the file or directory, and in what ways.

There are three categories of users, and three types of permissions, and hence, a total of nine permission bits when can be turned on or off.

The three user categories are:

User: The individual who owns of the file.

Group: The group that owns the file. Each individual user is on a Unix system belongs to at least one group. The owner of a file is usually a member of the group that owns the file.

World: All users who have access to the system.

The three types of permissions are **read permission**, **write permission**, and **execute permission**.

The nine permission bits for each file are arranged as shown in figure 4.2.

Special	User	Group	World
ugs	rwx	rwx	rwx

Figure 4.3: SUID, SGID and sticky Bits

Each bit that is '1' grants permission for a given type of access, and a '0' denies permission. For example, to give the owner permission to read and write a file, and deny any kind of access to other users, you would need permission bits of 110000000.

Permission bits are conveniently specified using octal numbers, since each octal digit represents three bits. Hence, each octal digit denotes the permissions for one category of users. For example, a permission value of 755_8 translates to 111101101_2. This gives the file's owner permission to read, write, and execute the file, while the group and world can only read and execute.

Permissions are set using the `chmod` command. For example, to make a file executable to the world, but only readable and writable to the owner, you would use the following command:

```
tcsh 1: chmod 711 file
```

Directories must be both readable and executable in order for users to access the files within them. Directories that are readable, but *not* executable may be listed, but not "entered". For example, to give the members of the group that owns a directory permission to access the files within it, use the following:

```
tcsh 1: chmod 750 directory
```

Set-On-Execute and Sticky Bits

Three special bits, called `SUID`, `SGID`, and `sticky`, can be specified by a fourth (leftmost) octal digit, or using addition mnemonic options. Figure 4.3 shows their positions relative to the permission bits.

If the u (SUID) or g (SGID) bit is set on an executable file, and another user runs the program, the process will take on the effective user ID or group ID of the program's owner. This allows ordinary users to run programs that write to system files, or files owned by other users. Programs such as mailers use this strategy to deliver mail to other users. You can also use this feature to allow other users to write into your own directory (using only *your* programs) without giving them write permission.

For example, to set the SUID and SGID bits on the program *a.out*, and allow others in your group to use the program under your user ID, use the following command:

```
tcsh 1: chmod 6710 a.out
```

If the **s** (sticky) bit is set on a program, the program is held in the system's swap space for a while after the program terminates. This allows the program to be started more quickly than if it had to be reloaded from the filesystem. This feature is obsolete on many systems, due to replacement by more intelligent caching systems that don't require specific programs to be marked.

If the sticky bit is set on a directory, the ability of users to delete or rename files within it is restricted. This is most useful for directories such as */tmp*, which must be world-writable, but do not allow users to delete each other's files.

Umask

Each Unix process has a **creation mode mask**, called a **umask**, associated with it. The umask affects the default permissions on newly created files. Each bit which is '1' in the umask will be set to '0' in the permissions of any newly created file. This provides users with a convenient way to ensure that their files are protected to the desired extent. The umask is controlled by the `umask` command, which normally appears in the shell startup script. (See section 4.11.) For example, if you want your new files to be readable and executable to the group and world, but not writable, you'll need a umask of 000010010_2, or 022_8.

```
tcsh 1: umask 022
```

4.4   The Shell Environment

We will focus on using the shell environment in this text, covering only a few essential commands for writing programs. Graphical and other menu systems vary widely in their appearance, and tend to be self-explanatory, so they will not be described here.

A shell program typically displays a simple prompt to indicate that it is waiting for a command.

Example

```
tcsh 1: _
```

The prompt can be anything, and in fact you can change it to anything you like. We will use the simple prompt "tcsh" to identify the shell as the **T-shell**. The number following tcsh is just a sequence number to let you know how many commands you have entered so far.

There are two families of shells in the Unix world. The two most common shells are **Bourne shell**, and **C shell**. **Korn shell** and **Bourne-again shell** are extensions of Bourne shell, while **T-shell** is an extended version of C-shell. If you're using a different shell, don't panic. Most of the examples used here apply to any Unix shell.

When you see the prompt, you can enter any Unix command. A Unix command begins with a program name, and may be followed by **switches** and other arguments. Switches control the behavior of the command. Each command has its own set of switches, but according to Unix convention, switches almost always begin with a '-'. Other arguments specify the data for a command to work with. Arguments are most often filenames, but may also be input data, or anything else the program needs.

Example:

```
tcsh 1: ls -al /etc
```

The `ls` command lists the files in a specified directory. The `-al` specifies two switches, -a and -l. The command could also have been typed as `ls -a -l /etc`. In fact, most Unix commands are pretty flexible in how switches are presented. You can either type them separately, or all in one lump. The on-line manuals provide detailed instructions on using each command. These are discussed in section 4.5.

The -a switch tells ls to list all files. Without the -a switch, `ls` does not list filenames beginning with a '.'. The -l switch tells `ls` to produce a long listing, which provides information like the file size, last modification time, and so on. Without the -l switch, `ls` will give only the filenames.

The argument, */etc*, tells `ls` which directory or files to list. If no argument is given, `ls` simply lists the files in the current working directory.

All Unix shells expect arguments to be separated by spaces. If you need to specify an argument that contains a space or tab character, the argument must be enclosed in single or double quotes. For example, typing

```
man regular expression
```

will cause the `man` command to search for two man pages; one called *regular*, and another called*expression*. The details of `man` are discussed in section 4.5 To make man search for a page about regular expressions, you would need to send both words as one argument to the man command, as follows:

```
man 'regular expression'
```

or

```
man "regular expression"
```

Single and double quotes are almost interchangeable in Unix shells. However, there is an important distinction. Certain characters, called **meta-characters**, have special meaning to the shell. These include $, *, \, ?, [,], and several others. If the $ meta-character appears between double quotes, it will be interpreted by the shell as a special character, and the string will be altered accordingly. Double quotes are therefore referred to as "soft quotes", since the shell penetrates them when searching for certain meta-characters. On the other hand, any string of characters enclosed in single quotes are taken literally as part of the string. Single quotes are therefore known as "hard quotes".

There are two types of commands accepted by a shell:

- **Internal commands** are part of the shell program itself.

- **External commands** are separate programs that are loaded and run by the shell.

Commands are generally implemented internally only if they need to affect the shell environment, or are extremely simple. Too many internal commands would make the shell an enormous program, which would require an enormous amount of memory. Since shells run almost constantly for hours or days at a time, and every user has at least one shell process going while they are logged in, it is important to keep their memory consumption as small as possible. Hence, most Unix commands are external.

After you type in a command and press *return*, the shell will either execute the command itself, or locate and run the program needed to execute it. For example, consider the following sequence:

```
tcsh 1: ls -a
.       ..          .login  .cshrc
tcsh 2: exit
```

The command `ls -a` lists all the files in the current directory. This is an **external** command, which is performed by the program in the file */bin/ls*.

The `exit` command is an internal command which tells the shell to terminate itself. This is one way to terminate your Unix session and log out of the system.

A basic Unix system has hundreds of commands, each with many options and arguments. At first, it may seem a bit intimidating, but as you gain experience, you will eventually become comfortable with the commands you use most frequently. For now, don't set out to memorize all the different commands and their options. The options are all documented on line, so you can always look them up at the moment you need them. To quote Albert Einstein, "don't fill your head with useless facts if you know where to find them". Of course, don't take this too far, and insist on remembering nothing about Unix. The more you know, the more time you can spend being productive, instead of sifting through manuals looking for the information you need.

It's good to know the names of a few commands that you use often, and especially, how to use the on-line manuals and other references you may have. Knowing which commands will be useful for each task at hand will make it easy to find the details when you need them. A list of common Unix commands is provided later in this chapter, so you can quickly determine which command to use.

4.5   Getting Help

The most important first step in learning to use Unix is learning how to obtain information on the available commands. Information on commands can be found either in a Unix textbook, or in the **on-line manuals**.

On-line manuals are references that come with *every* Unix system, and can be displayed right on your terminal whenever you need them. On-line manuals are the most convenient source of information, since they don't have to be carted around with you. Instead, they are always available when you need them, i.e. whenever you are logged into the system.

The standard on-line manuals can be accessed in two ways:

- The `man` command is used to obtain detailed information on almost any Unix topic. In order to use `man`, you have to know the name of the command or function. For example, to learn more about the man command, enter the command:

      tcsh 1: man man

  To learn more about the C `printf()` function, enter:

      tcsh 1: man printf

  The on-line manuals displayed by man, called **man pages** contain detailed technical information on the subject. Man pages are not always the best way to learn about a new subject, so it's good to have a book handy while you're a newbie. They *are* the best source of information for a particular system, however, and can generally be trusted as the final word on using your system.

- The `apropos` command lists Unix commands and functions related to a particular topic. On some systems, using `man` with the -k option simulates the apropos command. For example, if you want to know what command to use to compile a C program, enter:

      tcsh 1: apropos compile

or

```
tcsh 1: man -k compile
```

There are other forms on on-line documentation available for various Unix tools. The GNU **info** command is a more interactive alternative to the standard man pages. Man pages are simple formatted text files, which can be difficult to search through for specific information if the man page is large. `Info's` interactive interface makes it a little easier to navigate large documentation files and find the information you need.

HTML (Hyper-Text Markup Language) is a form of documentation with formatting and **linking** commands embedded in the text. By following the links, the user can quickly move to different sections in the same document, or even to different documents. In fact, HTML documents may contain links to other documents on computers all over the Internet. Such links use a special format known as a URL, or Uniform Resource Locator, to specify both the Internet host name and the filename of the document within that host. HTML is the language used to connect the **World Wide Web**, a large set of Internet hosts that run special software designed to exchange HTML documents. Whether HTML documentation is viewed on the WEB or locally on your own machine, it provides a highly intuitive method of browsing documentation.

4.6   Some Useful Unix Commands

The most difficult part of learning any system is getting started, and just finding out what it can do. To help you get going, the table below provides a brief description of many common Unix commands, grouped by their general purpose. This list will hopefully help you locate the commands you need. For more detailed descriptions, use the man command to read the on-line documentation, or consult a Unix user's guide. [16]

Moreover, for a complete list of commands on your Unix system, you can simply list your bin directories (/bin, /usr/bin, /usr/local/bin, ...) using the `ls` command.

Working with files as objects

ls	List files in a directory
cp	Copy files (files contents are duplicated)
ln	Link files - create another name
	for a file without duplicating contents.
mv	Move or rename files
rm	Remove files and directories

File output

cat	Copy (concatenate) files to standard output (screen)
more	View files one screen-full at a time
head	View first few lines of a file
tail	View last few lines of a file
od	Display file contents in octal, hexadecimal, decimal, ASCII
tee	Output file stream to two places at once

Printing files

lp	Print files (SYSV Unix)
lpr	Print files (BSD Unix)
lpq	Check printer queue
lprm	Cancel printer jobs (BSD Unix)

Interactive Editors

ex	Line oriented interactive editor
vi	Visual editor (full screen version of ex)
emacs	Sophisticated full screen interactive editor
pico	Simple, easy to use full screen interactive editor
ape	Another Programmer's Editor (Integrated Development Environment)

Processing file streams

sed	Stream editor (non-interactive, batch editor)
grep, fgrep, egrep	Search file stream for strings and regular expressions
sort	Sort a file stream
uniq	Remove duplicate lines from a sorted file stream
cmp	Compare file streams byte by byte

diff	Compare file streams line by line
cut	Extract portions of lines from a file stream
awk	Pattern matching and processing language
m4, cpp	Stream editors with embedded commands (markup)

Working with Directories

cd,	
chdir	Change current working directory
mkdir	Create a new directory
rmdir	Remove a directory (directory must be empty)
pwd	Print working directory
find	Locate files by name or other attributes

Getting help

man	Display manual on a topic (nroff -man format)
apropos	List manual topics related to a subject
info	GNU hypertext help system
whatis	Get short description of a command
lynx,	
netscape,	
mosaic	HTML/WEB browsers

User information

passwd	Change your password
who	List users currently logged on
w	List users and what they are doing
finger	Find out more about a user
chfn	Change your finger information
logname	Print login name for current shell
whoami	Print effective user id for current shell
su	Substitute user - change effective user id
last	Display recent login sessions for a user

Electronic Mail

mail	Send or receive mail
elm	Send or receive mail
pine	Send or receive mail
vacation	Set up automatic response to email while gone

biff	Ask to be notified when email arrives
uuencode	Encode a binary file for sending through email
uudecode	Decode a uuencoded message

Network tools

hostname	Display name of system
rlogin,	
telnet	Log in to another system on the network
ftp	Transfer files to/from another system
whois	Find out about someone on the net

Programming tools

cc	C compiler
ld	Linker
ld.so	Run time (shared object) linker
as	Assembler
pc	Pascal compiler
f77,f90	FORTRAN 77/90 compilers
lex	Generate lexical analyzer (scanner, tokenizer)
yacc	Generate language parser
indent	Reformat a C program so it looks nice
ar	Object code library archiver
cdiff	Special diff command for C source code
ape	Another Programmer's Editor (IDE)

Terminal tools

clear	Clear terminal screen
lock	Lock your terminal
tset	Initialize your terminal
reset	Reset terminal to default modes
stty	Change terminal settings
tty	Display device driver name for your terminal
window	Divide terminal screen into windows

File archiving

ar	Archiver used mainly for program libraries
tar	Create and manipulate archives of files
gzip	Compress files

gunzip	Uncompress files
zcat	Display compressed files
zmore	Display compressed files a screen at a time
zgrep	Search for strings in compressed files

Word Processing

nroff	Format text documents
groff	GNU version of nroff
spell	Find misspelled words in a file
ispell	Find misspelled words interactively
look	Look up a word in the spell dictionary

Controlling Processes

ps	Display list of running processes
kill	Terminate a process
nice	Run a process at low priority
at	Run a program at a set time
exec	Replace shell with a different program

Administrative

quota	Display disk usage and limits for a user
msgs	Display messages from the administrator

Time

date	Display current date and time
cal	Display a calendar
calendar	Set up system to send reminders

Miscellaneous

sh	The Bourne shell
csh	The C-shell
tcsh	The T-shell
ksh	The Korn shell
bash	Bourne again shell
bc	High-precision calculator
printenv	List environment variables

4.7   A Few Shortcuts with T-shell and Bash

The T-shell has an abundance of features designed to reduce the amount of effort needed to execute commands. A few of those features are described below. Most of the features described here are also incorporated into **bash**, the Bourne-again shell. For a more complete description, see the tcsh or bash man page.

4.7.1   Command History

The T-shell allows users to easily re-execute previous commands. For example, you can use the up-arrow (↑) key to redisplay previous commands, and then press *return* when you find the one you want.

An alternative is using history substitution. A history substitution command consists of an exclamation point (!) followed by a history specifier. For example, !! will execute the most recent command. !*string* will execute the most recent command beginning with the character sequence *string*. Command history is also available in C-shell.

Programmers using a simple text editor often repeat the edit-compile-execute sequence many times. Using T-shell, our command sequence might look like this:

```
tcsh 1: pico hello.c
...
tcsh 2: gcc -Wall hello.c
tcsh 3: a.out
...
tcsh 4: !p
pico hello.c
tcsh 5: !g
gcc -Wall hello.c
tcsh 6: !a

... and so on.
```

If you use an **Integrated Development Environment**, such as *APE* (section 5.5, you won't have to leave the editor to compile and run the program. Still, history substitutions will prove useful in other settings.

Character	Matches
*	Any sequence of characters
?	Any single character
[list]	Any single character in list
[c1-c2]	Any single character between c1 and c2

Table 4.1: File Globbing Meta-characters

4.7.2 File Specification: Globbing

Most Unix commands will accept a large number of files as arguments. For example, suppose you had the C programs *prog1.c*, *prog2.c*, *prog3.c*, *prog4.c*, and *emu.c* all in one directory. If you wanted to search all of the C programs for the `printf()` function, you might use the following command:

```
tcsh 1: fgrep printf prog1.c prog2.c prog3.c prog4.c emu.c
```

The shell provides us with a way to specify multiple filenames without typing all of them, called **global filename substitution**. Before each command is executed, the shell checks it for **meta-characters**. Expressions containing the meta-characters '*', '[', ']', and '?', are then replaced by the filenames or portions of filenames that they match. This replacement is often referred to as **globbing**. Table 4.1 describes some of the globbing meta-characters common to Unix shells.

Example:

Search all files in the current working directory that end in ".c" for the printf function.

```
tcsh 1: fgrep printf *.c
```

To search all files beginning with "prog" and ending in ".c", use the following command:

```
tcsh 1: fgrep printf prog*.c
```

To search only files prog1.c, prog2.c and prog3.c, type

```
tcsh 1: fgrep printf prog[123].c
```

or

```
tcsh 1: fgrep printf prog[1-3].c
```

If you also work with *DOS* systems, you should be aware that globbing in *DOS* is done by each individual application, rather than by the shell (`command.com`). This means that every program that uses globbing must contain special code for interpreting meta-characters, and the behavior will be somewhat different from Unix, since the shell passes all the command text to the program without modification.

4.8   Unix Input and Output

All programs must receive input and produce output in order to be useful.

When a program is running under Unix it is called a **process**. For example, emacs is a program, whether it's being used or just sitting around on the disk waiting to be used. Each time a user runs emacs, a new process is created, so if five people are using emacs, then there are five emacs processes running on the system.

4.8.1   File Streams

Each process has its own set of I/O **streams**, which can be used to input and output data. A stream is a hypothetical conduit through which data flows to or from an I/O device such as a disk or terminal. All processes have at least the following three standard streams:

- The **standard input** stream is normally connected to your terminal's keyboard. This is the stream used by most programs to receive input from the user.

- The **standard output** stream is normally connected to your terminal's screen. This stream is used to display output for the user to read.

- The **standard error** stream is also connected to the screen under normal circumstances. Most programs use the standard error stream to display error messages.

4.8.2 Redirection

You can easily reconnect of any of the streams to a different device or file using the shell's **redirection** capability.

For example, you can tell any program that normally sends output to the screen to send it to a file instead. Consider using the `ls` command to list the files in the current directory.

```
tcsh 1: ls
```

The ls command writes a listing of file to the standard output, so the command above will show the listing on your screen.

If you want the list to go to a file called *list*, instead of the screen, then you could use the '>' redirection operator:

```
tcsh 1: ls > list
```

You won't see any output on the screen, because the shell has disconnected the standard output stream from your terminal and connected it to the file *list*. Note that `ls` is totally unaware of where its output is going. The redirection is handled entirely by the shell.

You can view the list using the `more` command, as follows:

```
tcsh 2: more list
```

When you use redirection, the stream is only redirected for the command being executed. Remember that each process has its own set of standard streams, and redirecting the streams of one process will not affect any others. Hence, only the `ls` command above will send its output to the file, and the shell's output will not be affected.

As another example, you might want to save the error messages from `gcc` to a file. To accomplish this, you could redirect the standard error stream as follows:

```
tcsh 1: gcc -Wall prog1.c >& errors
tcsh 2: more errors
```

The '`>&`' operator actually causes both the standard output and standard error to be redirected to the same place.

Redirection works for input as well as output. The '`<`' operator instructs the shell to reconnect the standard input to a specified file or device. For example, the `fgrep` command, for reasons discussed in section 4.8.3, takes input from the standard input when no filenames are given as arguments:

```
tcsh 1: fgrep hello
```

The command above will read input from the keyboard until you type *ctrl+D* (simulating end of file on the standard input), and echo back any lines of input that contain the string "hello".

You can use redirection to make `fgrep` read a file *through the standard input stream*:

```
tcsh 1: fgrep hello < file.c
```

The command above will read the contents of *file.c* through the standard input stream, and echo any lines containing the string "hello".

Note that *file.c* is *not* and argument to the `fgrep` command. When the shell performs redirection, it removes the '`<`' and the filename that follows, leaving "hello" as the only argument to the `fgrep` command.

Pitfall: Redirection and Globbing

Consider the following command:

```
tcsh 1: fgrep hello < *.c
```

At first glance, you might think that the command searches all the C files in the current directory, much like:

```
tcsh 1: fgrep hello *.c
```

This is not the case. If the current directory contains the files prog1.c, prog2.c and prog3.c, then after globbing, the former command is expanded to:

```
tcsh 1: fgrep hello < prog1.c prog2.c prog3.c
```

The effect of redirection is to reconnect the standard input of **fgrep** to the file *prog1.c*. The other two files are then passed as arguments to **fgrep**. Recall that **fgrep** reads from standard input only if there are no filename arguments. In this case, however, there are two, so the **fgrep** command will search *prog2.c* and *prog3.c*, but not *prog1.c*.

4.8.3 Pipes

The shell's **pipe** facility is a faster way to perform tasks such as the output redirection example above. It allows us to run two or more commands simultaneously, and redirect the standard output of one command directly to the standard input of another. For example, instead of redirecting output to a file and then using more to view the file, you could pipe the standard output directly to the more command using the '|' (pipe) operator:

```
tcsh 1: ls | more
```

To pipe the standard error with T-shell, you use the '|&' operator:

```
tcsh 1: gcc -Wall prog1.c |& more
```

Commands like more, which can read input from the standard input, are called **filter programs**, because they are used at the receiving end of a pipe to filter the output of another command. In fact, *most* Unix commands can function as filters. Some other common filter commands, which are briefly described in section 4.6, include sort, diff, grep, awk, sed, and tee.

4.8.4 Named Pipes

For commands that are not designed as filters, Unix offers an alternative form of pipe, called a **named pipe**, or **FIFO file**. A named pipe is simply a pipe with a filename. It can be used as a substitute for an ordinary file in Unix commands that read input from or send output to a file that is specified by name.

Named pipes are created using mknod, or mkfifo.

```
tcsh 1: mkfifo mypipe
```

Individual commands can then be run with input or output channelled through the pipe. One of the processes must be run in the background (section 4.9), by placing a & character at the end of the command, so that you will be able to issue the second command while the first is still running.

Example:

The sequence of commands below demonstrates how to use a named pipe with two simple commands.

```
tcsh 1: mkfifo mypipe
tcsh 2: ls > mypipe &
tcsh 3: more mypipe
```

Named pipes are most useful for special program, as described in section 28.3, and for complex programs that cannot act as filters, such as LaTeX. Simple programs, such as those in the example above are more easily linked using the '|' operator.

4.8.5 Device Independence

Unix provides a standard interface between programs and I/O devices. A Unix program can read input from any input device, or send output to any output device, without requiring any changes to the program. In fact, Unix programs very often have no idea where their input comes from, or where their output goes. This device independence allows us to use old programs with new hardware, and easily port programs from one Unix system to another.

Device independence can be useful to the casual user as well as the programmer. For example, recall that you can redirect error messages to a file on disk as follows:

```
tcsh 1: gcc -Wall prog1.c >& errors
```

With device independence, you can actually redirect the errors to any output device you choose, if you just know the device name. For example, if your printer is attached to */dev/lp0*, you can send the errors directly to the printer:

```
tcsh 1: gcc -Wall prog1.c >& /dev/lp0
```

Although, it would be better to pipe print jobs to the print spooler, so they don't get mixed up with one another:

```
tcsh 1: gcc -Wall prog1.c |& lpr
```

You could even send the errors to another user's terminal screen, provided the system allows it. For example, if you want your friend Bob to see your error messages, but he's logged in from across town, you would first need to find out which tty device he is connected to:

```
tcsh 1: who
```

```
bob      ttyd1    Oct 20 11:32
loretta ttyd5    Oct 20 09:32
```

Then, you could use this information to send the errors directly to his terminal screen:

```
tcsh 2: gcc -Wall prog1.c >& /dev/ttyd1
```

Of course, this is a rather invasive way of showing Bob your errors. It would be more polite to redirect the errors to a file, and send them to Bob by email:

```
tcsh 1: gcc -Wall prog1.c >& errors
tcsh 2: mail Bob < errors
```

4.9 Job Control

Since Unix is a multitasking operating system, all Unix shells have the ability to control many processes at once.

Unix processes run either in the **foreground**, or the **background**. Unlike many other operating systems, such as *MVS*, there is no difference in the way foreground and background processes in Unix are written. The only difference between them is that a foreground process has control of the keyboard. There can be only one foreground process running under each shell process, because it doesn't make sense for multiple processes to compete for the same keyboard input.

You can run as many processes as you like in the background, by simply typing a '&' as the *last* character of the command. Don't get too crazy with background processes, though, because each process in the system slows it down for you and everyone else.

Pitfall: Babbling Background Processes

It's a good idea to redirect both the standard output and standard error of a background process, so it doesn't garble up your screen while you're working on something else. It's perfectly acceptable to Unix to have multiple processes sending output to the same terminal screen, but it's generally not a pretty sight.

When you run a process in the background, the shell will display a number, called the **job number**, and then immediately continue to accept commands. The job number is used only by the shell, and is independent from the **process ID** used by Unix. To find out the process ID of a job, use the `ps` command. The `ps` command will list the process ID and other information about all commands currently running from your terminal. (Including the `ps` process itself) You can then kill a background process if needed, using the `kill` command and the process ID.

Example:

```
tcsh 1: a.out >& myoutput &
[1]
tcsh 2: ps
PID TT  STAT    TIME    COMMAND
166 p0  Ss      0:01    tcsh
200 p0  R       0:02    a.out
201 p0  R       0:00    ps
tcsh 3: kill 200
```

If you have already started a process in the foreground, and it's taking too long, you have a few options besides sitting around waiting for it to finish.

You can always kill a foreground job by typing the **interrupt key**, which is usually *Ctrl+C*. The `stty` command can tell you what the interrupt key is currently set to.

You can also **suspend** the job by typing the **stop key**, which is usually *Ctrl+Z*. This will stop the job where it is without terminating it. You then have the option of continuing it in the future. If you want to continue the job in the foreground, type the internal shell command fg. To put it in the background, type bg. If there are no stopped jobs, but there are background jobs running, typing fg will bring the most recent job back into the foreground.

4.10   Shell Variables and Environment Variables

Both the shell and the operating system maintain a list of string variables, most of which are used to configure your environment.

Shell variables, as you might guess, are only accessible to the shell process that defined them. In C-shell and T-shell, variables are set using the internal shell command, set.

```
tcsh 1: set variable=value
```

Typing set without specifying a variable and value will list all the existing shell variables.

To set shell variables in Bourne shell and it's relatives Korn shell and Bourne-again shell, just type variable=value.

Most shells have some standard variables that configure the shell's behavior. Some of the more common variables include prompt, which defined the shell prompt, history, which defines how many previous commands the shell will retain for re-execution, and cwd, which holds the current working directory name. There are many other standard variables, and you can define new ones for your own use. Consult a Unix user's guide, or the man page for your shell, for more information on shell variables.[16]

Example:

The command below sets the shell prompt to "Unix shell: ".

```
tcsh 1: set prompt='Unix shell: '
```

or

```
bash 1: prompt='Unix shell: '
```

Environment variables are visible to both the shell process, and all of the processes executed under it, i.e. each **child process**. This provides a way for processes to communicate with their descendents. C-shell and T-shell use the internal `setenv` command to set environment variables.

```
tcsh: setenv TERM vt100
```

Note that setenv uses whitespace, rather than an '=', to separate the variable and value. Typing setenv with no arguments will list the currently defined environment variables, as does the external command `printenv`. To set environment variables in Bourne family shells, use the `export` command.

```
bash: TERM=vt100
bash: export TERM
```

Some of the standard variables include `PATH`, which determines which directories are searched for programs you wish to run, and `TERM` which many full-screen programs such as editors use to determine what type of terminal you are using.

With C-shell and T-shell, many variables, such as TERM and PATH, are duplicated as both shell and environment variables. Setting either one will cause its twin to be automatically updated.

4.11 Shell Scripts

Unix shells are more than just command executers. They are actually language interpreters, complete with variables and flow control statements. In fact, the C-shell gets its name from the fact that it resembles the C language.

If you have a sequence of commands that needs to be executed frequently, you can put them into a file, and have the shell execute the file as a program. The shell actually doesn't distinguish between reading from a file and reading from the keyboard. In fact, most Unix commands don't even know where their input is coming from, thanks to device independence. Typing commands on the keyboard is essentially having a shell program executed as you type it.

All shell scripts must contain a comment on the first line indicating which shell will be used to run it. Note that a new shell process is started to execute a script, rather than using the same shell that's taking your commands from the keyboard. This prevents shell variables in your interactive shell from being altered by statements in the script.

A comment in a shell script is any line beginning with a #. This applies to all Unix shells. The first line must contain the '#', followed by a '!', and the name of the shell.

Example:

```
#!/bin/csh
echo 'Look ma, I'm running a C-shell script!'
cc file.c >& errors
more errors
```

The script above can then be invoked by simply typing its name as with any other external command. The only catch is, the script must have execute permission set. This can be done using the `chmod` command, as follows:

```
tcsh 1: pico myscript
(type in the script, save and exit)
tcsh 2: chmod 755 myscript
```

You can also run the script as an argument to a shell:

```
tcsh 2: csh myscript
```

or using redirection:

```
tcsh 2: csh < myscript
```

The C-shell language is a sophisticated language worthy of a book of its own, so we won't attempt to cover it in detail. For more on shell programming, consult a Unix user's guide that covers shell programming. [16]

4.11.1 Startup Scripts: *.cshrc* and *.login*

There are two important scripts in every C-shell and T-shell user's directory. The commands in the file *.cshrc* are executed by every C-shell or T-shell process before it begins accepting command from the keyboard or script. The commands in the file *.login* are executed only by a login shell, and *after* those in *.cshrc*. The shell you use to enter commands on your terminal is usually a login shell. If you have more than one window on your terminal, it is possible to have an interactive shell that isn't a login shell. Shells invoked to run scripts are generally not login shells, so the .login file will not be read by them. However, the *.cshrc* file is read by every new C-shell or T-shell process, so it is effectively prepended to every shell script you run.

The *.profile* is analogous the the .cshrc file for Bourne family shells.

4.12 Advanced: Make

`Make` is a Unix utility program designed for automatically building an output file from several input files. This is especially useful when the output file is very large. By splitting the project into several smaller files, it becomes easier to edit, and the smaller modules can often be reused in other similar projects.

`Make` is most commonly used for building programs from separate source files, but `make` is useful for *any* project that builds an output file from many source files. This book, for example, was compiled from many *LATEX* source files and *Postscript* figures using `make`.

If you are only interested in using `make` for programming, then you may skip this section for now, and come back after reading chapter 11.

To use `make`, first write a *makefile*, which contains a list of **dependencies** with the following general form:

```
target: dependents
        command
```

The **target** is the name of a file to be built, the dependents are the files the target is built from, and the command is an ordinary Unix command which actually builds the target from the dependents.

The target must begin in column 1, and the commands must be indented. Some make programs require the command to be indented specifically with a *TAB* character: spaces cannot be used as a substitute.

Make uses the file-system's time stamps to determine if the target needs to be rebuilt. Each file in a Unix file-system is time stamped when it is modified; when a file is edited and saved, for instance. For each dependency in the makefile, if any of the dependents is *newer* than the target, then the command is executed. Assuming the command is correctly written, this will rebuild the target file, which in turn causes it to be time stamped as newer than all the dependents. Note that make knows nothing about your files or how they are put together. It simply executes the commands you provide when one of the dependents is newer than its target. It is entirely up to you to ensure that the targets are built properly.

The makefile is usually named *makefile* or *Makefile*. If this is the case, then typing the command

```
make
```

will execute the dependencies in the makefile. If the makefile is given a different name, then type

```
make -f filename
```

where *filename* is the name of the makefile.

Example:

A makefile to build the target *report.txt* by concatenating the source
files *intro.txt*, *body.txt*, and *concl.txt*. The makefile consists of a single
dependency naming the source files as dependents of *report.txt*, and
using the `cat` command to concatenate them.

```
report.txt: intro.txt body.txt concl.txt
        cat intro.txt body.txt concl.txt > report.txt
```

Makefiles tend to contain some natural redundancy. To alleviate the problems associated with this redundancy, you can use **macros** in the makefile. A macro is
defined at the beginning of the makefile as

```
name = text
```

and referenced in the makefile as `$(name)`. Macros make it much easier to modify
a makefile if you want to add more dependents or a new command. If macros are
being used, then only one change is required to the makefile, which reduces the
chances of introducing bugs.

Example:

Modify the makefile in the previous example using macros.

```
CMD = cat
DEP = intro.txt body.txt concl.txt

report.txt: $(DEP)
        $(CMD) $(DEP) > report.txt
```

If you want to add more dependents to this makefile, you need only modify the line defining `DEP`, instead of changing both the dependency line and its command.

As mentioned earlier, the most common use for `make` is in building programs from several source files. An example of using `make` in programming is given in chapter 11.

Part II

Programming in C

Chapter 5

Getting Started with C and Unix

Before you begin...

You should be familiar with the material on computer hardware and Unix presented in chapters 2, 3, and 4.

5.1   What is C?

C is a high-level programming language, commonly used to develop academic, scientific, and commercial software. Because C is a high level language, it is **portable**, meaning programs written in C can be run on more than one kind of computer. (See section 3.3) C programs must be **compiled**, that is, translated to machine language, so that they can be run *directly* by the computer hardware.

There are two flavors of the C language:

- Kernighan & Ritchie (K&R) C is the original C for Unix, developed at AT&T in the early 1970s as a systems programming language.

- ANSI C is the new C standard defined by the American National Standards Institute. This is the standard that most C compilers follow, and the one we will focus on in this book. In includes some very helpful new constructs and a somewhat cleaner syntax than K&R C.

Most C compilers in use today, and all C++ compilers, conform to the ANSI standard. You'll probably never use a K&R compiler, unless you find yourself working on an older Unix system. Still, we will cover K&R syntax for completeness.

5.2   C Program Structure

A C program consists of several different types of constructs, generally in the following order.

- Pre-processor directives

- Type definitions

- Function declarations

- Function definitions

Example:

A very simple C program:

```
/* This is a comment */

#include <stdio.h>        /* Preprocessor directive */
#include <sysexits.h>

/*****************************/
/* main() function definition */

int      main()

{
    char      name[40];         /* Variable definition */
```

```
          printf("What is your name? ");  /* Function call */
          fgets(name,39,stdin);           /* Function call */
          printf("Hello, %s",name);       /* Function call */
          return EX_OK;                   /* Return statement */
     }
```

Preprocessor directives are easy to recognize, since they always begin with the '#' character. They perform various tasks at **compile time**, while the program is compiling. For example, the #include directive inserts a file into your program during compilation. In the example above, the file */usr/include/stdio.h* is inserted in place of the line #include <stdio.h>. Other preprocessor directives are discussed in chapter 13.

Function definitions contain the statements of your program, which do the actual computations. The statements within a function are executed sequentially beginning at the top of the function.

Function calls are used to branch to a function and execute it. When the function is finished executing, the program returns to the point where the function was called from.

Function declarations are usually (and should be) contained in **header files**, such as stdio.h, which is included in the example above. Function declarations come in two forms. In K&R C, the function declaration states only the **return type** of the function. For example, the K&R declaration for fputs() is:

```
     int fputs();
```

The declaration informs the compiler what type of value the function returns, so that the return value is interpreted correctly. A K&R function declaration is known as an **allusion**, because it alludes to something which is defined elsewhere.

In ANSI C, a function declaration is called a **prototype**. Prototypes state both the return type of the function, and the types for each **argument**. For example, the prototype for the function fputs() is:

```
     int fputs(char *,int,FILE *);
```

Prototypes are much more powerful than K&R declarations, since they allow the compiler to verify all the details of each call to a function. Function declarations and definitions are discussed in greater detail in chapter 11.

Type definitions create new data types for use in your programs. They are also usually placed in header files. Type definitions are explained briefly in chapter 6. They are most extensively used with **structures**, which are discussed in chapter 18.

Comments are interspersed throughout the code to explain in simple terms how it works. This is necessary because program code is usually inundated with too much detail to be easily understood. A few good comments can often save a programmer from hours of tedious examination to determine how a program works. This is especially true for code written by someone else, and for code you wrote yourself a long time ago and probably don't remember very well. In either case, it will look unfamiliar, and comments will be greatly appreciated.

Programming with Style:

In the academic environment, a lack of comments will usually (and hopefully, for the sake of educational quality) result in a poor grade.

In the commercial environment, programs without comments end up being rewritten, rather than reused, because nobody besides the original author can possibly understand them. Even the original author won't be able to understand a program he or she wrote a long time ago, unless it contains helpful comments. Moreover, authors of poorly documented code are not respected their peers (whose time is often wasted struggling to decipher it), and often acquire a bad reputation, which *will* reach potential future employers.

Millions of dollars in productivity are lost each year, as programmers re-invent the wheel time and time again. These losses can be easily avoided if programmers invest a modest amount of time in documenting their code, so that they or others are able to easily reuse it in the future.

Comments, and many other matters of style are stressed throughout this text, so that you will be well equipped to build programs that stand the test of time.

A **return statement** exits a function, returning to the point where it was called from. The return statement in `main()` is somewhat special, since it causes the program to terminate. The return from `main()` sends an integer status value back to the shell (or other parent process). These return values are somewhat standardized. All C and C++ programs should include the header file *sysexits.h*, as in the example above, and use on the return values defined therein, such as `EX_OK` if the program ran successfully, when returning from `main()`. More program exit codes from *sysexits.h* are introduced as needed in later chapters.

5.3 A Word about Performance

C is a high-performance programming language, but the performance doesn't come automatically. It's up to you as a programmer to get the most out of the language by developing your knowledge and skills, and by taking time to evaluate the performance of each program you write. This evaluation can be done by comparison to similar programs, and comparison to an ideal. For example, compiler performance can be measured against other compilers (of the same language, of course), or against the `cp` (copy) command, which is limited only by disk speed. An ideal compiler would run as fast as `cp`. Of course, this isn't possible, since compilers use much more CPU time, but it provides a limit that a compiler writer can try to approach. There are many tools in the Unix environment for evaluating performance. The `time` command is the simplest, and probably the most frequently used. It can quickly provide you with an estimate of the CPU time and I/O time used by your programs. In addition, there are tools for measuring memory usage and I/O, and most compilers offer a **profiling** option to help you determine which functions in your program are the most active.

Performance of commercial software varies enormously. In one instance, the run time of a program was reduced from 14 hours to 10 minutes with a just a few hours of work by a talented consultant.

You can maximize performance in several ways. By far the most important is choosing the best **algorithms**, procedures for solving particular problems. Choosing a bad algorithm can slow down a program by a factor of 100 or 1000. For example, using **selection sort** instead of **quick-sort** would be a disaster when sorting a large list. The time required by selection sort for a list of N elements is proportional to N^2 (It is a $O(N^2)$ algorithm), whereas quick-sort is $O(N \times \log N)$. For a list of 1000 elements, N^2 is 1,000,000, whereas $N \times \log N$ is only 20,000. In most cases, the simplest, most straightforward method is the best.

Indiscriminate memory use can also seriously impact performance, especially on Unix and other multiuser systems, which may be running dozens of programs at once. If the system runs out of memory, it will begin swapping data between memory and disk. When you consider the fact that disks are 1,000,000 times slower than memory, the benefits of a program that minimizes memory use are obvious. There are many ways to keep memory use in check, including selecting the right algorithm, and using good coding practices. For instance, the merge-sort algorithm is highly efficient and very stable, but requires twice as much memory as quick-sort. As a result, merge-sort is rarely used for anything besides an academic exercise. Coding techniques you can use to save memory are discussed throughout the text in their appropriate sections. C programmers can also utilize features of the language to improve performance even further. It's often possible to double the speed of a C program, *without changing the algorithm*, through the use of pointers and other key features of the language.

Performance issues are further discussed in almost every chapter, in the context of each individual topic.

5.4   Some Early Warnings

As with any powerful tool, C has a few dangers. For example, some of the early library functions, such as `strcpy()`, should *never be used*, due to design flaws that can cause array overflows and other problems. Safer replacements are available, and should be used for all new C programs. It's even worth a little effort to update older code that uses these *dangerous* functions. In general, any function that copies data into an array without knowing the array's size, is dangerous and should be avoided. These functions will be pointed out along the way as the arise.

5.5   Coding and Compiling a C Program

5.5.1   Coding

To develop a program in the Unix shell environment, you can use a simple screen editor, such as `vi`, `emacs`, or `pico` to write the C program and save it to a file. Once saved to a file, the program must be compiled (converted to machine language) using the Unix command `cc`.

An **Integrated Development Environment**, or **IDE**, is a more sophisticated editor which provides an interface to programming tools, and many built-in editor features which make the programming process easier than it is with a simple text

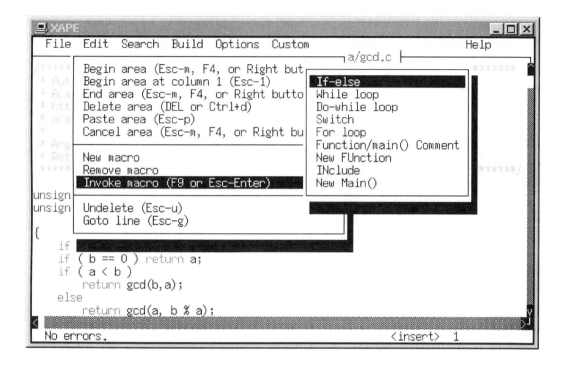

Figure 5.1: Another Programmer's Editor (APE)

editor. Programmers using an IDE can easily edit, compile, and test without ever leaving the editing environment. Figure 5.1 shows a screen shot of *Another Programmer's Editor*[tm], or *APE* for short. APE is a commercial IDE (currently free for academic use) which works with any programming language, and is available for many brands of Unix. This book was written using APE along with the *LA*T*EX* typesetting language. For more information on APE, visit *http://www.execpc.com/acadix*.

Commercial compilers (other than the standard `cc` command) usually come packaged with their own IDE, especially compilers for other operating systems such as *DOS* or *Windows*, which don't include the sophisticated shells, editors, and other programming tools that come with Unix. IDE's are the standard for developing on smaller platforms such as *DOS*, *OS/2*, and *Windows*, but are not (yet) as common in Unix programming. As the Unix market grows, however, IDE's will undoubtedly become more popular.

Programming should always be done *a little at a time.* In the old days, when computer resources were scarce, programmers often wrote entire programs on paper before typing them in, or entering them on punch-cards. The problem with this approach is that there is no way to test your ideas before expending an enormous amount of effort on writing code. This would often result in having to redesign large portions of a program after finding out it wouldn't work.

With today's technology, every programmer typically has a computer or terminal to work on. After planning the program thoroughly, you can easily do all of your coding right on the computer. The advantage with this strategy is that you can compile and test *very frequently.*

Tip of the trade: Small Steps

A good rule of thumb is to *write no more than 10 lines of new code before compiling and testing.* If something doesn't work as you expected, you can then alter your plan before wasting any more time following an unproductive approach.

By compiling frequently, you will never have to deal with more than a few error messages at a time, and you will learn quickly from your mistakes as you go. If you write a hundred lines of code all at once, you will undoubtedly have dozens of errors the first time you compile, and many of them may be for the same kind of error. Some compilers, including **gcc**, have a **syntax check** option, which instructs the compiler to quickly check the program for syntax without doing any translation to machine language. This option can save a considerable amount of time, especially for large source files.

By testing frequently, you will always know where to look for flaws in the program logic. If you write two hundred lines of new code without testing, and the program doesn't work, you now have two hundred lines of code to search through in order to find the error.

5.5.2   Compiling

As mentioned earlier, C programs must be converted from **source code** form to **machine code** by a compiler, before the computer can run them. Source code gets its name from the fact that it's the source of a compiler's input. The machine code output is stored in another file, called an **executable**, or **binary**. The default name

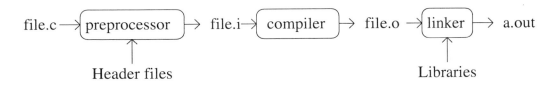

Figure 5.2: The C compiler phases

for the executable file in most Unix systems is *a.out*, although any filename can be specified, usually with the "-o filename" compiler option.

In Unix, `cc` is the standard command used to compile a C program. Each Unix version has it's own compiler, which may differ slightly from the rest. The compiler provided with a Unix system may be ANSI or K&R flavored, although most compilers in use today support the full ANSI standard. There are some third party commercial compilers available for certain brands of Unix, which offer more features than the standard compilers included with the operating system.

In addition, there is a free C compiler from the GNU[1] project, known as `gcc`. The GNU project is a world-wide group of programmers who donate software they've written to the community. Most GNU software is created as academic or personal learning projects, or in the commercial environment as in-house tools not intended for sale. The `gcc` compiler originated as an academic project in compiler design, and since then has had contributions from many different people around the world. Most GNU software is designed to run on Unix, but is often available for other platforms as well. GNU software is very popular in the academic environment, both because it is free, and the source code is available for students to study and modify.

Translating a C program to machine language actually involves three or more steps, all of which are performed behind the scenes by `cc`. (Figure 5.2)

1. The **preprocessor** finds and executes all the preprocessor **directives** in the program, such as `#include`, and `#define`. The modified program source code is then passed on to the true compiler.

2. The **compiler** translates the preprocessed source code to machine language. The output of the compiler is an **object code module**. Object code modules are not complete programs, so they cannot be executed.

---

[1]GNU stands for GNU's not Unix.

3. The last phase is the **linker**, which combines object modules into a complete executable program. Some object modules come from compiling your source files, and others, such as `printf()` and `fgets()`, come from **libraries**, archives of pre-compiled functions.

4. The **object code optimizer** examines and attempts to improve the efficiency of the object code. The optimizer phase is optional with most compilers. If you use the optimizer, it will take longer to compile, but the result will be a smaller and/or faster program. The results of optimization are often marginal, especially if the program is well-written to begin with. However, a good optimizer can sometimes triple or quadruple the performance of a computationally intensive program. I/O intensive programs are usually limited by the speed of the I/O devices they use, so the difference won't be as noticeable. Still, the optimized program may use significantly less CPU time, which will improve overall system performance for *all* processes. All programs should be compiled and tested with optimizations before being put into production.

All of these steps are performed automatically by the `cc` command, but it is still important to understand them, since you will need to work with header files and library files as a C programmer. Furthermore, chapters 4 and 11 discuss using the `make` utility, which is used to build programs from many separate source files. When using make, the compile and link steps must be performed separately, so you'll need to understand the compiling and linking processes in order to use `make`.

Compilers tend to have many command line options. We will use the "-Wall" option, which instructs `gcc` to generate as many warnings as possible at compile time, "-O" which instructs the compiler to run the optimizer, and the "-o" option, which specifies the name of the executable. For example, the following command produces an executable called "sort" from the source file "sort.c".

```
gcc -Wall -O3 sort.c -o sort
```

If no "-o" option is given the executable will be called a.out by default.

Pitfall: Biting the Hand that Feeds You

Programmers have been known to use compiler options to make warning messages go away, by simply telling the compiler not to report them.

This is not an intelligent way to program, however. Warning messages are there to *help* you in locating potential problems during compilation. It is *much, much, much* more difficult to locate errors based on outward signs of a program that compiles but doesn't function correctly. If you want to make your life easier, use compiler options such as "-Wall", which instruct the compiler to report as many warnings as possible. You can additionally use code analyzing programs such as `lint` to track down problems that the compiler might miss.

For a complete listing of compiler options, see the documentation for your compiler.

5.5.3 A First Example

We will assume the user is entering commands using the T-shell (`tcsh`), a shell commonly used with Unix, along with a simple editor such as `pico`. Both T-shell and `pico` are freely available and easy to use. If your Unix system does not have them installed, check with your system administrator. If they are not available, it won't be a problem. The examples used here will be generic enough to use with any shell or editor.

The prompt "tcsh #:" is the signal from `tcsh` that it is waiting for you to enter another Unix command. The number in the prompt is a sequence number to let you know how many commands you have entered so far.

Example:

Create a file *hello.c* using the `pico` editor, and compile it using `gcc`.

```
tcsh 1: pico hello.c

** Type in the sample program above, save, end exit **

tcsh 2: gcc -Wall hello.c
tcsh 3: a.out
What is your name? Bob
Hello, Bob!
tcsh 4:
```

First, use the `pico` editor to create the file hello.c. You may also use `emacs`, `vi`, or any other text editor available on your system.

Then compile it using `gcc -Wall hello.c`.

If the program compiles successfully, the machine language equivalent will be stored in the file *a.out*. All Unix programs are executed simply by typing the name of the machine language file. When you run the program, the machine language equivalent of each statement in the original C program is executed.

5.5.4   Handling Errors and Warnings

Programming usually involves making plenty of mistakes. Even experienced programmers are flabbergasted if they add more than a few lines to a program, and it actually works the first time they test it. In most cases, programs need to be edited and compiled many times before they run successfully. Section 4.7 describes some shortcuts with T-shell to make this cycle a little easier.

If you're lucky, you will get an error or warning message from the compiler. These are called **compile time** errors and warnings. Most compile time messages include the filename of the source code, the line number where the error was detected, and a statement describing the error. The most common type of compile time error is the **syntax** error, which is generally a misspelled keyword, missing operator, or something similar.

There is a clear distinction between compile time errors and warnings:

- A **compiler error** is a serious flaw in the program which prevents the compiler from completing the translation from source code to machine code.

- A **compiler warning** is issued by the compiler when it detects a *potential* problem with your program. The compilation will succeed in producing an executable file, but the program probably won't work properly. Warning messages should be taken very seriously, as they generally indicate real problems with the program. It's best to fix any problems that generate warnings before you move on and test the program.

If you're not so lucky, the program will compile successfully, but it won't work properly. These types of errors are called **run-time** errors, **logical errors**, or **semantic errors**, since they represent flaws in the *logic* or *meaning* of the program, rather than errors in the source code syntax. Run-time errors are much more difficult to locate and fix, but there are some techniques that are generally helpful. These techniques are discussed in chapter 19. For now, we will be using very short sample programs, which will generally not require any special techniques to debug.

Example:

Suppose you forgot the `#include` statement in the program above, and left off the `[40]` in the definition of `name`:

```
/* This is a comment */

/***************************/
/* main() function definition */

int     main()

{
    char    name[40];         /* Variable definition */

    printf("What is your name? ");  /* Function call */
    fgets(name,39,stdin);           /* Function call */
    printf("Hello, %s",name);       /* Function call */
    return EX_OK;                   /* Return statement */
}
```

When you compile this program, you will get the following warnings:

```
hello.c: In function main:
hello.c:7: warning: implicit declaration of
function 'printf'
hello.c:8: warning: implicit declaration of
function 'fgets'
```

These warnings indicate that the compiler does not know how a call to `printf()` or `fgets()` should look, so it is assuming that your calls on lines 7 and 8 are correct. Note that `printf()` and `fgets()` are merely **library functions**. Library functions are functions that have been previously written, and stored in a **library** file so that the compiler can find them. The standard library files are in the directories */lib* and */usr/lib*. Once placed in a library, they can be called from *any* program, without being defined in the program.

Since library functions are *not* part of the C language, the compiler does not automatically know what they should look like. That's where function declarations come in. The function declarations contained in */usr/include/stdio.h*, for example, show the compiler what `printf()` and `fgets()` return, and what types of arguments they should receive, so that the compiler can verify that your calls are correct. In this case, the program has compiled successfully, with a few warnings, but it will not run correctly. In particular, the `fgets()` function requires a string variable to store the name in, and the program only provides it with a single character variable.

You can eliminate the warning messages by finding out where `printf()` and `fgets()` are declared. An experienced C programmer will know this, but a novice may have to look it up in the on-line manuals or printed text (this book, for example). As you gain experience in C programming, you're knowledge of libraries and header files will naturally grow. For now, simply read the man page for the function to find out which header files are necessary. For example,

man printf

will provide you with the proper `#include` statements, and other information about printf.

If you add the proper `#include` and compile again, you now get the following:

```
hello.c: In main:
hello.c: 9: warning: argument passing of pointer from
integer lacks a cast
```

In English, you have attempted to pass an integer value to a function that expects a pointer on line 9. Note that a **char** is considered an integer in C, and an **array** is a pointer.

Compiler lingo may seem a bit confusing at first, but don't worry. These terms will become clearer as we discuss the basics of the C language. As your knowledge of C grows, so will your understanding of error and warning messages.

Writing a compiler that produces clear and meaningful error messages is a difficult task, since there are literally millions of possible errors a program could contain. For this reason, compilers try to use a few general error messages that fit a lot of cases, like "implicit declaration" and "syntax error". The good news is, the compiler does a pretty good job telling us *where* the error is. In most cases, that in itself is enough, and it generally doesn't take long to determine exactly what's wrong.

Chapter 6

Data Types

Before you begin...

You should be familiar with the material on binary number systems, computer hardware and software, and the basics of C programming presented in chapters 2, 3, and 5.

6.1   Introduction

Computers work with different **data types** for different purposes. For example, attendance at a baseball game could only be a positive integer value. It could not be 10,314.5 or -1. The value of π, however, is not a whole number, and must be stored as a real number.

It is extremely important to understand the available data types, so that you can choose the best data types for each variable and constant in your programs. Programmers often have to change poorly chosen data types later on, in order to make the program more efficient, reliable, or portable. Any time you modify a "finished" program, it becomes unfinished again, and will require re-testing. Therefore, make careful choices in designing the code to avoid these types of problems later on.

Computers offer several different data types, so that each **object** (piece of data) that your program uses can be represented in the most accurate and efficient way possible.

For example, computer floating point systems have a greater range flexibility than integers, but are much slower and less accurate.

6.2   Variables

A program's instructions and data objects are stored in the computer's RAM and ROM. When programming in machine language, we would access the objects in memory by specifying a binary memory address. Assembly language and high level languages allow us to identify memory locations by names, called **identifiers**, which are much more meaningful and easier to remember than numeric addresses. Identifiers are used by most languages to represent constants, data types, variables, and subprograms.

C identifiers must conform to a few simple rules, so that the compiler can distinguish them from other **tokens** of the language, such as keywords and punctuation:

- All identifiers must begin with a letter or the '_' character.

- Subsequent characters may be letters, digits, or the '_' (underscore) character.

- Each compiler has a maximum allowable length for identifiers. A typical maximum is about 32 characters, which is more than enough for most purposes. Longer names can be used with most compilers, but any characters beyond the maximum length are ignored.

An identifier which refers to an object in memory is called a **variable**. A program can change the value stored in a variable at any time, using an assignment or input statement. In C, and most other compiled languages, a variable must be **defined** before it is used. When defining a variable, you choose the data type and the name, and the compiler allocates a memory location.

A variable definition in C consists of a type specifier followed by one or more names:

```
type var1,var2, ..., varN;
```

Example:

```
#include <stdio.h>  /* I/O function declarations */
#include <sysexits.h>
#include <math.h>   /* #define for M_PI */

int     main()

{
    double  radius,area;    /* Define variables */

    /* Input the radius */
    printf("Enter the radius of the circle: ");
    scanf("%lf",&radius);

    /* Compute the area */
    area = M_PI * radius * radius;

    /* Print the result */
    printf("The area is %f\n",area);
    return EX_OK;
}
```

The radius and the area are stored in memory so the computer can perform calculations and later print the result. The definition

```
double radius,area;
```

defines two variables of type `double`, and names them `radius` and `area`.

When the radius is typed in by the user, the `scanf()` function will convert the input text to the proper binary format for an object of type `double` and store the value in memory at the address of `radius`. The next statement uses the value at address `radius` and the value of M_PI (π) to compute the area, and stores the result at address `area`.

Programming with Style:

Some programmers prefer to place each variable on a separate line, and comment the definitions to explain the purpose of the variable.

```
double  radius,      /* Radius of the circle */
        area;        /* Area of the circle */
```

Others aim at writing **self-documenting** code. By choosing descriptive variable names, and using clear input and output messages, we can greatly reduce the need for comments. With badly chosen names, you would need comments everywhere to explain what the code is doing.

As an example, see if you can determine what the following program does:

```
double  a,b,c,d,x;

printf("Enter a, b, c, and d: ");
scanf("%lf %lf %lf %lf",&a,&b,&c,&d);
x = sqrt((a-b)*(a-b) + (c-d)*(c-d));
printf("x is %f.\n",x);
```

Clearly, this code will need many comments to explain what the variables are for. Moreover, the input prompt doesn't give users a clue what to enter, and they will probably need to read the manual just to figure out how to use the program.

If we use more descriptive variable names, which describe the object contained in the variable, and more intelligent input prompts and output descriptions, the need for comments is greatly reduced:

```
double  x1,x2,y1,y2,dx,dy,distance;

printf("To find the distance between two points\n");
printf("enter the coordinates x1, y1, x2, y2: ");
```

```
scanf("%lf %lf %lf %lf",&x1,&y1,&x2,&y2);
dx = x2-x1;
dy = y2-y1;
distance = sqrt(dx*dx+dy*dy);
printf("The distance between the points is %f.\n",
       distance);
```

The second example is much more clear to both the programmer and the user. The user won't need anything but a basic knowledge of geometry, and any programmer who looks at the code will be able to understand it quickly.

In general, almost any program can be made user-friendly enough so that an average user can just walk up and use it without any training. Users don't want to, and shouldn't have to, read manuals to learn how to operate a software package. For example, writers should have no trouble figuring out how to use a word processor, and pilots should be able to figure out how to use weather reporting software without referring to the manuals. User-friendliness is one of the most important factors in making software sell, and it only takes a little effort from you as a programmer to understand and satisfy your users' needs.

6.3 C's Built-in Data Types

When discussing types, it is important to distinguish between **scalar** types and **aggregate** types. The word scalar is borrowed from mathematics, meaning dimensionless. Thus a scalar type represents a solitary value of some sort. Aggregate types represent groups of data such as linear lists or 2-dimensional tables. Aggregate types in C include arrays and structures, which are discussed in later chapters 15 and 18. The C language does not provide any built-in aggregate types, but it does provide the necessary high-level features for creating them.

C offers five built-in scalar data types, from which all aggregate types are built. Three of these types are integer types and the other two are floating point types, which support a subset of the **real numbers**.

Type	Bits	Format	Range
char	8	2's comp	-128 to +127
unsigned char	8	unsigned	0 to 255
short	16	2's comp	-32,768 to +32,767
unsigned short	16	unsigned	0 to 65,535
long	32	2's comp	-2,147,483,648 to 2,147,483,647
unsigned long	32	unsigned	0 to 4,294,967,295
Extended types			
long long	64	2's comp	$\pm 9.2233720 \times 10^{18}$
unsigned long long	64	unsigned	0 to 1.8446744×10^{19}

Table 6.1: Integer data types

Integer variables in C can be defined as either **signed** or **unsigned**. Using `unsigned` doubles the positive range of an integer type, while sacrificing the ability to represent negative values. This is often preferable to using a larger integer type, which reduces performance on some systems. Table 6.1 summarizes the integer data types and their ranges. See chapter 2 for an explanation of range and precision.

In addition, there is a **pseudo-type** called `int`, which represents either `short` or `long`, depending on the compiler. On a 16 bit compiler, `int` is equivalent to `short`. On a 32 bit or larger compiler, `int` is the same as `long`. The type `unsigned` by itself is equivalent to `unsigned int`.

Pitfall: The Unknown `int`

Many programmers make the mistake of assuming `int` is a particular size, usually 32 bits. It's a bad idea to make assumptions about the size of an `int`, even if you know which size *your* compiler uses. Try to write programs that will work exactly the same way regardless of the compiler. Virtually every C program that's written will eventually be compiled by other compilers. Unix programs in particular are likely to be compiled on a wide variety of different hardware platforms with different word sizes.

If you assume `int` is `long`, for example, your program won't run correctly when compiled with a 16 bit compiler. For example, the code fragment

below won't work on a typical *DOS* compiler, since the value 100,000 is
beyond the range of a 16 bit int.

```
int     c;

for (c=0; c<100000; ++c)
{
    ...
}
```

If you assume it is a short, then it will take up more space than you
expect when compiled with a 32 bit compiler. This will only be a problem
for large arrays, as demonstrated by the definition below.

```
int     list[500000];
```

The array list will require one megabyte of memory on a 16 bit system,
and 2 megabytes on a 32 bit system. Hence, this array should be defined
as short, to avoid wasting a megabyte of memory on 32 bit systems.

**The int pseudo-type should only be used if it doesn't matter
whether the variable is a short or a long.**

The int type exists for one reason; to provide easy, portable access to
the fastest data type on any machine. If you must make assumptions, be
pessimistic to be safe. Assume an int has the limited range of a short,
because this will be the case on some systems that your program will
run on. If this is not acceptable, then use long instead. Also assume
int takes up as much memory as a long, because, again, it will on some
systems. If this is not acceptable, then use short instead. If both of
these conditions are acceptable, then int is the best choice, because it
guarantees the fastest operations possible.

Similarly, an unsigned int is equivalent to either unsigned short or
unsigned long, and the same precautions apply.

The floating point types may vary from one system to another, but the IEEE floating
point standard is the most commonly used. The actual range of floating point types

Type	bits	Format	Range
float	32	IEEE	$\pm(1.2 \times 10^{-38}$ to $3.4 \times 10^{38})$
double	64	IEEE	$\pm(2.2 \times 10^{-308}$ to $1.8 \times 10^{308})$
Extended type			
long double	Hardware-dependent		

Table 6.2: Floating point data types

for your system can be found in the header file */usr/include/float.h*. The floating point types are outlined in table 6.2. Ranges are given for the IEEE standard. These also may vary for different CPU's. The `long double` type is available only on some platforms that support floating point formats larger than 64 bits. For example, the *Pentium* chip supports an 80 bit format, and some modern RISC chips and scientific computers support 128 bit formats. On computers with only 32 and 64 bit floating point formats, `long double` is equivalent to `double`.

6.3.1   Void

`Void` is a special type which can be used to define functions that don't return a value, and generic pointer variables, both of which are discussed in later chapters. The `void` type was not included in the original K&R C, but was adopted by the ANSI committee. Some older C programs may have `void` defined as `int` using a `#define` or `typedef`.

Tip of the trade: Word Boundaries

Each memory address in most modern computers holds one byte of data. Objects larger than one byte are typically aligned on *word boundaries* to minimize memory access time. For example, a word boundary for a 4 byte word, such as a `long`, will always have a memory address which is a multiple of 4. A word boundary for a `short` would be a multiple of 2, and a `char` could reside at any address. Word alignment wastes a (usually) small amount of memory in exchange for greatly improved performance. This is done because many types of computers restrict memory access to word boundaries in order to reduce the amount of wiring necessary. For example, if the addresses are restricted to multiples of 4, then the two lowest bits of each address are not needed, and two pins can be eliminated from the address bus and memory chips. When a program generates an address which is *not* a multiple of 4 then, the two lowest bits are not used to address the memory chips. If such a computer allows unaligned word access, then *two* four-byte words are actually accessed to satisfy the request, which will significantly slow down the program. For example, to access a `long` beginning at address 6 would require fetching the long from address 4, and the next one at address 8, and then pasting together the necessary bytes. RISC computers typically *require* all words to be aligned, while CISC computers just run slower if they aren't aligned. In either case, the C compiler usually aligns everything for best performance by default, so you don't have to worry about it.

6.4 Constants

6.4.1 Data Types of Constants

Constant values appearing in C programs have definite data types, just as variables do. The following rules explain how to identify the data type of a constant.

- Any sequence consisting of only the digits 0-9, and not beginning with 0, is a decimal `int`.

  Example: 255, 34

- Any sequence of digits beginning with 0 is considered an octal `int`.

  Example: 0100 is the same as 64, 011 is the same as 9

- 0x or 0X followed by a sequence of digits or letters a-f or A-F is considered a hexadecimal `int`.

  Example: 0xff or 0xFF is the same as 255 or 0377, 0XFFFF is the same as 65535 (On 16 bit systems, $65535 = 1111111111111111_2$, which is the same as -1_{10} in 2's complement)

- Any of the preceding integer constants followed by an 'L' is a `long`.

  Example: 0400L, 34L, 0xffL

Symbol	ASCII	Name
'\0'	0	nul
'\a'	7	bel (bell)
'\b'	8	bs (backspace)
'\t'	9	tab
'\n'	10	nl (newline)
'\f'	12	ff (form feed)
'\r'	13	cr (carriage return)
'\\'	\	backslash

Table 6.3: Standard escape sequences

The 'L' must be used whenever a **long** constant is called for, in order to guarantee portability of your programs. With most modern C compilers, **long** and **int** are the same, but if you assume this is *always* true, and leave out the 'L', your programs won't work properly with 16 bit compilers.

These are particularly useful for function arguments which require a **long** regardless of the compiler, such as the library function **lseek()**.

- A character constant is a single character between single quotes or an **escape sequence** between single quotes.

  An escape sequence is a \ followed by a special character or an octal number, such as \010 (8_{10}). An escape sequence is limited to three digits, and is taken as an octal value, even if it doesn't begin with a 0. For example, '\377' is equivalent to 255 decimal.

  Character constants in C are of type **int**, not **char**. Since the C language promotes all **char** values to **int** for arithmetic operations, a constant of type char would slow down the program. Therefore, the constants 'A', 65, \0100, and '\100' are all identical as far as the C compiler is concerned.

  Table 6.3 lists common escape sequences.

- Any sequence of digits containing a decimal point is considered a **double**.

  Example: 5.0, .713

- Any sequence followed by an e or E and integer is a DOUBLE in scientific notation

Example: 2.3e11 equals 2.3×10^{11}

- Any real constant followed by 'f' or 'F' is a float.

  Example: 2.3f, 2.3e10f

- Strings

  Although C does not support strings variables directly, it does support string constants. Any sequence of characters enclosed within double quotes is a null terminated string. (The compiler adds a '\0', or null byte to the end.) The C standard library functions all work with null terminated strings. The null byte must not be confused with the manifest constant NULL, which represents a *memory address*. The null byte is simply the character 0, and is best represented as '\0', not as NULL.

  All escape sequences can be used within a string constant, just as they are used in character constants.

  For example, the string constant "\020Bart\n" contains the decimal ASCII characters 16 66 97 114 116 10 0.

Pitfall: Unsigned Constants

Integer constants may be either signed or unsigned. It's possible to have two constants represent the same value in an assignment. For example, assigning 255 to a char variable has the same effect as assigning -1, because both constants are represented in 8 bit binary as 11111111_2. Similarly, assigning 65535 to a short variable or 4294967295 to a long variable will have the same effect. Assigning 254 to a char variable is the same as assigning -2, 253 is the same as -3, and so on. In all examples above, the positive value assigned was beyond the range of the signed integer type given. The maximum is +127 for char, +32767 for short, and +2147483647 for long. If a constant is too large for the signed type, C will automatically interpret it as an unsigned value, and copy the bits without any complaints. It's up to you to make sure the values you use are within the range of the data type.

6.4.2   Named Constants

Constants used in programs should be given names, rather than **hard-coded**. Using descriptive constant names will make the program more readable and self-documenting, just as descriptive variable names do.

Moreover, using named constants makes a program more **modifiable**, or easy to modify. This is especially true when a constant is used in many places throughout the program. A hard-coded constant that appears in 27 places will require 27 changes to the program when the value needs to be changed. It's easy to miss a few occurrences when making such changes, and this might cause some nasty run-time errors. By using a named constant, you only have to make *one* change, and then recompile to change the value throughout the program.

Constants can be named with the `#define` preprocessor directive, which has the following general form:

```
#define NAME    TEXT
```

The name follows the same naming rules as any other C identifier, and the text is taken as everything to the end of the line. When you compile the program, the preprocessor will simply substitute the text for the name wherever it's used.

Example:

A simple program to compute the area of a circle.

```
#include <stdio.h>
#include <sysexits.h>

#define PI      3.1415926535798943
#define PROMPT  "Please enter the radius: "

int    main()

{
    double  radius, area;
```

```
        /* Input radius */
        fputs(PROMPT,stdout);
        scanf("%lf",&radius);

        /* Compute area and print */
        area = PI * radius * radius;
        printf("The area is %f.\n",area);
        return EX_OK;
}
```

It is conventional to name constants with all upper-case letters so that they can be easily distinguished from variables, which are generally named with all lower case letters. This way, you will know at a glance what can be done with a given identifier, and where to look to find out it's type and value.

Named constants can also be defined on the command line when compiling, by using the -D compiler option. For example,

```
cc -Wall -DDEBUG=1 prog.c
```

is the same as having the line

```
#define DEBUG    1
```

in the program. Note that there is no space between the D and the constant name.

Named constants can also be defined using the const keyword in a variable definition:

```
const int debug = 1;
```

This method is not as flexible as #define, however, and is rarely used for this purpose. The const keyword is most often used with function arguments, as discussed in chapter 11.

Pitfall: Floating Point Constants

When writing constants, it is important to use all the precision available in the data type. For example, the definition

```
#define     PI   3.14
```

will ruin the precision of the program's results. The **double** data type is accurate to 16 digits on most computers. However, the results of your programs are at best only as accurate as the worst piece of data used to compute them. Because of round-off errors that occur during calculations, floating point results are usually less accurate than the input, so it becomes even more important to maximize the precision of the input and constants.

By using the constant 3.14, you would limit the precision of the result **area** to no more than three decimal digits. This program should be written with all values utilizing the full precision of the computer:

```
#define     PI   3.1415926535798943
```

Better yet, you can save yourself a lot of worry by using the standard header files, such as *math.h*. The standard headers define all kinds of useful constants for you, and will always use the full precision of the computer you are using. For example, math.h defines a constant called **M_PI** for the value of π, so you never have to define it or hard-code it yourself.

6.5   Initialization in Variable Definitions

Variables can be initialized in the definition by following the name with an assignment expression. For example, the definition

```
int     c = 0;
```

defines a variable named `c`, and sets the value to 0 before the first statement in the block is executed.

Strings can be initialized also. No dimension is needed if an initializer is present.[1] For example, in the definition below, the variable `lname` is automatically dimensioned to 12 characters, enough for the name "Von Neumann" and an null terminator byte, '\0'.

```
char    fname[10] = "Alfred";
char    lname[] = "Von Neumann";
```

6.6 Choosing the Right Data Type

Choosing the best data type for a given situation requires some thought, as well as a basic knowledge of computer hardware and compilers. Here are some general guidelines and reasons for choosing each data type. Some of the reasons given are clarified in section 8.3.

1. Always use an integer type instead of floating point if possible. Floating point operations typically take several times longer than the same operations on integers.

   For example, floating point addition requires the following three steps, much like scientific notation:

   (a) Equalize the exponents

   (b) Add the mantissas

   (c) Normalize the result

   An integer addition, on the other hand, is analogous to the second step alone. We can therefore expect that floating point addition takes about three times as long as integer addition.

---

[1]Some K&R compilers allow only `static` string variables to be initialized this way. Static variables are discussed in chapter 11.

If your computer doesn't have hardware support for floating point operations, then integer types may be as much as fifty times faster. Lack of floating point support was common in many older microprocessors, including all Intel processors up to the 486SX. Floating point support can be added to these processors by adding an 8087, 80287, 80387, or 80487 co-processor chip. The 486DX and Pentium processors have built-in floating point support.

2. Once it has been decided to use an integer type, use `int` if either a `short` or `long` will do. That's exactly what an `int` is — either `short` or `long`, depending on the compiler. Compilers are generally designed to use the optimal word size for the computer they are written for, although most *DOS* compilers use a 16 bit `int` by default, even if used on a 32 bit 80386, 80486, or Pentium processor. NEVER assume you know the size of an `int`, because it varies for different compilers, operating systems, and machines. The type of computer you write a program on is not necessarily the same as the one people will use it on, especially in the Unix realm. To play it safe, assume an `int` variable has the range of a `short`, in case the program is compiled on a 16 bit machine, and takes as much memory as a `long`, for the times it is compiled on a 32 bit machine. For more harping on this point, see section 6.3.

   The advantage of `int` is that it is guaranteed to give the fastest operations possible on any computer. On a 16 bit compiler, `int` will be the same as `short` to avoid multiple-precision arithmetic. On a 32 bit compiler, `int` will be the same as `long` to avoid time-consuming promotions. Promotions are discussed in chapter 8.

3. Use `short` only if it will save a substantial amount of memory. When your program is compiled with a 32 bit compiler, all `short` values are promoted to `int` when calculations are performed, which will slow down your program significantly. NEVER define a scalar `short` variable, unless that variable absolutely must be a 16 bit value for use with `scanf()` or for other technical reasons. `Short` should generally be used only for large arrays or other lists.

4. The `char` type is generally used only for strings, but may also be used as a very short integer to save space. If using `char` as an integer, apply the same rules as for `short`.

5. Use `long` only if a `short` does not have sufficient range. Otherwise, use `int`. For example, the distance from the earth to the sun is about 93,000,000 miles. This value cannot be stored in a `short`, so you can't define the variable as `short` or `int`. Use `long` to avoid potential problems. If you define it as

int, the program will work fine with 32 bit compilers, giving you lots of false confidence, and then mysteriously break down after being compiled with a 16 bit compiler.

Using long will slow down your program when it is compiled with a 16 bit compiler, since long is a 32 bit value. This requires multiple precision arithmetic, i.e. all calculations will require two or more machine instructions instead of one. Better to have a slow program, however, than one that doesn't work.

6. Sometimes using unsigned will provide adequate range so that it isn't necessary to use long. An unsigned variable has the same speed and size as its signed counterpart, but has twice the positive range, and cannot contain negative values. For example, attendance at a baseball game may be up to 50,000. This is larger than a short will handle (-32,768 to 32,767), so int would be a bad choice, and you might think to use long. On the other hand, this *is* within the range of an unsigned short (0 to 65,535).

Therefore, unsigned int is the best type for a scalar variable in this range, since it is the fastest available type and has adequate range on all systems. We would only use unsigned short for a large array, to save space. Long will also work, but will require multiple precision arithmetic on 16 bit systems, so it will be slow. It will also require more memory than the unsigned int on a 16 bit system.

7. When floating point is used, it's best to use double whenever possible for the sake of precision. Use float only if there isn't enough memory for double. Using float might also speed up the program on some older computers, but generally not enough to warrant the loss of precision. Most computers today have sophisticated floating point hardware that can process double values just as fast as float.

To demonstrate the difference in performance, consider the following loop, which simply counts to 10,000,000:[2] (We couldn't do this example with a single loop,

---

[2]Loops are described in chapter 10.

Data type	Execution time (seconds)
short	0.77
int	0.61
long	0.61
long long	1.52
float	3.52
double	3.52

Table 6.4: Execution times for various data types

because 10,000,000 is beyond the range of a `short`.)

```
for (count1=0; count1<1000; ++count1)
    for (count2=0; count2<10000; ++count2)
        ;
```

Table 6.4 shows execution times of the program using various data types for `count1` and `count2`, on a 486DX/66Mhz PC running FreeBSD. The program was compiled using `gcc` 2.7.2 with full optimizations.

Note that using `short` slows down the program slightly, because this is a 32 bit system, and the `short` values have to be promoted to `int` each time count1 and count2 are incremented. Since the 486 is a 32 bit CPU, and Unix is a 32 bit OS, `int` is equivalent to `long`, so we would expect them to perform equally. On a 16 bit machine, `int` and `short` would show the same performance, and `long` would be much slower. The performance of `long long` on a 32 bit system is analogous to using a `long` on a 16 bit system. Using `long long` requires multiple instructions for each operation, so it takes a little more than twice as long as `int`.

Furthermore, using `double` or `float` slowed the program down by a factor of almost six compared to `int`. The performance of `float` and `double` are identical because the 486 instruction set directly supports both 32 bit and 64 bit floating point.

Tip of the trade: Arbitrary Precision Integers

Some systems include an **arbitrary precision** integer library, which provides functions that can handle integers with unlimited range. While generally difficult to use, they are useful for many purposes where very large integers are needed, and the precision limitations of floating point cannot be tolerated. One example is cryptography, where large blocks of data are sometimes treated as huge integer values for encryption and decryption purposes. If your system doesn't have such a library, check your favorite GNU site: Odds are you can download one as an add-on.

6.7 Creating New Type Names: typedef

The `typedef` keyword in C is used to create a new name for a type. The general syntax is

```
typedef type-specifier type-name ;
```

Typedefs are **global**, meaning that typedefed names can be used throughout the program, not just in the vicinity of where they are defined. Typedefs should be placed in header files, so that they can be used in many different source files if needed. For programs small enough to be written entirely in one source file, the typedefs should appear above `main()`.

Typedefs are most often used with structures (chapter 18) to eliminate the need to write long, complicated type specifiers. Typedefs can also be used to create shorter names for relatively simple types.

For example, the system header file */usr/include/sys/types.h* contains the following typedefs aimed simply at saving us a little typing:

```
typedef unsigned char    uchar;
typedef unsigned short   ushort;
typedef unsigned int     uint;
typedef unsigned long    ulong;
```

Hence, if we `#include <sys/types.h>`, we can define `unsigned long` variables using `ulong` instead.

```
ulong    attendance;
```

We can also use typedefs to create more descriptive names. For example, we may want to use `char` for an array of tiny integers, instead of a string. If we define the array as

```
char    list[MAX_VALS];
```

it might be mistaken for a string variable.

We could use a typedef to make it more obvious:

```
typedef char    tiny_int_t;

int     main()

{
    tiny_int_t  list[MAX_VALS];
    ...
}
```

It is convention to use the suffix '_t' on type names so that they can be easily distinguished from variables. There are a few places in C programming where either a type name or a variable can be used, so it is often helpful to make a clear distinction.

Chapter 7

Simple Input and Output

Before you begin...

You should be familiar with the material on C data types presented in chapter 6.

7.1   The Standard I/O Streams

As discussed in chapter 4, every new process in Unix has three standard streams open from the moment the process is created. In a C program, the three standard streams are given the names `stdin` for the standard input, `stdout` for the standard output, and `stderr` for the standard error. These names are not C keywords, but are standardized variables defined in *stdio.h*.

The standard C library has many functions and macros which implicitly use `stdin` and `stdout`. These functions are the primary topic of this chapter. To send output to `stderr`, you must use generalized stream output functions and specify `stderr` explicitly. A few of the generalized functions are introduced here for use with `stderr`, and described in detail in chapter 21. Note that *none* of the I/O functions are part of the C language per se. In fact, C has no I/O capabilities whatsoever. All I/O is performed by library functions which ultimately utilize Unix system calls.

To use any of these I/O functions, you need to include the header file *stdio.h*, which contains prototype declarations for the I/O functions, and other necessary information for the compiler.

7.2   Single Character I/O

To input a single character from stdin, use the getchar() macro. To output a single character to stdout, use the putchar() macro.

Example:

The following program waits for the user to type a single character (followed by *return*), and then echoes the character to the screen.

```
#include <stdio.h>
#include <sysexits.h>

int     main()
{
    int     ch;

    ch = getchar();
    putchar(ch);
    return EX_OK;
}
```

Under normal circumstances, you will have to type the character *and press return* before the program responds. This is because a Unix terminal is normally operated in **cooked mode**. In cooked mode, the operating system collects an entire line of input from the terminal before handing it over to your program. Therefore, the program doesn't receive *any* input until you press return. This improves the efficiency of the system, and serves most purposes just fine. A few programs, such as editors, need to respond immediately when any key is pressed. These programs operate in **raw mode**. Terminal modes are discussed at length in chapter 26. For the sake of simplicity, all the examples we use in this and most other chapters are designed to operate in cooked mode.

7.3   String I/O

A strings in C is implemented as an **array** of characters. Arrays are covered in chapter 15. For now, we'll just demonstrate how to define a character array and use it with standard I/O functions.

Dangerous Function: `gets()`

The original standard I/O function designed to input an entire line of characters is called `gets()`. This function is generally regarded as unsafe, because it allows the user to input more characters than the array will hold. The generalized `fgets()` function is safer, because it requires you to specify the maximum number of characters.

The `fgets()` function reads characters until it encounters a newline ('\n') or until it has read the maximum number of characters specified. The newline character is included in the string. If you don't want the newline in your string, then the next best option is to write our own input function using a loop and `getchar()`. This will require knowledge of loops, arrays, and functions, which are covered in chapters 10, 15, and 11. You could also use `fgets()`, and remove the newline from the string after reading, but removing the last character in a string is a rather expensive search-and-destroy mission, so this isn't a very attractive option.

A sample function called `getline()` is shown below.

```
/* Input a string, and null terminate */
void    getline(char *string,int array_size)

{
    /* Read up to newline or to array limit */
    while ( ((*string = getchar()) != '\n') &&
            (--array_size > 0) )
        ++string;
    *string = '\0';   /* null terminate */
}
```

This function requires both the array argument, and the size of the array, so that it can avoid overfilling it. The `getline()` function will stop at `array_size`-1 characters to leave room for the null byte. For now, just type it into your programs to use it. In chapter 20, you'll learn how to add functions like `getline()` to your personal library so they can be automatically linked into any program that calls them.

Pitfall: Leaving the Cap Off

String input functions, and any other functions that create or copy strings, must null terminate the string, that is, place a '\0' character (null byte) at the end. If the null terminator is missing, certain string functions won't know where to stop reading characters, and may corrupt your data or cause the program to **crash**, i.e. to terminate abnormally before completing.

To output a string, you can use `puts()` or `fputs()`. The `puts()` function adds a newline to the output, which is generally undesirable when reading with `fgets()`, since the input string already contains one newline. If you don't want an extra newline printed after the output string, use `fputs()`.

Example:

```
#include <stdio.h>
#include <sysexits.h>

/* Prototype declarations */
void    getline(char *string,int array_size);

/* Main program */
int     main()

{
    char    name[40];   /* String variable */
```

```
        /* Get user's name */
        fputs("What is your name? ",stdout);
        getline(name,40);

        /* Say Hi */
        fputs("Hello, ",stdout);
        puts(name);
        return EX_OK;
    }


    /* Input a string, and null terminate */
    void    getline(char *string,int array_size)

    {
        /* Read up to newline or to array limit */
        while ( ((*string = getchar()) != '\n') &&
                (--array_size > 0) )
            ++string;
        *string = '\0';    /* null terminate */
    }
```

7.4 Numeric I/O

7.4.1 Output with `printf()`

To print numbers, or a formatted mixture of numbers and text, use the `printf()` function. This function builds an output string using a **format-string** and possibly some additional arguments, and then passed the string to `fputs()` for output.

Programming for Performance:

> The `printf()` function is well suited for printing numbers in ASCII format. It can also handle individual characters and strings, but this practice should be avoided if possible, since calling `putchar()` or `fputs()` directly is more efficient. In fact, every `printf()` call eventually leads to `putchar()` calls for each character, so printing characters with `printf()` is essentially taking the long way home.

The general syntax of a `printf()` call is:

```
printf(format-string,argument1,argument2,...);
```

The format string controls the appearance of the entire output sequence. It may contain ordinary text and escape sequences, which are printed verbatim, and one **place-holder** for each additional argument. Place-holders are special symbols in the format string that specify the data type and output format of the argument.

A place-holder is anything in the format string beginning with the '%' character, except for "%%", which represents the '%' character. The `printf()` function scans the format string from left to right, looking for '%' characters. Non '%' characters are simply copied to the output string. When a place-holder is encountered, `printf()` attempts to write the next argument into the output string according to the format specified by the place-holder.

The basic `printf()` place-holders are listed in table 7.1.

To print a decimal int argument, use the %d place-holder, as follows:

```
int     aardvarks = 15;

printf("Aardvarks = %d.\n",aardvarks);
```

The output of the code segment above is "Aardvarks␣=␣15.", where each ␣ represents a space character.

Place-holder	Data type	Output format
%d	int	Decimal
%u	int	Unsigned decimal
%o	int	Octal
%x	int	Hexadecimal with small letters
%X	int	Hexadecimal with capital letters
%c	int	ASCII character
%s	string (char *)	ASCII string
%f	float or double	Decimal
%e	float or double	Scientific Notation
%g	float or double	Like 'f' or 'e'
%p	Pointer	An address in hexadecimal

Table 7.1: Place-holders for `printf()`

Similarly, you can print **aardvarks** in octal by using the place-holder %o, or in hexadecimal using %x or %X. The two hexadecimal place-holders differ in that %X uses upper case letters A-F, whereas %x uses lower case.

The same place-holders used for **int** values are also used for any **char** and **short** values you may want to print as numbers, because the compiler promotes **char** and **short** values to **int** whenever they are passed to a function such as `printf()`. **Long** values, however, require the place-holder to be modified with the 'l' prefix, as describe later in this section.

Float and **double** use the same place-holder, much like **char**, **short** and **int**, because the compiler promotes **float** values to **double** when they are passed to a function.

To print a **float** or **double** value in plain decimal format, use the %f place-holder:

```
double  area;

...
printf("Area = %f.\n",area);
```

The scientific notation output format is the same as used for scientific notation constants, as described in section 6.4. For example, the plain decimal value 467.32

could be printed as `4.6732E2` using the %e place-holder instead of %f.

```
printf("Area = %e.\n",area);
```

The %g place-holder may produce output like either %f or %e, depending on which form is more compact.

Strings may be output using the %s place-holder. Remember, however, that it's more efficient to use `puts()` or `fputs()` to output a single string. Using `printf()` is only necessary if you need to output multiple items, or control the format of the output.

```
double   area = 4.5;
char     shape[20] = "circle";

    . . .
printf("The area of the %s is %f.\n",shape,area);
```

Pitfall: Arguments to `printf()` *and* `scanf()`

For most functions, the compiler uses a prototype declaration to check for a proper set of arguments. For example, the prototype for `fputs()` is

```
int fputs(char *,FILE *);
```

This informs the compiler that each call to `fputs()` should have a character pointer (string) argument followed by a FILE pointer argument. If you call `fputs()` with the wrong number or types of arguments, the compiler will produce an error message.

The difficulty with `printf()` and `scanf()` is that they accept a *variable* number of arguments. Any number of arguments is acceptable, as long as they match the place-holders in the format string. In order to properly check all of the arguments, the compiler would need to understand the format string. Since `printf()` and `scanf()` are not part of the C language, most compilers cannot do this, `gcc` being one notable exception.

The prototypes for `printf()` and `scanf()` are as follows:

```
int printf(char *,...);
int scanf(char *,...);
```

These prototypes inform the compiler that each `printf()` or `scanf()` call should have a string as its first argument, and anything goes after that. If the format string is missing, or preceded by a non-string argument, you will get a compiler error. If you use the wrong place-holder for a given argument, the compiler will not detect it, and your program will most likely exhibit some pretty odd behavior.

For example, the output of the following code segment is essentially unpredictable:

```
double  area = 51.0;

printf("%ld\n",area);
```

The `printf()` function will accept your word of honor that the argument following the format string is a `long`, then take the first 32 bits from the 64-bit variable `area`, and print whatever binary integer they represent. Since the bits in `area` are in floating point format, rather than 2's complement, the output will be gibberish. For example, the output produced by the code above when run under `gcc` on *FreeBSD* is 1717986918.

Place-holder Prefixes

To print a `long` value in any format, the place-holder must have a 'l' prefix:

```
long     aardvarks = 15;

printf("Aardvarks = %ld.\n",aardvarks);
```

Pitfall: Place-holders and Portability

If you are programming on a system where int and long are the same size, your programs will work fine when you print long values with int place-holders. However, the same programs may produce incorrect output when run on other systems. To avoid problems with porting your code, always make sure you use the 'l' prefix when printing long values, even if it isn't necessary on your own system.

The 'l' prefix can also be applied to floating point values, but it will either generate a warning message or be ignored by printf(). All floating point values are promoted to double when passed to a function, so there is no need for more than one floating point place-holder, unless your compiler supports long double. To specify a long double argument, prefix the format specifier with 'L'. Note that the 'l' prefix is *not* ignored by scanf(), for reasons discussed in section 7.4.2.

An integer constant preceding any specifier controls the width of the output field. If the argument value has fewer digits than the field width, it will be **right-justified**, with leading spaces to fill the rest of the field. If the argument value is wider than the field width specified, the field width is ignored, and the entire value is printed.

```
long     aardvarks = 15;

printf("Aardvarks = %5ld.\n",aardvarks);
```

The output of the code segment above is "Aardvarks␣=␣␣␣␣15.".

For floating point output, you can specify the number of decimal places, i.e. fractional digits, in addition to the field width, by adding a '.' followed by the number of decimal places. If the value printed contains more decimal places than you want printed, the output will be rounded (not truncated) to fit. Also note that the field width specifies the *total number of characters to be printed*, including the decimal point. For example, a place-holder of %10.2f specifies a field with up to 7 digits left of the decimal point, and exactly 2 digits to the right.

```
double  area = 12.45645;

printf("Area = %10.2f.\n",area);
```

The output is `Area⎵=⎵⎵⎵⎵⎵⎵12.46.`

Normally when a field width is given, the output is right-justified. If you want the item left-justified, such as `Aardvarks⎵=⎵15⎵⎵⎵.`, add a '-' prefix, as follows:

```
printf("Aardvarks = %-5ld.\n",aardvarks);
```

If you prefer leading 0's to leading spaces in integer or floating point output, such as `Aardvarks = 00015.`, use a field width beginning with '0':

```
printf("Aardvarks = %05ld.\n",aardvarks);
```

A '*' prefix denotes a variable field width, which is specified by an extra argument preceding the value to be printed.

```
int     field_width = 6, aardvarks = 15;

printf("Aardvarks = %*d.\n",field_width,aardvarks);
```

The variable field width is useful when you want to minimize the field width in order to fit the maximum number of columns on the screen.

7.4.2 Input with scanf()

The scanf() function inputs data in ASCII format, converts it into the appropriate binary format, and stores it in one or more argument variables. The scanf() function is essentially the converse of printf(), but uses a slightly different set of place-holders, which are listed in table 7.2.

Place-holder	Data type	Input format
%d	int	Decimal integer
%x, %X	int	Hexadecimal integer
%o	int	Octal integer
%i	int	Decimal, octal, or hexadecimal
%f, %e, %g	float	Decimal or scientific notation
%c	char	ASCII character
%s	char *	ASCII string

Table 7.2: Place-holders for `scanf()`

Pitfall: Leaving Without your Data

The return value from `scanf()` is the number of arguments successfully filled. Programs should always check the return value from `scanf()`. Otherwise, your program will continue, using whatever garbage data was in the variables before `scanf()` was called. To check this, you'll need an `if` or `switch` statement, both of which are covered in chapter 9. The examples in this chapter simply show you how to capture the return value. Chapter 9 demonstrates how to make use of it.

The most important thing to know about `scanf()` is that all of the arguments it receives must be **pointers**, i.e. addresses of variables. The `scanf()` function needs the *memory location* of each variable, not the *value*, so that it will know where in memory to place the input it receives from `stdin`.

Recall that `printf()` has no place-holders for `short` or `float`, because all `short` values are converted to `int` when passed to a function, and likewise all `float` values are converted to `double`. Since all arguments to `scanf()` are addresses, not values, *no promotions take place*, and a different place-holder is needed for *every* data type. Table 7.2 lists the common `scanf()` place-holders.

Most of the variables you pass to `scanf()` will need to be preceded by an **address operator**, '&', which specifies the address of a variable. For example:

```
int     age, args;
```

```
fputs("Please enter your age: ",stdout);
args = scanf("%d",&age);
```

Pitfall: Misplaced Input

It's easy to forget the address operator '&' when reading input into a numeric variable. For example, take a close look at the following code segment:

```
double   radius;
int      args;

args = scanf("%lf",radius);
```

Since scanf() is not part of the C language, most compilers don't know what type each argument should be, and won't detect this error. Instead, the *value* of radius will be interpreted as the *address* where you want scanf() to place the input value. This will often result in corrupted data in your program. If you're lucky, a segmentation fault will occur, leaving you with a core file that can be used to quickly pinpoint the error.

Remember that all arguments to scanf() must be addresses, so any scanf() argument without an address operator attached demands a closer look.

Strings in C are arrays, and array names *are* pointers, so no '&' is needed when passing a string to scanf().

```
int      age, args;
char     name[40];

fputs("Enter your name and age separated by a space: ",
```

```
        stdout);
args = scanf("%s %d",name,&age);
```

Pitfall: Strings and `scanf()`

Strings, like other data read by `scanf()` are delimited by whitespace, i.e. spaces, tabs, and newline characters. Hence, you cannot use `scanf()` to input a string that contains spaces or tabs. For example, the code fragment above cannot by used to enter both a first and last name. Doing so would cause `scanf()` to place the first name in `name`, and then attempt to place the last name in `age`, which of course, would fail, because age is a numeric variable. To input both a first and last name, you'll need two '%s' place-holders in the format string.

```
scanf("%s %s %d",fname,lname,&age);
```

Prefixing any integer place-holder with an 'l' will cause `scanf()` to convert the input to a `long` instead of an `int`. For example, a %ld is used to read a decimal `long`, and %lx to read a hexadecimal `long`.

The `float` place-holders %f, %e, and %g all behave the same way, as do the `double` place-holders %lf, %le, and %lg. All three can be used to read input in either plain decimal or scientific notation form.

An 'h' prefix in front of an integer place-holder will cause `scanf()` to convert input to a `short` instead of an `int`. For example, %hd is used to read a decimal `short`.

An 'h' prefix in front of a float place-holder has no effect, since there is no `short float` type. Hence, %hf is equivalent to %f.

Pitfall: Round Pegs and Square Holes

It is extremely important to use the correct place-holders for each argument variable in `scanf()`. As with `printf()`, most compilers won't notice if your place-holders don't match the arguments. Using an incorrect place-holder may cause a program crash, but will most often simply cause data corruption, since `scanf()` will convert the data into the wrong binary format for the variable.

The code fragment below compiles without errors or warnings on most systems, but the input is not properly converted to `long`, because a `float` place-holder is used:

```
long    emus;
int     args;

fputs("Enter the number of emus: ",stdout);
args = scanf("%f",&emus);
printf("%ld\n",emus);
```

Since the place-holder is %f, `scanf()` will convert the input text into binary floating point format. The program will then incorrectly interpret the bits as a 2's complement integer value, since the variable emus is defined as a signed long. For example, if the user enters '2', and the computer uses IEEE floating point format, `scanf()` will convert the ASCII input to the binary form 01000000000000000000000000000000, which is $+1.0 \times 2^1$ in 32-bit IEEE format.[1] The `printf()` call in the next line will interpret this bit pattern as an integer, since the %ld place-holder is used, producing a value of 2^{30}, or 1073741824_{10}. Note that the output will differ if your computer doesn't use IEEE floating point format, but the results will be just as confusing.

Input fields are delimited as follows: For each argument, `scanf()` will read characters until it encounters a whitespace character, the end of file, or any character which is invalid for the type of argument being read. For example, `scanf()` will stop reading an integer value when it encounters a whitespace character, the end of file condition (ctrl+D on the keyboard), or any non-digit character.

Any printable characters in the `scanf()` format string that are not part of a place-holder must be matched *exactly* by the input.

---

[1]See chapter 2 for an explanation of the IEEE standard.

A single whitespace character matches any number of whitespace characters in the input.

Pitfall: Trailing Whitespace and `scanf()`

Whitespace at the end of a format string should be avoided, since this will cause `scanf()` to continue reading and swallowing whitespace characters indefinitely. For example, consider the following code:

```
int     age, args;
...
args = scanf("%d ",&age);
```

The user of this program is expected to type in a number, and then press return. However, `scanf()` will discard the newline character as whitespace, and wait for more input. No matter how many times the user presses *return*, this program will never return from the `scanf()` function.

The %c place-holder allows `scanf()` to read a single character. However, you must use a `char` variable with %c. If you use a `short`, `int`, or `long`, only eight bits of the variable will be affected by `scanf()`. Furthermore, it is impossible to predict which 8 bits are affected, since it depends on whether the machine running the program is **big-endian** or **little-endian**[2], so these programs will behave differently on different platforms. The %c place-holder is an exception to the delimiter rules described above. When you use %c, the very next character in the input stream will be read into the argument variable, *even if it is a whitespace character.*

Example:

The `scanf()` call below will read two numbers with an operator between. If the user types any whitespace characters between the values and the

---

[2]The terms big-endian and little-endian refer to how the bytes of word are arranged in memory. Big-endian machines have the most significant byte at the lowest address. Most modern machines are little-endian, with the least significant byte at the lowest address.

operator, they will be absorbed by the whitespace surrounding the %c place-holder in the format string.

```
double  num1,num2;
/* Char variables are bad, since they get promoted, but
   this one is necessary for using %c in scanf() */
char    operator;
int     args;

printf("Enter <number> <operator> <number>: ");
args = scanf("%lf %c %lf",&num1,&operator,&num2);
```

Note that if you use the format string `"%lf%c%lf"` instead (note the lack of spaces), the user won't be able to type any whitespace *before* the operator, since the whitespace character itself would be input by the %c place-holder into `operator`. Whitespace typed *after* the operator would work, since `scanf()` will discard any leading whitespace while looking for the second number to match %lf.

Specifying a field width and precision in a `scanf()` format string is generally not useful, since most input is delimited by whitespace. Occasionally, you may want to extract a fixed number of digits from a long string of digits with no separators. In these cases, you can use a field width to tell `scanf()` to stop after reading the specified number of digits.

```
int     num1, num2, args;

args = scanf("%3d%9d",&num1,&num2);
printf("%d %d\n",num1,num2);
```

If the user enters 345643523324, the output will be 345 643523324.

Pitfall: Eating Leftovers Again

The `scanf()` function does not remove any characters from the input stream which follow an input value. Note that whitespace characters are removed if they come *before* an input value, but not if they come after. For example, in the following program segment, the user will enter a number followed by *return*. The program will fail, because `scanf()` leaves the *newline* character in the input buffer after reading the digits. The call to `fgets()` will then read the leftover *newline*, and leave a blank string in `address` instead of waiting for the user to enter their address.

```
int     age, args;
char    address[ADDRESS_MAX+1];

printf("Enter your age: ");
args = scanf("%d\n",&num);
printf("Enter your address: ");
fgets(address,ADDRESS_MAX,stdin);
```

To fix the problem, call `getchar()` following `scanf()` to clear the *newline* character from input buffer.

```
int     age, args, ch;

printf("Enter your age: ");
args = scanf("%d\n",&num);
getchar();  /* Remove dangling newline from input */
printf("Type 'y' to continue, 'q' to quit...");
ch = getchar();
```

You may be tempted to put a space at the end of the format string. This technique is acceptable when reading from a file, but not when reading from the keyboard. Recall that `scanf()` will read any number of whitespace characters to match one whitespace in the format string. As a result, `scanf()` won't return after reading the newline, since more whitespace could follow, and the program will be stuck in scanf() until the user types a non-space character.

7.5 Using fprintf() for Debugging

The most time-consuming part of programming is **debugging**, finding logic errors in your code, after it has been compiled successfully. It is often difficult to track down the problem when a program compiles successfully, but produces incorrect results or crashes.

One simple technique to help track down the problem is to insert fprintf() or fputs() statements in the program, to show intermediate results of calculations on stderr, or just to show how far the program is getting before it crashes.

Both of these can also be accomplished with a debugger, but sometimes it's just as easy to insert an fprintf() in the program and see what it does.

Pitfall: Lost Debug Output

Debugging messages printed by your program should go to stderr, not stdout. Output sent to stdout is collected in memory buffers until an entire line is received or until the output buffer is full. Then the buffer contents are sent to your terminal screen all at once. This buffering mechanism drastically improves the efficiency of the Unix I/O system by reducing the number of system calls, but can have ill effects on debugging statements. For example, if your program crashes immediately following a printf() call, the output from printf() may or may not appear on your screen. It may simply be left in the output buffer when the program dies.

Output sent to stderr is *unbuffered* by default, so by sending debugging messages to stderr, you ensure that they go directly to the screen. Even if your program crashes on the next statement, you'll be sure to see the debug output.

The following program sometimes crashes after receiving input, but we can't tell which statement causes the crash.

```c
#include <stdio.h>        /* For I/O functions */
#include <sysexits.h>
#include <string.h>       /* For strlen() */

void    getline(char *string, int array_size);

int     main()

{
    char    name[10];
    int     len;

    fputs("Please enter your name: ",stdout);
    getline(name,19);
    len = strlen(name);
    printf("%s, your name is %d letters long.\n",
            name, len);
    return EX_OK;
}


void    getline(char *string,int array_size)

{
    /* Read up to newline or to array limit */
    while ( ((*string = getchar()) != '\n') &&
            (--array_size > 0) )
        ++string;
    *string = '\0';   /* null terminate */
}
```

If you insert some `fputs()` statements, you can track down exactly where
the problem is occurring.

```c
#include <stdio.h>        /* For I/O functions */
#include <sysexits.h>
#include <string.h>       /* For strlen() */
```

```
void    getline(char *string, int array_size);

int     main()

{
    char    name[10];
    int     len;

    fputs("Please enter your name: ",stdout);
    getline(name,19);
    fputs("Back from gets()...\n",stderr);
    len = strlen(name);
    fputs("Back from strlen()...\n",stderr);
    printf("%s, your name is %d letters long.\n",
            name, len);
    return EX_OK;
}


void    getline(char *string,int array_size)

{
    /* Read up to newline or to array limit */
    while ( ((*string = getchar()) != '\n') &&
            (--array_size > 0) )
        ++string;
    *string = '\0';    /* null terminate */
}
```

Sending error messages to stderr also allows the debug output to be separated from the normal output, by using redirection with any Bourne-shell compatible. The Bourne-shell family can redirect any I/O stream if given the file descriptor number before the redirection operator. The normal descriptors are 0 for stdin, 1 for stdout, and 2 for stderr.

If you're using C-shell or T-shell, you can run a Bourne shell on top of it to perform the redirection:

```
tcsh: sh
sh: a.out 2> errs
sh: more errs
sh: exit
tcsh: _
```

By using the shell to separate the output, you won't have to visually scan through all your output looking for debugging messages.

Chapter 8

C Statements and Expressions

Before you begin...

> You should be familiar with the material on simple I/O statements presented in chapter 7.

Many languages, such as Pascal, FORTRAN, and BASIC have strict rules about how statements are formed. Most languages have three kinds of statements: assignment statements, subprogram calls, and flow control, each of which has strict syntactic rules. In addition, most languages has several types of expressions, such as Boolean (logical) expressions, integer expressions, string expressions, and floating point expressions.

C, on the other hand, makes no distinction between between one type of expression and another, and has no rigid syntax for assignment statements. In C, there are only flow control statements (chapters 9 and 10) and **expression** statements. Literally any expression can be made into a statement by placing a semicolon after it. For example, the program below is perfectly valid, and will compile and run without errors.

```
int     main()
{
    3;            /* This statement is a waste of ink */
    return 0;
}
```

The statement 3; serves no purpose, of course, but C wasn't designed to prevent programmers from writing nonsense. The design of C was aimed at giving the programmer as much freedom as possible, and also making the compiler as simple as possible. The fewer rules a language has, the simpler the compiler is, and the faster your programs will compile.

8.1   Simple Expressions

An **expression** in C is anything that has a value. Generally speaking, all expressions in C are created equal, and everything has a value, except a flow control statement.

As mentioned, some languages have many different types of expressions. For example, Pascal distinguishes between integer, real, character, and Boolean (true/false) expressions. You can't add an integer to a real, or a real to a character in Pascal. Pascal is consequently referred to as a **strongly typed** language. Pascal and many other languages attempt to hide hardware operations by making data types more abstract. In reality, however, a Pascal Boolean value is implemented as a binary integer with a value of 0 or 1, and character values are stored as integer ASCII values.

C, on the other hand, makes no attempt to hide the way data is stored at the hardware level. All data in C is treated as simple binary values, and you can freely mix all the C data types. The `char` type in C, for example, is simply an 8 bit integer, and can be treated like any other integer type. C doesn't have a Boolean type at all. The programmer simply uses integers: 0 represents *false* and any non-zero value represents *true*.

8.2 The C Operators

Strongly typed languages such as Pascal have different sets of operators for different types. There are operators such as `div` and `mod`, which produce the quotient and remainder for *integer* division, respectively, and '/', which divides two *real* numbers. There are also Boolean operators such as AND, OR, and NOT, which only work with true/false values.

In C, most operators are **polymorphic**, meaning the operator can be used with any data type.[1] For example, C uses '/' for both integer and real division, two operations which are very different in nature.

There are a few necessary exceptions, however. For instance, the `mod` operator, denoted as '%' in C, computes the remainder from an integer division. Since division of real numbers has no remainder, the '%' operator can't be used with `float` or `double` values.

Since all C operators work with the same data, any pair of operators could potentially interact within the same expression. For example, the && (logical AND) operator could appear next to a '/' (division) operator, or '=' (assignment) could appear next to '<' (less than). Which operation occurs first is not simply a matter of their order in the expression; you need to know the **precedence** and the **associativity** of each operator.

When two operators with different precedence interact, the one with the higher precedence is performed first. For example, in the expression

```
y = x + a * 5
```

the multiplication $a*5$ is performed first, since multiplication has a higher precedence than addition.

If a choice must be made between two operators with the same precedence, then the associativity rules come into effect. For example, consider the following expression:

```
z = a - 5 + b
```

Since addition '+' and subtraction '-' have the same precedence, associativity rules

---

[1]The term polymorphic comes from "poly" (many) and "morph" (form).

must be used to determine which one occurs first. The subtraction is performed first, since the associativity is *left to right* for both addition and subtraction.

Note that any two operators with the same precedence must also have the same associativity to avoid ambiguity.

8.2.1   Unary vs. Binary operators

A **binary operator** is one that performs an operation on two operands.

A **unary operator** operates on a single operand.

For example, consider the following statement:

```
y = 5 - x * -b
```

The '-' in front of the variable b is a *unary* minus, since it operates only on b. The '-' between 5 and x is a *binary* minus, since it operates on both the 5 and the x. Similarly, the '=' and '*' are both binary operators.

Tables 8.1 and 8.2 summarize the C operators. Do not attempt to memorize this table. In most cases, the precedence and associativity are fairly intuitive. If not, you can always group portions of the expression with parenthesis to make it easier to read. Using parenthesis is generally recommended, anyway, especially for complex Boolean expressions.

In the following sections, we will discuss some of the common operators used in C programs. Boolean operators, which are used primarily with if, switch and loop statements, are discussed in chapter 9. Additional operators such as array subscripts, pointer operators, structure binding operators, casts, sizeof(), and conditionals are also discussed in later chapters.

8.2.2   Math Operators

Most of the math operators in C are identical to their algebraic counterparts.

For example, in the statement:

```
y = a + b * c / d;
```

Operator	Operation	Precedence	Associativity
()	Grouping	Highest	left to right
[]	Array subscript binding	2nd	left to right
.	Structure binding		left to right
$->$	Structure pointer binding		left to right
Miscellaneous unary operators			
!	Boolean NOT	3rd	right to left
$\sim$	1's complement		right to left
++	Increment		nearest to furthest
$--$	Decrement		nearest to furthest
$-$	Unary minus		right to left
(type)	Type cast		right to left
*	Pointer dereference		right to left
&	Address of		Not applicable
sizeof()	Size of object		Not applicable
Math operators			
*	Multiplication	4th	left to right
/	Division		left to right
%	Mod (remainder)		left to right
+	Addition	5th	left to right
-	Subtraction		left to right
>>	Shift right	6th	left to right
<<	Shift left		left to right

Table 8.1: The C operators

Comparison operators

<	Less than	7th	left to right
>	Greater than		left to right
<=	Less or equal		left to right
>=	Greater or equal		left to right
==	Equal (comparison)	8th	left to right
!=	Not equal		left to right

Logical operators

&	Bitwise AND	9th	left to right
∧	Bitwise XOR	10th	left to right
|	Bitwise OR	11th	left to right
&&	Boolean AND	12th	left to right
||	Boolean OR	13th	left to right
? :	Conditional	14th	right to left

Assignment operators, etc.

=	Gets	15th	right to left
(op)=	var = var (op) val		right to left
,	Statement group	Lowest	left to right

Table 8.2: The C operators

the operations occur in the following order:

1. $b * c$

2. $(b * c)/d$

3. $a + ((b * c)/d)$

4. $y \leftarrow a + ((b * c)/d)$

The multiplication and division occur before addition, because they have a higher precedence. Multiplication and division have the same precedence, and both are left-associative, so the multiplication occurs before the division.

Grouping symbols in C work just as they do in algebra. For example, if you wanted the addition of a and b to occur first, you could parenthesize the expression as follows:

```
y = (a + b) * c / d
```

The '-' operator serves two functions. It may be a unary operator, negating a value, or a binary operator, subtracting one value from another.

The '%' operator produces the remainder of an integer division. For example, you may recall from early grade school math:

$$5 \div 2 = 2, \text{Remainder } 1$$

Later, you learned to use real numbers so

$$5.0/2.0 = 2.5$$

and you no longer needed remainders. Computers can perform both integer and real division. When using the '/' operator, the type of division that occurs depends on the data types of the operands. If both are integers, integer division is performed, otherwise real division is used. The full details of operator/data type interactions is discussed in section 8.3.

Example:

Try to determine the output of the code fragment below.[2]

```
double  v1,v2,v3;

v1 = 1/2;
v2 = 1.0/2.0;
v3 = 1.0/2;
printf("%lf %lf %lf\n",v1,v2,v3);
```

With the '%' operator, *both operands must be integers*, since there is no such thing as a remainder in real division.

Two operators unfamiliar from algebra are ++ and −−. These are the unary increment and decrement operators. In C, the *statement*

```
++c;
```

has the same effect as

```
c = c + 1;
```

This is also equivalent to

```
c++;
```

(which was the inspiration for the name of the C++ language.)

There is an important difference between placing the ++ before or after the variable, however. If the ++ operator appears to the left of the variable, the value of the

---

[2]Output is: 0.0 0.5 0.5.

expression is the incremented value. In other words, the variable is incremented *before* it is used. If the ++ appears to the right of the variable, the value of the expression is the original value of the variable. In other words, the variable is incremented *after* it is used. The −− operator behaves the same way.

This has important consequences when the ++ or −− operator is used in the middle of an expression.

Example:

```
int     mangos=1,baboons=1,fruits,apes;

fruits = ++mangos;
apes = baboons++;
printf("%d %d %d %d\n",mangos,baboons,fruits,apes);
```

Both `mangos` and `baboons` are initialized to 1, and incremented in subsequent statements. However, `mangos` is incremented *before* its value is assigned to `fruits`, so `fruits` gets a value of 2. On the other hand, `baboons` is incremented *after* its value is assigned to `apes`, so `apes` gets a value of 1.

The output is therefore:

2 2 2 1

8.2.3 Assignment Operators

The operator '=' performs an **assignment** to a variable. There must always be an **lvalue** to the immediate left of an assignment operator. The term lvalue refers to any *writable* memory address. This is usually a variable which was *not* defined with the **const** modifier. It could also be a dereferenced pointer, which are discussed in chapter 14, or an array element, which are discussed in chapter 15. The term lvalue is short for "left value", which comes from the simple fact that they may appear on the left side of an assignment operator.

Since C has no rigid statement format for assignments, an assignment operator can appear almost anywhere. There must always be an lvalue to the left of the assignment operator, but the assignment expression as a whole may be part of a larger expression.

Simple assignments are typical, such as the following:

```
mangos = 1.5;
```

Compound assignments are also possible, such as:

```
apes = baboons + gorillas = 5;
```

This works because the assignment expression itself has a value, which is the value assigned. The expression `gorillas = 5` assigns 5 to `gorillas`, and itself has the value 5, so this value can be added to **baboons**, with the sum being assigned directly to **apes**. Expressions like these may be a bit confusing to a beginner. To help clarify, you can rewrite it with parenthesis as follows:

```
apes = baboons + (gorillas = 5);
```

C also has the ability to combine any binary operator with the = operator to create special purpose assignment operators. For example, statements such as:

```
apes = apes + baby_apes;
```

are very common in programming. In order to reduce typing, and the potential for errors associated with redundant variable names, this expression can be written as:

```
apes += baby_apes;
```

The same idea can be applied to any of the binary operators, such as '*', '/', and so on.

8.3 Mixed Expressions

8.3.1 Implicit Conversions

Strongly typed languages such as Pascal do not allow mixing data types. For example, it is illegal in Pascal to add an integer to a real. The Pascal programmer must explicitly convert one of the operands to the same data type as the other using built in functions such as `round()`, `trunc()`, or `real()`.

C allows all data types to be freely mixed. When an operator is given two operands of different types, an implicit conversion, or **promotion**, takes place. Conversions must be done before the operation is carried out, because computers don't have hardware to perform operations on two values in different binary formats. For example, most computers have instructions for adding two integers or two floating point values, but not for adding an integer to a floating point.

A **mixed expression** is any expression that contains values of different data types. Mixed expressions can be both a blessing and a curse. While they save some time in typing program code, it is sometimes tricky to predict their behavior, and they are an additional source of semantic errors. To understand how an expression is evaluated by C, you must understand the types of implicit conversions that occur, and *when* they occur. This requires some knowledge of operator precedence and associativity.

C data types are given ranks for the purpose of promotion rules. In general, operands of a "lower" type are promoted to the "higher" type as needed during evaluation of the expression. Table 8.3 outlines the ranks of the standard data types when used in mixed expressions. Generally, the greater the *positive* range a type has, the higher its rank.

If you add a `double` and a `float`, the `float` value will first be promoted to `double`, and the machine will perform a `double` addition. Similarly, if you divide a `float` by an `int`, the `int` value is first promoted to `float`.

The only time an implicit **demotion** occurs is when a higher type is being assigned to a variable of a lower type. For example, if you assign a `double` expression to an `int` variable, the compiler has no choice but to convert the `double` value to an `int`, which may result in both the loss of fractional digits, and an integer overflow. Obviously, demotions are something to avoid as much as possible.

Type	Rank
long double	highest
double	2nd
float	3rd
unsigned long long	4th
long long	5th
unsigned long	6th
long	7th
unsigned int	8th
int	9th

Table 8.3: Data type ranking

Example:

```
int     a = 3, b = 2, c;
double  x = 3.5, y = 4.0;

c = x * a + a / b * y - 5;
```

In the code sample above, the following steps are necessary:

1. Promote the value of a from `int` to `double` (3.0).
2. $(x * a) = 3.5 * 3.0 = 10.5$
3. $(a/b) = 3/2 = 1$ (integer division)
4. Promote the result (a/b) from `int` to `double` (1.0)
5. $(a/b) * y = 1.0 * 4.0 = 4.0$
6. $(x * a) + ((a/b) * y) = 10.5 + 4.0 = 14.5$
7. Promote `int` 5 to `double` 5.0.
8. $(x * a) + ((a/b) * y) - 5.0 = 9.5$
9. Truncate the result (9.5) to `int` (9)
10. $c \leftarrow 9$

Of the ten steps performed in the example above, four were data conversions and six did some useful work. As a rough estimate, then, about 40% of the time is spent performing data conversions. You could greatly improve the execution speed of this statement by making all the values `double`, i.e. defining a and b as `double` and writing constants like 5.0 instead of 5. Of course, sometimes it isn't practical to define all the variables as `double`, but data mixing should be avoided as much as possible.

Note that `short` and `char` are not given ranks. These types are *always* promoted even if they are not being mixed with higher types. For example, if you add two `char` values, they will both be promoted to `int`, an `int` addition will occur, and the result will be truncated to a `char`. This involves a great deal of wasted time, and that's why scalar variables should *never* be defined as `char` or `short` unless absolutely necessary.

Example:

In the sample code below, the expression `promote_me + promote_me2` causes two promotions. The values retrieved from both `promote_me` and `promote_me2` are promoted to `int` before the addition takes place. This promotion could be avoided by defining both variables as `int` instead of `char` and `short`.

```
char    promote_me = 1;
short   promote_me2 = 2;
int     better;

better = promote_me + promote_me2;
```

Conversion between a signed integer type and the same size `unsigned` type does not cost any time. The binary format is not changed: the compiler simply generates `unsigned` machine instructions for subsequent arithmetic operations in the expression.

Example:

```
unsigned    c;

c = -1;
printf("c = %u\n",c);
```

Instead of printing -1, this program will print a very large integer value. Recall that -1_{10} is all 1's in 2's complement signed binary. The compiler simply copies the the signed integer -1 to the unsigned integer variable without changing it. The same bit pattern is subsequently interpreted as an unsigned binary value.

Note also that using %d instead of %u would cause `printf()` to interpret the value as a signed integer, and print -1 even though `c` is defined as `unsigned`.

8.3.2   Explicit Conversions: Casts

There are times when the default operation is not what you want. For example, if you divide two `int` variables, you may want a floating point division to be performed instead of an integer division. You can accomplish this by explicitly converting one or both values to `double` in the expression, so that you don't need to actually change the variable types.

Explicit data conversions are accomplished using a **cast**, which is simply a data type name enclosed in parenthesis.

Example:

Try to predict the output of the following program:

```
#include <stdio.h>
#include <sysexits.h>
```

```
int      main()
{
    int      x = 3, y = 4;
    double   percent;

    percent = x / y * 100.0;
    printf("percent = %f\n",percent);
    return EX_OK;
}
```

The correct answer is "`percent = 0.0`". The division of two integers, `x` and `y`, always produces an integer result, which is 0 in this case. If you want a *real* result, including fractional digits, you have to make at least one of the operands a floating point variable, or explicitly promote one of the values using a cast, as follows:

```
    percent = (double)x / y * 100.0;
```

This causes the value of `x` to be promoted to `double`. Since the program now divides a `double` by an `int`, the `int` will be implicitly promoted to `double` as well.

You could also explicitly promote *both* values:

```
    percent = (double)x / (double)y * 100.0;
```

The extra typing here has no effect, however, since promoting either `x` or `y` will cause the other to be implicitly promoted anyway.

Pitfall: Casting Expressions

You need to be careful about what you cast. A common mistake is to cast the *expression*, instead of a variable. For example,

```
percent = (double)(x / y) * 100.0;
```

The above statement will not achieve the desired effect, since the division occurs *before* the cast. The integer division will produce a result of 0, which will then be explicitly converted to `double`. Since the promotion of the result would have occurred anyway upon assigning the value to `percent`, the cast has absolutely no effect.

8.3.3   Advanced: Bitwise Operators

C provides a set of operators for performing bitwise logic operations, such as AND, OR, NOT, bit shifts, and complements. These operators utilize the logic portion of the arithmetic/logic unit; something few other high level languages can do. Pascal and FORTRAN programmers, for example, must resort to a form of mathematical trickery to shift or mask the bits in a variable.

Bitwise operators are commonly used in systems programming. Many Unix system calls receive or return 16 bit values containing several fields of smaller size. For example, the `system()` function returns a 16 or 32 bit status code. The lower 8 bits and higher 8 bits of this code have independent meaning, so we need to use bit operations to extract one of the two from the return value.

All of the bitwise operators are listed in tables 8.1 and 8.2.

1's Complement

The '~' operator performs a 1's complement inversion on a variable. This has the effect of inverting every bit. You may recall from chapter 2 that negating a 2's complement value involves inverting all the bits (1's complement inversion) and then adding 1. Therefore, all of the following statements have the same net effect:

```
c = ~c + 1;
c = -c;
c *= -1;
```

The 1's complement operator is typically used only in specialized applications such as cryptography or computer-aided design.

Shift operators

The '>>' operator performs an *arithmetic* shift right when shifting a signed value, and a *logical* shift right when shifting an unsigned value. The only difference between these two types of shifts is in what happens to the leftmost bit. In a logical shift, the leftmost bit is set to 0, while an arithmetic shift leaves it unchanged.

Both types of shifts have the effect of dividing a positive value by 2^{bits}, where *bits* is the number of positions the value is shifted. An arithmetic shift can also perform division on negative 2's complement values.

For example, in the statement

```
int     emus = -12;

emus = emus >> 2;
```

the bits in emus are shifted two positions to the right. The two rightmost bits are lost, and the leftmost bit remains unchanged. Hence, the final value of emus is -3.

The '<<' operator similarly shifts bits to the left. The leftmost bits are lost, and the rightmost bits are cleared. (Reset to 0)

Shifting bits N positions to the left has the effect of multiplying by 2^N for both positive and negative integer values.

C does not allow the bits of a floating point variable to be shifted, and will produce a compiler error if you attempt to do so. Shifting the bits of a floating point value would only foul up the sign, mantissa and exponent fields by moving bits from one field to another.

Programming for Performance:

Bit shifts can be a useful feature for improving performance, since bit shift instructions typically execute in a small fraction of the time of a multiply or divide instruction. Any time you need to multiply or divide by a power of two, using a shift operator is the most efficient way to do it.

AND, OR, XOR

The & operator performs a bitwise AND operation between a value and a **mask**. Each bit in the result is 1 only if the corresponding bits in *both* the value *and* the mask are 1. For example:

```
        0110100101    (value)
  AND   0011101010    (mask)
        0010100000    (result)
```

The **mask** is used to specify which bits in the other operand are to be retained, and which are to be cleared. For example, if you wanted to extract the rightmost 4 bits from a 16 bit status value and have 0's in the other bits, you would bitwise AND the status value with a mask of 0000000000001111_2 ($000F_{16}$), as follows:

```
    exit_code = status & 0x000f;
```

The variable `exit_code` receives the 4 rightmost bits of status, and all the remaining bits in `exit_code` are 0.

The | operator performs a bitwise OR operation between two operands. Each bit in the result is 1 if the corresponding bit in *either* the value *or* the mask is 1.

```
        0110100101    (value)
  OR    0011101010    (mask)
        0111101111    (result)
```

The OR operator is often used to *set* specific bits to 1 without affecting any other bits. For example, if you want to set bit 5 to one, you would bitwise OR the value with 100000_2 as follows:

```
    new_value = value | 0x20;
```

The variable `new_value` will have bit 5 set to 1. All other bits are the same as in `value`.

The '^' operator performs a bitwise XOR (Exclusive-OR) operation on two operands. Each bit in the result of an XOR is one if the corresponding bit in either operand is 1, but not they are both 1. In other words, the result bit is one if the operand bits are different.

```
        0110100101   (value)
XOR     0011101010   (mask)
        ----------
        0101001111   (result)
```

What C doesn't have

C has no logical shift right operator for signed integers, but it can be simulated by casting the value to **unsigned**. For example, to perform a logical shift right 2 positions:

```
c = ((unsigned)c >> 2);
```

Likewise, C has no circular shift operator. To simulate rotating a 16 bit value 3 positions to the left, you could use the following:

```
rotated = (value << 3) | ((value >> 13) & 0x07);
```

Pitfall: Confusing Bitwise and Logical Operators

A common mistake among C programmers is to confuse the bitwise operators '&' and '|' with the Boolean operators '&&' and '||'. Since C doesn't distinguish between Boolean values and binary codes, the compiler will happily do whichever operation you specify. These kinds of bugs are particularly hard to find. If you notice your program making rather strange decisions, or coming up with inexplicable bit patterns, double check your operators to see that you haven't pulled an accidental switcheroo.

Chapter 9

Decisions with `if` and `switch`

Before you begin...

> You should be familiar with the material on C expressions presented in chapter 8.

9.1 Program Flow

A C program consists of **expression** statements and **flow control** statements. An expression in C, as you may recall from chapter 8, is anything with a value. Any expression in C becomes a simple statement when it is followed by a semicolon. The normal flow of a program executes every statement in sequence from the top of the program down. Sometimes, however, there are decisions to be made, and certain statements may be executed *conditionally*, that is, only if the appropriate conditions are met.

Flow control statements are used to alter the normal top-down flow of execution. The **conditional** statements `if` and `switch` are used to select a group of statements to be executed either once or not at all. **Loops** are another type of flow control statement that cause a group of statements to be executed repeatedly. Loops are discussed in chapter 10.

Operator	Purpose
>	Greater than
>=	Greater than or equal
<	Less than
<=	Less than or equal
==	Equal
!=	Not equal

Table 9.1: Relational Operators

9.2   Boolean Expressions

An expression that has a value of either true or false is called a **logical** expression, or **Boolean** expression. Boolean expressions are named after George Boole, the inventor an algebraic system of logic known as **Boolean algebra**. Boolean expressions are used in `if` statements to make decisions.

Some languages, such as Pascal and FORTRAN, have a special data type for Boolean values. In Pascal, this type is called `boolean`. In FORTRAN, the type is called `logical`. In C, any data type can be used to represent Boolean values. A numeric value of 0 is regarded as false, and *any non-zero value* is taken as true.

9.2.1   Relations

Boolean expressions are most often formed by testing the **relation** between two values. A relation is any comparative statement made about two values that must be either true or false, such as "a is greater than b", or "name 1 is longer than name 2". Relational expressions in C are formed using the **relational operators**, outlined in table 9.1.

In C, relational expressions are `int` values. If the relation is true, the value of the expression is 1, and if it's false, the value is 0.

9.3 The if-else Statement

9.3.1 Statement Syntax

The if-else statement, sometimes called simply an if statement, is used to conditionally perform one or more statements. The general form is:

```
if ( Boolean expression )
    statement1;
else
    statement2;
```

If the Boolean expression evaluates to true (any non-zero value), then statement1 is executed. Otherwise statement2 is executed. In any case, *exactly one of the two statements will be executed.*

The else portion is optional, so the following form is also valid:

```
if ( Boolean expression )
    statement1;
```

If the else clause is omitted, then either statement1 is executed, or nothing happens at all.

Example:

Recall from chapter 7 that scanf() returns the number of arguments successfully filled. This example uses an if statement to check the success of a scanf() call.

```
char    name[NAME_MAX+1];

if ( scanf("%s %d",name,&age) != 2 )
    fprintf(stderr,"Error in input.\n");
```

Example:

Use an if-else statement to determine which fare to charge a passenger.

```c
#include <stdio.h>
#include <sysexits.h>

#define REGULAR_FARE    300.0
#define DISCOUNT_FARE   150.0

int     main()

{
    int     age, args;
    double  fare;

    /* Get passenger information */
    printf("Enter passenger's age: ");
    args = scanf("%d",&age);

    /* Check for kids discount */
    if ( age < 12 )
        fare = DISCOUNT_FARE;
    else
        fare = REGULAR_FARE;

    printf("Fare is %f.\n",fare);
    return EX_OK;
}
```

Pitfall: Round-off and Relational Expressions

Never use the operators $==$ and $!=$ with floating point values. Floating point types suffer from frequent **round-off errors**, which cannot be easily detected. Round-off errors result from the inability to express a particular value within a limited number of digits. For example, the value 1/3 cannot be accurately represented with a finite number of decimal digits. It's true value is $0.\overline{3}$, which means the 3's go on on forever. Similarly, it is impossible to represent the value 1/10 in binary, since this would require an infinite number of *binary* digits. This is why many business systems use **Binary Coded Decimal (BCD)** instead of floating point when working with dollar amounts. Numbers don't have to require an infinite number of digits to suffer from round-off error. For example, the binary value 5,000,000,231 has 10 significant digits, and thus cannot be accurately represented with a `float`, which is limited to about 7 decimal digits (24 bits to be precise) on most systems. This value would be rounded off to the nearest value with 24 significant bits or less, assuming IEEE `float` format.

Consider the following code fragment, which computes a simple time estimate given a calculated distance and rate. If rate is zero, the statement must not be executed, because division by zero would cause a program crash.

```
double  distance, rate, time;

...

if ( rate != 0.0 )
    time = distance / rate;
else
    printf("We're not movin' at all.\n");
```

If the value of the variable `rate` is rounded during calculations prior to the `if` statement, and ends up at 0.000000000000001 instead of 0.0, the `if` statement will fail to prevent the statement from being executed. Dividing by a miniscule value like 0.000000000000001 will most likely cause a floating point overflow, which in turn will generally cause the program to crash.

A better solution would be to check for a *minimum* allowable absolute value for rate, which would be determined by the accuracy of your rate measurement (experimental error), and the smallest value you can safely divide by, given the range of your floating point system.

```
#define EPSILON 0.000000000000010

double  distance, rate, time;

    ...

if ( abs(rate) < EPSILON )
    time = distance / rate;
else
    printf("It's gonna be a while.\n");
```

Programming for Performance:

Statistical studies have shown that the Boolean expressions programmers write into if statements are false about 60% of the time. Based on this fact, many compilers are optimized to produce an efficient else clause, sometimes at the expense of the if clause. You can take advantage of this by going with the flow, and writing Boolean expressions that are usually false. The performance gain will be slight, but may be worthwhile. To guarantee the results, you'll need to test your code with each compiler you use to make sure you are gaining performance, since this is not a rule in C compiler design. It's quite possible that a particular compiler will perform the if clause faster.

9.3.2 Compound Statements

Sometimes you may want to conditionally execute a *group* of statements, rather than just one. This is done using a **compound statement**, which is formed by grouping statements within curly braces. Compound statements are actually needed in most if statements, and it's a good idea to use them all the time.

Example:

Going back to our airline example, let's offer the kids some free peanuts in addition to the discount fare.

```
#define REGULAR_FARE    300.0
#define DISCOUNT_FARE   150.0
#define TRUE    1
#define FALSE   0

int     age, free_peanuts;
double  fare;
...

/* Kids get discount and 1/4oz bag of free peanuts */
if ( age < 12 )
{
    fare = DISCOUNT_FARE;
    free_peanuts = TRUE;
}
else
{
    fare = REGULAR_FARE;
    free_peanuts = FALSE;
}
```

There are no limits on how many statements can be grouped within curly braces, but it should generally be limited to a few, and never more than a screen full, or about twenty. If you find a need to group more than a screen full, then separate some or all of the statements and make a new function. Writing your own functions is discussed in chapter 11.

Programming with Style:

You may have noticed that the statements inside the if and else clauses are indented. The general practice is to align the if and else in the same column, and indent all the statements that are controlled by the if-else construct. That way, you can see at a glance which statements in your program are executed *conditionally*.

Indentation is not required by the compiler, but a poorly structured program is very difficult to read and debug. For example, try reading this:

```
if ( age < 12 )
{fare = DISCOUNT_FARE;
free_peanuts = TRUE;}
else{fare = REGULAR_FARE;
free_peanuts = FALSE;}
```

This program will compile and run, just like it's well-structured predecessor, but it's very difficult to read.

If you come across poorly written code, it can often be fixed using the GNU indent command. Indent is free, so if your system doesn't already have it, ask your administrator about getting it. A list of GNU sites is provided in appendix A.

Pitfall: Forgetting the Braces

It's a common mistake for beginners to forget to use compound statements under an if or else.

Forgetting the braces *between* an if and else will cause a compiler error.

Forgetting them under an `else`, or under an `if` with no `else` clause below it is a more serious problem, as demonstrated by the following code fragment:

```
if ( age < 12 )
{
    fare = DISCOUNT_FARE;
    free_peanuts = TRUE;
}
else
    fare = REGULAR_FARE;
    free_peanuts = FALSE;
```

This program is perfectly valid, but will not do what you might expect. In particular, the statement

```
free_peanuts = FALSE;
```

is *not* part of the `if-else` clause, and will *always* be executed. Hence, the kids won't get their peanuts.

Logical errors like this one are the hardest type of error to detect in a program, because they don't generate a compiler error, and the problems with the program output are not obvious. The best way to solve these problems is prevention; just be aware of hazards like these and be careful to avoid them.

Example:

Some decisions are critical to the continuation of the program. For example, consider a program that uses the quadratic formula

$$x = \frac{-b \pm \sqrt{b^2 - 4ac}}{2a}$$

to compute the roots of a second order equation. Since square roots don't exist for negative numbers, the value $b^2 - 4ac$ (the discriminant) must be greater than or equal to 0. If a computer program attempts to compute the square root of a negative number, the program will crash, unless special error handling techniques have been employed.[1]

```c
#include <stdio.h>  /* Input and output */
#include <sysexits.h>
#include <math.h>   /* Math functions - sqrt() */


int     main()

{
    double  a,b,c,root1,root2,discriminant,sq,two_a;
    int     args;

    printf("Enter coefficients A, B, and C: ");
    args = scanf("%lf %lf %lf",&a,&b,&c);
    discriminant = b*b - 4.0*a*c;
    if ( discriminant >= 0.0 )
    {
        /* 2*a and sqrt(discriminant) used twice */
        /* so we pre-compute and use variables */
        two_a = 2.0 * a;
        sq = sqrt(discriminant);

        /* Find roots */
        root1 = (-b + sq) / two_a;
        root2 = (-b - sq) / two_a;
        printf("Roots are %f and %f.\n",root1,root2);
    }
    else
        printf("Sorry, no real roots.\n");
    return EX_OK;
}
```

---

[1]Error handling techniques are covered in section 28.2.

Pitfall: The '=' Imposter

A common mistake among C programmers is using the assignment operator, '=', in an `if` statement, instead of the comparison operator, '=='. Since assignment expressions are legal *anywhere* in C, this type of error may go unnoticed by the compiler. Some compilers will generate a warning if the warning level is set high enough. (e.g. gcc with the -Wall option), but many will accept the code with no complaints. The code fragment below will demonstrate:

```
int     artichokes;

...

if ( artichokes = 0 )
    printf("Time to order more artichokes.\n");
```

Instead of comparing `artichokes` to 0, statement *assigns* 0 to the variable `artichokes`. Since the value of an assignment expression is the value assigned, the expression is always 0 (false), the `printf()` statement will *never* be executed, and your database will continually tell you that you're out of artichokes until the program is fixed.

There are some instances where you may intentionally perform an assignment within an `if` statement, to save a value computed in the expression. This is often used in `if` statements and `while` loops to shorten the code. For example:

```
if ( (args = scanf("%d",&age)) != 1 )
{
    fprintf(stderr,
            "Input error: %d values read.\n",args);
    exit(1);
}
```

C operator	Boolean operation
&&	AND
||	OR
!	Logical NOT

Table 9.2: Boolean Operators

If the expression involves operators other than the assignment operator, then the assignment expression will need to be parenthesized, since assignment operators have very low precedence. Without parenthesis, the statement above would read as

```
if ( args = (scanf("%d",&age) != 1) )
    . . .
```

This would assign `args` a value of true or false instead of the number of arguments read.

9.3.3   Building Bigger Boolean Expressions

Decisions often need to be made based on more than just a simple relation between two values. Boolean expressions can be infinitely complex, but Boolean algebra can express any combination of relations with just three Boolean operators: AND, OR, and NOT. The C equivalents are listed in table 9.2.

An expression of the form `A AND B` is true only if the operands A and B are *both* true. For example, the expression:

> "Fish swim" AND "Pigs fly"

is false, because pigs don't fly.

An expression of the form `A OR B` is true if either A or B is true. For example

> "Fish swim" OR "Pigs fly"

A	B	A && B	A || B	! A
false	false	false	false	true
false	true	false	true	true
true	false	false	true	false
true	true	true	true	false

Table 9.3: Truth Table for Boolean Operators

is true, because fish do swim, and only one of the two operands to OR needs to be true to make the whole expression true.

NOT is a *unary* operator which gives the opposite of a Boolean value. For example,

NOT "Pigs fly"

is true, because the statement "Pigs fly" is false.

Table 9.3 lists all the possible forms of AND, OR, and NOT expressions.

Example:

Returning to our previous sales example, you may in time discover that artichokes just aren't selling. The relation (`artichokes == 0`) isn't sufficient motivation to purchase more artichokes. Instead, you would like to satisfy *both* of two conditions before ordering another shipment.

1. We're out of artichokes
2. We've sold at least one artichoke since the last inventory check

Since we want to satisfy both conditions, the AND operator is used:

```
int     artichokes, artichokes_sold;

. . .

if ( (artichokes == 0) && (artichokes_sold >= 1) )
    printf("Time to order more artichokes.\n");
```

```
else
    printf("Don't bother with the artichokes.\n");
```

Suppose that instead of thinking about when to order more artichokes, you were thinking of when *not to order* them. In this case, you might say that no order is needed if *either* there are artichokes in stock, *or* if they aren't selling. The code below illustrates how this would be coded.

```
int     artichokes, artichokes_sold;

...

if ( (artichokes > 0) || (artichokes_sold == 0) )
    printf("Don't bother with the artichokes.\n");
else
    printf("Time to order more artichokes.\n");
```

Programming for Performance:

When using the logical operators && and ||, the order of the operands can make a difference in performance, since in many cases it will not be necessary to evaluate both expressions. For example, consider the following code segment:

```
if ( (column >= MIN) && (column < MAX) )
    statement;
```

If the first expression is false, i.e. if column is less than MIN, then the entire expression must be false, and the second relation, (column < MAX), will not be evaluated. All C compilers compliant with the K&R or ANSI standards will evaluate the expression on the left first, and will not needlessly evaluate the rest of the expression once the outcome is known.

Therefore, you want to consider which of the two relations is more likely to be false, and place it *first* in the overall expression. If for example, if it's likely that `column` will be greater than or equal to `MAX`, but it's unlikely to be less than `MIN`, then the above statement should be rearranged as follows:

```
if ( (column < MAX) && (column >= 0) )
    statement;
```

Similarly, when using ||, it's best to place the relation that is more likely to be *true* first, because, if the first relation is true, then the second need not be evaluated.

Programming for Performance:

Boolean expressions can often be simplified by using the right data type. For example, consider the following code segment:

```
int     column;

...

if ( (column >= 0) && (column < MAX) )
    statement;
```

Converting the value of `column` to `unsigned` will cause the the relation (`column >= 0`) to always be true. Therefore, it can be eliminated:

```
int     column;

if ( (unsigned)column <= MAX )
    statement;
```

Casting an `int` to `unsigned` will not alter the bit pattern, so the cast requires no CPU time. It merely tells the compiler to use `unsigned` comparison and branch instructions. If `columns` is negative, it's `unsigned` counterpart will be larger than the largest possible signed `int`, hence it is *guaranteed* to be larger than `MAX`, assuming `MAX` is properly defined within the range of an `int`.

Tip of the trade: DeMorgan's Rules

Many relations involving the NOT operator in C can be simplified to make them more readable or more efficient, either by reversal of the if and else clauses, or using DeMorgan's laws. These laws state the following: Given two Boolean values, A and B,

> NOT (A AND B) is the same as (NOT A) OR (NOT B)
> NOT (A OR B) is the same as (NOT A) AND (NOT B)

Suppose you had initially written your artichoke inventory program as follows:

```
if ( !((artichokes == 0) && (artichokes_sold >= 1)) )
    printf("Don't bother with the artichokes.\n");
else
    printf("Time to order more artichokes.\n");
```

This code is a little confusing, and also less efficient than the first example, since the if statement must perform an extra NOT operation when evaluating the Boolean expression.

You could simplify it by eliminating the '!' operator and switching the two printf() calls.

Or, by applying DeMorgan's law and simplifying, you could write it as follows:

```
if ( (artichokes != 0) || (artichokes_sold < 1) )
    printf("Don't bother with the artichokes.\n");
else
    printf("Time to order more artichokes.\n");
```

9.3.4 Nested if Statements

It is often necessary (or just plain convenient) to use an if statement inside another if statement.

When nesting if-else statements, each else corresponds to the most recent if, unless curly braces are used to group statements differently. Nested if statements are another way of checking multiple relations, as we did with the AND and OR operators, but they have an important advantage: Using a nested if statement, the program can take more than just two possible actions.

Example:

The previous inventory check example told you whether or not to order more artichokes, but it didn't tell you *why*. It may be because you're well stocked, or because they aren't selling. The following example will provide the user with better information:

```c
if ( artichokes == 0 )
{
    if ( artichokes_sold >= 1 )
        printf("Time to order more artichokes.\n");
    else
        printf("Artichokes aren't selling.\n");
}
else
    printf("We're OK on the artichokes for now.\n");
```

Programming with Style:

Even though braces are not necessary with nested if statements, it's always a good idea to use them. Nested if statements, especially those with else clauses, can look very confusing otherwise, and it might not be obvious which if each else belongs to.

9.4   Switch

The `switch` statement can be used in place of a long sequence of `if-else`'s where a variable needs to be compared to many possible values.

Programming for Performance:

> Using `switch` statements instead of long chains of nested `if` statements will often greatly improve performance. Some C compilers build an **address table** for a `switch` statement, which can be used to branch directly to the matching case, rather than compare the expression to every case constant until a match is found.[2] This is not a rule in C compiler design, so a performance boost isn't guaranteed.

The general syntax of a `switch` statement is as follows:

```
switch (expression)
{
    case    constant1:
        statements;
        break;
    case    constant2:
    case    constant3:
        statements;
        break;
    default:
        statements;
        break;
}
```

The `expression` must be an integer C type, i.e. `char`, `short`, `int`, `long`, `long long` or any `unsigned` variant. Floating point types are not allowed in `switch` statements, because the `switch` construct only checks for equality to a case. This would be equivalent to using the `==` operator with floating point values in an `if`

---

[2]Address tables are discussed along with function pointers in chapter 15.

statement, as described in the Pitfall on *Round-off and relational expressions*, page 177.

If the value of `expression` matches one of the case constants, the program branches to the first statement below that constant. Execution will continue down until a `break` statement is encountered. If the value of `expression` does not match any of the `case` constants, the program branches to the first statement under `default`.

Note that the program will *not* automatically jump out of a `switch` block before the next `case`. Instead, it will continue to execute the statements in every `case` below until a `break` is encountered. This behavior allows multiple case constants to be used for the same purpose, as demonstrated in the next example.

Example:

You might write a calculator program using nested `if-else` statements as follows:

```c
#include <stdio.h>
#include <sysexits.h>
#include <math.h>

#define EPSILON 0.00000000001

int     main()
{
    double  a,b,result;
    char    operator;   /* Must by char for scanf().
                           Otherwise, would prefer int
                           to avoid promotions */
    int     args;

    printf("Enter an expression of the form ");
    printf("<number> <operator> <number>: ");
    args = scanf("%lf %c %lf",&a,&operator,&b);
    if ( operator == '+' )
        result = a + b;
    else if ( operator == '-' )
        result = a - b;
```

```
        else if ( (operator == '*') || (operator == 'x') )
            result = a * b;
        else if ( operator == '/' )
            /* Prevent division by too small a number */
            if ( abs(b) > EPSILON )
                result = a / b;
            else
                fprintf(stderr,"Cannot divide by 0.\n");
        else
            fprintf(stderr,"Invalid operator: %c.\n",
                    operator);
        printf("The result is %f\n",result);
        return EX_OK;
    }
```

The same program could be written with a switch statement:

```
    #include <stdio.h>
    #include <sysexits.h>
    #include <math.h>

    #define EPSILON 0.00000000001

    int     main()
    {
        double  a,b,result;
        char    operator;    /* Must by char for scanf().
                                Otherwise, would prefer int
                                to avoid promotions */
        int     args;

        printf("Enter an expression of the form ");
        printf("<number> <operator> <number>: ");
        args = scanf("%lf %c %lf",&a,&operator,&b);
        switch(operator)
        {
            case    '+':
                result = a + b;
```

```
                    break;
            case    '-':
                result = a - b;
                break;
            case    '*':
            case    'x':
                result = a * b;
                break;
            case    '/':
                /* Prevent division by too small a number */
                if ( abs(b) > EPSILON )
                    result = a / b;
                else
                    fprintf(stderr,"Cannot divide by 0.\n");
                break;
            default:
                fprintf(stderr,"Invalid operator: %c.\n",
                    operator);
        }
        printf("The result is %f\n",result);
        return EX_OK;
    }
```

Pitfall: Missing the Exit Ramp

As mentioned earlier, a break statement is required to exit a switch block without executing all subsequent statements. It is common for C programmers to forget break statements in a switch.

For example, in the code below, if the user enters the operator '+', execution will continue through *all* the cases, including the default, and the error message will always be printed.

```
    switch(operator)
    {
```

```
case     '+':
   result = a + b;
case     '-':
   result = a - b;
case     '*':
case     'x':
   result = a * b;
case     '/':
   /* Prevent division by too small an number */
   if ( abs(b) > EPSILON )
       result = a / b;
   else
       fprintf(stderr,"Cannot divide by 0.\n");
default:
       fprintf(stderr,"Invalid operator.\n");
}
```

9.5   Advanced: The Conditional Operator

The conditional operator can often be used in place of an `if` statement to produce more compact code. The general syntax is as follows:

```
(condition) ? (value if true) : (value if false)
```

Example:

You can assign the *minimum* of two values to a variable using a simple `if` statement:

```
if (a < b)
    c = a;
else
    c = b;
```

You could also accomplish the same task in a single line using a conditional:

```
c = (a < b) ? a : b;
```

Note that there is little or no difference in efficiency between an `if` statement and a conditional expression. In fact, many compilers will generate exactly the same machine code in either case. The conditional operator is simply a convenience that allows us to write shorter source programs, and perform conditional operations within expressions. The opportunities to use the conditional operator are diverse, and often require a bit of imagination.

Example:

Consider the age-old dilemma of writing programs that use plural forms in their output. Using an `if` statement always seems a bit of a nuisance just to get one extra 's' printed:

```
if ( artichokes_sold != 1 )
    printf("We sold %d artichokes this month.\n",
            artichokes_sold);
else
    printf("We sold 1 artichoke this month.\n");
```

This dilemma is solved by the conditional operator:

```
printf("We sold %d artichoke%s this month.\n",
        artichokes_sold,
        artichokes_sold == 1 ? "" : "s");
```

Chapter 10

Repetition: Loops

Before you begin...

You should be familiar with the material on `if` statements presented in chapter 9.

Computers are best suited for performing simple, repetitive tasks, because they're fast and extremely accurate. (Two qualities we humans sorely lack.) As a result, most computer programs involve repeated execution of groups of statements, known as **iterating**, or **looping**. Each individual repetition is called an **iteration**. Algorithms and programs that use loops are described as **iterative**.

Programming for Performance:

Loops are a very useful tool that *should be avoided as much as possible.* Loops are the *only* construct in programming that are essential to making a program excessively slow. There is really no such thing as a slow computer: Software is the reason for slow response times in virtually every case. To put things into perspective, consider the following facts: A typical Pentium processor can execute about twenty million instructions per second. Some RISC processors can run hundreds of million instructions per second. Hence, a program devoid of loops, even if it were millions of lines long, would complete in a small fraction of a second. As you've probably noticed, most programs take far longer than this.

To complete any journey, there are an infinite number of different paths you can follow, the shortest of which is always a straight line. The more you deviate from the straight path, the longer it takes to reach your destination. Programs can be thought of in a similar way, following an **execution path** from a starting point to a destination. In order to reduce the amount of CPU time used by a program, you must shorten the execution path of the program. This means either reducing the number of instructions executed, or using instructions that require less time (e.g. use a shift instruction rather than a multiply or divide instruction). With very few exceptions, you cannot select which machine instructions you use when you program in a high level language. The compiler makes this selection for you. You can, however, easily reduce the number of instructions executed, by simply reducing the number of statements executed at the source code level.

When writing any program, always look for algorithms that don't require loops. A loop in the execution path means your program is literally going in circles. Nothing else you do as a programmer will affect the performance of your code as much as unnecessary loops.

If there are no loop-free algorithms to do the job, then use an algorithm that minimizes the number of iterations. For example, to sort a list of 1000 items, the **quicksort** algorithm will require about $1000 \times \log_2(1000)$, or roughly 10,000 comparisons. The **selection sort**, on the other hand requires 1000^2, or 1,000,000 comparisons to sort the same list. Similarly, a **binary search** on a list of 1000 items requires no more than $\log_2(1000)$ (about 10) comparisons, while a **linear search** (searching from end to end) could require up to 1000. These algorithms are discussed briefly in chapter 23. For more information, consult a text on algorithms and data structures.

Finally, if you must run around in circles, you'll want to make the circle as small as possible. In a program, this means placing as few statements as possible inside each loop. An example of this is presented in section 10.3.

There are also many hidden loops in software you may be familiar with, in places where you might not expect a loop to be necessary. Many of the mathematical functions, such as `sin()`, `cos()`, `pow()`, `exp()`, etc. use loops to compute values using numerical analysis techniques. Virtually all array processing requires loops. Strings, as you may recall from chapter 7, are arrays of characters. As a result, most string functions, such as `fgets()`, `fputs()`, `strlen()` and `strcpy()`, use loops. Whenever you use a library function, it's a good idea to look into how it works, and if it will adversely affect performance, look for some alternatives.

10.1 The Universal Loop - `while`

The `while` loop is used to execute a statement repeatedly as long as the specified **condition** remains true. As in `if` statements, the loop may use either a simple statement or a compound statement.

The basic syntax of a while loop is:

```
while (condition)
    statement;
```

The `while` loop is similar to an `if` statement in that it executes the statement only if the condition is true (non-zero).

A loop, however, executes the statement *repeatedly* until the condition becomes false. If the condition is false to begin with, the loop will iterate zero times, i.e. the statement is never executed.

The `while` loop is sometimes called the universal loop, because it can be used to implement *any* iterative task. Other types of loops are sometimes more convenient, but a `while` loop can always be used in their place.

Example:

Print the squares of all integers from one to ten.

```
#include <stdio.h>
```

```
#include <sysexits.h>

int     main()
{
    int     c;

    /* Initialize loop variable */
    c = 1;

    /* Continue as long as c <= 10 */
    while ( c <= 10 )
    {
        printf("%d squared is %d\n",c,c*c);
        ++c;
    }
    return EX_OK;
}
```

In the program above, the variable c is initialized to 1. The loop is
then entered, since the condition c <= 10 is true. Each iteration prints
the value of c and c squared, and increases the value of c. When c
becomes 11, the condition c <= 10 becomes false, and the loop terminates. Control then passes to the statement following the loop, in this
case, return 0;.

Pitfall: Infinite Loops

When writing a while loop, you must be careful to design it so that one
of the statements inside a while loop will eventually cause the condition to become false. Otherwise, the loop will never terminate. A loop
that never terminates is called in **infinite loop**, and is a very common
problem in virtually all types of programming.

In the example above, the statement ++c; will eventually cause the condition c <= 10 to be false, so the loop will terminate when c is 11. It's

fairly common for programmers to forget to increment a variable in a
while loop, as follows:

```
c = 1;
while ( c <= 10 )
{
    printf("%d squared is %d.\n",c,c*c);
}
```

This program will continue to print "1 squared is 1." until you kill
it by typing Ctrl+c. In this case, it's easy to see what's wrong as you
watch the program run. If the program didn't produce this repetitive
output, however, it wouldn't be so obvious.

Programming for Performance:

Using a loop introduces some additional overhead cost to the program,
because loop variables must be updated, and the condition must be
checked during each iteration. Some programmers prefer to use a technique called **unrolling the loop**, writing several redundant statements
in place of a short loop. This will eliminate the cost of maintaining a
loop variable, and can significantly increase the speed of a program in
some cases. In fact, some intelligent compilers will unroll a loop if it can
be determined at compile time that there are relatively few iterations.

Programming with Style:

As with an if statement, the statements inside a loop should be indented, to show that they are controlled by the loop. This makes it
easy to see at a glance where the loop begins and ends. Also, place a
comment above each loop explaining the purpose of the loop as a whole.
Some brief comments inside the loop explaining individual statements
are also helpful.

In general, loops should begin and end in a single screen, or about twenty
lines of code, so that the entire loop can be viewed at once while debugging. If the loop becomes larger than this, you can either rearrange the
code to make the loop smaller, or take out a section of code and make
it into a separate function. [1]

Example:

The program below is a similar to the Unix `vis` (or `cat -v`) command,
which simply copies the standard input to the standard output one character at a time. Any control characters in the file are made visible by
printing an octal escape sequence instead of the character. This program
reads characters from the standard input until `getchar()` returns the
`EOF` flag, signaling that there are no more characters to read.

---

[1] Functions are discussed in chapter 11.

Note: EOF is *not* a character. In fact, there is no special character to mark the end of a Unix file. EOF is merely an int constant (usually -1) that is returned by getchar() and some other I/O functions and macros when they detect that the end of input has been reached.

```c
#include <stdio.h>
#include <sysexits.h>
#include <ctype.h>  /* iscntrl() */


int     main()

{
    int     ch;

    /* Loop until end of file */
    while ( (ch=getchar()) != EOF )
    {
        /* Is ch a control character? */
        if ( iscntrl(ch) )
            printf("\\%03o",ch); /* Print octal */
        putchar(ch);             /* Print character */
    }
    return EX_OK;
}
```

10.2 The do-while Loop

The do-while loop is similar to the while loop, except that the condition is checked *after* the loop statement is performed, rather than before.

The general syntax is as follows:

```c
do
    statement;
while (condition);
```

Since the statement is executed before the condition is checked, the do-while loop always iterates *at least once*, unlike the while loop, which won't execute it's statement at all if the condition is false to begin with. If you want to set up a loop that's guaranteed to iterate at least once, the do-while is the loop to use.

Example:

Since users often make mistakes entering data, enclosing input in a loop to verify valid input is always a good practice. The program fragment below will continually ask the user to enter their birth date until they get it right. A program must make at least one attempt to input a piece of data, so the do-while is ideal for this situation.

```
#include <stdio.h>
#include <sysexits.h>

int     main()

{
    unsigned int     month,day,year;
    int              args;

    do
    {
        /* Prompt user for input */
        fputs("Enter your birth date as MM/DD/YYYY: ",
            stdout);

        /* Read in precise format MM/DD/YYYY */
        args = scanf("%02u/%02u/%04u",&month,&day,&year);

        /* If incorrect format, print error message */
        if ( args != 3 )
            fputs("Input error.  Please try again.\n",
                stderr);
    }   while ( args != 3 );
    return EX_OK;
}
```

To implement the same loop using a `while`, you would have to artificially force the loop to execute at least once. This is known as *priming the loop*.

```
/* Prime the loop - set args to anything but 3 */
args = 0;

while ( args != 3 )
{
    fputs("Please enter your birth date as MM/DD/YY: ",
            stdout);
    args = scanf("%02d/%02d/%02d",&month,&day,&year);
    if ( args != 3 )
        fputs("Input error.  Please try again.\n",
            stderr);
}
```

It's easy to forget to prime a `while` loop, and if you do forget, it may be difficult to track down the problem. Using a `do-while` to eliminate the need for priming is a great way to avoid a lot of debugging frustration.

10.3 The `for` Loop

10.3.1 Basic Syntax

The `for` loop is essentially a `while` loop with all the loop overhead packaged in the first line. The general form is

```
for (initializer; condition; control)
    statement;
```

This general form is equivalent to the following generalized while loop:

```
initializer;
while ( condition )
{
    statement;
    control;
}
```

The **condition** is the same as you would use in a while or do-while loop. The loop will continue to iterate until the condition becomes false.

The initializer is executed *once*, before the loop begins its first iteration. The initializer is usually used to set up a loop counter or other variable which is used inside the loop, and possibly in the condition as well. It can also be used to prime the loop if necessary.

The control is executed at the *end* of each iteration, *after* the statement in the loop. The control usually causes the condition become false at some point.

Example:

Print the squares of all integers from 1 to 100.

```
#include <stdio.h>
#include <sysexits.h>

int     main()

{
    int     c;

    for (c=0; c<=10; ++c)
        printf("%d^2 = %d\n",c,c*c);
    return EX_OK;
}
```

Compare this to the equivalent program using a `while` loop:

```
#include <stdio.h>
#include <sysexits.h>

int     main()

{
    int     c;

    c=0;
    while ( c<=10 )
    {
        printf("%d^2 = %d\n",c,c*c);
        ++c;
    }
    return EX_OK;
}
```

As you can see, the `while` version is slightly longer. In addition, when using a `while` loop, it's easy to forget the initialization statement `c = 0`, or the increment `++c`. The `for` loop is a little safer, since it's rigid format reminds you about these small but important details.

There is absolutely no difference between placing a statement in the control, or at the end of the loop statements. The control is only present to remind the programmer to fill in the necessary control statements. Using a `while` or `do-while`, such statements are easy to forget, since they seem so insignificant compared to the "interesting" work the loop performs.

Likewise, there is no difference between placing a statement before the loop or in the initializer.

For example, the following is equivalent to the example above:

```
#include <stdio.h>
#include <sysexits.h>
```

```
int     main()

{
    int     c;

    c=0;
    for ( ; c<=10; )
    {
        printf("%d^2 = %d\n",c,c*c);
        ++c;
    }
    return EX_OK;
}
```

Of course, this defeats the purpose of using a `for` loop, but it hopefully helps to
clarify the roles of the initializer and control, as well as demonstrating the similarity
of `for` and `while`.

10.3.2   Doing More with `for`

The statement grouping operator ',' is often used in `for` loops to initialize more
than one variable, and perform more than one operation in the control.

Example:

Print factorials from 1! to 10!. Each factorial is computed using the value from the previous iteration by multiplying by N, i.e. N! = (N-1)! * N. 0! is defined as 1. Since factorials are rather large numbers, we'll use long to ensure adequate range for 10!, which is 3,628,800, well beyond the range of an int on a 16 bit compiler.

For factorials beyond 12!, we'll need to use a floating point type like double, which will provide the necessary range (although it will only be accurate to about 16 digits). Note that each factorial with more than 16 significant digits is less precise than the previous one, because multiplying an imprecise value by N increases both the value *and* the error by a factor of N. A solution to this problem is presented in section 15.6, page 323.

```
long    n,nfac;

for (n=1, nfac=1; n<=10; ++n, nfac *= nfac)
{
    printf("%ld! = %ld\n",n,nfac);
}
```

Just for demonstration, you could also pull some of the statements out of the initializer and control, as follows:

```
long    n,nfac;

nfac = 1;
for (n=1; n<=10; ++n)
{
    printf("%ld %ld\n",n,nfac);
    nfac *= nfac;
}
```

Pitfall: Round-off in Relationals Again

A common mistake, also mentioned in chapter 9, is to use the == or !=
operators with floating point values in loops. As with `if` statements
and other Boolean expressions, these operators must *never* be used with
floating point values in loops.

For example, see if you can predict the behavior of the following loop:

```
#include <stdio.h>
#include <sysexits.h>

int     main()

{
    double  x;

    for (x = 0.0; x != 1.0; x += 0.1)
        printf("%20.16f\n",x);
    return EX_OK;
}
```

If you're like most programmers, you would expect it to print the numbers from 0.0 to 0.9, in increments of 0.1. The actual output is shown
below:

```
0.0000000000000000
0.1000000000000000
0.2000000000000000
0.3000000000000000
0.4000000000000000
0.5000000000000000
0.6000000000000000
0.7000000000000000
0.7999999999999999
0.8999999999999999
0.9999999999999999
```

```
1.0999999999999999
1.2000000000000000
1.3000000000000000
1.4000000000000001
...
```

Because of round-off error, the loop misses the value 1.0, and will continue on forever. The variable x will eventually reach a value that has 16 significant decimal digits to the left of the decimal point, and adding 0.1 will have no effect since there is no room for a 17th significant digit.

No matter what you do, round off will occur in this loop, since the decimal value 1/10 cannot be represented perfectly in binary. It's similar to trying to represent 1/3 in decimal - an infinite number of digits would be needed. You can get the loop to terminate *about* where it should by simply changing the operator from != to <:

```
for (x = 0.0; x < 1.0; x += 0.1)
    printf("%f\n",x);
```

Note that this loop will perform one extra iteration, since round off error brings x to 0.9999999999 instead of 1.0. This isn't a serious problem for this program, however, and is certainly preferable to an infinite loop. Floating point is an imperfect data type, so it is very difficult to predict the exact outcome of any program that uses it. In most cases however, if you take a little care, the outcome will be very close to what you expect.

Programming for Performance:

One of the most blatant of all common mistakes is to place statements inside loops that don't need to be there. Consider the following code fragment:

```
double  val, avg;
```

```
int     count;

/* Compute the average of a list of values */
while ( scanf("%lf",&val) == 1 )
{
    total += val;
    ++count;
    avg = total / count;
}
```

Computing the average is a *one time operation*, which can and should be done *after* the loop has finished.

```
double  val, avg;
int     count;

/* Compute the average of a list of values */
while ( scanf("%lf",&val) == 1 )
{
    total += val;
    ++count;
}
avg = total / count;
```

Obviously, executing a statement 100,000 times, when it only needs to be executed once, is going to slow the program down tremendously. When you write any loop, keep in mind that any statement inside a loop is potentially millions of times more expensive than the same statement on the outside.

10.4   Nested Loops

It is often necessary to place a loop inside another loop. For instance, programs that use multidimensional arrays, or produce **ordered samples** or **permutations**, will use nested loops. Multidimensional arrays are discussed in chapter 15. For now, we'll just present a simple example demonstrating nested loops.

Example:

The following code fragment prints every possible ordered sample of three letters. A similar program could be used to generate license plate numbers using letters and digits.

```
int     letter1,letter2,letter3;

for (letter1 = 'a'; letter1 <= 'z'; ++letter1)
    for (letter2 = 'a'; letter2 <= 'z'; ++letter2)
        for (letter3 = 'a'; letter3 <= 'z'; ++letter3)
            printf("%c%c%c\n",letter1,letter2,letter3);
```

The output is as follows, trimmed down to the essentials under the assumption that you don't want to look at 26^3 lines of gibberish:

```
aaa
aab
aac
...
aba
abb
abc
...
zaa
zab
zac
...
zzy
zzz
```

You may have noticed that `letter1`, `letter2` and `letter3` are defined as `int`, rather than `char`, even though they are meant to contain

character values. As discussed in chapter 6, `char` and `short` values are
promoted to `int` whenever a mathematical operation (such as ++) is performed on them. Therefore, you should never define a variable smaller
than `int` unless it is necessary for `scanf()` or some other esoteric reason.

Programming for Performance:

When using nested loops, it is particularly useful to optimize the *inner*
loops, since the statements inside the innermost loops are executed many
more times than those in more outer loops. For example, consider the
following generic nested loop:

```
for (row=0; row<1000; ++row)
{
    statement1;
    for (col=0; col<1000; ++col)
    {
        statement2;
    }
}
```

`Statement1` is only executed 1,000 times, compared to 1,000,000 times
for `Statement2`. If you have limited time available to spend optimizing
the code, then obviously `statement2` is where you should focus your
efforts.

More specific examples are included in chapter 15.

Chapter 11

Functions

Before you begin...

> You should be familiar with the material on loops presented in chapter 10.

11.1   Subprograms for Modularity

The example programs shown so far have been in the neighborhood of ten or twenty lines long. Real programs, however, typically range from a few thousand to more than a million lines of source code.

In order to tackle programming challenges of this magnitude, you need to break the problem down into smaller pieces, or **modules**. This process should begin *before* the coding phase, using the **stepwise refinement** approach discussed in section 3.3. Stepwise refinement is important for large projects, because people can only effectively deal with a relatively small amount of information at once. By breaking a large problem into many smaller ones, you convert an overwhelming task into a series of simple tasks that can easily be tackled *one by one*.

Attempting to tackle a large programming project without using stepwise refinement would be about the same as trying to swallow a chicken sandwich whole, or trying to lift an old sidewalk block and carry it on your back to the dump. Either way,

215

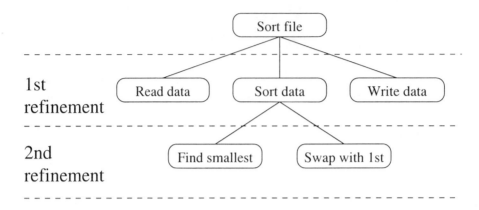

Figure 11.1: A simple problem refinement

you won't get anywhere, and you'll probably be in pretty bad shape following the attempt. It would be smarter to eat your chicken sandwich one small bite at a time, and use a jack-hammer to break the concrete slab into smaller pieces before trying to move it.

The same concept applies to programming. If you plan the programming process first, you can break it into smaller pieces, and attack each piece of the job individually. This **divide and conquer** approach is what makes sophisticated software possible.

For small programs, you may only go through a few refinements, breaking the problem into fewer than a dozen modules. Figure 11.1 shows how the problem of sorting the contents of a file might be broken down.

For larger programs, you may go through many levels of refinement, and end up with hundreds of modules. Note that the number of modules will grow very quickly (exponentially, in fact) as you refine the problem, so even a complex problem can be pulverized to a large number of very small sub-problems in relatively few steps.

For example, if you refine each step into exactly five smaller steps (of course, it never quite works out this way), then the second level of the design will have 5 modules, the third will have 25, the fourth 125, the fifth 625, and the sixth level will have 3125 modules. Figure 11.2 shows the modules produced by just two refinements when breaking each module down into exactly five smaller modules.

Even the largest programs will generally require no more than five to 10 levels of refinement if well planned. Studies have show that most programs have no more than seven levels, and some RISC CPU's are accordingly designed to efficiently

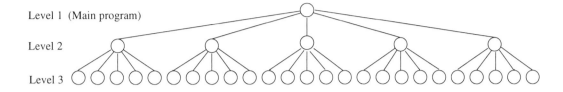

Figure 11.2: Modules for three levels of refinement

handle up to seven levels of refinement in the programs they run.

Subprograms are used to implement the modules. Hence, figure 11.1 could represent either a hypothetical refinement of a complex problem, or an actual program structure. In C and C++, all subprograms are called **functions**. Other languages have more than one kind of subprogram. For example, Pascal has both functions and **procedures**, while FORTRAN has functions and **subroutines**. There is very little difference between the different types of subprograms, and no need to dwell on the syntactic details of various languages. The concept of how to use subprograms is the important point to be taken from this chapter.

11.2   Reusability and Encapsulation

There are several reasons for using subprograms. One, discussed above, is to divide a problem into smaller pieces, which can be written and tested individually. Many functions created for this reason might only be used once in the program, and might never be used in another program.

An equally important advantage of subprograms is the **reusability** of program code that is packaged into subprograms. There are many common tasks that a given program must perform in more than one context. There are also tasks that must be performed by many different programs. For example, printing a string to `stdout` is something that many programs do, and may be done at several points within the same program. Imagine what C programming would be like without the `fputs()` function. Instead of writing

```
fputs(string,stdout);
```

you would have to duplicate the following lines of code every time you wanted to print a string:

```
char    *p;

for (p=string; *p != '\0'; ++p)
    putc(*p,stdout);
```

Worse yet, try to imagine having to retype the code of a complicated function such as `printf()`, which consists of hundreds of lines of source code. By *packaging* the code to print a string into a function, you can reuse it both within the program, and in other programs. Eliminating redundancy in this way reduces programming effort and program size at the same time.

One of the most important aspects of C programming is the use of **libraries**. A library is an archive of reusable functions which are stored in such a way that they can be used by other programs without being recompiled. Creating and managing libraries is the topic of chapter 20.

Encapsulation is an important cornerstone in **object oriented programming** (**OOP**). In OOP, the primary focus of programming is on the **objects**, or pieces of data, used in a program. In contrast, **procedural** programming focuses on the **algorithms**, objects being the secondary concern. You can use either approach when programming in any language. We will discuss important concepts of both approaches in this and the remaining chapters.

The idea behind encapsulation is to package a *data type* and all the *operations* that go with it into one tidy bundle. In programming, this means writing a set of **member functions** for each data type, to implement all the operations that can be performed on it.

For example, consider a simple data type such as `int`. The operations that go with `int` include addition, subtraction, multiplication, division, negation, comparison, copying, reading, and printing, to name a few. Most of these operations are handled by built-in C operators, but the read and print operations are performed by library functions such as `scanf()` and `printf()`.

The combination of a data type and all its member function is referred to as a **class**. OO languages such as C++ have special facilities for implementing classes. While C has no such facilities, you can easily apply the class concept in C programming by simply writing a set of member functions for each data type you use. Neither C nor C++ forces programmers to use classes, but it's a very useful concept and worth considering in all programming settings.

Using strict encapsulation, *all* operations on an object are done using the member functions of its class. For example, the C library contains many functions for manipulating strings, such as `strlen()` for finding the length of a string, `strcpy()` for copying a string, and so on. If you wanted to do something more, such as capitalize the letters in a string, you could write a simple loop directly into the program to do it.

```
#include <stdio.h>
#include <sysexits.h>
#include <ctype.h>

#define MAX_LEN 100

int     main()

{
    char     name[MAX_LEN+1], *p;

    /* Input string */
    fputs("Please enter your name: ",stdout);
    fgets(name,MAX_LEN,stdin);

    /* Capitalize each word in name */
    for (p=name; *p != '\0'; ++p)
        if ( isalpha(*p) && ((p == name) || isspace(p[-1])) )
            *p = toupper(*p);

    puts(name);
    return EX_OK;
}
```

However, this would violate the idea of encapsulation. Instead, write a new member function which will capitalize *any* string object. Once this function is written, it will be easy to capitalize any string in any program you write hereafter.

```
#include <stdio.h>
```

```
#include <sysexits.h>
#include <ctype.h>

#define MAX_LEN 100

char    *strcapitalize(char *name);

int     main()

{
    char    name[MAX_LEN+1];

    /* Input string */
    fputs("Please enter your name: ",stdout);
    fgets(name,MAX_LEN,stdin);

    /* Capitalize each word in name */
    strcapitalize(name);

    puts(name);
    return EX_OK;
}
```

As you may have already guessed, reusability is one of the major motivations behind encapsulation and OOP.

11.3   Writing Functions

Functions in C are both **declared** and **defined**. The **definition** of a function contains the function body, i.e. the statements that make up the function. The **declaration** exists only to give the compiler enough information to check the syntax of a function *call*. Both definitions and declarations can be done in two forms, which are discussed in the following sections.

11.3.1 Function Definitions

A function definition has two possible forms, depending on the flavor of C you are using. The two forms differ in how the **formal arguments** are defined.

ANSI C uses the following general form:

```
<return type>  name(formal argument definitions)

{
    body
}
```

K&R C is the older standard, and uses a slightly different form:

```
<return type>  name(formal argument names)
formal argument definitions

{
    body
}
```

Choosing a Form

All ANSI compilers are required to recognize K&R syntax constructs, so any compiler can handle the K&R form. A strict K&R compiler, on the other hand, won't recognize the ANSI form. Strict K&R compilers are nearly extinct, so using the ANSI form isn't likely to cause any portability problems. In addition, there is a free GNU tool called *unproto* which converts ANSI code to K&R form. Unproto is generally used as a filter to convert ANSI code to K&R form and then feed it directly to a K&R compiler. Unproto is available at many GNU sites (see appendix A). Another consideration is that ANSI C++ compilers are only required to recognize ANSI C constructs, and hence may not handle K&R constructs properly, if at all.

The return type of a function may be any *scalar* type, either built-in or user defined. Functions cannot return **aggregate objects**. Aggregate types include arrays and structures, which are discussed in chapters 15 and 18. They can, however, return

pointers to aggregate objects. A pointer is a memory address, which is a always scalar value, regardless of what it points to. Pointers are discussed in chapter 14.

The formal arguments may be any data type, including arrays and structures, although passing structures is not allowed in strict K&R C. Passing structure objects is also inefficient, since it requires copying potentially large blocks of memory. Hence, it's common practice to pass a **pointer** to a structure instead, since this is more efficient and more portable.

Finally, the types `char`, `short`, and `float` are not normally used as formal arguments, for reasons discussed in section 11.5.3.

11.3.2   A First Example

Example:

We'll begin with a simple program that prints N! for all values of N from 1 to 10.[1] This example uses a simple function that computes N! for any non-negative integer N, provided N! is within the range of a `double`. We use `double`, even though all factorials are integers, because factorials can be extremely large, and `double` has a greater range than any integer type in C.

Note that this example presents the simplest and *most inefficient* way to write a factorial function. A much better factorial function is presented in section 15.5.

The following is a top-down design which describes the overall program in detail:

1. Initialize N to 1

2. Compute N!

   (a) Initialize factorial to 1

   (b) Multiply factorial by all numbers from 2 to N

3. Increment N

---

[1]N! (pronounced "N factorial") is a function defined for any value of $N \geq 0$. 0! is defined as 1, and all others are defined as $(N-1)! \times N$. For values of N greater than 0, N! is the product of all integers from 1 to N.

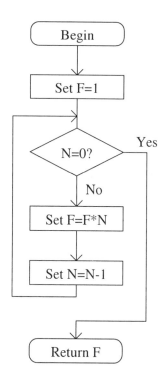

Figure 11.3: Flow chart for computing N!

4. Repeat until N is greater than 10

Figure 11.3 shows the flow chart for computing a single N! value (Step 2 in the top-down design). Expanding the flowchart to represent the overall program is left as an exercise.

In most cases, the top-down design should translate naturally to an arrangement of subprograms. The details of any step that is broken down should be packaged into functions, so that they don't clutter up the program at the current level. Each step in the first level of refinement should correspond to one or two statements in `main()`. Hence, steps 1, 2, 3, and 4 represent the main program below.

```
#include <stdio.h>
#include <sysexits.h>

double  factorial(int n);
```

```
int     main()

{
    int     c;
    double  f;

    for (c=1; c<=10; ++c)
    {
        f = factorial(c);
        printf("%d! = %f\n",c,f);
    }
    return EX_OK;
}
```

Steps 2a and 2b represent the body of the `factorial()` function. The function definition for `factorial()` can be written in ANSI form as follows:

```
double  factorial(int n)

{
    double  f = 1;

    while ( n > 1 )
        f *= n--;
    return f;
}
```

or in K&R form:

```
double  factorial(n)
int n;

{
    double  f = 1;
```

```
        while ( n > 1 )
            f *= n--;
        return f;
    }
```

Note that using this function makes the program less efficient than the version presented in chapter 10 (page 209), because the function computes each factorial from scratch. The chapter 10 version computes each new factorial using the previous factorial value, which requires only a single multiplication. There is a solution to this problem, using a function, which makes the program more efficient than either version so far. This example requires the use of an array, and is presented in section 15.5.

11.3.3   Declaring Functions: Allusions and Prototypes

Some languages, such as Pascal, don't require function declarations. Pascal programs are typically contained in a single file, and each subprogram must be *defined* before it is called. Therefore, the compiler, which reads the program from top to bottom, knows everything about each subprogram before it encounters a call to it.

In C, you are not required to *define* functions in any particular order. In fact, C functions are usually defined in several different source files, which are compiled separately. Thus, the compiler often sees calls to functions for which it has not seen a definition. If a function is called in a program before it is defined, or if it is defined in a different file, then the compiler must encounter a *declaration* of the function prior to the call.

When a program is divided among several source files, the function declarations should be placed in a header file, which is included in each source file. This will ensure that all the necessary function declarations are seen by the compiler when compiling any of the source files.

The K&R function declaration for the factorial function above would be written as follows:

```
    double  factorial();
```

The K&R declaration, called an **allusion**, provides the compiler with the return type, but says nothing about the arguments the function expects.

Pitfall: Limitations of Allusions

When using an allusion, the compiler cannot detect errors in the argument list of a function call. For example, the call:

```
f = factorial(2.0);
```

is incorrect, since 2.0 is a double value, and the function requires an int argument. This type of error will slip past the compiler, and will most likely be difficult to track down. The factorial function in this case will simply misinterpret the floating point formatted bits of the double value 2.0 as a simple int, which will produce some very odd results. For example, if the machine uses the IEEE double format, the value 2.0 would be stored in memory as $00000000000010\cdots00$. If an int is 32 bits, the program will take either the first 32 bits, which are $00000000000010000000000000000000_2 = 524288_{10}$, or the latter 32 bits, which are all 0, depending on the byte ordering the machine uses for large values.

The ANSI declaration, called a **prototype** prevents incorrect function calls by providing a description of the argument list:

```
double factorial(int);
```

This prototype declaration states that the function requires one argument, which must be an int. If the wrong type of argument is given, as in the call shown above, the compiler will generate an error message.

Tip of the trade: Prototype Arguments

The name of each argument may also be shown in the prototype, but is ignored, since a declaration doesn't actually use the argument variable.

```
double factorial(int n);
```

A prototype declaration with argument names is identical to the first line of the *definition*. This is in fact why the name is allowed in a prototype; so that you can create a prototype easily by cutting and pasting the first line of the function definition.

Since the formal argument name in the prototype is ignored, it doesn't even have to match the name used in the function definition. Hence, you are free to change the names of formal argument variables in your function definitions, and there's no need to bother updating the prototypes as long as the types of the arguments are not changed.

An even better way to create prototypes is to use a prototype generating tool such as cproto, which is available for free under the GNU public license. If your system doesn't have cproto, visit one of the GNU sites listed in appendix A to obtain a copy.

Example:

Now that we've covered the basics of using functions, let's put it all together. The complete factorial program is written as follows:

```
#include <stdio.h>
#include <sysexits.h>

/* Prototype declaration for factorial. */
double  factorial(int);

/***************************/
```

```
/* Definition of main program */

int     main()

{
    int     c;
    double  f;

    for (c=1; c<=10; ++c)
    {
        f = factorial(c);
        printf("%d! = %f\n",c,f);
    }
    return EX_OK;
}


/***************************/
/* Definition of factorial */

double  factorial(int n)

{
    /* 0! = 1, so initialize to 1 */
    double  f = 1;

    /* Multiply by values from 2 to n */
    while ( n > 1 )
        f *= n--;
    return f;
}
```

Pitfall: Accidental Allusions

A common mistake made by ANSI C programmers is *inadvertently* using
a K&R declaration for functions that have no arguments. If a function

has no arguments, the prototype must be written with `void` in the argument list:

```
int     print_intro(void);
```

This tells the compiler that the function `print_intro()` does not take any arguments. The declaration

```
int     print_intro();
```

is interpreted as an allusion (a K&R declaration), even by ANSI compilers, because ANSI C is backward compatible with the K&R standard. As a result, the compiler won't check the argument list in calls to `print_intro()`, and won't tell you if your argument list is wrong.

This problem is especially common among C++ programmers using C compilers, since the declaration rules are different for C++. Since C++ is *not* K&R compatible, a declaration with no arguments is considered to be a prototype with a `void` argument list, not an allusion. If you use C++, it's a good idea to get in the habit of using `void` in prototypes, so that you won't forget it when you use a C compiler.

11.3.4 Function Calls

Each time a function is called, the value of each argument is copied to the corresponding **formal argument variable** inside the function. In the example above, the variable c in `main()` is the argument, and n in `factorial()` is the formal argument variable. When `factorial()` is called in the statement

```
f = factorial(c);
```

the value of c is first copied to n, and then the function body is executed. When the function is done executing, the program returns to complete the statement that called the function.

Function calls can appear almost anywhere in a C program, except for void functions, which can't appear where a value is expected. For example, the variable f in main() is used only to improve readability. You could also have written main() as follows:

```
int     main()

{
    int    c;

    for (c=1; c<=10; ++c)
        printf("%ld! = %f\n",c,factorial(c));
    return 0;
}
```

This would shorten the program considerably, but makes the print() statement somewhat cluttered. Which style you use is a matter of personal preference.

11.4   Local Variables

Each function in a C program, including main(), has it's own set of variables. The variables defined in one function are not accessible to other functions. Different functions may use the same variable names. For instance, a variable called f in main() is separate from f in function factorial(). That is, each function's f uses a different memory address. This also applies to formal argument variables. The *only* difference between a formal argument variable and other local variables in a function, is that the formal arguments are initialized to the values of the corresponding arguments in the function call.

If you want to make information in one function available to another function, it must be passed in as an argument or sent back as the function's return value, or through a pointer argument.[2]

Example:

The main() function and factorial() function below each have a local variable called n. Although the two variables have the same name, they

---
[2]Pointer arguments are discussed in chapter 14.

represent different memory locations, so decrementing n in factorial() has no effect on the variable n in main(). When the factorial() function is called, the value of n in main() is copied to the formal argument variable n in factorial(). Using the same name for an argument and formal argument variable is a common practice, but it is important to remember that they are distinct variables.

```
#include <stdio.h>
#include <sysexits.h>

double  factorial(int n);

int     main()

{
    int n;

    for (n=1; n<=10; ++n)
        printf("%d! = %f\n",n,factorial(n));
    return EX_OK;
}

/**************************/
/* Definition of factorial */

double  factorial(int n)

{
    double  f = 1;

    while ( n > 1 )
        f *= n--;
    return f;
}
```

Figure 11.4 shows the contents of memory after the last iteration in main().

Address	Contents	Name
1000	11	n in main()
	...	
1100	1	n in factorial()

Figure 11.4: Two variables called **n**

The rules about local variables apply to `main()` just as they do in any other function. In fact, the only special quality of `main()` is that it's the first function called when a program is executed. Otherwise, it's just like any other function in the program. It can even be called by other functions, although there is usually no reason to do this.

11.5   Arguments

11.5.1   Privacy

Formal argument variables in C are ordinary local variables, so the formal argument holds a private copy of the value passed in. They only differ from other local variables in that they are initialized to the argument values given in the function call. Otherwise, they can and should be treated like other local variables.

Pitfall: Needless Redundancy

A common mistake among inexperienced C programmers is to duplicate the values of formal argument variables using other local variables, which only makes the program longer and slower. Many programmer's are phobic about modifying the contents of formal argument variables. This may stem from the fact that other languages, such as Pascal, FORTRAN, and C++, support **reference arguments**, in which case the programmer must be careful about modifying the formal argument's value. In C, however, modifying a formal argument *never* has any side effects outside the function. The reasons for this are discussed in section 11.5.2.

Consider the following example:

```
double  factorial(int n)

{
    double  f = 1, c;

    for (c=n; c>1; --c)
        f *= c;
    return f;
}
```

The local variable c in this program is unnecessary. It only adds to the complexity of the source code, and makes the program slightly slower. The previous examples of factorial functions, which made direct use of the formal argument variable, were both simpler and more efficient.

11.5.2 Argument Passing: Behind the Scenes

The argument passing strategy used by C is called **pass by value**, meaning the *value* of each argument is passed to the corresponding formal argument variable when the function is called. An alternative strategy used by other languages, such as FORTRAN and Pascal, passes the *address* of the argument, so that the function can actually access the memory location of the argument outside the function. This strategy is called **pass by reference**, since the formal argument variable actually *refers to* the argument, rather than being a copy of it.

Figure 11.5 demonstrates how memory is used in argument passing for the factorial program when n in `main()` has a value of 5. The addresses shown for each variable are representative examples of the addresses that the compiler would choose.

```
#include <stdio.h>
#include <sysexits.h>

double  factorial(int n);

int     main()
```

Beginning of `factorial()`...

Address	Contents	Name
1000	5	c
	...	
1100	5	n

End of `factorial()`...

Address	Contents	Name
1000	5	c
	...	
1100	1	n

Figure 11.5: Pass by value

```
{

    int     c;

    for (c=1; c<=10; ++c)
        printf("%d! = %f\n",c,factorial(c));
    return EX_OK;
}

double  factorial(int n)

{

    double  f = 1;

    while ( n > 1 )
        f *= n--;
    return f;
}
```

Passing arguments by *reference* is often useful, since it allows a function to manipulate several values outside of it's own set of local variables, in essence *returning* multiple values to the calling function. Since only one value can be formally returned from a function, reference arguments are necessary for functions like `scanf()`, which need to send back multiple values in many cases.

C has no pass by reference formal arguments. Instead, if you want to pass the address of a variable in C, you do it explicitly, using pointers, which are discussed in chapter 14. Reference arguments make a program more abstract, which would be out of character for C. For example, in Pascal or C++, it is *impossible* to tell if an argument is being passed by value or by reference just by looking at the subprogram call. You would have to see the subprogram definition or documentation to determine how the argument is passed. In C, however, the nuts and bolts are always visible. Arguments being passed by reference are either defined as pointers, or have an & operator attached, as in the example below:

```
scanf("%d",&num);
```

Techniques for defining functions that accept pointer arguments, like `scanf()`, are discussed in chapter 14.

11.5.3 Promotions in Argument Passing

You should rarely, if ever, see formal arguments defined as `char`, `short`, or `float`. This is because C programs promote these types when they are passed to functions, just as when they are used in mathematical operations. When you pass a `char` or `short` to a function, it's value is automatically promoted to `int`. Similarly, when you pass a `float`, it is promoted to `double`. If you do use `char`, `short`, or `float` for formal arguments, then many more promotions are likely to occur inside the function as the formal argument variables are used in expressions. Hence, doing the promotions in advance, when the function is called, ultimately enhances program performance.

Argument promotions also increase programming flexibility, since you can pass a `char` or `short` value to an `int` formal argument, or a `float` to a `double` formal argument without a cast. This is also the reason that `printf()` uses the same place-holders for `char`, `short` and `int` arguments (%d, %o, %x, etc.), and for `float` and `double` arguments (%f).

11.5.4 Multiple Arguments

When more than one argument is passed to a function, the *position* of each argument determines which formal argument variable receives it's value. The first argument that appears in a function call is copied to the first formal argument variable, and so on.

Example:

Use a simple function to compute 2^{50} by repeated multiplication. **Note: This is a very inefficient way to compute a power. A much better example is given in section 11.9.**

The argument 2.0 is copied to formal argument variable `base`, and 50 is copied to formal argument variable `expo`.

```c
#include <stdio.h>
#include <sysexits.h>

double pow(double base,int expo);

int     main()

{
    printf("2^50 = %f\n",pow(2.0,50));
    return EX_OK;
}

/* Simple, but very slow pow() function */
double pow(double base,int expo)

{
    double  p = 1;

    /* The most naive method to compute base^expo */
    while ( expo-- > 0 )
        p *= base;
    return p;
}
```

11.6   Library Functions

Definitions for standard library functions such as `printf()` and `puts()` are pre-compiled, and stored in library files, such as */usr/lib/libc.a*, and */usr/lib/libm.a*. These libraries are automatically searched by the linker, so the necessary definitions are extracted and linked into your program as needed.

The standard libraries contain hundreds or thousands of functions, designed for every type of programming. For example, on FreeBSD 2.1, the standard library, */usr/lib/libc.a*, contains over 570 functions. The math library, */usr/lib/libm.a*, contains more than 150 additional functions. These are just two examples of the many libraries found on Unix systems. One of the most important aspects of becoming a proficient C programmer is learning *what's available* in the libraries. No one can memorize all the available functions, but by knowing in general what the libraries contain, you can avoid re-inventing the wheel.

One of the most important rules in C programming is *check the libraries before writing a function yourself.* Odds are, there is a function, or a simple combination of a few functions that will accomplish what you need. You can follow the example of electrical engineers in their design of digital circuits. Very rarely does an engineer design a new circuit from scratch. Instead, they search through references like the *TTL Data Book* first, in hopes of finding a simpler solution. There is no *Library Function Data Book* for us to search, but you can gather the information you need on line, by using the `man` and `apropos` commands, as well as simply looking into the directories containing libraries, and looking into the libraries with the `ar` command. For example, to list the functions available in *libc.a*, type

```
ar t /usr/lib/libc.a | more
```

This will provide the names of all the functions available. You can then use the `man` command to get detailed information on any functions of interest.

Many modern systems provide some or all of their library functions in **dynamic libraries**, which have a ".so" extension, followed by a version number. To list the contents of these libraries, use the `nm` command. For example:

```
nm /usr/lib/libc.so.2.2
```

The *declarations* for library functions in *libc.a* are found in the system header files, such as *stdio.h*, *string.h*, and so on. There are many header files associated with the library *libc.a*, while some other libraries have only one or a few associated headers. For example, *libm.a* contains math functions, such as `sin()`, `cos()`, `exp()`, and so on. Most or all of these functions are declared in *math.h*, along with the defined constants and type definitions that go with them.

It is also important for C programmers to learn how to build and maintain their own libraries. Techniques for building both static and dynamic libraries are discussed in chapter 20.

11.7   Documenting Functions

A well-written, **self-documenting** program can usually get by with one verbose comment explaining each function, and a few brief comments inside. Writing a self-documenting function means choosing a descriptive name for the function, and for all the variables used inside. Good, consistent code formatting is also important. Use consistent indentation, and leave blank lines between major sections of the function, such as loops or `if` statements, to create modularity at an even lower level than the function itself.

A **cohesive function** is one with a *singular purpose that is described completely by the function's name*. If you have difficulty coming up with a name for a function, it probably means the function is too large and complicated. You'll need to split the function into two or more separate functions so that each one has a unique purpose, which can easily be described with a short name. Cohesiveness is an important concept in software engineering. The more cohesive your functions are, the more **maintainable** your code will be. A maintainable program requires minimal effort in debugging and enhancing the program.

Connectivity is another important concept, which evaluates how information is exchanged between functions, or how well the pieces fit together. If you restrict information exchange to formal arguments and return values, your program will be well connected.

Information exchange can also be accomplished via global variables, but this is considered a bad practice since it reduces the modularity of the code, making it difficult to maintain. Global variables also make it possible for one function to have side effects on others that use the same global variables. Side effects are one of the most frustrating problems to overcome in the debugging process. This is another reason to *never* use global variables in your programs.

11.8 Top-down Programming and Stubs

Never begin writing code without having a written plan to follow. Always think through how the program will work in general, and write an *outline* before beginning the coding phase.

Once coding begins, it should be a simple translation process. Still, you can expect to make plenty of mistakes while writing the code. For this reason, coding should be done *a little at a time*, and new code should be compiled and tested frequently during development. A good rule of thumb is to write no more than ten lines of new code at a time before compiling and working out the errors. If you are using a modern integrated development environment (IDE), such as APE, compiling frequently is a simple matter.

When programming with subprograms, each subprogram must be declared *and* defined before a program will compile successfully. You might think this would make it difficult to test every 10 lines of new code. However, function definitions don't have to be *complete* in order to compile. You can follow the idea of coding a little at a time, and still make the compiler happy by using **top-down programming**.

Top-down programming simply means writing function *calls* before writing the function definitions. Hence, the main() is always written first, and the functions it needs are initially written as **stubs**. A stub is nothing more than a blank function definition. It has the essential elements needed to compile, but few or no statements in the body.

Top-down programming and stubs make it easy to produce modular code. As each function you are writing approaches the size of a screen, you can stop it from growing any further by simply relegating the rest of its work to a new function, for which you insert a call and a stub. You can then test the code you have so far, and afterwards move on to filling in the next stub. This may seem like procrastination, since you find yourself writing a lot of stubs, and continually putting off writing any real code. However, this method leads to a much better organized program.

Example:

> In coding the factorial program above, you can begin by writing the
> main() function, and supplying a stub for factorial, just to make the

program compilable. Writing `main()` first helps clarify the details of
the next level of refinement. In other words, how the factorial function
should work is determined by how you design `main()` to call it.

```c
#include <stdio.h>
#include <sysexits.h>

/* Declaration for factorial */
double  factorial(int);

/*****************************/
/* Definition of main program */

int     main()

{
    int     n;
    double  f;

    for (n=1; n<=10; ++n)
    {
        f = factorial(n);
        printf("%d! = %f\n",n,f);
    }
    return EX_OK;
}

/*********************/
/* Stub for factorial */

double  factorial(x)
int x;

{
    /* Bogus return value to avoid compiler warnings */
    return 0.0;
}
```

This program obviously won't print a table of factorials, but it will compile and run. You can now work out errors in the main program before beginning to write the `factorial()` function.

11.9 Advanced: Recursion

Recursion is the art of defining something *in terms of itself*. Recursive definitions may sometimes seem tricky or confusing. However, if used carefully, recursion can be extremely useful in simplifying complex concepts.

For example, the expression b^{100} can be described as multiplying b by itself 100 times. This is easy to do using a loop which begins with 1, and iterates 100 times, multiplying by b each time. However, there is a much more efficient way to compute an integer power.

Any integer power can be described *recursively*, in terms of smaller powers. For example, $b^{100} = (b^{50})^2$. This only works for even powers, but odd powers are solved with a simple extension. For example, $b^{101} = b^{100} \times b = (b^{50})^2 \times b$. You need only compute b^{50} *once*, and then multiply the result by itself. Using a loop, this will take about half the multiplications needed to compute b^{100} with a simple loop. You can save even more time by recursively applying the same technique to compute b^{50}, b^{25}, b^{12}, and so on until you reach a **base case** that cannot be divided any further. In computing integer powers, the base case can be b^1 or b^0.

This is an example of **divide and conquer computation**, and is analogous to our divide and conquer approach to planning a program. Instead of 100 multiplications that a simple loop would perform, this algorithm does one multiplication for each time it divides the exponent in half. The total number of multiplications is approximately $log_2(exponent)$, since this is how many times you can divide the exponent by 2.

Recursion in programming is implemented by functions that call themselves repeatedly until the base case is reached.

```
#include <stdio.h>
#include <sysexits.h>

double   pow(double base,int expo);
```

```
int     main()

{
    double  base=2.0;
    int     expo;

    for (expo=0; expo<=32; ++expo)
        printf("%f\n",pow(base,expo));
    return EX_OK;
}



/* Divide and conquer power function */
double  pow(double base,int expo)

{
    double  p;

    /* If base case, no more recursive calls */
    if ( expo == 0 )
        return 1.0;
    else
    {
        /* Get base ^ (expo/2) using recursion */
        p = pow(base,expo/2);
        if ( (expo & 1) == 0 )     /* Even expo */
            return p*p;
        else                       /* Odd expo */
            return p*p*base;
    }
}
```

What makes recursion so useful in programming is the fact that many difficult algorithms are easily expressed recursively. For example, The divide and conquer method for computing powers can be implemented without recursion (i.e. iteratively), but the iterative version isn't nearly as simple and elegant. Many other algorithms, such as quicksort, mergesort, and binary search, are also more easily expressed recursively, and are usually implemented with recursion.

Given an iterative function, and a recursive function that implements the same algorithm, the recursive version *always* takes more time and memory resources, due to the added overhead of all the function calls. Recursion essentially uses function calls to iterate. Function calls are far more costly than loops in terms of both time and memory, due to the time spent passing arguments and branching to and from the function body, and the additional memory allocated for local variables and such each time the function is called.

If the function is large, the overhead of the calls won't be a significant fraction of the computing time. If the function is very small, however, it can be very significant. For example, factorials can be computed recursively as follows:

$$N! = (N - 1)! \times N$$

```
double  factorial(int n)

{
    if ( n == 0 )
        return 1.0;
    else
        return factorial(n-1) * n;
}
```

This function is *so* short, the overhead of calling it actually takes up more time than the computations done inside the function.

In addition, this recursive function implements the same algorithm as the iterative version, and therefore can't offer any performance advantage. Since the factorial function is easy to define and code iteratively, there is no advantage to using recursion here.

These facts make `factorial()` a bad candidate for recursion. In fact, the iterative version of factorial is about twice as fast as the recursive version. In larger functions, such as `qsort()` (quick-sort), the iterative version is only marginally (a few percent) faster, and is very difficult to program. Hence, most implementations of quicksort use recursion.

Another consideration is the number of **levels of recursion**, the number of times the function calls itself before reaching the base case. If a function is likely to go through many levels, it will consume a lot of time and memory, since new memory is allocated for local variables, arguments, etc., each time the function is called. In these cases, it is often worth some extra effort to implement an iterative version instead. If the function will generally go through only a few levels of recursion, then there is no point spending extra programming effort writing an iterative version. Binary search is a good example. This function is extremely simple when written recursively, and never requires many levels or recursion. When searching a list of 1,000,000 items, the binary search will only go through 20 levels of recursion at the most.

Tip of the trade: Recursion in Other Languages

The C language uses a particularly simple and efficient function calling method. Other languages, notably C++ and PL/1, exert a great deal more effort calling functions, due to the complexity of information that they pass to the function. Therefore, if you are using a complex language such as C++, you may want to be a little more conservative about using recursion.

11.10   Advanced: Scope and Storage Class

11.10.1   Scope

The **scope** of a variable describes where in the program it can be used. As discussed in section 11.4, most variables are available throughout, and only in, the function in which they are defined. The true scope of a variable in a C program is from the point where it is declared or defined, to the end of the *block* it is declared or defined in.

This usually means the variable is in scope to the end of the function. However, a variable can be defined locally inside *any* block delimited by curly braces. In other words, variables can be defined immediately following any { character within a function body. Defining variables in this way puts the definition closer to where the variable is used, and may make the code a little easier to read. It also avoids allocating memory for variables that may not be needed, although usually a trivial amount. On the other hand, each instantiation (allocation) takes a small amount of time, so to maximize performance, it's best to define all your variables at the beginning of the function. This will allow the program to allocate all the memory needed at once.

If two variables with the same name are both in scope, the variable with the narrower scope is used. Since most C variables are defined at the beginning of the function, however, the compiler rarely has to make such a choice.

Example:

Consider the following code fragment:

```
{
    int     c = 5;

    if (c > 0)
    {
        int     c = 2;

        printf("%d\n",c);
    }
}
```

There are two variables named `c` in scope for the `printf()` call, so the compiler must decide which one to use. The actual output is 2, since the variable `c` defined inside the `if` statement has the narrower scope.

11.10.2 Storage Class

Variables in C have several different possible **storage classes**. The storage class determines how and where the variable's contents are stored, and when the variable is **instantiated**, i.e. when memory is allocated for it.

Each process running under Unix has four memory segments, as shown in figure 11.6.

Figure 11.6: Memory segments of a Unix process

1. The **text segment** contains the program instructions.

2. The **data segment** contains the program's static data, such as constant values and `static` variables, which will be described shortly.

3. The **stack segment** is used for the program's local variables, argument passing, and return addresses when functions are called.

4. The **heap** is used for dynamic memory allocation, discussed in chapter 15.

Static

A `static` variable uses memory space in the *data* segment. `Static` variables are instantiated the moment the program begins execution, and remain in existence until the program terminates. Thus, `static` variables can retain their contents between function calls.

If a `static` variable definition contains an initializer, it is initialized *only* when the program is loaded.

Example:

> Demonstration of `static` variable initialization. The `static` variable `calls` is initialized to one when the program begins, and incremented each time the function is called.

```
void    count_calls()

{
    static int  calls = 1;

    printf("I've been called %d times.\n",calls);
    ++calls;
}
```

Auto

Auto is the default storage class for all local variables. Auto variables use memory space in the *stack* segment. They are instantiated upon entering the block in which they are defined. For example, the local variables defined at the beginning of a function are instantiated when the function is called, by allocating additional stack space. Auto variables are destroyed when the function returns, and the same stack space is reused for different variables in the next function called. Figure 11.7 shows the system stack contents at several instants during the execution of the program below:

```
void    fn1(void), fn2(void);

int     main()

{
    int     a,b;

    fn1();
    fn2();
    return 0;
}

void    fn1()

{
```

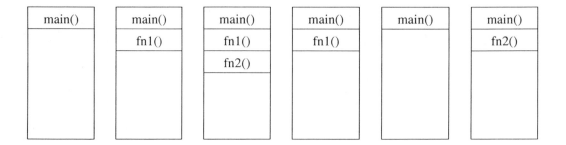

Figure 11.7: Stack contents during program execution

```
    int      c;

    fn2();
}

void    fn2()

{
    int      d, e;
    return;
}
```

Auto variables conserve memory, since they don't take up any memory space when they aren't being used. They do require a small amount of time during execution to allocate the memory, however, so they are slightly slower than static variables. The difference is usually very slight, since allocating stack space is a simple task, and is generally only done once, at the beginning of a function's execution. All the variables defined at the beginning of a function can be allocated in one operation. It makes no difference if there are two or twenty. Auto variables defined with narrower scope, e.g. inside if statements or loops, will require a separate allocation step, and therefore may slow down the program slightly.

If an auto variable definition has an initializer, it is reinitialized every time it is instantiated. For example, auto local variables at the beginning of a function that have initializers are reinitialized each time the function is called. This is an important distinction between static and auto variables, and is often the primary reason for choosing one over the other.

Example:

The factorial function below needs f initialized each time it is called. If f were defined as a `static` variable, the function wouldn't be reliable after the first call, since f would contain a leftover value from the previous call, instead of 1.0.

```
double factorial(int n)

{
    double f = 1.0;

    while ( n > 1 )
        f *= n--;
    return f;
}
```

Register

`Register` variables use a CPU register instead of memory if a register is available. This is theoretically advantageous, because retrieving data from a register inside the CPU is essentially instantaneous. That is, data requested from a CPU register is always available at the next clock tick. In a 300Mhz CPU, this translates to 3.3 nanoseconds. A typical memory chip, on the other hand, takes up to 70 nanoseconds to respond to a read request. This means the CPU may have to spend up to 22 clock ticks waiting for data to arrive from memory.

The `register` keyword was often used in the past to make programs faster, by using registers for the most frequently accessed variables in a function. Loop control variables generally fall into this category, as shown below:

```
register int    c;
```

```
for (c=0; c<1000; ++c)
{
    ...
}
```

There are some important things to know about the `register` keyword, however.

First, the `register` keyword is only a request: There is no guarantee that a variable defined as `register` will actually get to use one.

Next, the & operator cannot be used on a variable with register storage class, since the variable does not represent a memory address.

Most importantly, today's machine code optimizers can make much better use of registers through **register caching** than is possible at the source code level, so the `register` keyword is obsolete. Register caching is a technique used by compilers which keeps a copy of a frequently used variable in a register for quick access. The same register can be used to cache several variables in the same scope, depending on which is being used most frequently in a given section of the program. These sections are often as small as a few lines. Therefore, using the `register` keyword will most likely *slow down* your program by hogging registers that could be put to better use. If you see a variable defined as `register`, it's usually a good idea to change it to an `auto` or `static` variable, and compile the code with the -O (capital O) option to ensure the optimizer is invoked.

Const

The `const` modifier marks a variable as *read-only*. A variable definition with the `const` modifier *must* have an initializer, since the variable cannot be assigned a new value by any C statement. The `const` modifier can be used to define simple constants, as shown in chapter 6, but is most commonly used with pointer arguments, which are discussed in section 15.7.

Volatile

The `volatile` modifier informs the compiler that a variable might be altered *at any time* by forces outside the function. For example, a variable that is used in a **signal handler** function could be altered when the program is interrupted by the appropriate signal. Signals are discussed in detail in chapter 27. Signal handlers exhibit

asynchronous execution, meaning that the program does not decide *when* signal handlers are executed. In other words, they are not called explicitly within the program, but instead are called by the operating system when appropriate signals occur in the system. When the signal is received, the kernel immediately discontinues the program and executes the handler function assigned to the type of signal received. When the signal handler completes, the program is resumed exactly where it left off. This could happen during execution of *any* of the millions of instructions in the program, and the program will be completely unaware that anything has happened. Because signal handlers may be part of the program, they could potentially alter the contents of variables in the program.

Under normal circumstances, the optimizer can determine what types of code rearrangements are safe to perform. This is not the case for variables that may be modified by signal handlers, however. When a variable is defined as `volatile`, the compiler will not perform optimizations such as register caching, because it is impossible to know when the variable might be updated, and thus impossible to ensure that the cached copy in the register is up to date.

11.11 Advanced: The `inline` Request

The `inline` keyword is a modifier used to eliminate the overhead of function calls. Inlined functions work essentially the same way as macros, which are discussed in chapter 13. The body of the function is *substituted* for each function call, instead of being branched to and returned from.

If you use inlining, the source code for the function must be made available to the compiler, so it can be inserted into the program. Inlining is practical for small functions, but for larger ones, it can dramatically increase the size of the executable program, since the function body is duplicated everywhere the function is called.

Chapter 12

Programming with make

Before you begin...

> You should be familiar with the material on the basics of the Unix `make` command, the operation of the C compiler, and functions presented in chapters 4, 5, and 11.

12.1   Using Separate Source Files

Imagine making a small change to a 50,000 line C program, and then waiting 10 minutes for it to compile, only to find out you omitted a semicolon. This is what would happen today, if large programs were written using a single source file. In the early 1970's, when Unix was first designed, compiling 50,000 lines of code would have taken many hours. Clearly, this was not, and still is not, an acceptable way to go about programming.

In order to avoid situations like these, most C programs are divided into many small source files which can be compiled separately into **object modules**, which are then linked together to build the executable program. When changes are made to a source file, *only that source file needs to be recompiled*. This reduces the compile time to a small fraction of what it would take to recompile the entire program. For example, if a program is split into ten equally sized source files, then compile time is reduced to about one tenth of what it would be if the whole program were contained in one file. The smaller you make your source files, the less time you'll spend waiting for your programs to compile. As a rule of thumb, each source file should generally contain no more than a few hundred lines of code. In many cases, each source file will contain only one function definition.

To build an executable file, you need to compile each source file separately *without linking*, and then link all the object files together to create the executable program.

To compile each file without linking, use the -c option with cc. This will produce an unlinked **object file** with a ".o" extension. These object files are then linked together using a separate command, to form the executable program file.

For example, if you want to build a program called *sort* from source files *sort.c* an *swap.c*, you could use the following sequence of compile and link commands:

```
(tcsh) 10: gcc -Wall -c sort.c
(tcsh) 11: gcc -Wall -c swap.c
(tcsh) 12: gcc sort.o swap.o -o sort
```

If you later make changes to the file *sort.c*, you only need to recompile this file, and then relink. There is no need to recompile *swap.c*, since *swap.o* already contains the latest machine code translated from *swap.c*.

```
(tcsh) 20: gcc -Wall -c sort.c
(tcsh) 21: gcc sort.o swap.o -o sort
```

Pitfall: Compiler Compatibility

It has become fairly common to have more than one compiler and linker installed on the same system. In particular, many Unix systems have both the vendor's compiler, cc, and the GNU compiler, gcc available.

It is important to realize that the object code formats produced by two compilers often have important differences, and may not be compatible. If you try to link object files produced by cc with those produced by gcc, you may run into trouble. Also, linking gcc object modules using cc or vice versa may cause problems, since the one linker may not recognize some features of the other's object modules. The safest route to follow is to compile all the source modules with the same compiler, *and* use the same command to link them.

12.2 Using make

Compiling separate source files by hand is a cumbersome process, and it's easy to lose track of which files need to be recompiled. Programmers in the IBM mainframe environment, which has no tools like make, often recompile hundreds of unmodified source files just to be certain that all the object files are up to date. The Unix make command can be used to automate the building of an executable from its source file dependents.

A makefile for a program will typically contain a link dependency and several compile dependencies. The link dependency is generally listed first. You can also use macros in the makefile so it will be easy to modify later.

Example:

Create a makefile for the *sort* program. The file *sort.h* is included in both *sort.c* and *swap.c*, so both object files need to be rebuilt if *sort.h* is modified. Therefore, *sort.h* is listed as a dependent for both object files.

```
sort:   sort.o swap.o
        gcc sort.o swap.o -o sort

sort.o: sort.c sort.h
        gcc -Wall -c sort.c

swap.o: swap.c sort.h
        gcc -Wall -c swap.c
```

As described in section 4.12, macros help eliminate redundancy and reduce the chances of errors in the makefile. The makefile above could be written with macros as follows:

```
OBJS    = sort.o swap.o
CC      = gcc
COPTS   = -Wall -c

sort:   $(OBJS)
        $(CC) $(OBJS) -o table

sort.o: sort.c sort.h
        $(CC) $(COPTS) sort.c

swap.o: swap.c sort.h
        $(CC) $(COPTS) swap.c
```

Before a dependency is executed, make will check each dependent to see if it appears as a **target** in a subsequent dependency. For example, before executing the link command to produce the file sort, make will check to see if either of the dependents *sort.o* or *swap.o* need to be rebuilt first. Hence, if you edit *sort.c* and then run make, make will detect that *sort.o* is out of date, and execute the command:

```
gcc -Wall -c sort.c
```

It will then note that the new *sort.o* is newer than *sort*, and will execute the link command:

```
gcc sort.o swap.o -o sort
```

To develop a program then, first create a makefile, then edit source files as needed, and then simply type make at the Unix prompt:

```
tcsh: make
```

You'll never need to keep track of which files need to be recompiled, because make will figure it out for you.

It is very important, however, to maintain the makefile correctly. You have to make sure that all the dependents are listed for each target file, and that the commands given for each dependency correctly build the target. It's very easy, for example, to forget to list some of the header files as dependents. If one is left out, `make` will not rebuild the target after that header is modified, and you will likely be testing an out-of-date executable. Section 12.4 discusses some alternatives to maintaining a makefile by hand.

12.3   Using Header Files

Header files are especially important when programming with multiple source files. Any information that might be needed by more than one source file belongs in a header file, which can be included in each source file that needs it. For example, the type definitions, function definitions, and macro definitions for the `sort` program could be placed in a header called *sort.h*, and both *sort.c* and *swap.c* would contain the line

```
#include "sort.h"
```

Each source file should generally contain only #includes and function *definitions*. All the #defines, typedefs, and prototypes belong in the header files.

12.4   Makefile Generators

Using `make` is a great way to automate program building, but maintaining a makefile can be tedious, and faulty makefiles can cause serious problems when you are trying to debug your latest changes.

There are several free software tools available for creating "perfect" makefiles given a list of source files. All of these tools are based on the C preprocessor's ability to identify the headers an object (.o) file is built from.

The simplest of the makefile generators is `genmake`. To use `genmake`, simply `cd` to the directory containing the source files, and type `genmake`. Genmake will automatically generate a simple makefile which builds a program from *all* the source files in the current directory. If there are any source files in the directory that are not part of the project, they must be moved out of the directory before running `genmake`.

Imake is a highly sophisticated program which generates complex makefiles using a template file called an *imakefile*. Imake uses a default filename of *Imakefile*. The primary advantage of imake is that the imakefiles are highly portable. This is important because header files and libraries are sometimes located in different places on different systems. In ordinary makefiles, these pathnames must be hard-coded. Imake generates an appropriate makefile for each system by determining the system dependent parameters. Imake is especially popular for X Windows[1] applications, which often use many different header files and libraries on different systems.

---

[1]X Windows is the Unix graphical program interface, and is covered in chapter 29.

Chapter 13

The C Preprocessor: cpp

Before you begin...

> You should be familiar with the material on Unix basics and C functions
> presented in chapters 4 and 11, respectively.

13.1   Macros and Constants: `#define`

Any identifier defined using the `#define` directive is technically called a macro.
However, defined identifiers can be divided into two groups:

- A **named constant** is a simple identifier which is replaced by some other
  text.

- What we commonly call a **macro** is a defined identifier followed by arguments.
  These types of macros are more like functions than constants.

The general form of a macro definition is:

`#define` *identifier(formal arguments) text*

The C preprocessor simply substitutes the *text* for the identifier and arguments
wherever the macro is referenced.

The formal arguments are optional. If not present, then the macro defines a simple constant. You have already seen many examples of constant definitions, such as

```
#define PI      3.1415926535897943
#define PROMPT  "Please enter your full name"
```

The identifier follows the same rules as other identifiers in C, as outlined in section 6.2. The text can contain virtually anything, and is terminated by the end of the line. If you need to define a macro whose text is longer than a single line, you must place a backslash at the end of each line to be continued. For example,

```
#define BIG_STRING "This string is too long to fit on one"\
                   "line, so it is broken into four parts,"\
                   "which are concatenated by the compiler"\
                   "since they're end to end."
```

It's conventional to use all upper case letters in macro names so that they may be easily distinguished from variables and functions. It's important to recognize macros, because they sometimes have side effects not associated with functions.

Tip of the trade: Alternative to #define

All Unix C and C++ compilers have a -D (define) command-line option which has the same effect as #define. If you want to define a constant that changes often, or is used in many files, it might be too much trouble to edit the source or header file that contains it. For example, you may want to define a constant that tells the compiler what platform standards to follow:

```
#define PLATFORM FreeBSD
```

Since this would need to be edited for every platform the program is compiled on, it may be easier to use the -D option in the makefile or on the command line:

```
gcc -Wall -DPLATFORM=FreeBSD file.c
```

Pitfall: Tricky Macro Bugs

Since the text substitution process occurs *before* the program is compiled (hence the name *pre*-processor), the preprocessor may output faulty C code if macros are badly defined. Thus, errors that appear far into your program can often be traced back to a faulty macro. For example, the following macro definition lacks a closing quote. This is perfectly acceptable to the preprocessor, since it doesn't place any restrictions on the content of the text, but the substituted text will cause compiler errors wherever it appears.

```
#define OOPS    "Look ma, one quote!
```

The statement

```
puts(OOPS);
```

is expanded by the preprocessor to

```
puts("Look ma, one quote!);
```

which will not compile. The compiler error will point to the `puts()` statement, not the macro. Note that using all upper case letters for the name `OOPS` makes it obvious that it's a macro, and thus you'll instantly know that the macro definition needs to be checked.

If the identifier being defined is followed by one or more formal argument variables, then the arguments given to the macro are substituted for the formal argument wherever it appears in the text.

Example:

Consider the following macro which uses the conditional operator (chapter 8) to compute the absolute value of a number:

```
#define ABS(n) ( (n) < 0 ? -(n) : (n) )
```

Now, let's see how it's used in a program:

```
dist = ABS(x2 - x1) * 5;
```

As discussed in chapter 5, the preprocessor is the first phase of program compilation. The preprocessor substitutes the expression `x2 - x1` into the text for the formal argument `n`, and then substitutes the modified text for `ABS(x2 - x1)`. The preprocessor expands this statement to the following:

```
dist = ( (x2 - x1) < 0 ? -(x2 - x1) : (x2 - x1) ) * 5;
```

Many of the so-called standard library "functions" are actually implemented as macros. One good example is `getchar()`. This macro is defined in *stdio.h* as follows:

```
#define getchar() getc(stdin)
```

To make things even more interesting, `getc()` is a macro itself, which demonstrates that macros can *use* other macros. Because there are some situations where a macro can't be used, the standard library provides true function versions of most common macros. For example, `fputc()` is a true function that behaves exactly like the `putc()` macro. One such situation is where a **function pointer** is called for.[1]

---

[1]Function pointer are discussed in chapter 17.

Pitfall: Macros with Arguments

It's important to enclose the formal argument in parenthesis each time it appears in the text of the macro, and to enclose the entire macro text in parenthesis as well. Otherwise, the C operator precedence rules may produce something unexpected.

For example, suppose you define the `ABS()` macro without parenthesis as follows:

```
#define ABS(n)   n < 0 ? -n : n
```

Now suppose you then write the following statement in your program:

```
distance = ABS(x2 - x1) * 5;
```

This statement will expand to the text shown below.

```
distance = x2 - x1 < 0 ? -x2 - x1 : x2 - x1 * 5;
```

There are two serious flaws in this statement. First, since there are no parenthesis around the argument `x2 - x1`, the statement computes `(-x2) - x1`, instead of `-(x2 - x1)` as you might expect.

Second, since there are no parenthesis around the entire text, the 5 is not multiplied by the result of the macro, but instead becomes part of the `else` expression, `x2 - x1 * 5`. Furthermore, since multiplication has higher precedence than subtraction, the result is `x2 - (x1 * 5)`, instead of `(x2 - x1) * 5` as you might expect.

Errors like these are extremely difficult to isolate in a program, since they are hidden from our view by our use of the faulty macro, and produce code that compiles, but does not produce the correct results. By always using parenthesis as shown earlier, you can easily avoid these types of computational errors.

Tip of the trade: Viewing cpp output

In order to debug macros, you sometimes need to examine the actual code that they expand to. This can be done using the -E compiler option, which instructs `cc` to run *only* the preprocessor, and show its output on `stdout`. Since this tends to produce a lot of blank lines, it's a good idea to pipe the output through `uniq`, to compact it a bit. The `uniq` command eliminates consecutive duplicate lines. In a computer program, only blank lines are likely to be identical and consecutive, so this won't likely eliminate anything important.

```
cc -E prog.c | uniq | more
```

This will allow you to see exactly what the code is doing, and will expose any flaws in the design or use of a macro.

13.2   Functions vs. Macros

Functions are very useful for both refining a problem and reducing program size by virtue of their reusability. However, there is a cost to using functions. Every time a function is called, your program has to spend time passing arguments, saving the return address, and branching to and from the function.

For large functions, this overhead cost is usually an insignificant fraction of the overall time spent executing the function. Furthermore, if the function is called infrequently, the overhead cost won't add up to much.

For very small functions, however, the time it takes to call the function can account for the *majority* of the total time needed to execute it. In cases like these, it is often better to use a macro. Macros are used very much like functions, but instead of being *called*, they are *expanded* in place by the preprocessor. In other words, the preprocessor replaces the macro call with the macro text. There are no arguments to pass, return address to save, or branch instructions to call and return from the macro. The time savings can be significant if the macro is called many times, such as when it appears inside a loop.

Example:

Consider the following C program:

```
#include <stdio.h>
#include <sysexits.h>

int     main()

{
    int     x = 5;

    printf("%d\n",abs(x));
    return EX_OK;
}

int     abs(int n)

{
    if ( n < 0 )
        n = -n;
    return n;
}
```

Translated to *optimized* VAX assembly language, it would look something like the code below. Pay special attention to the comments on the right if you are not familiar with assembly language.

```
format: .ascii "%d\n\0"

main:
        movl    #5,x
        pushl   x               ; Pass argument via stack
        calls   abs             ; Push stack frame and
                                ; branch to abs
```

```
        pushl   r0          ; Pass abs() return value
                            ; to printf()
        pusha   format      ; Pass format to printf()
        calls   printf
        movl    #0,r0       ; Return value for main()
        ret                 ; Return to OS

abs:
        movl    -8(sp),r0   ; Get argument from stack
        cmpl    r0,#0
        bge     pos         ; If r0 > 0, skip neg
        neg     r0          ; Negate r0
pos:
        ret                 ; Return to point of call
```

The function call to abs() requires the execution of a push instruction
to pass the argument, a calls instruction to go to the function, a movl
instruction inside the function to retrieve the argument from the stack,
and a ret instruction to return to main. Thus, four instructions are
needed to call the function, while the body of the function contains only
three (cmpl, bge, neg). Furthermore, the VAX calls instruction is
extremely sophisticated, and most other types of CPU's would require
several instructions in it's place. Hence, the majority of the time spent
executing this function is overhead cost. To make matters worse, many
functions require push and pop instructions to save and restore the contents of registers they use.

All of the instructions needed for function calling can be eliminated by
implementing ABS as a macro instead of a function.

```
#include <stdio.h>
#include <sysexits.h>

#define ABS(n) ( (n) >= 0 ? (n) : -(n) )

int     main()

{
```

```
int     x = 5;

printf("%d\n",ABS(x));
return EX_OK;
}
```

The preprocessor would expand this to the following:

```
int     main()

{
    int     x = 5;

    printf("%d\n",(x) >= 5 ? (x) : -(x) ));
    return 0;
}
```

The corresponding VAX machine code is shown below. Note the absence of the pushl, calls and ret instructions in the sequence that computes the absolute value of x. The instructions that made up the body of the abs() function, are now inserted directly into main(), and there is *no overhead* involved in executing them. Imagine the difference this will make if abs() or ABS() is used inside a loop that iterates a few million times.

```
format: .ascii "%d\n\0"

main:
        movl    #5, x       ; Pass argument via stack
        movl    x, r0       ; Get macro argument x
        cmpl    r0,#0       ; Check for negative
        bge     pos
        neg     r0          ; Make positive
pos:
        pushl   r0          ; Pass value to printf()
        pusha   format      ; Pass format to printf()
```

```
calls   printf
movl    #0,r0           ; Return value for main()
ret                     ; Return to OS
```

Tip of the trade: C vs. C++ function calls

One of the major differences between C and C++ is the way functions
are called. In C++, function calls are more complex and time consuming than in C. Be aware that if you compile a C program using a C++
compiler, you may be using the more expensive function call mechanism
employed by C++. If you want to maximize the speed of your programs, check the documentation of your C++ compiler to find out how
to compile C programs using C calling conventions.

Another advantage of macros is their **type independence**. Because macros perform a simple text substitution, the formal arguments of a macro are typeless, and
can be replaced with any type of argument value.

Example:

The following code demonstrates how the same macro can be used with
both `int` and `double` values.

```
int     x, ax;
double  y, ay;

ax = ABS(x);
ay = ABS(y);
```

The expanded text is

```
int      x, ax;
double   y, ay;

ax = ( (x) < 0 ? -(x) : (x) );
ay = ( (y) < 0 ? -(y) : (y) );
```

If you used a function to compute the absolute value of a number, it might look like this:

```
double  abs(double x)

{
    return x < 0 ? -x : x;
}
```

Since the formal argument x is defined as a double, you can't use this function to compute the absolute value of any other type, unless you use a cast to force a conversion of the argument to double, which would slow things down even further.

```
int     x1, x2, distance;
...
distance = abs((double)(x2 - x1));
```

Since floating point operations are several times slower than integers *and* suffer from round-off problems, converting an integer to floating point is never a desirable solution. The most efficient solution would be to duplicate the function for every other data type that you use, but this is a lot of extra work. For something as simple as the abs(), macros are the way to go.

Pitfall: Argument Side Effects

One of the dangers in using macros is their potential for side effects. Consider the following use of the ABS() macro:

```
y = ABS(c++);
```

At first glance it looks perfectly innocent, but if you view the expanded text, you see a different story:

```
y = ( (c++) < 0 ? -(c++) : (c++) );
```

The conditional operator uses the expression (c++) once to compare to 0, and *again* in either -(c++) if it was negative, or just (c++) if it was positive. As a result, the variable c gets incremented *twice*. This isn't the least bit apparent from looking at the original source code. You have to see the expanded code to identify the problem. This is one reason macro names are normally capitalized to distinguish them from functions: If you didn't know ABS() was a macro, you would never think to look at the expanded text to track down this problem. Knowing that ABS() is a macro, you should avoid using ++ or -- in the argument, and take a different approach:

```
y = ABS(c);
++c;
```

As a general rule, ++ and -- should never be used in an argument to a macro, unless you can determine for certain that it won't have any such side effects.

13.3   Header Files: #include

The #include directive causes cpp to insert another input file, called a **header file**, into its output stream, which is then passed to the compiler. This is one of the mechanisms employed by C programmers to separate code into different files.

Header files are given a ".h" extension in C. The name of the header file may be enclosed in either brackets or double quotes. If enclosed in brackets, the pathname of the file is assumed to begin in the directory */usr/include*. For example, the directives

```
#include <stdio.h>
#include <sys/types.h>
```

insert the files */usr/include/stdio.h* and */usr/include/sys/types.h* into the cpp output.

If enclosed in double quotes, the pathname of the file is appended to the current working directory.[2] For example,

```
#include "protos.h"
```

inserts the file *./protos.h* into the cpp output.

Header files are a very important part of C programming. As mentioned earlier, most C programs are split into many different source files. Any information that is needed by more than one source file should be contained in a header file, which can be included in each source file that needs it. The following constructs should generally be placed into header files:

- All defined macros and constants

- All function *declarations* (i.e. prototypes or function allusions)

- Type names defined with typedef

- Some #includes, used with extreme caution

- Small *inline* function *definitions*

Information that is only needed in a single source file should not be placed in a header file. This includes the following:

- All function definitions, except small *inline* functions

---

[2]See chapter 4 for a definition of the current working directory.

- Most `#includes`

Placing function definitions in a header file will cause them to be recompiled many times, which is generally a waste of time. Worse yet, if a header containing a function definition is included in two files that are part of the same program, the linker will produce a *duplicate definition* error, since same function name appears twice in the object code. Function definitions that are useful in many programs should be compiled separately, and placed in an **object code library**, so that they can be linked into other programs without being recompiled. Building libraries is discussed in chapter 20.

Pitfall: Hidden `#includes`

Using `#include` in header files is dangerous, since this can lead to the same header file being inadvertently included many times in the same file. For example, if *stdio.h* is included in the file *sort.h*, then the following would cause *stdio.h* to be read twice by the preprocessor:

```
#include <stdio.h>
#include "sort.h"
```

Since *stdio.h* is a very large header file, this can significantly slow down compilation. It's not apparent from this view that *sort.h* contains a duplicate `#include`. The only way to find out is to examine *sort.h* and all others like it. Since this is more trouble than most programmers are willing to go through, it's best to simply not have any hidden `#includes` in your programs. A technique for safely using `#include` within header files is discussed in section 13.4.

13.4   Advanced: Conditional Compilation

One of the most powerful features of the preprocessor is **conditional compilation**. This feature allows you to *conditionally* exclude sections of code from being compiled.

13.4.1 #if

The `#if` directive works much like the `if` statement, except that it operates during the preprocessing phase, rather than at run time. The condition used by `#if` is a constant or preprocessor macro. Like the C language, a value of 0 is considered false, and any non-zero value is true.

Example:

Consider the following code fragment, which shows the number of items input, as a debugging aid:

```
#define DEBUG   1

int     main()
{
    int     count;
    double  some_num;

    count = scanf("%lf",&some_num);
    if ( DEBUG )
    {
        fprintf(stderr,"%d items read.\n",count);
    }
    ...
}
```

If `DEBUG` is set to a non-zero value (true), the statement is executed. If `DEBUG` is 0 (false), the statement will not be executed, but program performance will be slightly degraded since the `if` statement has to check the value of `DEBUG` at run time before deciding to skip the statement.

You can perform essentially the same task during the preprocessing phase using `#if`:

```
#define DEBUG   1
```

```
int     main()
{
    ...
#if DEBUG
    fprintf(stderr,"%d items read.\n",count);
#endif
    ...
}
```

The `#if` directive checks the value of DEBUG during preprocessing. If
DEBUG is false, then the statements between `#if` and `#endif` *are not
output by the preprocessor.* Since the statements aren't passed on to the
compiler, no corresponding machine code is generated. The program is
thus smaller and faster than the same program compiled with DEBUG set
to 1, or with an `if` statement in place of the `#if` directive.

If you don't like the idea of having to edit the program to switch debugging on or
off, you can use the -D compiler option as follows when you want the debugging
code included:

```
cc -Wall -DDEBUG=1 prog.c
```

This will eliminate the need to define DEBUG inside the program.

13.4.2   Preprocessor Operators

The `#if` directive recognizes many of the same operators as the C language, such
as '==', '<', and '>'.

Example:

If a program has many debugging statements, you may want to enable
some of them, while disabling others. This can be accomplished by
using two or more debugging levels. Debugging level 1 could enable
some debugging statements, while level 2 enables all of them.

```
#define DEBUG 2

int     main()

{
    int     count;
    double  new_item;

    ...
#if DEBUG >= 2
    /* Display only if debug level > 1 */
    fprintf(stderr,"%d items read.\n",count);
#endif
    ...
#if DEBUG
    /* Display for any debugging level */
    fprintf(stderr,"Latest item is %f.\n",
            new_item);
#endif
    ...
    return EX_OK;
}
```

The #if directive supports the same comparison operators as the C language proper, as well as the logical operators !, ||, and &&. Complex expressions are rare in #if directives, so we won't get into too many details here. It's good to be aware that #if can handle a great deal more, though, in case you need it in the future.

13.4.3 #ifdef and #ifndef and defined()

Debugging statements can also be turned on or off with the #ifdef or defined() preprocessor directives. Each of these checks to see if a macro is defined at all, regardless of the value.

Example:

This program uses `#ifdef` to control a debugging statement.

```
#define DEBUG    /* Just needs to exist */

int     main()
{
    ...
    #ifdef DEBUG
        fprintf(stderr,"%d items read.\n",count);
    #endif
    ...
}
```

The same effect can be achieved using `#if` and `defined()`:

```
#define DEBUG    /* Just needs to exist */

int     main()
{
    ...
    #if defined(DEBUG)
        fprintf(stderr,"%d items read.\n",count);
    #endif
    ...
}
```

Again, you can use the -D compile option instead of a `#define`.

```
cc -Wall -DDEBUG prog.c
```

The `#ifndef` directive is the opposite of `#ifdef`: It causes the preprocessor to output code when a value is *not* defined. This is most often used to avoid redefining a macro, or to disable code for one particular operating system that lacks support for a common feature. Examples of both are shown in section 13.4.4.

The `defined()` function is useful when more than one condition must be checked. The `defined()` function is generally used in conjunction with the !, || and && operators. For example:

```
#if defined(DEBUG) || defined(VERBOSE)
    fprintf(stderr,"%d items read.\n",count);
#endif
```

13.4.4 Improving Portability

Conditional compilation is also useful for side-stepping system dependencies. For example, there are a few differences between ANSI C and K&R C which require code to be written differently for the two systems. One of these differences is the way functions are declared and defined. One solution is to simply write K&R code, since the ANSI compiler can deal with either form. However, this doesn't take advantage of helpful ANSI features such as prototypes. In order to write code that takes full advantage of both ANSI and K&R compilers, you can use conditional compilation to select one form or the other. In addition, you'll need to use the `#else` directive, and the predefined `__STDC__` macro, which is always defined as true for ANSI compilers, and undefined for non-ANSI compilers.

```
#ifdef __STDC__             /* Use prototypes */
double  pow(double,int);
int     abs(int);
#else                       /* Use allusions */
double  pow();
int     abs();
#endif
```

Another method for selecting declaration styles, which doesn't require duplicate declarations for every function, is using a **guard macro**. A guard macro eliminates unsupported features from the code. For example, to eliminate prototype features when ANSI support is not available, you can define a __PROTO macro as shown below. If __PROTO is already defined, redefining it will produce a preprocessor warning, so we'll add a check for __PROTO.

```
#if !defined(__PROTO) && defined(__STDC__)
#define __PROTO(p)  p
#else
#define __PROTO(p)  ()
#endif
```

We then write each declaration in the following form:

```
double  pow __PROTO((double,int));
```

When compiling on an ANSI compiler, __STDC__ is defined, so the declaration will expand to a prototype:

```
double  pow (double,int);
```

On a non-ANSI compiler, __STDC__ will be undefined, so the declaration will expand to an allusion:

```
double  pow ();
```

Note that an extra set of parenthesis are needed along with the __PROTO macro, as in:

```
double  pow __PROTO((double,int));
```

This is necessary to make multiple items, such as (double,int) appear as a single argument to the macro, since the macro uses a single formal argument p to represent all the function arguments. For the same reason, the text in the macro definition may be written as p rather than (p): The inner parenthesis provided in each reference to the macro will be included in the expanded text, so the prototype will be complete.

In some rare instances, you'll need to be fussy about which type of operating system you're compiling on. For example, there may be different limits imposed by different systems. The #elif directive serves as an else-if conditional where many different actions are needed.

Example:

The code fragment below defines FILE_NAME_LEN to a size appropriate to each operating system the code is compiled under.

```
#if defined(MSDOS) || defined(WINDOWS)
#define FILE_NAME_LEN    8
#elif defined(COHERENT) || defined(OS2)
#define FILE_NAME_LEN    14
#else
#define FILE_NAME_LEN    128
#endif
```

This code should be compiled with the -D option to define one of the system types. For example

```
cc -Wall -DCOHERENT prog.c
```

13.4.5   Nesting #include Efficiently

Each standard header file defines a unique constant, so that the preprocessor can detect when that header has already been included. These constants are checked within the header to prevent everything from being redefined. For example, the header *stdio.h* is organized as follows:

```
#ifndef _STDIO_H_    /* Prevent everything below from */
#define _STDIO_H_    /* being redefined. */
```

```
...

Header contents
...
#endif
```

While this prevents duplicate definitions, it *does not* prevent the header from being opened and read twice during compilation. The preprocessor still needs to read through the header file in search of the `#endif` to match the `#ifndef _STDIO_H_`, and the compile time will still be degraded.

To prevent the file from being redundantly included in the first place, you can use a similar technique any time an `#include` is used in a header file.

Example:

If something in the header *protos.h* requires a definition contained in *stdio.h*, the #include should be written as follows:

```
/* protos.h */
...

#ifndef _STDIO_H_    /* Prevent reading stdio.h twice */
#include <stdio.h>
#endif

/* Prototypes */
int     read_num __PROTO((FILE *));
double pow __PROTO((double,double));
int abs __PROTO((int));
    ...
```

The `#ifndef` surrounding the `#include <stdio.h>` prevents the preprocessor from opening *stdio.h* if it has already been processed, so the header will not be opened and read more than once.

13.5 Advanced: Other Directives

The following directives are rarely used, and are included here only for completeness.

The #error directive is an ANSI feature which prints an error message to `stderr` during preprocessing.

Example:

```
#if defined(MSDOS) || defined(WINDOWS)
    #define FILE_NAME_LEN   8
#elif defined(COHERENT) || defined(OS2)
    #define FILE_NAME_LEN   14
#elif defined(UNIX)
    #define FILE_NAME_LEN   128
#else
    #error "No platform defined - cannot compile."
#endif
```

The #error directive simply gives us earlier warning about potential problems. These types of problems would otherwise surface at link time or run time.

The #line directive sets the internal line number maintained by `cpp`. This is rarely necessary, except in programs that write programs, such as `lex` and `yacc`. These programs use the #line directive to ensure that compiler errors generated from the code they produce will reflect the correct line number.

The #pragma directive is used to alter the behavior of the compiler in system specific ways, such as controlling structure alignment or special optimizations. Each compiler has its own set of pragmas. For details on the use of #pragma, consult the documentation of your compiler.

13.6 Advanced: The Paste Operator:

ANSI preprocessors have the ability to paste two or more tokens together to form a single token.

Example:

Consider the following macro definition:

```
#define GAME(game_num)  game_##game_num
```

In a program, you can use a macro like this to generate different variable names. For example, the statement

```
printf("Game 1 attendance = %d\n",GAME(1));
```

expands to

```
printf("Game 1 attendance = %d\n",game_1);
```

Uses for this operator are limited, but it can be helpful in saving some typing when the pasted argument is common to several tokens in an expression.

13.7   Advanced: Predefined Macros

The C preprocessor has several built-in macros, which expand to the text listed below:

__DATE__   The current date
__FILE__   The source filename
__LINE__   The line number in the source file
__STDC__   1 for ANSI compilers, 0 for non-ANSI
__TIME__   The current time

Individual compilers may have other built-in macros which can be checked to take advantage of special features. Check your compiler documentation for a complete listing.

Chapter 14

Pointers

Before you begin...

> You should be familiar with the material on functions presented in chapter 11.

14.1   Pointers: This Stuff is BIG!

Pointers are one of the most important topics in programming in many languages, and a major cornerstone in C programming. Each language deals with pointers differently. Many languages, such as Pascal and C++ provide facilities for **abstracting** pointers, that is, allowing the programmer to use them without understanding what's really happening at the hardware level. C, on the other hand, treats pointers as exactly what they are; memory addresses. As a result, the uses for pointers in C are quite diverse. This chapter will only cover basic and essential pointer use, and some of the later chapters, especially those on arrays and structures, will discuss how pointers are used in more advanced settings.

Regardless of the language you use, a solid understanding of how programs address memory is an important part of becoming a proficient and productive programmer. Programming in C will help you to develop this understanding, as you work directly with memory addresses, rather than the abstract and limited analogs offered by some other languages. Although there have been many attempts to make programming easier through abstraction, there is really no escape from the need to understand how pointers and related constructs work behind the scenes. The sooner you commit yourself to achieving this understanding, the more enjoyable and productive your career in programming will be.

Unfortunately, many programmers find pointers difficult to understand. However, like binary numbers, pointers are *inherently simple*. The difficulty many programmers have with pointers stems from their lack of understanding of basic concepts like memory addressing. In other words, they have not yet committed themselves to *understanding* how pointers work *behind the scenes*. These concepts are not hard: They are probably *new*, however, so you need to spend a little time *thinking* about them and *experimenting* with them. It is often difficult for a programmer to spend time reading, studying, and experimenting for the sake of learning a concept, when they feel they should be getting some work done. However difficult it is to motivate yourself, you *must* dedicate some time to read, study, and experiment with pointers until you understand them thoroughly. If you don't, you'll never be as proficient as you could be in C or any other programming language. You'll be surprised how little time it takes to master pointers, and moreover, you'll be astonished by the amount of time and frustration you save by understanding them well.

As a further exercise, consider learning to program in assembly language, in order to develop a deeper understanding of what goes on after your program has been translated to machine code, and is being run by the CPU. Although the demand for professional assembly language programmers is low, knowing assembly will make you a better programmer in all languages. Because of the drastic differences between high-level languages and the machine code that compilers translate them to, a program's behavior can never be understood completely by looking at the source code. It will inevitably be necessary at some point to understand what goes on at the underlying hardware level.

Many C textbooks deserve a share of the blame for confusion about pointers, since most do not adequately explain how pointers work. Many, in fact, present pointers along with arrays, because pointers and arrays have a practical relationship. While this provides an interesting and unifying theme for seasoned programmers, it may be confusing for a beginner to be burdened with two new concepts simultaneously, and at the same time be expected to appreciate the pragmatic relationship between them. Our goal in this chapter is to provide a clear and simple explanation of *pointers*, and nothing more. Arrays, and the associated *uses* of pointers, are discussed in chapter 15.

14.2   Pointer Basics

A **pointer** is a variable which holds the **memory address** (the location in RAM) of an object, rather than the object itself. Technically, memory addresses can also be thought of as objects, and they often are when manipulating the contents of pointer variables. However, the actual *data* a pointer *points to* (i.e. whose address it contains), is usually the object of interest. In other words, pointers are simply an *indirect* way of referring to data objects. Hence, the use of pointers to access objects is often called **indirection**.

In C, pointers are not as abstract as they are in most other languages. The C language provides the programmer virtually unlimited power and flexibility with pointers. The flexibility C offers with pointers is one of the major reasons that C programs *can be* much more efficient than the equivalent program in another language. If you don't make use of pointers, however, your C code won't be as efficient as it could be.

The binary format of a pointer is the same as that of an unsigned integer. Like the `int` and `unsigned int` types, however, the size of a pointer varies from one system to another. Furthermore, a pointer isn't always the same size as an `int`. Never make any assumptions about size of a pointer, since they are certain to be false for some systems, and *never* assign pointer values to integer variables, or vice versa.

14.3   Defining Pointer Variables

A pointer variable is defined by simply placing a '*' in front of the variable name. For example,

```
int     *ptr = NULL;
```

defines `ptr` as a *pointer to an int*. The variable `ptr` will hold the *memory address* of an integer, *not* the integer itself. A cardinal value of `NULL` is assigned to `ptr` for reasons discussed later.

Pitfall: Pointer Variable Definitions

A common mistake among both novice and experienced C programmers is to forget the '*' on the second pointer variable when defining two pointers at once. Consider the definition statement below:

```
int      *p1,p2;
```

The definition above defines `p1` as a pointer to an `int`, and `p2` as an `int`. If you want both variables to be pointers, they must both be given an '*', as follows:

```
int      *p1,*p2;
```

The '*' is part of the *variable* in a definition, not the *type*. This allows both pointers and data variables to be defined in the same definition statement, as follows:

```
int      age, *ptr = NULL;
```

If you prefer not to have to type a '*' for every variable, you can use a typedef to create a pointer type, as outlined in section 14.6.

14.4   Using Pointers: Indirection

To assign a pointer the address of a variable, you can use the **address operator**, '&'. For example, the code below assigns the address of the variable x to the variable `ptr`.

Variable	Address	Contents
x	2000	5
ptr	2004	2000

Figure 14.1: `ptr` contains the address of x

```
int      x = 5;
int      *ptr = NULL;

ptr = &x;
```

Following this assignment, `ptr` contains the address of x, as shown in figure 14.1.

Once assigned the address, the variable `ptr` can be used to access the `int` object in x. Accessing a data object through a pointer is called **indirection**, or **dereferencing** the pointer. This is done using the **dereference operator**, '*'. Note that this is the same token used in the definition of a pointer variable, but it serves a completely different purpose when used in an expression.

Thus, the statement

```
*ptr = 5;
```

has the same effect as

```
x = 5;
```

Similarly, the statement

```
printf("%d\n",*ptr);
```

has the same effect as

```
printf("%d\n",x);
```

Programming for Performance:

Referencing an object *indirectly* through a pointer is slower than referencing it *directly*. When using a dereferenced pointer such as *ptr, the
program must first retrieve the address of the object from the pointer
variable, and then retrieve or write the object itself. CPU's vary immensely in their support for indirection, but regardless, it would be
faster to use x directly than to use *ptr.

Note that pointers can *improve* efficiency immensely when used with
arrays and structures, since they can be used in place of constructs that
are far more expensive than indirection. This is discussed further in
chapters 15 and 18.

Pitfall: Uninitialized Pointers

Like any variable, pointer variables contain garbage until they are initialized. The effects of using an uninitialized pointer are quite different,
however. Dereferencing an uninitialized pointer attempts to access some
unknown, essentially random memory address, which will often result in
a **segmentation fault**, an illegal attempt to access memory outside the
program's memory space. If a segmentation fault occurs, the operating
system will terminate the process, and create a **core file**, which contains
a memory image of the program for use in debugging. More information
on core files is provided in chapter 19.

Until a pointer can be given a useful address, it should be given the value
NULL, preferably in the variable definition.

```
#include <stdio.h>

int     main()

{
    int     *ptr = NULL;
```

```
      . . .
    }
```

NULL is defined as a constant in *stdio.h*, and sometimes in other headers as well. The NULL pointer constant is used as a cardinal value with all kinds of pointers, to indicate that a pointer does not point to a data object. Note that NULL is not a C keyword, but is defined in the header *stdio.h*, usually as

```
#define NULL    (void *)0
```

Although NULL is almost always defined as 0, you should never substitute 0 for NULL in your programs. Doing so will reduce readability, and may result in a compiler warning, since the constant 0 has type int, and should not be assigned to a pointer variable.

The NULL pointer doesn't have any meaning to the C compiler, but it serves as a conventional flag value that you can check to see if a pointer really points to anything. For example, the code below avoids accessing an uninitialized pointer by first checking for NULL:

```
    int     *ptr = NULL;
    . . .

    if ( ptr != NULL )
        printf("%d\n",*ptr);
```

If ptr were not initialized to NULL, there would be no way to check the validity of it's contents, and and thus no way to prevent the ensuing segmentation faults.

In protected mode operating systems such as Unix, the hardware validates every memory reference, so dereferencing a bad pointer will most likely result in a segmentation fault eventually. If the garbage address happens to be a within the process' memory space, data corruption will often occur, and your program may produce incorrect output. Each time the program is run, the garbage address will probably be different, so eventually, a segmentation fault will expose the problem.

In a real mode system, like *MS-DOS*, no address checking is performed by the hardware. As a result, using a garbage pointer can corrupt *any* part of memory, including the program's code, and the kernel's code and data. As a result, *DOS* systems often have to be rebooted following pointer errors in an ordinary program. In these situations, it is usually impossible to know what caused the problem, so these types of bugs may persist for a long time. It is also common for programs ported from *DOS* to Unix to cause frequent segmentation faults, because they contain bugs that went unnoticed in the *DOS* environment. With a little patience and a good debugger, these types of errors can be worked out rather quickly.

Pitfall: Mixing Pointers and Integers

Pointers, like all other data types in C, can be used in mixed expressions. It's common practice to add integer offsets to a pointer, but this is the *only* way pointers and integers should be mixed. Furthermore, this practice is only useful when using pointers with arrays, which are discussed in chapter 15.

Since pointers and integers may have different sizes, you should *never* assign a pointer to an integer, or vice versa. Doing so can result in **truncation**, i.e. a loss of significant bits. For example, some workstations use a 32 bit `int`, and a 64 bit address. If a 64 bit pointer is copied to a 32 bit `int`, the high-order 32 bits are lost. Any subsequent attempt to use this address will result in serious problems. Similar problems occur under *DOS* and 16 bit Windows when using the compact, medium, large, and huge memory models, which use a 16 bit `int` and a 32 bit address.

Programming with Style:

While it is generally safe to assume that `NULL` is defined as the value 0, it's not a good idea for the sake of readability to take advantage of this fact. Since C essentially treats integers, Booleans and pointers the same, you as the programmer need to make it obvious which type a variable is at all times. For example, consider the following code fragment:

```
int *ptr = NULL;
...

if ( !ptr )
{
    printf("%d\n",*ptr);
    ...
}
```

If `ptr` is NULL, i.e. 0, it will be viewed as false, and the program will not attempt to dereference it. While writing code like this may seem clever, it also misleads anyone viewing the program, by implying that `ptr` is a Boolean value. If, in fact, it is a pointer, write the `if` statement to demonstrate it clearly, as follows:

```
if ( ptr != NULL )
{
    printf("%d\n",*ptr);
    ...
}
```

This code fragment makes it obvious that `ptr` is a pointer variable, even without looking at the definition. Typing a few extra keystrokes to make your code readable will go a long way in improving your karma.

14.5   Pointers as Function Arguments

As you have seen with the `scanf()` function, pointers are often useful as function arguments. We'll now examine a simple use of pointers in a function.

Many applications, such as sort programs, need to swap the contents of two variables. This is a relatively simple task, requiring only three statements:

```
int      x, y, temp;

...
temp = x;    /* Save value of x before overwriting it */
x = y;
y = temp;
```

Usually, there is little motivation to write a function to replace three lines of code. However this is such a common task in programming, it's worth writing a swap() function just to improve readability a bit.

A novice programmer might write the program as follows:

```
#include <stdio.h>
#include <sysexits.h>

void     swap(int a,int b);

int      main()

{
    int      x = 10, y = 5;

    swap(x,y);
    printf("x = %d, y = %d\n",x,y);
    return EX_OK;
}


void     swap(int a,int b)

{
    int      temp;

    temp = a;
    a = b;
    b = temp;
}
```

At the beginning of `swap()`...

Variable	Address	Contents
x	1000	10
y	1004	5
...		
a	1510	10
b	1514	5

End of `swap()`...

Variable	Address	Contents
x	1000	10
y	1004	5
...		
a	1510	5
b	1514	10

Figure 14.2: A useless swap function

Since all arguments in C are *passed by value*, a only receives a *copy* of x, and b receives a *copy* of y. Hence, this function only swaps the local variables a and b, and has no effect on x and y. Figure 14.2 shows a memory map of the program.

In order for this function to work, it must know the *addresses* of x and y, so that it can exchange the contents of the two memory locations. In order to do this, you need to pass the addresses of both x and y as arguments, as follows.

```
int     main()

{
    int     x = 10, y = 5;

    swap(&x,&y);
    printf("x = %d, y = %d\n",x,y);
    return EX_OK;
}
```

The formal arguments a and b must be defined as pointers to receive the addresses

Beginning of `swap()`...

Variable	Address	Contents
x	1000	10
y	1004	5
...		
a	1510	1000
b	1514	1004

End of `swap()`...

Variable	Address	Contents
x	1000	5
y	1004	10
...		
a	1510	1000
b	1514	1004

Figure 14.3: A useful swap function

of x and y, and dereferenced when used inside the function, to access the contents of arguments such as x and y:

```
void    swap(int *a,int *b)

{
    int     temp;

    temp = *a;
    *a = *b;
    *b = temp;
}
```

Figure 14.3 shows a memory map for the new program.

Note that a and b contain *addresses*, not integers. The contents of x and y are never duplicated when `swap()` is called. Instead, the function *reaches out* to access the variables x and y in `main()`.

14.6 Typedef and Pointers

Some programmers prefer to use `typedef` to create pointer types. This has the advantage of eliminating the need for a '*' in the variable definition, thus eliminating a potential pitfall.

Others prefer not to introduce new type names unless it significantly reduces typing, or makes the program more readable. In addition, modern compilers will issue warnings if you attempt to use an `int` where a pointer is expected, so a forgotten '*' in a variable definition is usually discovered at compile time, which further reduces the motivation for defining pointer types.

Example:

Using `typedef` to create a pointer type.

```
typedef int * intptr_t;

int     main()

{
    int        x, y;
    intptr_t   p1, p2;

    ...
    p1 = &x;
    p2 = &y;
    ...
    return 0;
}
```

Note that both `p1` and `p2` are pointers. By using the user defined type `intptr_t`, we no longer need to place a '*' before each variable being defined as a pointer.

Pitfall: Creating Type Names with #define

You may be tempted to use **#define** in place of **typedef** to create new type names. While this can be useful, and generally has the same effect as **typedef**, there are problems that arise from the fact that a macro is a simple text substitution. Consider the following code fragment:

```
#define intptr_t int *

int     main()

{
    intptr_t    p1, p2;
    ...
```

Since **intptr_t** is a macro, it is simply replaced by the macro text, which produces the following **cpp** output:

```
int     main()

{
    int     *   p1, p2;
```

Note that **p2** is *not* defined as a pointer, since the macro will not place a '*' before each variable for you. The preprocessor simply replaces the token **intptr_t** with the text **int *** and then merrily copies the variable list as is.

Chapter 15

Arrays and Strings

Before you begin...

> You should be familiar with the material on loops and pointers presented in chapters 10 and 14.

The goal of this chapter is to demonstrate many of the common ways that arrays are defined and used in C. Since strings are implemented as arrays, several examples of manipulating strings are also included in this chapter. For a discussion of the string functions provided with the standard C library, see chapter 22.

15.1 One Dimensional Arrays

In order to perform certain algorithms efficiently, it is necessary to store large amounts of data in memory. For example, consider a program which reads in a list of 5 numbers, and then prints the list *backwards*. In order to print the first input value *after* the second, the program has to remember both values. The same applies to the second and third, third and fourth, and so on. Hence, *all* the input values must be stored somewhere simultaneously so that they can be retrieved in reverse order, after the last item has been input. They could, theoretically, be stored in a file on disk, but reading a file backwards is difficult and inefficient, since disk files are designed primarily to be read and written *sequentially*, from beginning to end.

Up to now, you've been limited to *scalar* variables, variables that hold a single value. You could implement this algorithm using scalar variables as follows:

```
#include <stdio.h>
#include <sysexits.h>

int     main()
{
    int n0,n1,n2,n3,n4;

    scanf("%d %d %d %d %d",&n0,&n1,&n2,&n3,&n4);
    printf("%d %d %d %d %d",n4,n3,n2,n1,n0);
    return EX_OK;
}
```

This is a rather awkward solution for anything more than a few values, however.

Instead of using **scalar** variables as in the example above, you can define an **array** variable to hold all the values, as follows:

```
#define MAX_LIST_SIZE    5

int     list[MAX_LIST_SIZE];
```

This array will hold up to five integer values. In other words, it has a **dimension** of 5.

Programming with Style:

> The dimensions of an array should always be specified using a named constant, such as MAX_LIST_SIZE, so that it can be easily changed later if needed. Array sizes tend to be reused in many places throughout the program: You may define many arrays of the same size, and you'll definitely need to use the array size to limit loops that manipulate the array. If you use a named constant, then one simple change to a #define

Address	Element
1000	list[0]
1004	list[1]
1008	list[2]
1012	list[3]
1016	list[4]

Figure 15.1: A typical array

is all you'll need to change the size. Named constants also make the program more self-documenting, since they are more descriptive than a hard-coded number.

To select an individual element within the array, you use a **subscript**, also sometimes called an **index**. The subscript is an *integer* value which states the position of the element in the array. Floating point types cannot be used as subscripts, since there is no such thing as a 1.5^{th} element in a list. Any floating point variables would have to be converted to an integer value, and round-off error might cause the wrong element to be accessed.

The term subscript is borrowed from mathematics, where it is common to denote a set of values using a single name with subscripts, such as x_0, x_1, x_2, x_3, and so on. In C, subscripts are used essentially the same way. However, it's impossible to type a true subscript on most terminals, so the **subscript operator**, [ ] is used as substitute. For example, in C, you would type x_0 as x[0], x_1 as x[1], and so on.

When an array variable is instantiated, a **contiguous** block of memory is allocated to hold all the values. In other words, all the elements of an array are stored in consecutive memory cells. For example, x[1] is at the memory address following x[0], x[2] follows x[1], and so on. Figure 15.1 depicts a memory map for the array `list`, assuming a 32 bit integer.

The address of an array element is calculated as the address of the first element, known as the **base address**, plus the subscript times the size of an element. For example, the memory address of `list[3]` in figure 15.1 is

$$1000 + (3 \times sizeof(int))$$

This is in fact what happens each time a program uses an array subscript Note that `sizeof(int)` could be either 2 or 4, depending on the compiler. Figure 15.1 assumes a 32 bit compiler, so an `int` is 4 bytes long.

Programming for Performance:

The address calculation that must occur when you use an array subscript is one important reason to avoid using the subscript operator whenever possible. Consider the following code fragment:

```
x = list[c];
y = list[c] * a;
```

Each reference to `list[c]` requires an address calculation. The second array subscript can be eliminated, since `x` is equal to `list[c]` at this point in the program:

```
x = list[c];
y = x * a;
```

Using `x` instead of `list[c]` is much more efficient. This example demonstrates that not all C statements are created equal. Watch out for expensive constructs like array subscripts, since they tend to translate to slower machine code.

The lowest possible subscript for an array in C is always zero, and the highest is the size of the array, minus one. Thus, the valid subscripts for the array `list` range from 0 to 4.

Using an array and a loop, you can rewrite the input reversal program as follows:

```
#include <stdio.h>
#include <sysexits.h>

#define MAX_LIST_SIZE    5
```

```
int     main()

{
    int list[MAX_LIST_SIZE];
    size_t  s;

    /* Read values list[0], list[1], ... */
    for (s=0; s < MAX_LIST_SIZE; ++s)
        scanf("%d",&list[s]);

    /* Count down and print.  Cast to long since */
    /* size_t is unsigned, always >= 0. */
    while ( (long)--s >= 0 )
        printf("%d ",list[s]);
    return EX_OK;
}
```

Generally, the loop control variable also serves as the subscript for selecting array elements in a loop, although the subscript may be *any* integer expression.

Programming for Performance:

Any algorithm that requires non-sequential access to data will benefit greatly from storing the data in an array, provided the amount of data is within reason. When you decide whether or not to load a large amount of data into memory, you must maintain a balance between two factors:

1. Will doing so significantly improve program performance, assuming all the data will fit in available RAM?

2. Will doing so affect the *system's* performance, by hogging too much memory, and causing processes to compete for memory resources?

It is important to remember that Unix is a multiuser, multitasking operating system, which may have dozens of programs running at once. Thus, individual programs may have only a small fraction of the systems memory and other resources available to them at a given time. Those that demand fewer resources will run much faster, since they won't have to wait for resources to become available. Generally speaking, the smaller a program is, the faster it is likely to run.

When a Unix system runs out of RAM, it will begin **swapping** blocks of RAM out to disk to make room. Since a typical disk is about 100,000 to 1,000,000 times slower than RAM, *nothing* compares to swapping when it comes to slowing a system down. Programs that have to wait for their data to be swapped back into memory may run hundreds or thousands of times slower than they would if they fit into available RAM. The CPU, on the other hand, is rarely a performance bottleneck, so using an algorithm that is 10% slower is a good trade-off for saving a substantial amount of memory.

Never make assumptions about how many processes will be running at once, or about how much memory the user's system has, and *always* try to minimize the amount of memory your programs use. You may be programming on a workstation with 256 megabytes of RAM, where you are the only user, but some of your end-users may be supporting dozens of users on a system with far less memory.

You may be tempted to think that this becomes less important as memory prices drop, but this is not the case. History has shown that any increase in memory or disk size is quickly used up by a corresponding increase in the complexity of programs, and the number of programs being installed and used. In the Unix environment, the number of *users* on an individual system is also likely to increase over time, so it will always be important to optimize programs.

Programming for Performance:

Virtually all array operations require loops. Sometimes these loops are hidden from the high-level language programmer inside functions such as `strlen()` or `strcmp()`. The fact that a function uses an array almost certainly means that it performs some sort of loop. For example, the `strlen()` function looks something like this:

```
size_t  strlen(char string[])
```

```
    {
        char    *p;

        for (p=string; *p!='\0'; ++p)
            ;
        return p-string;
    }
```

Don't be fooled by the lack of *visible* loops in a program that uses arrays. If you're looking to optimize a program, look at the library functions it uses, and consider whether or not they would need to use loops. If so, then look for alternatives that won't require use of these functions.

One way to eliminate calls to `strlen()`, for example, would be to save the string length in a variable at some previous point in the program, such as when the string is read in.

Pitfall: Wimpee Subscript Variables

One of the most commonly used data types for array subscripts is `int`. This causes problems, however, when dealing with large arrays. Since the maximum value of a signed `int` is only 32,767, you can't use an `int` to access the higher elements of an array larger than 32k elements. An `unsigned int` subscript can reach as high as 65,535, or 64k. For larger arrays, you have to use `long` or `unsigned long` subscripts.

Many programs written on 32 bit systems, using `int`, will fail to work properly when ported to a 16 bit system, such as *MS-DOS*. It is important to remember that an `int` is a short on some systems, and to explicitly use `long` where the range of a `short` is inadequate.

There is a special type defined in *stdio.h* called `size_t`, which provides a reliable, efficient, and portable way to specify an array subscript on any system. `Size_t` is an unsigned integer type which parallels the size of a memory address on each system, so it is guaranteed to be large enough to index any array.

Address	variable
1000	list[0]
1004	list[1]
1008	list[2]
1012	list[3]
1016	list[4]
1020	s

Figure 15.2: Memory map for array

Pitfall: Runaway Subscripts

Some languages, such as Pascal, will issue an error if the program attempts to use a subscript that is beyond the bounds of the array. Subscript checking has a cost, however. A program is slowed down significantly if it has to validate the subscript every time an array is referenced. C is designed to *trust the programmer*, in favor of producing more efficient machine code. In line with this tenet, C programs *do not* check array subscripts. They simply calculate the address of an element as described above, and happily attempt to read or write whatever address is computed.

For example, consider the following code fragment:

```
int     list[5];
size_t  s;

for (s=0; s<=5; ++s)
    scanf("%d",&list[s]);

while (--s > 0 )
    printf("%d\n",list[s]);
```

Figure 15.2 shows how the variables will probably be mapped into the process' memory space.

The highest valid subscript for the array list is 4, but the subscript variable s reaches 5, because the program mistakenly uses <= instead of <. When the program attempts to access the element `list[5]`, it computes the address as follows:

$$1000 + 5 \times 4 = 1020$$

As a result, the `scanf()` function will place the input value into `s`, causing data corruption, and the `while` loop which follows will start with an essentially random value in `s`.

Programs that use arrays need to *somehow* ensure that the array subscripts remain in-bounds. With some loops, like the `scanf()` loop above, this comes naturally. You simply have to make sure the loop ends before it reaches the end of the array.

With loops that don't perform a fixed number of iterations, however, you need to add another loop condition to avoid array overflows.

The program below reads values until the user types *Ctrl+D*, which simulates end-of-file when reading from the keyboard. Although the program informs the user to enter no more than MAX_LIST_SIZE values, it wouldn't be wise to assume they never will. You can make the program **idiot-proof**, by preventing the loop from going through more than MAX_LIST_SIZE iterations. Simply check the subscript *in addition* to watching for the EOF signal.

```
#include <stdio.h>
#include <sysexits.h>

#define MAX_LIST_SIZE    5

int     main()

{
    int     list[MAX_LIST_SIZE];
    size_t  s = 0;

    printf("Enter up to %d integers, then <ctrl>+D.\n",
            MAX_LIST_SIZE);
    while ( (scanf("%d",&list[s]) != EOF) &&
            (s < MAX_LIST_SIZE) )
```

```
            ++s;
        ...
        return EX_OK;
    }
```

When defining an array, you need to give some thought to the appropriate size. Because arrays are fixed in size at compile time, you often have to make compromises between memory use and functionality.

If the array is defined too small, the program will be limited in it's capabilities, so you always want to define an array large enough for the largest likely scenario. However, it's easy to go too far when choosing an array size. If the largest case likely is 10,000 elements, then don't define an array to hold 100,000, because the program will be using 10 times more memory than it needs.

The best solution to balancing memory use and functionality is **dynamic memory allocation**. Using dynamic allocation, you can determine the size of the array at *run-time*, rather than at compile time, and in many cases, allocate exactly the amount of memory needed. Dynamic memory allocation is discussed in chapter 16.

Programming for Performance:

> Lastly, a word of advice about using arrays in general: Don't do it. Like loops, arrays increase the overhead and complexity of a program, as well as imposing limitations on the amount of data it can process. If there is an efficient way to implement a program *without* using arrays, then by all means, use it. Remember, *the simplest solution is usually the best!*

> For example, suppose you want to compute the average of a list of numbers. The very fact that you are thinking about a list might trick you into using an array. However, if you examine the algorithm for finding an average, you find that there is no need to store all the values at once:

> 1. Input a value
> 2. Add value to sum
> 3. Add one to count

4. Repeat until all values entered

5. Divide sum by count

The program is best written as follows:

```
#include <stdio.h>
#include <sysexits.h>

int     main()

{
    double   num, sum = 0.0;
    unsigned long    count = 0;

    puts("Enter values to average.");
    puts("Then type <ctrl>+D.");
    while ( scanf("%lf",&num) == 1 )
    {
        sum += num;
        ++count;
    }
    printf("The average is: %f\n",sum/count);
    return EX_OK;
}
```

This program is simple, efficient, and imposes no limitations on how many values you can average.

15.2 Arrays and Pointers

An array definition, like a scalar definition, allocates memory for an object, and assigns it a data type and a name. There is an important difference, however, between the names of scalar variables and array variables. The name of a scalar variable refers to the scalar *object*. To refer to the *address* of a scalar variable, you use the & operator.

```
int     x;

printf("%d\n",x);    /* Print object x */
printf("%p\n",&x);   /* Print address of x */
```

An array name, on the other hand, is actually a *pointer constant*, which refers to the address of the first element in the array.

```
int     list[MAX_LIST_SIZE];

printf("%p\n",list);    /* Print address of list */
```

In fact, it isn't even possible to refer to an entire array as an *object* in C. You might intuitively think that dereferencing an array name would produce the array object. However, since the array name points to the first element in the array, dereferencing it will only produce the first element. That is, *list has exactly the same meaning as list[0].

Tip of the trade: Arrays and &

One peculiarity in the C language is that the & operator has no effect when used with an array name. For example, &list has the same meaning as list. Since there is no practical use for the address of a constant, it really doesn't make any sense to use an expression like &list in a program. Nevertheless, the designers of C decided to accept it, by simply ignoring the & operator in this context.

One interesting and very useful aspect of C programming is the fact that array names and pointer variables are almost *completely interchangeable*. For instance, array names can be dereferenced like pointer variables, and the subscript operator, [ ], can be used with pointers variables the same way it is used with arrays. The *only* difference is that an array name is a *constant* pointer, so you can't make it point to anything other than the first element of the array that it refers to. For example, the statement

```
++list;
```

is illegal, and will generate a compile error.

15.2.1 Pointers Instead of Subscripts

Let's begin with a fundamental law of arrays and pointers in C:

> Anything that can be accomplished with an array subscript can also be accomplished with a pointer, and the pointer version will be faster.

Array subscripts are actually a redundant feature in C. Array subscripts in C primarily offer programmers a familiar construct from other languages such as FORTRAN, Pascal, or BASIC. An array name with an attached subscript is much like a dereferenced pointer. The distinction is that a subscripted pointer has to be computed at run time, which significantly slows down the program. Since C provides the ability to work with addresses directly in the same way you would work with array subscripts, there is little reason to ever use subscripts to access an array in C. Hence, the [ ] operator should generally be used only in variable definitions, and avoided in C expressions.

This is one of the most important performance issues in C programming. Given this fact, you may wonder why anyone uses array subscripts at all. The reason is simple; convenience. Working with array subscripts tends to be more intuitive than working with memory addresses for some programmers. It's easier to grasp the concept of an object's position in a list, than it's overall position in memory. You can think of an array subscript as a *high-level pointer*, one that indirectly points to an element in an array, by denoting it's position in the list. Furthermore, other languages like Pascal, FORTRAN, and BASIC *require* the use of subscripts with arrays. They don't have the same flexibility with pointers offered by C. When programmers switch from another language to C, array subscripts are familiar, and therefore inviting.

When working in C, however, it's best to use pointers instead of subscripts in most situations, and especially when performing intensive calculations on array elements.

Consider the following loop, which performs a linear search on an array:

```
#define MAX_LIST_SIZE    100
```

```
int     main()

{
    long    list[MAX_LIST_SIZE], key;
    size_t  c;

    ...

    /* Search list */
    for (c=0; c<MAX_LIST_SIZE; ++c)
        if (list[c] == key)
            printf("Found key in element %d.\n",c);
    ...
}
```

Each time the program accesses an element `list[c]`, it must calculate the address of that element, so it can compare the value at that location to `key`. The calculation, as mentioned earlier, is the base address of the array + the subscript times the size of each element:

$$address = list + (c \times sizeof(long))$$

Hence, each access to the array using a subscript requires one *addition* and one *multiplication*[1] to compute the address, in addition to incrementing the subscript variable and whatever operation is performed on the array element.

You can accomplish the same task using a pointer variable, which will point to each array element *directly*:

```
#define MAX_LIST_SIZE    100

int     main()
```

---

[1]If the size of the data type is a power of 2, as is the case for all of C's built-in types, then the compiler can use a bit shift instruction in place of the multiplication instruction. Since bit shifts are many times faster than multiplications, this reduces the impact of using subscripts. It is still much faster to use pointers, however, since this will completely eliminate the instructions generated by subscript notation.

```
{
    long    list[MAX_LIST_SIZE], *p, *list_end, key;

    /* Search list */
    list_end = list+MAX_LIST_SIZE;
    for (p=list; p < list_end; ++p)
        if (*p == key)
            printf("Found key in element %d.\n",p-list);
    ...
}
```

To understand this example, you need to understand **pointer arithmetic**, that is, how *integer* values are added to pointers, as in the expression list+MAX_LIST_SIZE or ++p. In order to ensure the pointer always points to the beginning of a valid object, the value added to the pointer is actually the integer value times the *size of the type* pointed to. For example, the statement ++p actually adds 4 (sizeof(long)), to the pointer p, rather than 1, so that p will point to the next long in memory. Similarly, the expression list+MAX_LIST_SIZE represents the memory address list+400, not list+100.

So, in the example above, ++p correctly advances the pointer from one array element to the next. If list begins at address 10,000, then list+MAX_LIST_SIZE represents the address 10,400, and the loop will terminate when p contains this address.

The pointer version of this program ran about 27% faster than the subscripted version above on a 486 PC, using gcc with full optimizations on both versions. The actual amount of improvement will depend on a number of factors, such as what compiler you are using, the hardware capabilities, the data type of the array, and what optimizations were done by the compiler.

Tip of the trade: More on Subscripts

Just for the sake of demonstration, let's examine one more way to code this program. Instead of using list[c], you could achieve the effect of the subscript operator *manually*, by explicitly computing and dereferencing each address:

```
#define MAX_LIST_SIZE    100
```

```
int     main()

{
    long     list[MAX_LIST_SIZE], key;
    size_t  c;

    /* Search list */
    for (c=0; c<MAX_LIST_SIZE; ++c)
        if (*(list+c) == key)
            printf("Found key in element %d.\n",c);
    ...
}
```

The term list+c computes the address of element list[c], and the
dereference operator produces the value at that address. The expression
*(list+c) has *exactly* the same meaning as list[c], so there is no
advantage to using this syntax. However, the basic idea is useful in a
similar situation. Consider the following loop:

```
#define MAX_LIST_SIZE    100

int     main()

{
    long     list[MAX_LIST_SIZE];
    size_t  c;

    /* Input list */
    for (c=0; scanf("%ld",&list[c]) == 1; ++c)
        ;
    ...
}
```

The expression &list[c] is actually a somewhat redundant way of specifying the address of an array element. By itself, list[c] first computes

the address of an element, and then dereferences it automatically. You then use the & operator to revert back to the address. If the address is what you want, you can just ask for it in the first place, instead of going from address to object, and back to address again:

```c
#define MAX_LIST_SIZE    100

int     main()

{
    long    list[MAX_LIST_SIZE];
    size_t  c;

    /* Input list */
    for (c=0; scanf("%ld",list+c) == 1; ++c)
        ;
    ...
}
```

The expression `list+c` is the same as `&list[c]`, without the redundancy.

15.2.2 Using Subscripts with Pointer Variables

The subscript operator [ ], although used primarily for arrays, can actually be used with *any* address value. For example, given the following variable definitions, all of the expressions below are valid:

```c
#define MAX_LIST_SIZE    10

double  list[MAX_LIST_SIZE],
        *ptr = list+5;

list[0] = 0L;
ptr[0] = 0L;            /* Same as *ptr or list[5] */
ptr[-1] = 0L;          /* Same as list[4] */
```

```
(ptr+5)[-5] = 0L;   /* Same as *ptr */
```

Keep in mind that these examples serve to demonstrate what you *can* do in C, not necessarily what you might *want* to do. The expression `(ptr+5)[-5]` for example, is the same as `*ptr`, since the +5 and -5 cancel each other.

Let's now examine an example which is known to be useful. Consider the following loop, which shifts the contents of an array up one position. This operation would be necessary for inserting an element into a sorted list, although it is *very* inefficient, since it requires looping and moving large amounts of data. It's usually easier and more efficient to build the list in random order, and sort it afterwards with an efficient sort algorithm such as `quicksort()`.

```c
#define MAX_LIST_SIZE   100

int    main()

{
    double  list[MAX_LIST_SIZE];
    size_t  c;

    /* Shift elements up one position */
    for (c=1; c<MAX_LIST_SIZE; ++c)
        list[c-1] = list[c];
    ...
}
```

You can reduce the use of subscripts as follows:

```c
double  list[MAX_LIST_SIZE], *p, *end_list;

/* Get address of last element in list */
end_list = list+MAX_LIST_SIZE;

/* Shift elements up one position */
for (p = list+1; p < end_list; ++p)
    p[-1] = *p;
```

Note the use of a negative subscript to specify the element *before* the one pointed to by `ptr`. You could eliminate subscripts altogether by using two separate pointer variables, as follows:

```
double  list[MAX_LIST_SIZE], *src, *dest, *end_list;

/* Get address of last element in list */
end_list = list+MAX_LIST_SIZE;

/* Shift elements up one position */
for (src=list+1, dest=list; src < end_list; )
    *dest++ = *src++;
```

15.3   Typedef and Arrays

If you need to define many arrays of the same type and dimension, then using a `typedef` can save you some work and eliminate some of the potential for mistakes.

Example:

The program below demonstrates how to create an array type called `list_t` for use in defining arrays of 100 `doubles`.

```
#define MAX_LIST_SIZE    100

typedef double list_t[MAX_LIST_SIZE];

int     main()

{
    list_t  list;
    ...
}
```

Remember that type names are *global*, so they can be used in any function to define variables. For large projects consisting of multiple source files, the `typedef` can be placed in a header file to make it available in all the source files.

15.4   Advanced: More Fun with Pointers

Pointers are very often dereferenced and incremented at roughly the same time. You can use this technique to reduce the size and complexity of the source code by combining these operations into a single statement.

For example, consider the array search example presented earlier. Instead of using a `for` loop, it could be done by initializing the pointers when they are defined, and then using a `while` loop:

```
#define MAX_LIST_SIZE     100

int     main()

{
    long    list[MAX_LIST_SIZE],
            *p = list,
            *endlist = list+MAX_LIST_SIZE,
            key;

    /* Initialize list */
    while ( p < endlist )
        if (*p++ == key)
            ...
}
```

Since the `++` operator comes after `p`, `p` is incremented *after* the value `OL` is assigned to `*p`. Note that both the `*` and `++` operators act directly on the pointer variable. In contrast, consider the following expressions:

```
++*p;
*++p;
```

The first expression will actually increment the *object that* p *points to*, not the address in p, because the ++ operator acts on the expression *p, not p directly. It is equivalent to ++(*p). The second expression, *++p, will increment p, and then dereference the new address in p. It is equivalent to *(++p).

There are many potentially confusing expressions that can be formulated using pointers and the operators that work with them. It is important to understand the rules of precedence and order of evaluation when they apply. If an expression is somewhat confusing, it is often better to break it up into two or more statements to make it more readable. Keep in mind that reducing the size of the source code doesn't necessarily reduce the size of the machine code. For example,

```
*++p = 0L;
```

and

```
++p;
*p = 0L;
```

will most likely produce exactly the same compiler output. The only advantage to the former is that it's easier to type. The latter, however, is less likely to cause confusion, and preferred by most programmers.

15.5 Arrays and Functions

Since an array name is a pointer, when a program passes an array to a function, it only passes the *address* of the first element. There is no way to pass an array object by value in C: You can *only* pass a pointer to it. Passing arrays by value would be inefficient due to the added time and memory needed to duplicate the array.

Consider the following program which passes an array called list to the function print_list():

```
#define MAX_LIST_SIZE    1000

int     main()
```

```
{
    double  list[MAX_LIST_SIZE];
    size_t  listsize;

    ...
    print_list(list,listsize);
    ...
}
```

There are two ways to define the formal argument variable that receives the array. First, it can be defined as an array:

```
void    print_list(double list[], size_t listsize)

{
    double  *p;

    for (p=list; p<list+listsize; ++p)
        printf("%f\n",*p);
}
```

Note that the array dimension is omitted in a formal argument, because a formal argument definition doesn't have to allocate any memory for a new array. It only allocates enough space for a copy of the array's *address*. Since C doesn't check array subscripts anyway, the dimension serves no purpose in a formal argument.

Furthermore, the argument passed in could be an array of any size, so it doesn't make sense to fix the size of the formal argument. You can specify a dimension if you like, but it will be ignored by the compiler.

The formal argument could also be defined as a pointer variable. Defining list as a pointer variable allows you to use it as a local variable in the function:

```
void    print_list(double *list, size_t listsize)

{
    while ( --listsize > 0 )
```

```
        printf("%d\n",*list++);
}
```

Using an *array* called `list`, you need to define a local pointer variable (such as `p`) to access the array elements, since the expression `list++` would be illegal with an array name.

Pitfall: Pointers to Doomed Objects

As mentioned in chapter 11, a function can only return a *scalar* object. Hence, it isn't possible to return an array. A function *can* return a pointer to an array, but this must be done with caution. A function must *never* return the address of an **auto** variable, since this memory space is immediately freed for use by other functions when the function returns. Any data stored in a local **auto** variable is likely to be overwritten by the next function called, since it will use the same stack space for its own variables.

For example, the `read_list()` function below returns the address of the local array `list`, which ceases to exist immediately after the return.

```
#define LIST_SIZE        10000

int     main()

{
    double  *list;
    size_t  listsize;

    ...
    list = read_list(&listsize);
    ...
}

double  *read_list(size_t *listsize)

    {
```

```
        double  list[MAX_LIST_SIZE], *p;
        size_t  l;

        for (p=list, l=0; (scanf("%lf",p) == 1) &&
                    (l < MAX_LIST_SIZE); ++p, ++l)
            ;
        return list;    /* A bad idea */
    }
```

A function may return the address of a **static** object, an object allocated with
malloc(), or an object that was received as an argument.

For example, the function below is a bit safer:

```
    double  *read_list(size_t *listsize)

    {
        static double  list[MAX_LIST_SIZE];
        double  *p;
        size_t  l;

        /* Read until EOF encountered or array is full */
        for (p=list, l=0; (scanf("%lf",p) != EOF) &&
                    (l < MAX_LIST_SIZE); ++p, ++l)
            ;
        return list;    /* This is OK, but risky */
    }
```

While it's safe, in an immediate sense, to return the address of a **static** object,
this is generally regarded as a bad practice, because it's difficult for other functions
to know if the object has recently been modified. Any pointer to a **static** variable
returned by a function should be regarded as pointing to temporary data. For
example, a few library functions, such as **tmpnam()**, which returns the generated
name of a temporary file, sometimes return pointers to internal **static** variables.
This data must be copied to a different, more permanent location if it will be
needed in the future, since the next call to **tmpnam()** may overwrite the contents of
its internal **static** array.

Example:

```
char    *filename1, *filename2;

filename1 = tmpnam(NULL);
...
filename2 = tmpnam(NULL);
```

Both `filename1` and `filename2` point to the same `static` buffer defined inside `tmpnam()`, which will ultimately contain the name generated by the *second* call. The name generated by the first call is overwritten.

The argument to `tmpnam()` is actually the address of a character array. If it is not `NULL`, then `tmpnam()` will copy the generated filename into the address specified. Using this feature will allow us to receive two different filenames, as follows:

```
char    filename1[L_tmpnam+1],filename2[L_tmpnam+1];

tmpnam(filename1);
tmpnam(filename2);
```

Some library functions (such as `readdir()`) don't give you the option of specifying an array to put the data in. Instead, they *always* return a pointer to an internal `static` array. If this were the case with `tmpnam()`, we could use `strlcpy()` to circumvent the problem:

```
char    filename1[L_tmpnam+1],filename2[L_tmpnam+1];

strlcpy(filename1,tmpnam(NULL),L_tmpnam);
strlcpy(filename2,tmpnam(NULL),L_tmpnam);
```

Also note that using `static` arrays increases the memory requirements of a program, since they exist throughout the lifetime of the process. An `auto` array only takes up memory space until the program exits the block in which the array is defined.

The best solution for the read_list() function, and any similar function, is to have the calling function provide the memory space to put the list in. There is little use in returning the array address in this setting, so we'll use the function's return value to return the list size instead. Also, we will pass in the size of the array from main(), so that the read_list() function can be safely used for arrays of different sizes.

```
#define LITTLE_LIST_MAX      100
#define BIG_LIST_MAX         10000

int     main()

{
    double  little_list[LITTLE_LIST_MAX],
            big_list[BIG_LIST_MAX];
    size_t  littlesize,bigsize;

    ...
    littlesize = read_list(little_list,LITTLE_LIST_MAX);
    bigsize = read_list(big_list,BIG_LIST_MAX);
    ...
}


size_t  read_list(double list[],size_t max_list_size)

{
    double  *p;
    size_t  l;

    /* Read until EOF encountered or array is full */
    for (p=list, l=0; (scanf("%lf",p) != EOF) &&
                (l < max_list_size); ++p, ++l)
        ;
    ...
    return l;
}
```

15.6 Lookup tables

Another use for `static` arrays is for storing pre-computed data to be looked up at a later time. This speeds up execution times dramatically in some situations, as demonstrated by the following example. This is essentially like using a `DATA` block in FORTRAN or BASIC.

Example:

The function below uses a `static` array to store pre-computed factorial values. Such an array is called a **lookup table**, since the values are looked up, rather than computed at run time. Since the array is `static`, it is initialized before the program begins executing, and retains it's data as long as the program is running.

By using a lookup table, you avoid the need to use a loop or recursion to compute each factorial value. Tests on a 486 computer showed this function to be about *500 times faster* than the iterative factorial function presented in section 11.3.2. The real version uses a lookup table of 171 values. Only 8 are shown here for simplicity.

The factorial function is a good candidate for a lookup table, since factorials are expensive to compute, and 171! is the largest that can be computed in the range of a `double`, so the lookup table is fairly small.

```
double factorial(int n)

{
    static double f[8] =
        { 1, 1, 2, 6, 24, 120, 720, 5040 };

    if ( n < 8 )
        return f[n];
    else
        return -1;
}
```

Note that it is difficult to compute precise factorial values using floating point variables, due to round-off error. To maximize the accuracy of the larger factorials, the table should be constructed using a multiple precision utility such as the Unix bc calculator language.

15.7   Pointer Arguments and `const`

The `const` modifier is often used with formal arguments that point to arrays. Using `const`, you can protect the array contents from side effects, or protect the pointer in case the address needs to be preserved. The placement of the `const` keyword is crucial to how it is interpreted. A simple trick for determining the meaning is to *read the definition backwards*, saying "pointer" when you read the * operator. For example, consider the following definition:

```
const double *list;
```

When read backwards, it says "list is a pointer to a double constant". In other words, the `doubles` in the array are marked as constant, so the function cannot change the values in the array.

The definition

```
double const *list;
```

has exactly the same meaning. Read backwards, "list is a pointer to a constant double", which says essentially the same thing.

The last possibility is

```
double * const list;
```

This definition states that the *pointer* cannot be changed, but the array object *can* be changed. Read backwards, "list is a constant pointer to a double". This is essentially the same as defining `list` as an array, since an array name is a constant pointer. The array definition is generally preferred, since it is less confusing.

The first two definitions of `list` would be suitable for a function like `print_list()`. Looking at a call to `print_list()`, a programmer wouldn't expect the list to be modified. If you define the function as follows,

```
void    print_list(const double *list, size_t listsize)

{
    ...
}
```

then any attempt to modify the contents of the array inside `print_list()` will cause a compile time error. It's a good practice to use `const` as often as possible to prevent yourself from inadvertently introducing side effects into functions. Since array objects cannot be passed by value, this is the only way to protect them.

15.8 Multi Dimensional Arrays

Multidimensional arrays are arrays with two or more dimensions. The most common uses include *matrix* and *table* manipulation in applications such as scientific programming or spread-sheets, and arrays of strings in other applications.

Technically, C doesn't support arrays with more than one dimension. This is another example of the elegant simplicity of the C language design. Although C has no features to specifically support multidimensional arrays, they can be implemented using an *array of arrays*. For example, the following definition defines a two-dimensional array:

```
double  mat[MAX_ROWS][MAX_COLS];
```

The definition states that `mat` points to an array of `MAX_ROWS` arrays, each of which is itself an array of `MAX_COLS` type double values. The elements of a two dimensional array are stored in **row-major** ordering, meaning that all the elements of the same row are in contiguous memory locations. Hence, the first subscript specifies the row in the matrix, and the second specifies the column. Figure 15.3 depicts the general format of a matrix. Figure 15.4 depicts a two dimensional array as it resides in memory.

$$
\begin{bmatrix}
mat_{0,0} & mat_{0,1} & \cdots & mat_{0,N-1} \\
mat_{1,0} & mat_{1,1} & \cdots & mat_{1,N-1} \\
 & & \cdot & \\
 & & \cdot & \\
 & & \cdot & \\
mat_{M-1,0} & mat_{M-1,1} & \cdots & mat_{M-1,N-1}
\end{bmatrix}
$$

Figure 15.3: General format of a $M \times N$ matrix

Address	Element
1000	array[0][0]
1008	array[0][1]
.	
.	
.	
1072	array[0][9]
1080	array[1][0]
1088	array[1][1]
	.
	.
	.
1720	array[9][0]
.	
.	
.	
1792	array[9][9]

Figure 15.4: A 10 by 10 array of `doubles`

The expression mat[r][c] represents the double value in the matrix at row r and column c. The name mat is a pointer to the first element. It is essentially equivalent to &mat[0][0]. Mat[r] is a pointer of type double * to the first element of row r, i.e. to mat[r][0]. Hence, mat[0] represents the same address as mat.

Example:

Read a matrix into a 2-dimensional array. The input has the number of rows and columns of the matrix on the first line, followed by the matrix elements on subsequent lines:

```
3 4
5.7     2.3     -0.1    4.9
-9.8    6.2     0.0     4.1
3.7     8.6     9.0     10.4
```

First, we'll demonstrate the program using subscripts. Then we'll improve on this by using pointers to address the matrix elements, which will improve performance.

```c
#include <stdio.h>
#include <sysexits.h>

#define MAX_ROWS    100
#define MAX_COLS    100

int     main()

{
    double  mat[MAX_ROWS][MAX_COLS];
    size_t  rows,cols,r,c;

    /* Input and check size of matrix */
    scanf("%u %u",&rows,&cols);
    if ( (rows > 100) || (cols > 100) )
    {
        fputs("Matrix input is too large.\n",stderr);
```

```
        fputs("Limit is 100 x 100.\n",stderr);
        return(1);
    }

    /* Input matrix into array */
    for (r=0; r<rows; ++r)
        for (c=0; c<cols; ++c)
            scanf("%lf",&mat[r][c]);

    /* Print matrix */
    for (r=0; r<rows; ++r)
    {
        for (c=0; c<cols; ++c)
            printf("%f ",mat[r][c]);
        putchar('\n');
    }
    return EX_OK;
}
```

Using pointers, the program could be written as follows:

```
#include <stdio.h>
#include <sysexits.h>

#define MAX_ROWS     100
#define MAX_COLS     100

int     main()

{
    double  mat[MAX_ROWS][MAX_COLS];
    size_t  rows,cols,r,c;
    double  *rowp,*colp, *end_mat, *end_row;

    /* Input and check size of matrix */
    scanf("%d %d",&rows,&cols);
    if ( (rows > 100) || (cols > 100) )
    {
```

```
            fputs("Matrix input is too large.\n",stderr);
            fputs("Limit is 100 x 100.\n",stderr);
            return(1);
        }

        /* Input matrix into array */
        end_mat = (double *)mat + rows * MAX_COLS;
        for (rowp=(double *)mat; rowp<end_mat; rowp+=MAX_COLS)
        {
            /* Compute end address of this row */
            end_row = rowp + cols;
            for (colp=rowp; colp<end_row; ++colp)
                scanf("%lf",colp);
        }

        /* Verify matrix read using subscripts */
        for (r=0; r<rows; ++r)
        {
            for (c=0; c<cols; ++c)
                printf("%f ",mat[r][c]);
            putchar('\n');
        }
        return EX_OK;
    }
```

Since each row of the array contains MAX_COLS double values, you need to add MAX_COLS to rowp to advance it to the beginning of the next row. The inner loop stops at rowp+cols, which is equivalent to &mat[r][cols] in the subscripted version. The outer loop stops after the last row that contains useful data, which is pointed to by end_mat.

When passing a multidimensional array to a function, the dimensions cannot be omitted from the formal argument definition. The compiler needs to know the number of columns in each row, so it can determine the address where each row begins. Hence, the *first* dimension – the number of rows – can be omitted, but all others must be specified, and must match the argument being passed in.

```
void read_mat(double mat[][MAX_COLS],size_t *rows,size_t *cols);
{
    ...
}
```

Arrays of arrays are a quick convenient way to store multidimensional data. However, they can waste vast amounts of memory when there is a wide range of possibilities for the amount of actual data. For example, suppose you write a program that uses matrices anywhere from 3×3, up to 1000×1000. If you use an array of arrays, it will have to be defined as 1000×1000 to handle the largest possible matrix. If you use an 8-byte `double`, this array will require *eight megabytes* of memory, even when the program is only processing a 3×3 matrix. Allocating blocks of memory so much larger than needed places a strain on the system that can slow it down for everyone.

This problem can be solved using **dynamic memory allocation**, which allows a program to allocate exactly the amount of memory it needs. This topic is covered in the chapter 16.

Chapter 16

Dynamic Memory Allocation

Before you begin...

> You should be familiar with the material on arrays presented in chapter 15.

One of the major problems with fixed-size arrays is they usually aren't fully utilized. Fixed sized arrays must always be made large enough for the largest possible case, regardless of how much data is actually stored in them.

In order to minimize the amount of memory a program demands, you must use **dynamic memory allocation**. Dynamic memory allocation allows a program to request a block of memory *after* it has determined how much it will need.

16.1   Dynamic Allocation: `malloc()` and `alloca()`

All dynamic memory allocation is performed by either `malloc()` or `alloca()`. These two functions differ in *where* they allocate memory, but otherwise behave very similarly.

The `malloc()` function is the most commonly used allocation function. It allocates memory in the **heap** segment[1], and maintains a table describing which portions of

---

[1]See section 11.10 for a description of the heap and stack segments.

the heap are in use, and which are free. Memory allocated with `malloc()` is freed when the process terminates, or when it is explicitly released by the process using the `free()` function. Memory allocated with `malloc()` has `static` storage class, so it can be used by different functions, and retains it's contents between function calls, just like a `static` variable.

Programming for Performance:

> One of the most common errors when programming with `malloc()` is forgetting to free the memory when it is no longer needed. As a result, many programs hoard memory, gathering more and more heap space until they terminate. Freeing memory as soon as it is no longer needed will help minimize your program's impact on system performance.

The `malloc()` function has a rather high overhead cost in both CPU time and memory use. Each call to `malloc()` must maintain a table describing allocated and free memory blocks, which requires both CPU time and memory to keep track of the blocks. The cost can run especially high in programs that call `malloc()` frequently to allocate small blocks of memory, as when using linked lists[2] and related structures.

For this reason, many programmers prefer to use the less expensive `alloca()` function. The `alloca()` function allocates memory in the stack segment. This is the same segment which contains a function's local `auto` variables, the function's return address, and arguments that were passed in. Memory space allocated with `alloca()` has `auto` storage class, so it is freed automatically when the function returns. Like an auto variable, this memory can only be used by the function that called `alloca()` to allocate it, and its descendents. Using `alloca()` is a much more efficient way to allocate memory, since no tables have to be maintained for the stack, and the memory is automatically freed when the function returns, so there is little chance that the program will hoard memory that isn't being utilized.

16.2   Basic Usage

Both `malloc()` and `alloca()` allocate a requested number of *bytes* of memory. The argument to either function is usually the number of items to allocate, times the

---

[2]Linked lists are described in section 18.5.2.

size of the data type for the array being allocated.

Both functions return the starting address of the allocated memory block, or NULL if the requested memory cannot be allocated.

Both functions are usually prototyped in *stdlib.h*.

Example:

The program below allocates an array just big enough for a list of numbers, and then inputs the list into the array.

The input consists of the number of values, followed by the values themselves.

```
5
2.3 0.9 8.7 4.6 -1.5
```

```c
#include <stdio.h>
#include <stdlib.h>
#include <sysexits.h>

size_t  read_list(double **list);

int     main()

{
    size_t  listsize;
    double  *list;

    listsize = read_list(&list);

    free(list);
    return 0;
}

/*
 * Allocate memory for a list and read in the values
 */
```

```
size_t  read_list(double **list)

{
    int     ch;
    size_t  listsize;
    double  *temp, *p;   /* Use temp in place of */
                         /* *list to simplify code */

    /* Get size of list */
    scanf("%d",&listsize);
    do
    {
        temp = (double *)malloc(listsize * sizeof(*temp));
        if ( temp == NULL )
        {
            puts("Out of memory.  Try again? (y/n) ");
            if ( (ch = getchar()) == 'n' )
                exit(EX_OSERR);
        }
    }   while ( (temp == NULL) && (ch == 'y') );

    /* Read until EOF encountered or array is full */
    for (p=temp; p<temp+listsize; ++p)
        scanf("%lf",p);

    *list = temp;         /* Return pointer to list */
    return listsize;      /* Return list size */
}
```

Note that you need to send the *address* of the pointer variable `list`
to `read_list()`, just as we would with a data variable, so that the
`read_list()` function can modify the address in the pointer variable.
In other words, pointer variables are treated *no differently* than data
variables in C.

When specifying the size of any item, it's best to use the `sizeof()` operator, rather than make assumptions about the size of an item, even if the item is a standard data type. For example, for a `double`, you could usually get away with writing

```
temp = (double *)malloc(listsize*8);
...
free(temp);
```

since the `double` type is almost always 8 bytes. However, it is possible that a particular compiler will use a different size for `double` in order to best utilize hardware features, so hard-coding the size of a type reduces portability of a program. It would be preferable to write

```
temp = (double *)malloc(listsize*sizeof(double));
...
free(temp);
```

The argument to `sizeof()` can be either a type name or an expression of the given type, such as an element of the array being allocated. An expression is generally preferable, because if you change the data type of the expression, then `sizeof(expression)` will still be valid. For example, consider the following code fragment:

```
float   *list;
size_t  listsize;

list = (float *)malloc(listsize*sizeof(float));
...
free(list);
```

If you change the definition of `list`, it's easy to forget to change the type in `sizeof()` to correspond:

```
double  *list;
size_t  listsize;
```

```
list = (double *)malloc(listsize*sizeof(float));
...
free(list);
```

The code above will compile cleanly, but will not allocate enough memory for the array, which may lead to a segmentation fault, or worse yet, data corruption and incorrect output. If you use `sizeof(*list)` instead of `sizeof(float)`, then the argument to `malloc()` will consequently be adjusted when you change the definition of list:

```
float   *list;
size_t  listsize;

list = (float *)malloc(listsize*sizeof(*list));
...
free(list);
```

Note that `list` must be dereferenced in `sizeof()`. Writing `sizeof(list)` instead of `sizeof(*list)` would give you the size of a pointer rather than the size of the data.

An even better way to make a program easy to change (modifiable) is to define a type name to be used throughout:

```
typedef double  float_t;

int     main()

{
    float_t *list;
    size_t  listsize;

    list = (float_t *)malloc(listsize*sizeof(float_t));
    ...
    free(list);
}
```

If you want to change the program to use `float` instead of `double`, only the `typedef` statement needs to be changed, and everything that follows will be properly adjusted when you recompile.

Pitfall: Ask Not, and Ye Shall Not Receive

A common mistake when using `malloc()` and `alloca()` is to forget the `sizeof()` portion in the size of the requested block, which generally means the program will ask for less memory than it really needs. For example,

```
size_t  listsize;
double  *list;

list = (double *)malloc(listsize);
...
free(list);
```

It's important to remember that `malloc()` allocates the number of *bytes* you specify, not the number of *items*. If listsize is the number of `doubles` the program needs, then the call above will allocate 1/8 of the needed memory, assuming an eight byte `double`. This will most likely lead to an eventual segmentation fault, or data corruption.

For this reason, some programmers prefer to use `calloc()`, since it requires two arguments. The `calloc()` function requires the number of items *and* the size of an item as separate arguments, rather than the product of these values as a single argument.

```
size_t  listsize;
double  *list;

list = (double *)calloc(listsize,sizeof(*list));
...
free(list);
```

If you omit one argument, an ANSI compiler will produce an error message, since your call won't match the prototype.

The down side of `calloc()` is that it initializes the memory block to all zeros, (the 'c' in `calloc()` is for clear) which is usually a waste of time. Hence, `calloc()` should only be used if you actually need a block of memory which is cleared from end to end.

A better alternative is to define a simple macro or function which *requires* both the count and size arguments, but doesn't waste time initializing the memory. This way, the preprocessor will notify you in the event you omit something.

```
#define MALLOC(n,s)      malloc(n*s)
...

    list = (float_t *)MALLOC(listsize,sizeof(float_t));
    ...
    free(list);
```

You could also define the macro to take an item count and a *type*:

```
#define MALLOC(n,type)\
        (type *)malloc(n*sizeof(type))
...

    float_t *list;

    list = MALLOC(listsize,float_t);
    ...
    free(list);
```

Programming for Performance:

Calling any allocation function with a constant argument is usually pointless. For example, consider the following code fragment:

```
#define MAX_LIST_SIZE    100
#define MALLOC(n,t)      ((t *)malloc(n*sizeof(t)))
...
float_t *list;

/* A dumb idea, usually */
list = MALLOC(MAX_LIST_SIZE,float_t);
...
free(list);
```

This is a silly thing to do, because it carries the expense of dynamic memory allocation, and has the essentially same effect as defining an array, as follows:

```
static double  list[MAX_LIST_SIZE];
```

The only possible advantage to using malloc() this way is that the dynamically allocated array can be freed or resized at some later time.

Similarly, using alloca() in this way is *exactly* the same as defining an auto array, since both use the stack, and are instantiated at run time. If the size of an array is going to be fixed at compile time, just define an array, rather than increase the complexity of the code using dynamic allocation.

16.3 How malloc() Keeps Track: Heap Tables

The malloc() and free() functions maintain a table which keeps track of all the allocated and free memory in the process' heap area. The more often a program calls malloc() and free(), the larger and more complex this table becomes, and the more **fragmented** the heap becomes. As a result, calls to malloc() become progressively slower as memory is continually allocated and freed.

Therefore, calling malloc() to allocate many small blocks of memory will degrade performance, especially if the blocks are different sizes. If all the blocks are the same size, then malloc() can usually reuse them after they have been freed.

Data structures such as the **linear linked list** and **trees**, which are allocated one node at a time, have a high overhead cost because of the extensive heap management needed.[3] If the amount of memory needed can be determined *before* the memory is allocated, then it's best to allocate an array with a *single call* to `malloc()`. In addition, arrays are easier to manipulate and faster than linked structures, because they allow random access (you can access any element instantly), whereas linked lists only allow sequential access (to get to the Nth element, the program must loop through the first $N - 1$ elements).

If the list size is not known ahead of time, you can use `malloc()` to allocate an *estimated* list, and then use `realloc()` to extend it later if needed. Be aware, however, that `realloc()` is *very* expensive. The `realloc()` function actually allocates an entirely new block, copies the contents of the old block to it, and then frees the old block. This is expensive in terms of both copying time and heap fragmentation. In general, if using `realloc()`, try to design the program so that it won't have to call `realloc()` more than a few times. It's better to waste a small amount of memory than to call `realloc()` too frequently. This means starting with a generous allocation to begin with, and adding fairly large chunks with `realloc()` so that the memory block won't have to be extended any time soon. A good strategy often used is to double the list size each time `realloc()` is called. This way, the list can grow exponentially with relatively few calls to `realloc()`. The *worst* approach would be to allocate one more node using `realloc()` for each item read.

Another problem with `realloc()` is that it moves existing data. If you have any other pointer variables pointing into a block of allocated memory, they will be invalid following a call to `realloc()`, and will have to be reset to point to the same offset within the new block.

The `realloc()` function can also be used to "trim" an allocated array. Quite often, it isn't possible to know how large an array to allocate in advance, so you have to allocate (or reallocate) more than is actually needed. Once all the contents have been loaded into the array, there may be space left over. The `realloc()` function can then be used to *reduce* the size of the array in order to minimize memory use.

---

[3]These data structures are covered in chapter 18.

Example:

```
#include <stdio.h>
#include <stdlib.h>
#include <sysexits.h>

#define INITIAL_SIZE    100
#define MALLOC(n,t)     ((t *)malloc(n*sizeof(t)))
#define REALLOC(l,n,t)  ((t *)realloc(l,n*sizeof(t)))

typedef double  float_t;

int     main()

{
    float_t *list, *p;
    size_t  list_size = INITIAL_SIZE;

    list = MALLOC(list_size,float_t);

    /* Read values until a negative value is entered */
    p = list;
    while ((scanf("%lf",p) == 1) && (*p >= 0.0))
    {
        /* Extend array if full */
        if ( ++p - list == list_size )
        {
            /* Fastest way to double list size */
            list_size <<= 1;

            /* Move list to bigger quarters */
            list = REALLOC(list,list_size,float_t);

            /* Array list has been moved, so reset p */
            p = list+list_size;
        }
    }
```

```
        /* Trim the list */
        list = REALLOC(list,list_size,float_t);

        /* Check */
        for (p=list; *p >= 0.0; ++p)
            printf("%f\n",*p);
        free(list);
        return EX_OK;
    }
```

16.4 Pointer Arrays

The **pointer array**, an array of pointer variables is a very popular data structure in C and C++ programming. Pointer arrays can be used to implement both linear lists and multidimensional lists, such as matrices.

Using pointer arrays for linear lists shares the same memory allocation problems as linked lists, in that many small blocks of memory must be allocated. Pointer arrays do, however, have an advantage over linked lists in that they allow random access. This is an important reason why pointer arrays are so widely used in C programming.

16.4.1 Pointer Arrays and Matrices

Suppose you write a program that uses a multi-dimensional array:

```
    #include <stdio.h>

    #define MAX_ROWS    1000
    #define MAX_COLS    1000

    int    main()

    {
```

```
    double   mat[MAX_ROWS][MAX_COLS];
    size_t   rows,cols,r,c;

    /* Input matrix size */
    scanf("%d %d",&rows,&cols);
    if ( (rows > MAX_ROWS) || (cols > MAX_COLS) )
    {
        fprintf(stderr,"Sorry, maximum is %d x %d.\n",
            MAX_ROWS,MAX_COLS);
        return(1);
    }

    /* Input matrix into array */
    for (r=0; r<rows; ++r)
        for (c=0; c<cols; ++c)
            scanf("%lf",&mat[r][c]);
    ...
}
```

The array `mat` requires $1,000,000 \times sizeof(double)$, bytes, which is 8 megabytes of memory on most systems. This is true whether the actual matrix is 1000×1000, or 3×3. You can significantly reduce the memory overhead by using a pointer array, and allocating each row dynamically, as follows:

```
#include <stdio.h>
#include <stdlib.h>
#include <sysexits.h>

#define MAX_ROWS    1000
#define MALLOC(n,t) (t *)malloc(n*t)

int     main()

{
    float_t *mat[MAX_ROWS];
    size_t   rows,cols,r,c;

    /* Input matrix size */
```

```
    scanf("%u %u",&rows,&cols);
    if ( rows > MAX_ROWS )
    {
        fprintf(stderr,
            "Sorry, maximum is %d rows.\n",MAX_ROWS);
        return(1);
    }

    /* Allocate each row and input the data */
    for (r=0; r<rows; ++r)
    {
        /* Allocate new row */
        mat[r] = MALLOC(cols,float_t);
        if ( mat[r] == NULL )
        {
            fputs("Out of memory.\n",stderr);
            exit(EX_OSERR);
        }

        /* Use a pointer to move through new row */
        for (c=0; c<cols; ++c)
            scanf("%lf",&mat[r][c]);
    }
    ...
}
```

Assuming the size of a pointer is 4 bytes, the pointer array `mat` requires only 4 kilobytes of memory. In addition, the program uses the value of `cols` to allocate the minimum amount of memory required to contain each row.

For a 1000×1000 matrix and 8 byte `double`, the total memory requirement will be 4K for the pointers + 8 megabytes for the actual data, which is 4K more than the 2-D array version. For a 3×3, the total memory will be 4K + a mere 72 bytes, which is a trivial amount of memory for any system.

Figure 16.1 visually demonstrates the organization of a pointer array containing a matrix.

Note that by using a pointer array, you have also eliminated the limit on the number of columns the matrix can contain. You can go one step further to eliminate the

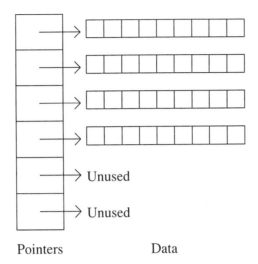

Figure 16.1: Schematic of a Pointer Array Matrix

limit on the number of *rows*, by dynamically allocating the pointers as well:

```c
#include <stdio.h>
#include <stdlib.h>
#include <sysexits.h>

#define MALLOC(n,t)   (t *)malloc(n*sizeof(t))

int     main()

{
    float_t **mat;
    size_t  rows,cols,r,c;

    scanf("%d %d",&rows,&cols);
    mat = MALLOC(rows,float_t *);
    if ( mat == NULL )
    {
        fputs("Out of memory.\n",stderr);
        exit(EX_OSERR);
    }

    /* Allocate each row and input the matrix */
    for (r=0; r<rows; ++r)
    {
        mat[r] = MALLOC(cols,float_t);
        if ( mat[r] == NULL )
        {
            fputs("Out of memory.\n",stderr);
            exit(EX_OSERR);
        }
        for (c=0; c<cols; ++c)
            scanf("%lf",&mat[r][c]);
    }
    ...
}
```

In both cases, you can still use the same subscript notation to access the data as you did with the multidimensional array, since mat[r] is a pointer to the first element in a row, which itself is an array.

If you use direct pointers, however, the input loop will be somewhat different than the example given for multidimensional arrays:

```
#include <stdio.h>
#include <stdlib.h>
#include <sysexits.h>

#define MAX_ROWS    100
#define MAX_COLS    100

int     main()

{
    double  **mat;
    size_t  rows,cols,r;
    double  **rowp,*colp,*end;

    /* Get matrix size and allocate pointer array */
    scanf("%d %d",&rows,&cols);
    mat = (double **)MALLOC(rows,sizeof(*mat));
    if ( mat[r] == NULL )
    {
        fputs("Out of memory.\n",stderr);
        exit(EX_OSERR);
    }

    /* Allocate each row and input data */
    for (rowp=mat; rowp<mat+rows; ++rowp)
    {
        *rowp = (double **)MALLOC(cols,sizeof(**rowp));
        for (colp = *rowp; colp<*rowp+cols; ++colp)
            scanf("%lf",colp);
    }
}
```

Another advantage to using a pointer array is that you can switch two rows of a matrix without actually moving any data. This is a common practice in some numerical algorithms, such as Gauss elimination.

With a two dimensional array, you would have to use the `memcpy()` function to swap the entire contents of two rows, as follows:

```
double  temp[MAX_COLS];

memcpy(temp,mat[r1],cols*sizeof(float_t));
memcpy(mat[r1],mat[r2],cols*sizeof(float_t));
memcpy(mat[r2],temp,cols*sizeof(float_t));
```

With `MAX_COLS` defined as 1000, each `memcpy()` call above uses a loop to move up to 8K of data from one location to another - a very expensive operation. With a pointer array, you need only swap the pointers, which is a scalar operation and may be literally thousands of times faster:

```
double  *temp;

temp = mat[r1];
mat[r1] = mat[r2];
mat[r2] = temp;
```

16.5   Pointer Arrays and Strings

Arrays of strings can also be implemented as two-dimensional arrays or as pointer arrays. Again, a lot of time and memory can be saved by using pointer arrays.

Consider the following program:

```
#include <stdio.h>
#include <stdlib.h>
#include <sysexits.h>

#define MAX_NAMES      10000
#define MAX_NAME_LEN   40

int     main()
```

```
{
    char    names[MAX_NAMES][MAX_NAME_LEN+1];
    size_t  count;

    /* Input names */
    count = read_names(names);

    /* Sort names */
    selection_sort(names,0,count-1);
    ...
}



/*
 * Recursive selection sort
 */

void    selection_sort(char names[][MAX_NAME_LEN+1],
                       int first,int last)

{
    int     lowpos;
    char    temp[MAX_NAME_LEN+1];

    if ( first < last )
    {
        /* Find smallest element */
        lowpos = findlow(names,first,last);

        /* Swap smallest with first */
        strcpy(temp,names[lowpos]);
        strcpy(names[lowpos],names[first]);
        strcpy(names[first],temp);

        /* Sort remaining elements */
        selection_sort(names,first+1,last);
    }
}
```

```
/*
 * Get position of alphabetically lowest name
 */

size_t  findlow(char names[][MAX_NAME_LEN+1],
                size_t first,size_t last)

{
    ...
}



/*
 * Read in names from stdin
 */

size_t  read_names(char names[][MAX_NAME_LEN+1])

{
    ...
}
```

This `selection_sort()` function literally moves entire strings in order to swap two strings in the array. If you use a pointer array, you can swap the pointers instead, which will be many times faster. For example, if the average string length is twenty characters, then swapping the scalar pointers will be at least twenty times faster than swapping the whole strings, and probably more, due to the loop and function call overhead of `strcpy()`.

```
#define MAX_NAMES       10000

int     main()

{
    char    *names[MAX_NAMES];
```

```
        size_t   count;

        count = read_names(names);
        selection_sort(names,count);
        ...
}


/*
 * Recursive selection sort
 */

void     selection_sort(char *names[],
                        int first,int last)

{
    int      lowpos;
    char     *temp;

    if ( first < last )
    {
        /* Find smallest element */
        lowpos = findlow(names,first,last);

        /* Swap smallest with first */
        temp = names[first];
        names[first] = names[lowpos];
        names[lowpos] = temp;

        /* Sort remaining elements */
        selection_sort(names,first+1,last);
    }
}
```

In addition, **read_names()** can be designed to allocate the minimum amount of memory needed for each string when using pointer arrays. If the average string length is 20 characters, this cuts memory use from 400k to just over 200k.

16.6   Command Line Arguments: `argc` and `argv`

C programs are capable of receiving arguments from the shell command line (or from the parent process in other ways which are covered in chapter 27). For example, when you compile a C program, you type a command such as

```
gcc -Wall -O3 prog.c
```

Each token in the command, delimited by spaces or tabs, is called a *command-line argument*.

The `main()` function in C has a facility for accessing the arguments within a command. Until now, we've shown the `main()` function without any formal arguments:

```
int     main()

{
    ...
}
```

However, there are three optional arguments for `main()`, called `argv`, `argc`, and `envp`.

```
int     main(int argc, char *argv[], char *envp[])
```

Programs in the Unix environment are executed using the `execve()` system call, which is described in chapter 27. This function first loads the program (or a portion of it) into memory, and then calls `main()`, sending the three arguments shown above.

If no formal arguments are defined in `main()`, then the argument values passed in by `execve()` are ignored. If command line arguments are to be processed, you need to define `argc` and `argv`. The `envp` argument contains pointers to environment variables, and is not necessary to process command line arguments.

When you type a Unix command at the shell prompt, the shell separates the command into a list of arguments, and constructs a pointer array, with one pointer to each argument string.

Since a command can have any number of command line arguments, the number of arguments is passed to `main()`, and received in `argc`.

The pointer array `argv` receives the pointers to each of the arguments from the command line. The first pointer, `argv[0]`, points to the name of the command, `argv[1]` points to the first command-line argument, and so on. The last argument is `argv[argc-1]`. `Argv[argc]` is set to NULL, to provide an alternative way of determining where the end of the argument list is. Figure 16.2 depicts the `argv` array for the `gcc` command above.

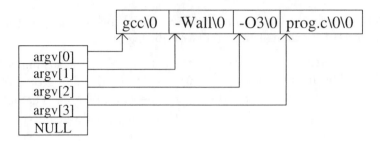

Figure 16.2: The argv array

Example:

The following program uses a "-d" command-line switch to turn on debugging features.

```
int     main(int argc,char *argv[])

{
    int     debug = 0;
    char    **p;

    /* Look for switches in arg list */
    for (p = argv+1; p!=NULL; ++p)
        if ( strcmp(*p,"-d") == 0 )
            debug = 1;
    ...
    if ( debug )
        fprintf(stderr,...);
}
```

The command name pointed to by **argv[0]** has many important uses. For example, programs are often renamed. By using **argv[0]** instead of a hard-coded program name, you can provide a better help message when the program is invoked incorrectly:

```
/* gcc */
int     main(int argc,char *argv[])

{
    if ( argv < 2 )
    {
        fprintf(stderr,"Usage: %s <filename>\n",argv[0]);
        return -1;
    }
    return 0;
}
```

Furthermore, the same program may be invoked using different names. For example, the editor **vi** is actually a full screen (VIsual) version of the line editor **ex**. The two editors are really links to the same program, but it's behavior is controlled by which name is used to invoke it. The **main()** function in **vi/ex** might look something like this:

```
int     main(int argc,char *argv[])

{
    if ( strcmp(argv[0],"vi") == 0 )
        mode = VISUAL;
    else
        mode = LINE;
    ...
    return 0;
}
```

Other examples of such links include **gzip** and **gunzip**, **at** and **batch**, and the **netpbm** collection of graphics conversion utilities.

16.7   The Environment: envp

The **envp** pointer array contains pointers to each of the environment variables defined for the process.

The environment is actually a single character array containing concatenated string
of the form **name=value**. A copy of this array is inherited by each Unix process
from it's parent via the **execve()** system call. The names in the environment are
separated by '\0' characters, and the end of the environment is marked by two
adjacent '\0' characters. For example, the environment may contain the following
text:

```
TERM=vt100\0PRINTER=lp0\0SHELL=tcsh\0PATH=/bin:/usr/bin\0\0
```

The **envp** array is an array of pointers to the beginning of each *name*, such as **TERM**
or **PRINTER**. Programs can use this array to directly access their environment string.

Example:

A **printenv** program.

```
#include <stdio.h>

int     main(int argc,char *argv[],char *envp[])

{
    char    **p;

    for (p=envp; *p!=NULL; ++p)
        puts(*p);
    return 0;
}
```

The **envp** array is rarely used for accessing individual environment variables. A
simpler alternative is to use the **getenv()** function, which returns a pointer to the
string *value* of any variable. For example, to determine the value of the TERM
variable:

```
    char    *term_type;
```

```
term_type = getenv("TERM");
```

Since envp is a local variable in `main()`, it would have to be passed to other functions in order for them to use it. Most of the time, calling `getenv()` is easier, although not quite as efficient.

Chapter 17

Advanced: Function Pointers

Before you begin...

You should be familiar with the material on pointer arrays presented in chapter 16.

17.1 Simple Function Pointers

C has the rather unusual ability to work with pointers to *functions* as well as pointers to data objects. The most common use for function pointers is passing the address of one function to another, so that the second function can call the first.

For example, the `qsort()` library function sorts an array of *any* type of data. In order to do this, it needs to know how many objects there are, the size of each object, and *how to compare two objects*. The size and count are simple integer values, but the last piece of information specifies an *algorithm*, not a simple numeric feature of the data. This algorithm is supplied to `qsort()` as a pointer to a comparison function. The address of a function is specified by supplying the function name with no argument list. For example, `printf()` represents a call to the `printf()` function, while `printf` (note the lack of trailing parenthesis) represents the address of the `printf()` function within your program. There is no need to use the `&` operator to determine the address of a C function.

Example:

The program below uses the `qsort()` library function to sort a list of `long` values. The function `long_cmp` takes *pointers* to the two objects to compare, and returns a positive value if the first argument is larger than the second, a negative value if the first is smaller than the second, or zero if they are equal. This return value conforms the requirements of `qsort()`, as does `strcmp()` and other standard library functions for comparing data.

```
int     long_cmp(long *l1,long *l2)

{
    return *l1 - *l2;
}


int     main()

{
    long    list[MAX_VALS];
    int     count;
    int     (*cmp_func)() = long_cmp;

    count = read_list(list);
    qsort(list,count,sizeof(long),cmp_func);
    ...
}
```

The `qsort()` function is an example of a **polymorphic** function, since it is capable of sorting arrays of any data type. Polymorphism is one of the cornerstones of object oriented programming. Object oriented languages such as C++ provide features which make it easier to create polymorphic functions. More on this in chapter 30.

17.2 Function Pointer Tables

An interesting alternative to using a `switch` statement is the function pointer table. A function pointer table is an array of function pointers, each pointing to one of several functions with a similar purpose. By using a function pointer table, a switch statement can be replaced with only one or a few lines of code. The value that would be used in the `switch` is instead used as a subscript to the table.

Example:

Use a `switch` statement to select a calculator operation.

```
#include <stdio.h>

/* Prototypes */
void    add(double,double);
void    subtract(double,double);
void    multiply(double,double);

int     main()

{
    /* Scalar char variables are generally a bad idea,
       but it's necessary here for scanf() */
    char    op;
    double  a,b;

    printf("Enter expression: ");
    scanf("%lf %c %lf",&a,&op,&b);
    switch(op)
    {
        case    '+':
            add(a,b);
            break;
        case    '-':
            subtract(a,b);
            break;
        case    '*':
```

```
                multiply(a,b);
                break;
        default:
            fprintf(stderr,"Invalid operator: %c\n",
                    op);
            break;
    }
}


void    add(double a, double b)

{
    printf("The sum is %f.\n",a+b);
}


void    subtract(double a, double b)

{
    printf("The difference is %f.\n",a-b);
}


void    multiply(double a, double b)

{
    printf("The product is %f.\n",a*b);
}
```

The following program uses a function pointer table in place of the switch statement.

```
#include <stdio.h>

#define MAX_FUNCTIONS    100

/* Type name for pointer to void function */
```

```
typedef void (*funcptr)(double,double);

/* Prototypes */
void    init_tab(funcptr []);
void    add(double,double);
void    subtract(double,double);
void    multiply(double,double);

int     main()
{
    /* Array of pointers to void functions */
    funcptr table[MAX_FUNCTIONS];

    unsigned char    op;
    double  a,b;

    /* Initialize pointer table */
    init_tab(table);

    printf("Enter expression: ");
    scanf("%lf %c %lf",&a,&op,&b);
    if ( (op < MAX_FUNCTIONS) && (table[(int)op] != NULL) )
        (*table[(int)op])(a,b);
    else
        fprintf(stderr,"Invalid operator: %c\n",op);
    return 0;
}


void    init_tab(funcptr table[])

{
    int     c;

    /* NULL all entries */
    for (c=0; c<MAX_FUNCTIONS; ++c)
        table[c] = NULL;

    /* Set valid entries */
```

```
        table['+'] = add;
        table['-'] = subtract;
        table['*'] = multiply;
    }
    ...
```

Using a function pointer table may greatly improve the performance of a program, since it provides an immediate branch to the correct function for the small cost of one array reference. A `switch` statement, on the other hand, is often equivalent to a series of `if` statements, which can take a long time, especially for the later cases. Note, however, that a function pointer table is only practical if the switch value has a fairly small range, otherwise the pointer array may consume too much memory. Also, modern compilers do an excellent job optimizing `switch` statements. Some may even convert the switch to an address table behind the scenes. Hence, you may not notice any improvement in performance after converting a `switch` to a function pointer table.

Chapter 18

Structures and Unions

Before you begin...

You should be familiar with the material on dynamic memory allocation
and pointer arrays presented in chapter 16.

18.1   Structures

A wide variety of programs work with bundles of related data, such as names,
addresses, and phone numbers, or stock numbers, prices, and sales figures. A group
of related items could be kept in separate variables, but it's more convenient to
bind them into a single aggregate variable. For example, a database program for
keeping track of customers might manage hundreds of pieces of information about
each customer. If you had to pass these hundreds of variables to a function to print
the information, the program would become a calamity.

Example:

Suppose we kept a database of insurance clients. For each client, we would keep dozens of pieces of information. Each function in the program would have to be passed some of this information, and a few, such as the `print_client()` function shown below, would have to be passed all of it. As you can see, the argument list is so large, it's virtually unmanageable.

```
void    print_client(char *first_name,
                     char *last_name,
                     char *middle_name,
                     char *street,
                     char *city,
                     char *state,
                     char *country,
                     int age,
                     double auto_value,
                     int doors,
                     and so on...
                     );
{
    ...
}
```

A **structure** is an aggregate object, like an array, meaning that it contains multiple items. However, the items in a structure, called **fields**, or **members**, don't all have to be the same type. Furthermore, each field is referenced by name, rather than by subscript.

18.1.1   Structure Templates

A structure **template** is a type definition which defines the members of a structure type. Structure templates are usually defined in header files using a `typedef`.

Example:

The following type definition defines a structure type that contains some basic information about a tennis player:

```
typedef int gender_t;

/* Define template for player */
typedef struct
{
    int         world_rank;
    gender_t    gender;
    char        first_name[MAX_NAME_LEN+1];
    char        middle_name[MAX_NAME_LEN+1];
    char        last_name[MAX_NAME_LEN+1];
}   player_t;
```

Structure objects can then be defined using the new type name.

```
int     main()

{
    player_t    player;
    ...

    return EX_OK;
}
```

As mentioned in chapter 6, it is conventional to end each type name with "_t", so that the identifier is easily recognized as a type name in any context.

Tip of the trade: Minimizing Structure Size

For alignment purposes, it's best to define the fields with the larger *data type* first, since larger data types tend to have stricter boundaries. If you define a **short** preceding a **long**, for example, the compiler may have to include padding between them so that the **long** begins on a long word boundary. More on this in section 18.8.

To access the fields in a structure, use the structure variable name followed by the **structure binding operator**, '.', and then the field name.

Example:

The code fragment below initializes a **player_t** structure:

```
int     main()

{
    player_t    player;

    strlcpy(player.first_name,"Poncho",MAX_NAME_LEN);
    strlcpy(player.last_name,"Gonzales",MAX_NAME_LEN);
    player.world_rank = 1;
    ...
    return EX_OK;
}
```

Note that the structure binding operator has higher precedence than any operator, except for the array subscript operator, [], and parenthesis. (See table 8.1, page 157.) As a result, a structure name bound to one of it's members is treated as a unit in most expressions. For example, the expression

```
++player.world_rank;
```

increments the member `player.world_rank`, rather than attempting to increment the structure `player`. This is equivalent to

```
++(player.world_rank);
```

Similarly, `*player.first_name` is equivalent to both `*(player.first_name)` and `player.first_name[0]`.

You can also define structure variables directly, without defining a template first:

```
struct
{
    int     world_rank;
    char    first_name[MAX_NAME_LEN+1];
    char    last_name[MAX_NAME_LEN+1];
}   player1, player2;
```

However, each variable definition would require typing all the structure members again, which would defeat the purpose of using a structure.

Strictly speaking, K&R C allows only two operations on structures. You can take the address of a structure using &, or access the members of a structure. In reality, most compilers that are classified as K&R will allow some additional operations such as whole structure assignment, or run-time initialization.

ANSI C ,on the other hand, allows structures to be treated as scalar variables in most respects. Hence, they may be assigned as a unit, passed to functions, initialized at run time, and so on. The details are discussed in subsequent sections.

18.1.2   K&R: Structure Tags

The original C language didn't support `typedef`, so structure templates were defined using a **structure tag**.

Example:

Defining a K&R structure template.

```
struct player_st
{
    int     world_rank;
    char    first_name[MAX_NAME_LEN+1];
    char    last_name[MAX_NAME_LEN+1];
};

int     main()

{
    struct player_st player;

    ...

    return EX_OK;
}
```

A structure tag is very much like a type name, except that it must *always* be preceded by the word `struct`. Structure tags are rarely used any more, and have been largely replaced by `typedef`. However, some older C headers and library functions still use structure tags for backward compatibility.

18.1.3   Copying Structures

In ANSI C, you can copy structures using an assignment operator, as follows:

```
player_t    player1, player2;
    ...

player1 = player2;
```

K&R C doesn't allow this, so you may have to use the `memcpy()` function, which copies a specified number of bytes from one memory address to another:

```
player_t    player1, player2;
...


memcpy(&player1,&player2,sizeof(player1));
```

Again, K&R compilers are hard to find these days, and those few that are still in use tend to support structure assignments anyway, so using `memcpy()` probably won't be necessary.

18.2 Pointers to Structures

Wherever structures are being used, you can expect to find pointers as well. Pointers to structures have many uses. Some are essential, while others improve efficiency. A pointer to a structure is defined and used much like a pointer to any other type.

Example:

The program below defines a structure pointer and assigns it the address of a structure.

```
int     main()

{
    player_t    player,*ptr;

    ptr = &player;
}
```

Referencing a structure member through a pointer using the '.' operator is a little tricky. You can't simply attach a dereference operator to the structure pointer, because the binding operator has a higher precedence than the dereference operator. For example, the statement

```
printf("World rank = %d\n",*ptr.world_rank);
```

is equivalent to

```
printf("World rank = %d\n",*(ptr.world_rank));
```

This attempts to dereference the member world_rank, which is not a pointer, so the compiler will produce an error message. What we want to do here is dereference the variable ptr, and then extract the member world_rank from the object pointed to. To accomplish this, we can parenthesize the expression so that the dereference occurs first:

```
printf("World rank = %d\n",(*ptr).world_rank);
```

Because this is such a common situation, and it's so easy to forget the parenthesis, C provides a second binding operator specifically for use with structure pointers. Instead of using '.', and having to parenthesize the expression, you can use the **pointer binding operator**, '->', as follows:

```
printf("World rank = %d\n",ptr->world_rank);
```

The -> operator serves the same purpose for structure *pointer* variables that the '.' operator serves for structure variables. As you will see shortly, structures are frequently referenced via pointers, so the -> operator will become very familiar as you gain experience with C.

18.3 Structures, Functions, and OOP

K&R C does not allow structures to be passed to functions, so you have to pass pointers instead.

ANSI C allows structures to be passed to functions, but this should be done with caution, since copying a large structure to the formal argument variable is very time consuming. If the structure is very small, then passing the structure by value won't hurt performance, and may even help, since directly referencing a copy of the structure inside the function will be faster than referencing it through a pointer. Large structures should never be passed by value unless there is a clear need to be duplicate the structure.

One of the primary themes in object oriented programming (OOP) is **encapsulation**, the binding of a data type to it's operations. Encapsulation can be achieved in C by writing a set of **member functions** for each structure type. Only member functions should access the members of the structure. Furthermore, member functions should *only* access the members of one type of structure, i.e. a function should not be a member of more than one data type. Programs that use the data type can then do so much more easily, since all the common operations on the data type can be performed using simple function calls.

Generally, member functions should be kept separate from the program, preferable in an object library, so that the data type and it's member functions can be used in other programs.[1] The type definition and function *declarations* can be placed in a header file which goes along with the library. To help discipline yourself in this respect, you should immediately create separate source and header files to contain all information and member functions for a particular structure type. Any time you need to reference the structure, define a new member function or macro along with the appropriate declarations.

Example:

The program below uses member functions to input data into and print a `player_t` structure.

Note that it is necessary to pass the *address* of the structure object to the `read_player()` function, since it has to load values into the structure.

The `print_player()` function could receive either a pointer or a structure object, but we'll use a pointer to avoid duplicating the structure contents. Passing a pointer eliminates the privacy of the argument, and makes it possible for `print_player()` to have side effects on the structure. Hence, we'll use the `const` modifier to protect the formal argument

---

[1]Chapter 20 describes how to create object libraries.

from modifications.

```c
#include <stdio.h>

#define MAX_NAME_LEN    40

/* Player structure */
typedef struct
{
    int     world_rank;
    char    first_name[MAX_NAME_LEN+1];
    char    last_name[MAX_NAME_LEN+1];
}   player_t;

/* Prototypes of player_t member functions */
void    read_player(player_t *ptr);
void    print_player(const player_t *ptr);

/* Prototypes of non-member functions */
void    getline(char string[],int maxlen);


int     main()

{
    player_t    player;

    read_player(&player);
    print_player(&player);
    return EX_OK;
}


/****************************************
 * Read a player's info into a structure
 ****************************************/

void    read_player(player_t *ptr)
```

```
{
    /* Input name */
    fputs("First name? ",stdout);
    getline(ptr->first_name,MAX_NAME_LEN);
    fputs("Last name? ",stdout);
    getline(ptr->last_name,MAX_NAME_LEN);

    /* Input ranking information */
    fputs("World rank? ",stdout);
    scanf("%d",&ptr->world_rank);
}



/**********************************
 * Print a player's info to stdout
 *********************************/

void    print_player(const player_t *ptr)

{
    printf("Name: %s %s    World rank: %d\n",
            ptr->first_name,ptr->last_name,
            ptr->world_rank);
}



/************************************
 * Input a string, and null terminate
 ***********************************/

void    getline(char string[],int maxlen)

{
    size_t  c = 0;

    /* Read up to newline or to array limit */
    while ( ((string[c] = getchar()) != '\n') &&
            (c < maxlen-1) )
        ++c;
```

```
        string[c] = '\0';    /* null terminate */
    }
```

Using encapsulation minimizes the number of functions that directly access the members of a particular structure. This tends to reduce the overall size and complexity of the program, and thus *minimizes the impact of making changes to the structure*. Programs that don't use encapsulation, but freely access structure members everywhere, will require extensive modification for even minor changes to the structure definition.

Example:

Suppose we changed the structure so that there was only one name member, instead of separate members for first and last names. All statements that access the members first_name and last_name will have to be edited to use the new combined member. If the access is restricted to member functions, then the number of changes necessary will be minimized.

A print_name() function for the structure with separate names would appear as follows:

```
void    print_name(player_t *ptr)

{
    printf("%s %s",
           player->first_name,player->last_name);
}
```

After the change to a single name member, the function would become:

```
void    print_name(player_t *ptr)

{
    fputs(player->full_name,stdout);
```

```
    }
```

In programs that use the structure type, there may be many calls such
as:

```
    print_name(&player);
```

Note that *none* of these calls will need to be edited! If we had not used
a member function to print the name, but instead had used `printf()`
directly throughout the program, the impact of the change could be
enormous: Every occurrence of printf() that accessed either `first_name`
or `last_name` would have to be updated. Instead, one simple change to
the member function `print_name()` did the trick.

As with any function, small member functions can be implemented using macros
to maximize performance. This will still utilize the concept of encapsulation by
eliminating direct references to structure members in your program.

Example:

Use a macro to print the name in a `player_t` structure.

```
    #define PRINT_NAME(player)\
        printf("%s %s",player.first_name,player.last_name)
```

Note that '\' characters are necessary after each line except the last in
order to continue the macro definition on the next line.

If the structure is later modified to use a full name member instead of
separate names, we can still use a PRINT_NAME() macro, following a
simple modification:

```
    #define PRINT_NAME(player)\
        fputs(player.full_name,stdout)
```

Many C compilers also support **inlining**, which can be used as an alternative to macros form enhancing the speed of programs that use small functions. Inlining is used heavily in C++ programs for small member functions. Note, however, that not all C compilers support this, so it may not improve performance on some systems.

The main focus of *C++* and *JAVA* programming is an extension to the structure, called a **class**. A class is very much like a structure, except that the member functions are explicitly bound to the class, and are called using a somewhat different syntax. Classes are described in chapter 30.

18.4   Nesting Structures

Structures can and often do contain other structures as members. Defining a structure with members that are also structures is called **nesting** structures.

Example:

The code below demonstrates how to define and use a simple nested structure.

```
typedef struct
{
    int     serve_percentage;
    int     aces;
    int     wins;
    int     losses;
}   stats_t;

typedef struct
{
    stats_t stats;  /* Nested structure */
    char    first_name[MAX_NAME_LEN+1];
    char    last_name[MAX_NAME_LEN+1];
}   player_t;

int     main()
```

```
    {
        player_t    player;

        ...

        printf("Aces = %d\n",player.stats.aces);
        ...
        return EX_OK;
    }
```

According to object oriented design methodology, each structure should have it's own set of member functions. Expressions such as `player.stats.aces` would violate the encapsulation principle, since the function that contains this statement is accessing the members of two different structure types, namely `player_t` and `stats_t`.

A common practice in C++ programming is the use of `get()` and `set()` member functions to access structure members from non-member functions. You can apply the same technique in C using functions or macros.

Example:

The program below uses get and set macros to access `stats_t` fields. As a result, `main()` does not access members of the `stats_t` structure directly. Hence, main() could be considered a member of the `player_t` type, since this is the only structure type whose members are accessed within `main()`.

```
    #define GET_ACES(stats)      ((stats).aces)
    #define SET_ACES(stats,r)    ((stats).aces = (r))

    int    main()

    {
        player_t    player;
```

```
          ...
       SET_ACES(player.stats,4);
       printf("Aces = %d\n",GET_ACES(player.stats));
          ...
    }
```

Like other member functions and macros, using `get()` and `set()` will minimize the number of changes needed in the program following changes to the structure.

Programming for Performance:

> If you use a function for `get()` or `set()` instead of a macro, it should be `inlined` if possible, to eliminate the overhead of calling such a trivial function.
>
> ```
> inline int      get_aces(stats_t &stats)
>
> {
>     return stats->aces;
> }
> ```
>
> Recall that the body of an inlined function is substituted for the function call, much like a macro. This eliminates the extra machine instructions needed by non-inlined functions to pass arguments, save and restore the return address, and branch to and from the function.

18.5   Lists of Structures

A linear list can be implemented using either a simple array, a linked list, or pointer array.

18.5.1 Arrays of Structures

Arrays are generally the easiest implementation, but they waste a lot of memory if the size of the list isn't known ahead of time. The whole array must be allocated at once, either automatically or using `malloc()` or `alloca()`, and must be made large enough for the largest possible list size. Arrays have the advantage of being **randomly accessible**, that is, you can access any element at any time, and the code for doing so is straightforward. Thus, using a simple array is easy and efficient in terms of CPU time, but possibly inefficient in terms of memory use.

To access the structures in an array, you'll need a subscript or pointer variable. The placement of the subscript is very important, since the subscript operator is always bound to the identifier to it's immediate left. Note that the subscript operator has a higher precedence than the structure binding operators. To subscript the array of structures, place the subscript on the name of the *structure array*. To subscript a member of the structure, place the subscript after the *member name*.

Example:

The function below demonstrates how to use subscripts with an array of `player_t` structures. The function assigns a null byte to the first character in the name of each player.

```
void    init_list(player_t players[])

{
    size_t  p;

    for (p=0; p<MAX_PLAYERS; ++p)
        players[p].name[0] = '\0';
}
```

Programming for Performance:

You may recall from chapter 15 that using subscripts slows down a program, since the address of each element must be computed at run time using the following formula:

$$address = base + subscript \times sizeof(type)$$

If the size of the type is a power of two, as is the case for built in types like `short`, `int`, `long`, and `double`, the multiplication can be achieved using a less expensive shift operation. The size of a structure type, however, is rarely a power of two, so an expensive multiply instruction is needed to compute the location of each element in an array of structures.

If you use a pointer, you can eliminate this expensive address computation:

```
#define MAX_PLAYERS 256

void    init_list(player_t players[])

{
    player_t    *p, *end = players+MAX_PLAYERS;

    /* Initialize names to null string */
    for (p = players; p < end; ++p)
        *p->name = '\0';
}
```

Note that the expression `*p->name` is equivalent to `p->name[0]`.

18.5.2   Linked Lists

A basic **linear linked list** is a data structure where each element contains a pointer to the next element. Variations on linear linked lists include **doubly linked lists**, where each element also points to the previous element, and **circular linked lists**, where the last element points back to the first. Non-linear linked lists include **trees** and **graphs**. Our discussion will be limited to the basic linear linked list. Extensive discussion of linked lists is a topic for a course in data structures. Figure 18.1 depicts a simple linear linked list.

Figure 18.1: A Linked List

Programming for Performance:

A major disadvantage of linked lists is that they can only be accessed *sequentially*. For example, to access the fifth element in a linked list, you have to start at the head, and then jump to the second, third and fourth on the way to the fifth. Another disadvantage is that code for working with linked lists tends to be complicated. Given the fact that programmer time is the most expensive aspect of software development, keeping things simple is generally the best approach, and thus, using linked lists should be avoided unless they can offer substantial benefits over other list implementations.

To implement a linked list, you need to define a **self-referencing structure**; a structure containing a pointer to another structure of the same type. The type definition of self-referencing structures has a hitch: Since the type name isn't given until *after* the structure definition, it can't be used to define a structure member. For example, the following structure definition is invalid, since it attempts to use list_t to define the member next before list_t has been defined.

```
typedef struct
{
    int     number;
    list_t  *next;
}   list_t;
```

You can use a structure tag to work around this problem:

```
typedef struct list list_t;
```

```
struct list
{
    int     number;
    list_t  *next;
};
```

This type definition is valid because the type **struct list** is unambiguous, even though the structure has not been defined yet. The compiler only needs to know that it's a structure in order to define the type list_t.

To define a linked list, you need a special pointer to the first element, called the **head** pointer. The head pointer points to the first element in the list. The first element then points to the second, the second points to the third, and so on. The last element usually has its **next** pointer set to NULL.

New elements can be added at any point, but the simplest and most efficient method is to insert them at the head. Adding new nodes to the end, or anywhere between existing nodes, requires scanning through the list to *find* the correct position, which introduces an extra loop into your program. If the new nodes *must* be added to the end, a pointer to the **tail** should be maintained in addition to the head pointer, to eliminate the need to loop through the list every time a new node is added.

Example:

> The program below inputs records and stores them in a linked list. It then prints the contents of the list. This example uses an exceedingly simple structure. Linked lists are usually used only for lists of much larger structures, to minimize the cost of the extra pointer that goes with every element. A linked list of integers, for example, is about twice the size of an array of integers, since each element consists of both an integer and a pointer. This makes the array implementation much more attractive. On the other hand, for a structure of 100 bytes or more, adding a four or eight byte pointer does not significantly increase the structure size.
>
> ```
> #include <stdio.h>
> #include <sysexits.h>
> ```

```
#include <stdlib.h>

#define MAX_NAME_LEN    40

/* Safe memory allocation */
#define MALLOC(nelem,type)  malloc(nelem*sizeof(type))

/* Player structure */
typedef struct player player_t;
struct player
{
    int         world_rank;
    char        first_name[MAX_NAME_LEN+1];
    char        last_name[MAX_NAME_LEN+1];
    player_t    *next;
};

/* Prototypes */
player_t  *read_list(void);
void    print_list(player_t *);
void    free_list(player_t **);

int     main()

{
    player_t  *head = NULL;

    head = read_list();
    print_list(head);
    free_list(&head);
    return EX_OK;
}


/*
 * Read a list into a linked list,
 * and return a pointer to head.
 */
```

```
player_t  *read_list()

{
    player_t  *temp, *head = NULL, new_player;

    while ( scanf("%s %s %d",new_player.first_name,
                    new_player.last_name,
                    &new_player.world_rank) == 3 )
    {
        /* Allocate memory for new node */
        temp = (player_t *)MALLOC(1,player_t);

        *temp = new_player; /* Copy to allocated node */
        temp->next = head;  /* Point new head to old */
        head = temp;        /* New node is new head */
    }
    return head;
}


/*
 * Print the contents of a linked list.
 */

void    print_list(player_t *ptr)

{
    /* Start at head and stop at NULL pointer */
    while ( ptr != NULL )
    {
        printf("%s %s %d\n",ptr->first_name,
                            ptr->last_name,
                            ptr->world_rank);
        ptr = ptr->next;
    }
}

/*
 * Free all nodes in the list
```

```
    */

    void    free_list(player_t **head)

{
    player_t    *dead_head = *head,
                *next_node = *head;

    /* Start at head and stop at NULL pointer */
    while ( next_node != NULL )
    {
        next_node = dead_head->next;
        free(dead_head);
        dead_head = next_node;
    }

    /* Mark list as empty */
    *head = NULL;
}
```

As described in chapter 16, there is a high cost to allocating nodes one at a time, since the `malloc()` and `free()` functions must maintain a table to manage the heap. Efficiency may also be degraded due to the sequential nature of linked lists. If the program needs to access list elements in random order, then using a linked list will require a loop for each node accessed. Using an array will eliminate the need to search through the list for the desired location, and greatly improve the speed of the program.

18.5.3 Pointer Arrays

Pointer arrays combine the ease of use and random accessibility of an array with the minimal memory use of a linked list. Each node can be allocated individually as needed, in order to minimize memory use. Note, however, that doing so will incur the same memory allocation costs as linked lists. Once the list is allocated, however, you can access any node randomly, just like an ordinary array. Referencing an object through a pointer array is slightly slower than an ordinary array, due to

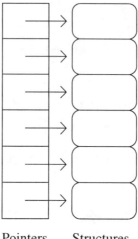

Pointers   Structures

Figure 18.2: A Structure Pointer Array

the cost of dereferencing the pointer. This difference is rarely noticeable, however, so performance of a pointer array is generally about the same as a simple array.

Example:

The program below reads a list of records into a pointer array, as depicted in figure 18.2, and then prints the list on the standard output.

The `read_list()` function shows how to access list elements using subscripts to a pointer array, while the `print_list()` and `free_list()` functions access the members using a pointer to the pointer array for better efficiency.

```
#include <stdio.h>
#include <sysexits.h>
#include <stdlib.h>
#include <unistd.h>

#define MAX_NAME_LEN    40

/* Use a generous list size - they're only pointers */
#define MAX_LIST_SIZE    1000
```

```
/* Safe memory allocation */
#define MALLOC(nelem,type)  malloc(nelem*sizeof(type))

/* Player structure */
typedef struct
{
    int         world_rank;
    char        first_name[MAX_NAME_LEN+1];
    char        last_name[MAX_NAME_LEN+1];
}   player_t;

/* Prototypes */
void    read_list(player_t *list[]);
void    print_list(player_t *list[]);
void    free_list(player_t *list[]);

int     main()

{
    player_t  *list[MAX_LIST_SIZE];

    read_list(list);
    print_list(list);
    free_list(list);
    return EX_OK;
}




/**************************************************
 * Read a list of inventory items into a pointer
 * array.  Mark the end of * the list with NULL.
 **************************************************/

void    read_list(player_t *list[])

{
    player_t    new_player;
    int         list_size, c = 0;
```

```c
    /* Read list items until EOF (ctrl+D) */
    for (list_size=0; c != EOF; ++list_size)
    {
        /* If input from keyboard, prompt user */
        if ( isatty(fileno(stdin)) )
        {
            fputs("Enter player number and name",stdout);
            puts(" or <ctrl>+D when finished.");
        }

        /* Input a record */
        c = scanf("%s %s %d",
                    new_player.first_name,
                    new_player.last_name,
                    &new_player.world_rank);

        /* If valid entry, add to list */
        switch(c)
        {
            case    3:
                list[list_size] =
                    (player_t *)MALLOC(1,player_t);
                *list[list_size] = new_player;
                break;
            case    EOF:
                break;
            default:
                fprintf(stderr,"Invalid entry.");
        }
    }

    /* Mark end of list */
    list[list_size-1] = NULL;
}


/*****************************************
 * Print list contained in pointer array.
```

```
                   ****************************************/

    void     print_list(player_t *list[])

    {
        player_t  **p;

        for (p = list; *p != NULL; ++p)
        {
            printf("%s %s %d\n",
                    (*p)->first_name,
                    (*p)->last_name,
                    (*p)->world_rank);
        }
    }


    /***********
     * Free list
     ***********/

    void     free_list(player_t *list[])

    {
        player_t  **p;

        for (p=list; *p != NULL; ++p)
            free(*p);
    }
```

18.6 Initializing Structures

Structure initializations work much like array initializations. Simply enclose a comma-separated list of initial values in braces following the variable definition, as shown below.

```
typedef struct
{
    int     world_rank;
    char    first_name[MAX_NAME_LEN+1];
    char    last_name[MAX_NAME_LEN+1];
}   player_t;

int     main()

{
    player_t player = { 1, "Pete", "Sampras" };
    ...

    return EX_OK;
}
```

K&R compilers technically cannot initialize `auto` structure variables. However, most K&R compilers have extensions beyond the K&R standard, so this may not apply to your compiler. If your compiler doesn't support this feature for `auto` variables, you can make the variable `static`, provided this won't require too much memory. Otherwise, an initialization member function can be used.

```
    init_player(&player,1,"Pete","Sampras");
```

Arrays of structures can be initialized by using nested groups of braces, as follows:

```
player_t    player[] =
            {
                {1, "Pete", "Sampras"},
                {2, "Michael", "Chang"}
            };
```

Similarly, nested structure initializations use nested braces to enclose the nested member data:

```
typedef struct
{
    int     rank;
    int     serve_percentage;
}   stats_t;

typedef struct
{
    stats_t stats;
    char    first_name[MAX_NAME_LEN+1];
    char    last_name[MAX_NAME_LEN+1];
}   player_t;

int     main()

{
    player_t    player =
                    {{1, 56}, "Pete", "Sampras"};
    ...
}
```

18.7   Advanced: Unions

A **union** is a block of memory with multiple names and data types. The definition of a union looks much like the definition of a structure, but the effect is very different.

With a structure, each member has it's own memory location. With a union, however, all the members share *the same memory location.*

Unions are used primarily for two purposes:

- To subdivide a large object into several smaller ones

- To conserve memory

18.7.1   Unions for Subdividing Objects

Unions can used to subdivide a large object into smaller ones in order to extract or set portions of the object. For example, consider the following union:

```
typedef union
{
    long    longword;
    char    bytes[4];
}   split_t;
```

The members `longword` and `bytes` share the same memory location, so each element in the array `bytes` is actually one of the 4 bytes in `longword`.

The problem with this union is that you can't be certain which element of `bytes` corresponds to which byte of `longword`, because it depends of the type of machine. On a **big-endian** machine, the higher order bits of a word (the big end) are stored at the lowest address. For example, if a `long` is stored at address 100, then bits 24-31 of the `long` are at address 100, bits 16-23 are at 101, bits 8-15 are at 102, and bits 0-7 are at address 103. On a **little-endian** machine, the lower bits are at the lowest address.

Hence, `bytes[0]` in the union above may represent either bits 0-7 or bits 24-31 of `longword`.

This is actually a portable way for a program to find out if it is running in a big-endian or little-endian machine. If you load the value 1 into `longword`, then bit 0 will be set to 1, and the rest will be 0. On a little-endian machine, `bytes[0]` will be 1, and the rest will be 0. In a big-endian machine, `bytes[3]` will be 1, and the rest will be zero.

```
#define LITTLE_ENDIAN    endian_check.bytes[0]
#define BIG_ENDIAN       endian_check.bytes[3]

split_t endian_check;

endian_check.longword = 1;

if ( BIG_ENDIAN )
```

. . .

If you need to reference specific bits of an integer value, this should be done using the bitwise operators. For example, to extract the lowest and second lowest bytes of a longword, you could use the bitwise AND and shift operators as follows:

```
long    longword;

printf("The low byte is: %d\n",
        longword & 0x000000ff);
printf("The second lowest byte is %d.\n",
        (longword & 0x0000ff00) >> 8);
```

The bitwise operators are guaranteed by the C standard to treat the left operand (longword in this case) as a binary integer value, so >> will shift bits toward the low order end whether the machine is big-endian or little endian. The mask values used with the & operator are integer constants, so the rightmost digits are guaranteed to be the lower bits.

18.7.2 Unions for Conserving Memory

Unions are used to conserve memory in situations where there are unused variables or structure members in certain circumstances, and there are large amounts of data to store. For example, suppose we maintain a large inventory of clothing. For each clothing item, we would use a structure variable to hold the features. All items will have many common properties, such as color, cost, retail price, brand name, and so on. However, some items will have features not used by others. For example, mens jeans use waist and inseam to specify size, while womens jeans might use a simple integer to specify size. We could define the structure as follows:

```
typedef struct
{
    double  cost;
    double  retail;
    gen_t   gender;
    int     womens_size;
```

```
        int     inseam;
        int     waist;
        char    brand[MAX_NAME_LEN+1];
    }   jeans_t;
```

The size would then be shown as follows:

```
    jeans_t jeans;

    if ( jeans.gender == MENS )
        printf("Size: %d waist x %d inseam.\n",
               jeans.waist,jeans.inseam);
    else
        printf("Size: %d.\n",jeans.womens_size);
```

For variables that describe womens' jeans, the members `inseam` and `waist` are not used. For mens' jeans, the member `womens_size` is not used. If there are a large number of items in the inventory, the wasted memory can be significant. We can reduce the size of the structure by nesting a union inside the structure, so that two of the fields can share the same memory space.

```
    typedef struct
    {
        double  cost;
        double  retail;
        gen_t   gender;
        union
        {
            int     womens_size;
            struct
            {
                int     inseam;
                int     waist;
            }   mens_size;
        }   size;
        char    brand[MAX_NAME_LEN+1];
```

```
}   jeans_t;
```

The size would then be shown as follows:

```
jeans_t jeans;

if ( jeans.gender == MENS )
    printf("Size: %d waist x %d inseam.\n",
            jeans.size.mens_size.waist,
            jeans.size.mens_size.inseam);
else
    printf("Size: %d.\n",jeans.size.womens_size);
```

Note that this example *does not* use encapsulation, and should be rewritten using get() and set() functions to make it more modifiable. It is only presented this way to demonstrate the use of unions in the simplest possible way.

An **anonymous union** is a union within a structure which doesn't have a name. The members of an anonymous union are referenced as members of the structure in which the union is nested. Anonymous unions are useful to simplifying the code by reducing the number of identifiers in a structure reference. For example, if we use an anonymous union for the structure above, we could eliminate the name size from all references to inseam, waist, and womens_size.

```
typedef struct
{
    double  cost;
    double  retail;
    gen_t   gender;
    union
    {
        int     womens_size;
        struct
        {
            int     inseam;
            int     waist;
        } mens_size;
```

```
        };
        char    brand[MAX_NAME_LEN+1];
}    jeans_t;
```

The size would then be shown as follows:

```
jeans_t jeans;

if ( jeans.gender == MENS )
    printf("Size: %d waist x %d inseam.\n",
            jeans.mens_size.waist,jeans.mens_size.inseam);
else
    printf("Size: %d.\n",jeans.womens_size);
```

18.8   Advanced: Structure Alignment

Structure members, like all other variables, are aligned on appropriate word boundaries either out of necessity or to maximize efficiency of memory access. This is due to the fact that many computers can really only access memory in 4 byte chunks. If a single byte is read from memory location 5 on a 32 bit machine, for example, the hardware actually reads addresses 4 through 7, and throws away the three unwanted bytes. If a longword is read from address 5, then the longwords at addresses 4 and 8 must both be read, bytes 5 through 8 are pasted together, and bytes 4, 9, 10, and 11 are thrown away. Moreover, many RISC computers *require* all longwords to be located at longword boundaries, i.e. addresses which are a multiple of 4.

As a result, some structures have to be **padded** with unused space between members, so that each member is properly aligned. Furthermore, the size of a structure is generally rounded up to the next longword boundary, so that the next variable in memory begins at a longword boundary. Any time a member with a larger data type follows a member with a smaller data type, chances are padding will be required. For example, if a `long` member follows a `char` or `char` array which doesn't end on a longword boundary, padding will be used to ensure the `long` is properly aligned.

Since the order of the members within a structure may be important, compilers will not rearrange members to minimize the structure size. Some optimizers are capable of doing this, but only if given permission through the use of #pragma, or special compiler switches.

By arranging the members of a structure carefully, you can minimize the size of each structure, by reducing or eliminating the need for padding between members. The general rule of thumb for arranging structure members is *put the larger data types first.*

Note that we are referring to the size of the *data type*, not the size of the object. For example, a string should generally come *after* a long, since char is smaller than long, even though the string itself is probably much larger than a long.

Example:

Consider the following structure:

```
typedef struct
{
    char     home_runs;
    float    average;
    char     hits;
}   stats_t;
```

Three bytes of padding are needed after the member home_runs in order to align the member average on a float boundary. (Recall that the size of a float is usually 4 bytes) Assuming a 32 bit machine, three more bytes of padding will be placed after the member hits to round to entire structure up to a longword boundary, so the total size of the structure is twelve bytes, even though only 6 bytes are actually used.

Figure 18.3 shows the memory alignment of the stats_t structure for a variable beginning at memory address 1000.

If you rearrange the members, you can reduce the size of the structure significantly:

```
typedef struct
{
    float    average;
```

Address	Used for
1000	home_runs
1001	padding
1002	padding
1003	padding
1004	average
1005	average
1006	average
1007	average
1008	hits
1009	padding
1009	padding
1009	padding

Figure 18.3: Structure alignment

```
    char     home_runs;
    char     hits;
}   stats_t;
```

Char members don't need to be aligned, so no padding is needed between the members. Two padding bytes are placed after hits to round the structure size up to a longword boundary, but we can't do any better than this. The rearranged structure, therefore, requires 8 bytes, instead of 12 as did the previous arrangement. In a list of 1,000,000 such structures, the latter arrangement will save four megabytes of memory. Figure 18.4 shows the alignment of this optimal version for a structure variable beginning at memory address 1000.

One further note about structure padding: Different computers may have different boundary requirements for objects such as shorts and doubles. As a result, the same structure may be aligned differently by different compilers.

If a structure is *dumped* to a file in binary format using write() or fwrite(), the actual format can vary from one computer to another. If you want such binary files to be portable from one computer to another, great care must be taken to ensure the structure alignment is the same in all cases. This can often be done using explicit

Address	Used for
1000	average
1001	average
1002	average
1003	average
1004	home_runs
1005	hits
1006	padding
1007	padding

Figure 18.4: Structure alignment

padding, i.e. defining `char` members between fields to force padding, or by using the #pragma directive to control how structure alignment is performed by a particular compiler. See your compiler documentation for information on using the #pragma directive.

18.9 Advanced: Bit Fields

Structure members in C can actually be defined as virtually any number of *bits*, within the limit of the largest available integer type.

This can be used to access a particular group of bits within a larger value by name, as opposed to extracting them using bitwise operators.

Bit fields can also be used to conserve memory where large arrays of structures are used.

Programming for Performance:

> Keep in mind that accessing bit fields requires some extra work with bit instructions behind the scenes, so the program will be somewhat slower than one that uses whole integer structure members. Unless you are working with a large list of objects, using bit fields may not improve the situation.

To align bit fields, the compiler packs as many consecutive members as possible into each word, but does not allow any bit field member to cross a word boundary. The boundaries are determined by the type used to define the bit field. The types are usually unsigned integer types.

As with all structures, the arrangement of the bits fields can affect the total size of the structure.

Example:

Consider the following structure template:

```
typedef struct
{
    unsigned short  a : 4;
    unsigned short  b : 3;
    unsigned short  c : 10;
    unsigned short  d : 7;
}   example_t;
```

The members a and b will be contained in the first short word, followed by nine bits of padding to fill out the first `short`. The member c will be in the second short word followed by six bits of padding. The member d will be in the third short word, followed by another nine bits of padding. The total structure size is therefore six bytes.

If you rearrange the fields, you can reduce the amount of padding needed:

```
typedef struct
{
    unsigned short  a : 4;
    unsigned short  b : 3;
    unsigned short  d : 7;
    unsigned short  c : 10;
}   example_t;
```

This arrangement can pack members a, b, and d all into the first short word, followed by two bits of padding. The member c occupies the second `short`, followed by six bits of padding. The total structure size is thus only four bytes instead of six.

Chapter 19

Debugging

Before you begin...

> You should be familiar with the material on functions presented in chapter 11.

Of all the phases of programming (planning, coding, debugging, testing), debugging is probably the most time consuming and intellectually difficult. Debugging is both an art and an experimental science, where the programmer must determine the cause behind often vague or misleading outward signs of trouble.

Debugging techniques fall into one of a few general categories:

- Good old fashioned thinking.

- Code manipulation and experimentation.

- Use of a **debugger**, a program designed specifically for debugging other programs.

Regardless of the technique used, debugging is a two-step process:

1. It is extremely important to focus the initial effort on determining *where* the problem is. If a program is producing incorrect output, there could be many

potential causes. In a large program with many variables, there are too many possible points of failure to consider. Hence, it's important to narrow down the search to the smallest possible segment of code.

2. Once the location of the bug has been determined, it will be easier to identify *what* the problem is, and come up with a solution.

19.1 Thinkin' it Through

The first step in any debugging session is to consider carefully how the program is misbehaving, and from these outward signs, try to determine *where* in the program the problem may be. If you know the code well, it will often be obvious where the problem is, as soon as you look at the program output. For example, if a selection sort program (see section 16.5) is printing the list in descending order when you wanted ascending, then odds are the problem is with the `findlow()` function giving you the largest value instead of the smallest.

If a program crashes, you can often get an idea where it went awry by noting what was the last thing the program did successfully, and then tracing through the code up to that point.

Other times, particularly when debugging unfamiliar code, figuring out where to look for the problem is half the battle. In these cases, you will probably need to resort to other techniques to give you some clues about where the problem lies.

19.2 Making Programs Talk: Debug Code

We need to consider how to get more information out of a program, when the normal output isn't providing enough clues about where the problem might be.

The age-old and still common technique of adding output statements is one you can always count on. This technique uses functions like `fputs()` and `fprintf()` to display intermediate results of the program's work, so that you can track its progress and determine where the problem is occurring.

Debug statements may simply tell you that the program has made it to a certain point in its execution path, or may print the values of some key variables that you suspect might contain faulty information. Sometimes it's even helpful to print the values of some variables that you *don't* expect to be faulty or enlightening. You never know what they might tell you, until you take a look.

Pitfall: Lost Debug Output

All debugging output should be sent to `stderr`, not stdout. Output sent to `stdout` is normally line buffered, and may not make it to your screen if the program crashes, even though the output statements may have been executed. Thus, you may be misled about where the program is crashing if you use `printf()` or `puts()` to print debug output. If you use `stdout`, you'll need to use `fflush()` immediately after the debug output statement, so that the output will appear on your screen before the program proceeds any further.

```
puts("Back from sort_list().");
fflush(stdout);
```

Using `stderr` makes this unnecessary, since `stderr` is normally unbuffered, i.e. all output sent to `stderr` is *immediately* written to the screen.

```
fputs("Back from sort_list().\n",stderr);
```

Example:

The program below crashes before producing any output.

```
int     main()

{
    size_t      list_size;
    widget_t    list[MAX_WIDGETS];

    list_size = read_list(list,MAX_WIDGETS);
    sort_list(list,list_size);
```

```
      print_list(list,list_size);
      return 0;
}

   ...
```

In order to determine where the problem is, we can add some debugging
code, as follows:

```
int      main()

{
    size_t       list_size;
    widget_t     list[MAX_WIDGETS];

    list_size = read_list(list,MAX_WIDGETS);

    /* Debug output for read_list */
    fputs("Back from read_list().\n",stderr);
    fprintf(stderr,"list_size = %d\n",list_size);
    printf("Raw list is:\n");
    print_list(list,list_size);
    fflush(stdout);

    sort_list(list,list_size);

    /* See if sort_list survived */
    fputs("Back from sort_list.\n",stderr);

    print_list(list,list_size);
    return 0;
}

   ...
```

If you don't want debugging code to bog down your program, you can
use **#if** or **#ifdef** to turn it on or off, as discussed in section 13.4.1.

```
int     main()

{
    size_t      list_size;
    widget_t    list[MAX_WIDGETS];

    list_size = read_list(list,MAX_WIDGETS);

#ifdef DEBUG
    /* Debug output for read_list */
    fprintf(stderr,"Back from read_list.\n");
    fprintf(stderr,"list_size = %d\n",list_size);
    printf("Raw list is:\n");
    print_list(list,list_size);
    fflush(stdout);
#endif

    sort_list(list,list_size);

#ifdef DEBUG
    /* See if sort_list survived */
    fprintf(stderr,"Back from sort_list.\n");
#endif

    print_list(list,list_size);
    return 0;
}

    ...
```

As an alternative to using preprocessor directives, some programs use C `if` statements to control debugging code. When used in conjunction with a command-line switch, these can be used to turn debugging code on or off *without recompiling*. An example of this is presented in section 16.6.

19.3   Unix Debuggers: Which One?

19.3.1   Debugger Features

A popular alternative to inserting debugging code into programs is using a **debugger**, a special program designed to test and analyze other programs. Using a debugger, you can control and examine your program's operation *without* adding any code, and in most cases, without recompiling it. Debuggers can read, understand, and control other programs, often making use of extra information inserted by the compiler.

Unfortunately, Unix debuggers don't follow any well-defined standards such as the ANSI C standard or the POSIX operating system standard. Hence, each Unix system has it's own debugger with features and an interface that may be vastly different from the rest. Nevertheless, most debuggers offer a certain set of common features, regardless of the platform or language. We'll discuss a few of these features below.

Breakpoints are stopping points that can be introduced into a program using a debugger. When a breakpoint is established, and the program is executed *under the debugger's control*, the program will stop at the breakpoint, and control returns to the debugger. You then usually have the option of resuming the program from the breakpoint using further debugger commands, if desired.

Tracebacks show the function call sequence up to the point where a process terminated. Some tracebacks also state the exact line in the source code where the termination occurred. Tracebacks are most commonly used with a **core** file, which is often produced when a program crashes. The core file contains an image of the process' memory contents at the time of a program crash. This includes the system stack, which contains the return addresses of each function in a calling sequence up to the point where the crash occurred. Thus, the traceback can show which function the program was executing when it crashed, and all the function calls leading to it from `main()`.

Variable watching allows the debugger to peek at the contents of particular variables, provided the memory address of the variable is known. Some debuggers allow variables to be watched while the program is running, while others allow this at breakpoints or after program termination.

In order to fully utilize a Unix debugger, each source file to be debugged must be compiled with the "-g" option. This option instructs the compiler to include vital information in the executable file that the debugger can use to provide you with usable feedback.

19.3.2 Types of Debuggers

Symbolic debuggers make use of the **symbol table** included in the executable file, which states the relative address within the program of each `external` identifier. This generally includes all functions and `static` variables. `Auto` variables reside on the stack, and their actual memory address may be different each time the function is called. Thus, these addresses cannot be determined at compile time, and are not included in the standard symbol table. Nevertheless, some debuggers allow you to check the values of auto variables, provided the block they are defined in is active. (So that the variables are actually allocated space on the stack at that moment) Symbolic debuggers can typically help you pinpoint problems to a particular function, although not to the exact line of source code.

Source-level debuggers provide more detailed information with respect to the program source code. In addition to a symbol table, source-level debuggers require, at the least, a **line-number map**, which can be used to determine the source filename and line within the source file for every instruction in the executable. Tracebacks in source-level debuggers will often show the exact line of code where a crash occurred. In addition, some source level debuggers allow you to visually step through a program, essentially watching the source code statements being executed one by one.

As mentioned earlier, there are many different debuggers available on different Unix platforms, and in some cases, many debuggers for the same platform.

Section 19.4 introduces you to `gdb`, the GNU debugger. We discuss `gdb` because it is the only debugger available for virtually *all* Unix platforms, and because it has a fairly complete set of features to explore. Note that there some commercial debuggers are much easier to use than `gdb`, since they may provide a menu-driven interface. Some may also provide capabilities not found in `gdb`. Whatever flavor of Unix you use, it will be worth your while to explore the features of it's debuggers.

Pitfall: Compiler-Debugger Compatibility

> If you install a second compiler, such as **gcc**, or a second debugger, such
> as **gdb** on your system, you need to be careful about mixing them with
> the native tools. Proper debugging requires a high level of compatibility
> between the information produced by the compiler and that which is
> understood by the debugger. Your native debugger may not understand
> all the code and tables produced by **gcc**, and likewise, **gdb** may not
> understand all the output of your native compiler. Whatever compiler
> and debugger you use, make sure they are part of the same system, and
> you'll avoid a lot of headaches.

19.4   The GNU Debugger: gdb

The GNU debugger, **gdb**, is a command-driven, source-level debugger which can be
used in conjunction with any GNU compiler, such as **gcc**, **g++**, or **g77**. This section
introduces some of the common uses for **gdb**. More detailed information can be
found in the **gdb** man page, or by looking up **gdb** under the **GNU** **info** help facility.
For a quick reference to commands, you can also type **help** at the **gdb** prompt.

19.4.1   Running Programs under gdb

There are two common ways to use debuggers such as **gdb**. One is to enter the
debugger environment and run your program under the debugger's control. The
other, discussed in section 19.4.2 is to make use of the *core* file produced by Unix
when a program crashes.

To run your program under **gdb**, simply run **gdb** with the name of your program as
an argument. For example, if the program *sort.c* were compiled to an executable
named *sort*, then the following command would be appropriate:

```
tcsh 1: gdb sort
```

This will place you into the debugger's command interpreter, where you can now test the program under gdb's control by entering commands at the (gdb) prompt.

Perhaps the most important command to know when learning gdb is help:

```
(gdb) help
```

Gdb uses a command-driven interface, which is not as easy for beginners as a menu-driven system would be. Hence, it is important to know where to get information *quickly* when you need it. The help command will provide a brief synopsis of each gdb command, which is often enough, once you know the basics of how the debugger works. If more information is needed, you can always refer to the man page or use info.

Running your Program

To run your program under gdb, simply type run, followed by any command line arguments you wish to pass to the program.

```
(gdb) run arguments
```

This will execute the program under the watchful eye of gdb. If the program crashes or is stopped (by you), gdb will be able to provide information about the program's execution.

Setting Break Points

To set a break point in your program, use the break command, followed by a function name.

Example:

Suppose you want to see if the sort program is getting through the read_list() function successfully. This could be done by setting a break point at the *next* function call following read_list():

```
(gdb) break sort_list
Breakpoint 1 at 0x168c: file sort.c, line 51
```

This will cause the program to stop at the call to `sort_list()`. After the program stops at the first break point, you can continue execution using the `continue` command.

Break points are often useful in determining where a program is running into trouble. To do so, place a break point at or before a suspected problem area, and then run the program. If the program reaches the breakpoint without incident, place another breakpoint further along the execution path, and run it again.

```
(gdb) break sort_list
Breakpoint 1 at 0x168c: file sort.c, line 51
(gdb) break print_list
Breakpoint 2 at 0x17b6: file sort.c, line 68
(gdb) run
1 6 3 9
<ctrl+D>
Breakpoint 1, sort_list (list=0xefbfb808, list_size=4)
at sort.c:51
51  for (start=0; start<list_size; ++start)
(gdb) continue
Breakpoint 2, print_list (list=0xefbfb808, list_size=4)
at sort.c:68
68  for (c=0; c<list_size; ++c)
```

Continue adding breakpoints until the problem manifests itself. The problem must then be between the last two breakpoints.

To remove break points that are no longer needed, use the `clear` command:

```
(gdb) clear sort_list
Deleted breakpoint 1
```

The program will no longer stop at the first breakpoint, so you won't need to use `continue`.

Break points can also be used to stop the program for the purpose of examining some of it's variables using other **gdb** commands. Note in the example above that gdb displays the source code of the line where the break occurred, and the values of formal argument variables within the block.

To exit **gdb**, type `quit`.

Tip of the trade: Abbreviations for two-finger Typists

Gdb, like many other interactive Unix programs, accepts abbreviated commands. When entering any command at the gdb prompt, you really only need to type as many letters as needed to distinguish it from other **gdb** commands. For example, run can be abbreviated as r, since it's the only command beginning with 'r'. Similarly, `continue` can be abbreviated `cont`.

19.4.2 Using the *core* File

A **core** file contains a snapshot of a process' memory contents at the time it was terminated by Unix due to a segmentation fault, bus error, or other unrecoverable error.[1] Core dumps can also be produced intentionally using the **abort()** function.

The most common name for a core file is *core*. Some systems have expanded on this to prevent the core dumps of one process from overwriting previous core files. For example, *FreeBSD* core dumps are given the name *program.core*, where *program* is the name of the executable file that crashed. *DEC Unix* takes this a step further by adding the host name to the core filename. This is helpful on systems that support NFS (Network File Systems) because two different Unix hosts with access to the same server disk may dump core files in the same directory.

The most common use of a core file is to determine the location of the statement that caused the program to crash. You could attempt to reproduce the problem by

---

[1]The man page on `signal()` lists the error conditions that normal result in a core dump.

running the program again under gdb with the same input, but there is no guarantee the problem will occur again. For example, the problem may have been caused by an uninitialized variable, which would contain different garbage values each time the program is run. The program may crash on some garbage values but not others. The core file, on the other hand, provides information on the most recent execution that *did* have a problem, so there is no need to make it happen again.

Example:

Suppose the sort program above crashed and produced a core file while *not* running under gdb. In order to make this happen, we changed line 58 of the program to:

```
list[100000000] = temp;
```

This causes a segmentation fault or bus error[2], accompanied by a core dump, since 100000000 is well beyond the bounds of the array list.

You can load the program *and* core file into the debugger as follows:

```
tcsh 1: gdb sort core
```

On *FreeBSD* systems, this would be:

```
tcsh 1: gdb sort sort.core
Core was generated by 'sort'.
Program terminated with signal 10, Bus error.
#0 0x1786 in sort_list (list=0xefbfb820, list_size=4)
at sort.c:58
58   list[100000000] = temp
```

Note that the exact line number where the problem occurred is immediately displayed.

Once inside gdb, you can use the **where** command to trace the function calls from the point of failure back to main().

---

[2]Both of these errors result from the program referencing an invalid memory address.

```
tcsh 1: gdb sort core
Core was generated by 'sort'.
Program terminated with signal 10, Bus error.
#0  0x1786 in sort_list (list=0xefbfb820, list_size=4)
at sort.c:58
58                  list[10000000] = temp;
(gdb) where
#0  0x1786 in sort_list (list=0xefbfb820, list_size=4)
at sort.c:58
#1  0xefbfd78c in end ()
#2  0x1607 in main (argc=1, argv=0xefbfd78c)
at sort.c:27
```

Most debuggers have the equivalent of a **where** command, although it may be under a different name. Under **gdb**, for example, the **where** command is a synonym for **backtrace**. Other debuggers may use **traceback**, or just **t**.

Core files have many other uses in addition to performing a backtrace. For more information, consult your debugger's documentation.

Part III

Unix Library Functions and Their Use

Any experienced C programmer can tell you that libraries are central to all C programming. The C language itself is actually very small, with only about 30 keywords. The design of C follows a minimalist approach, placing only what's necessary into the language so that it remains simple and efficient. Anything that could be handled by a function was left out of the language, so that it wouldn't bog down the compiler.

Even common features such as I/O and string handling proved to be unnecessary for the compiler to handle, and are handled by library functions instead.

Implementing a feature as a library function rather than a built-in language component has several advantages:

- It's one less item for the compiler to recognize and process, so the compiler remains simple.

- All functions share a common interface, which reduces the learning curve for new users.

- If a feature proves inadequate in any way, it's easy to replace, since no changes to the compiler are required.

The standard C libraries have grown and evolved immensely since C was conceived in the early 1970's. Today, a typical C compiler comes with thousands of library functions, which perform a wide variety of tasks, such as I/O, mathematical computations, database management, graphics, and much more.

This part describes how to build libraries under Unix, and provides an overview of the standard libraries. The Unix libraries contain many more functions than can possibly be covered in detail in any single book. The goal here is not to describe each of the thousands of functions, but to provide you with an understanding of the major areas covered by the Unix libraries, so that you can become **self-sufficient**. Each major group of library functions is discussed, and the most common functions are outlined in a clear and simple manner.

The ultimate source of information on Unix library functions is the online manuals, accessed via the `man` command. Here you'll find all the details on each function. However, man pages are often a poor source of information for beginners: They tend to contain far too much detail to sift through, assume the reader is knowledgeable on the subject, lack code examples, and are very often just poorly written.

This part of the text is meant to serve as a starting point, which will provide you with a basic understanding of topics like process control, I/O, and device control, and the associated library functions. You will then be better prepared to comprehend and utilize the man pages effectively, if you need to dig deeper into the subject. In many cases, this text and the man pages will be the only references you need. A few topics, however, such as X Windows programming and networking, may require a separate, specialized text dedicated to the subject, particularly if you intend to program in one of these areas for a living.

Chapter 20

Building Object Code Libraries

Before you begin...

You should be familiar with the material on functions presented in chapter 11.

20.1   Working with Libraries

20.1.1   Creating Libraries

Every time you write a new function, you have a choice:

1. Add the function to the current program.

2. Add the function to a library.

Whenever possible, new functions should be placed in a library instead of directly in the program, so that they will be readily available to future programs. Unfortunately, many programmers don't know how, or don't think to do this, and as a result, thousands of functions are either pasted into new programs and recompiled, or completely rewritten.

The cost of maintaining redundant source code is time and money down the drain. The more redundant code you produce, the lower your productivity drops as time goes by. If, on the other hand, you get in the habit of building personal libraries, your productivity will *increase* over time, and your job will be much more interesting, since you'll be working on new things rather than reinventing the wheel and maintaining redundant code.

20.1.2   Static or Dynamic?

There are two types of libraries:

Static libraries are archives of object files which are searched by the linker (the last phase of compilation). The object file containing the function of interest is extracted from the archive and inserted into the executable file by the linker.

Dynamic libraries, also called **shared object** libraries in the Unix world, are also archives of object files, but are linked in a different way. When you compile a program to use shared objects, the linker does not insert the object file into the executable file. Instead, it merely inserts a tag which instructs the **loader** to find the object file at runtime. This results in smaller executable files, and can save a lot of disk space, since the same library functions are not being redundantly inserted into every executable file that uses them. Dynamic libraries can also save memory, since shared objects can even be shared by processes *after* they've been loaded into memory. When a process requests a shared object, the system can first check to see if it has already been loaded into memory by another process, and thus avoid unnecessary I/O.

Dynamic libraries have some disadvantages as well. For one thing, linking programs at run time creates extra overhead for the system, and leads to slower program startup, since the program must now be pieced together from several sources. One popular shared object format, called ELF (Extended Link Format), has earned the nickname "Expensive Link Format" as a result of it's high overhead costs.

Another problem with shared objects is that the shared object libraries must be present on every system along with the programs that use them. This doesn't present a problem with the standard libraries, which are part of every system anyway, but if used for special purpose libraries, it means more files to install with each software shipment. It's often easier to use static libraries to keep the installation of programs simple. The shared object libraries must also be located in a special directory, where the loader can find them. This means they must be installed by the administrator, or you'll need to specify a search path for libraries, similar to the `PATH` variable used to find executables.

Finally, shared object libraries may need to be present in several versions, to accommodate executables from both current and older versions of the compiler and/or library. Hence, shared object library files often have version numbers appended to their names.

20.1.3   Creating Static Libraries

Static libraries are created with the `ar` command. Building a library is very much like building a program from several source files, with two minor differences:

- None of the source files may contain a `main()` function.

- The linker is replaced by `ar`, and usually followed by `ranlib`.

Example:

Suppose you've created a few new string handling functions to supplement those in the standard library. They might include `strdup()`, which copies a string to a block of memory allocated by `malloc()`, `strlcat()`, a safer version of `strcat()` which takes the size of the destination array into account, and `strblank()`, which returns `true` if a string contains only whitespace.

Since all of these functions may be useful to many different programs, they should be placed in a library so that they can be easily utilized by other programs without being recompiled.

To build the library, you need to:

1. Compile each file separately to an object module.
2. Archive the object modules into a static library, using `ar`. The name of the library file must end with ".a".
3. **Randomize** the library, using `ranlib`. This builds a sort of table of contents for use by the linker, `ld`, which must be able to search the library for particular functions quickly and extract the object files it needs.

This process can be done using make, and is almost identical to the process of building a program. The following makefile demonstrates how to archive these three functions into a library:

```
OBJS = strdup.o strlcat.o strblank.o

# Build library archive and randomize
libstrings.a: $(OBJS)
        ar r libstrings.a $(OBJS)
        ranlib libstrings.a

# Build object modules to be placed in library
strdup.o: strdup.c strings.h
        gcc -c -Wall strdup.c

strlcat.o: strlcat.c strings.h
        gcc -c -Wall strlcat.c

strblank.o: strblank.c strings.h
        gcc -c -Wall strblank.c
```

This makefile will automatically rebuild the library *libstrings.a* whenever one of the source files is modified.

You can link library functions into any program that needs them by simply supplying the "-L" and "-l" link options. The "-L" option specifies the directory containing the library file. The "-l" option specifies the filename of the library, minus the "lib" prefix and ".a" suffix.

For example, to compile a simple program and link in the string functions in *libstrings.a*, use a command similar to the following:

```
gcc -Wall prog.c -L~/C/Lib -lstrings
```

If you build the program using a makefile, then these options should appear in the link command. You may also want to specify the library as a dependent of the executable, so that the program will be rebuilt when the library has been altered.

```
OBJS = main.o sort.o

sort: $(OBJS) ~/C/Lib/libstrings.a
        gcc -o sort $(OBJS) -L~/C/Lib -lstrings

main.o: main.c
        gcc -c -Wall main.c

sort.o: sort.c
        gcc -c -Wall sort.c
```

The contents of a static library can be listed using **ar** with the "-t" option. It is often useful to sort the output so that function names are easier to find.

```
ar -t libstrings.a | sort | more
```

Tip of the trade: Special Options with **ar**

> Some versions of **ar** include a randomize option, which eliminates the need for an explicit **ranlib** command in the makefile. If you use such an option, however, your makefiles may not be portable to all the systems you use the library on.

20.1.4 Creating Dynamic Libraries

The process of creating dynamic libraries is very similar to that for static libraries. Most of the details of using shared objects are handled automatically by the linker and loader, so working with dynamic libraries is fairly straightforward.

Shared object libraries are structurally more similar to executable files than to static libraries. Hence, the building of a shared object library is usually handled by the linker, **ld**, rather than **ar**. For example, to create a shared object library for the string functions above on FreeBSD, you could use the following link command in the makefile:

```
ld -Bshareable -o libstrings.so.1.0 $(OBJS)
```

This link command places references to the library, and to the functions of interest within the library, into the executable.

To use the shared object library in a program, you use the same syntax as you did for a static library:

```
sort: $(OBJS) ~/C/Lib/libstrings.so.2.2
      gcc -o sort $(OBJS) -L~/C/Lib -lstrings
```

The file *libstrings.so.1.0* must be present on every system which runs programs that use it (e.g. `sort`). It must also be in an appropriate directory (in the search path for shared object libraries) so that the loader can find it. For example, any shared object libraries on a FreeBSD system that are not installed in the standard directories must be specified in the `LD_LIBRARY_PATH` environment variable, which contains a colon-separated list of directories similar to that in `PATH`.

Note that the name of the shared object library ends in ".so" rather than the ".a" used by static libraries.

Each Unix system may have a slightly different syntax for building shared libraries. Check the documentation for `ld` on your system for details.

Listing the contents of a shared object library is done with the `nm` (name list) command, which lists the external symbols in any type of object file, but most often in executables and libraries.

```
nm libstrings.so
```

Chapter 21

Files and File Streams

Before you begin...

You should be familiar with the material on basic I/O presented in chapter 7. Some knowledge of functions, arrays, and structures, presented in chapters 11, 15, and 18 is also helpful, but not essential.

21.1   FILE Streams

All Unix input and output is performed by the `read()` and `write()` functions, which simply read and write a specified number of characters to or from a file or device. The `read()` and `write()` functions each perform a **system call**, a request for service from the Unix kernel. Each system call made by a process is costly, and in many cases, the program will be **blocked** while it waits for service from the kernel. When a process is blocked, it relinquishes control of the CPU, and goes into a queue of processes waiting for service from the device it requested. Service from most I/O devices is very slow compared to CPU speed. For example, a typical hard disk takes about 10 milliseconds to find a requested block of data. On a machine executing 100 million instructions per second, this is a delay of 1,000,000 instruction cycles; enough to run a small program from start to completion. Once the I/O request has been completed, the process goes to *the end of the line* of processes waiting to use the CPU. Hence, programs that make frequent system calls spend a lot of time waiting in system queues, and don't generally utilize their full share of CPU time.

These types of processes are called **I/O bound**, and generally take much longer to complete than a **CPU bound** process, which spends most of its time using the CPU. The purpose of streams is to shift the behavior of programs from the I/O bound state, toward a more CPU bound state, so that it will complete its work faster.

`FILE` streams are a buffering mechanism designed to minimize the number of I/O system calls a program has to make. A program that uses `FILE` streams reads data from, and writes data to its own memory buffers, usually one character at a time. Since memory access doesn't require a system call, this type of buffered I/O can be done very quickly, and *without* blocking. Only when an input buffer is empty, or an output buffer is full, do the programs issue the `read()` or `write()` system calls. A typical `FILE` stream buffer is 1024 characters. Hence, a program that uses `read()` directly to request single characters from the kernel will make 1024 times as many system calls as one that uses `FILE` streams.

Note, however, that using `FILE` streams to read or write large blocks of data will be much *slower* than using `read()` or `write()` directly, since the stream must perform extra work to move data to and from the memory buffers. Stream I/O should only be used where relatively few characters are being read or written at once.

By making it more efficient to read and write single characters, `FILE` streams make many forms of formatted I/O practical, such as those used by `printf()` and `scanf()`. This chapter explains how `FILE` streams work, and provides an overview of the many `FILE` stream functions provided in the Unix C libraries.

21.2   The `FILE` Structure

The `FILE` type is a structure similar to the following:

```
typedef struct
{
    char    *buff;       /* I/O buffer */
    char    *p;          /* Next available character */
    size_t  bytes;       /* # of characters present */
    size_t  buffsize;    /* Size of the buffer */
    short   flags;       /* Stream parameters */
```

```
    short    file;      /* File descriptor buffered
                           by this structure */
}   FILE;
```

The member `buff` is a pointer to the memory buffer used to store the characters between `read()` or `write()` calls.

The pointer `p` points to the next available character to be read from the buffer, or the next available position a character can be written to.

The member `bytes` is the number of characters currently in the buffer. When a stream is open for reading, a `read()` system call is issued when `bytes` becomes 0. For streams open for writing, a `write()` call is issued when `bytes` equals `buffsize`, i.e. when the buffer is full.

The member `flags` contains various information about the stream, such as whether the end of the file has been reached, or what type of buffering is being used.[1]

The member `file` is the file descriptor used in the underlying `read()` or `write()` calls.

Most Unix systems define additional members in the `FILE` structure, which are not relevant to this discussion. To learn more about them, you can examine the file */usr/include/stdio.h* on your system.

Every newly created Unix process has, at least, the three standard `FILE` streams, called `stdin, stdout,` and `stderr`. Each of these is a variable of type `FILE *`, i.e. a pointer to a `FILE` structure. The functions that deal with the `stdin` and `stdout` streams are discussed in chapter 7.

The remainder of this chapter deals with functions that create, destroy, and manipulate `FILE` streams for the purpose of performing buffered stream I/O.

21.3 Basic Stream I/O Functions

21.3.1 Opening a File: `fopen()`

Synopsis: *FILE *fopen(char *pathname,char *mode);*

Return value: A pointer to the new `FILE` structure, or `NULL` if the file could not be opened for any reason.

---

[1]Buffering is covered in section 21.6.1.

This function performs a system call.

The `fopen()` function creates a `FILE` structure, allocates the associated memory buffer using `malloc()`, and issues an `open()` system call.

The `pathname` argument is the full or relative pathname[2] of the file you wish to open.

The `mode` argument specifies which types of operations you want to perform on the stream. The standard modes are as follows:

"**r**": Reading only.

"**w**": Writing only. If the file already exists, it is overwritten.

"**a**": Writing only. If the file already exists, new data is *appended* to the end of the file.

"**r+**": Both reading and writing. The stream is initially positioned at the beginning of the file, and the file contents may be overwritten.

"**w+**": Both reading and writing. Any existing file contents are erased before the first read or write operation. (i.e. the file is truncated.)

"**a+**": Both reading and writing. Like "r+", except the stream is initially positioned at the *end* of the file.

When a file is opened with "w" or "w+", the file contents are erased. However, the file retains its original identity, so if any other hard links (See `ln`, section 4.6) exist to the file, they are also affected. If you wish to create a *new* file, the existing file must be removed using `remove()` or `unlink()` before it is opened.

21.3.2 Closing a File: `fclose()`

The `fclose()` function closes a file using the `close()` system call, and frees all memory allocated for the `FILE` structure. Any data remaining in the stream buffer is written to the output device before the file is closed. Files should be closed at the earliest possible time to ensure the safe storage of your output data, and in some cases, to free the output device for use by other processes.

---

[2]See section 4.3.2 for definitions of pathnames.

21.3.3 Reading Characters: `getc()` and `fgetc()`

Synopsis: *int getc(FILE *);*

Return value: The next character in the stream, or `EOF` upon end of file

 This function may perform a system call.

The `getc()` macro reads and returns a single character from a `FILE` stream. Given the `FILE` structure definition above, `getc()` would be defined as follows:

```
#define getc(strm)\
    ((strm)->bytes-- == 0 ? fillbuf(strm) : *(strm)->p++)
```

The macro first checks to see if `bytes` is 0, i.e. if there are no more characters left in the buffer. If so, the macro calls the `fillbuff()` function, which would issue a `read()` system call to fill the stream buffer, and reset the `bytes` and p members. The `fillbuff()` function must also return the first character read, or the `EOF` constant if the end of file was reached. If `bytes` is not zero, the next character in the buffer is returned, `bytes` is decremented, and the pointer `p` is advanced to the next buffer position.

The `getc()` macro is called by most other stream input functions, so virtually every character a program reads through a stream passes through `getc()`. For this reason, `getc()` must be very fast, which is why it is implemented as a macro.

In some cases, you may need to use a real function to input a character from a stream. This might be the case, for example, if you need to use a pointer to an input function. (See chapter 17.) For these cases, there is a true function called `fgetc()`, which does the same job as `getc()`, although quite a bit slower, due to the overhead of calling the function.

21.3.4 Writing Characters: `putc()` and `fputc()`

Synopsis: *int putc(int ch,FILE *stream);*

Return value: The character written, or `EOF` to indicate an error.

This function may perform a system call.

The `putc()` macro is the output counterpart to `getc()`. The `putc()` macro places a character into an output stream buffer, and, if the buffer is full, issues a `write()` system call to empty the buffer. The `putc()` macro can be defined as follows:

```
#define putc(c,strm)\
    (strm)->bytes++ == (strm)->buffsize ?\
        flushbuf(strm) : *(strm)->p++ = (c)
```

The `flushbuf()` function is called when the buffer is full, and is responsible for issuing the `write()` system call, and reinitializing the output buffer.

Note that there are other possible definitions for the macro, depending on the type of output buffering in effect for the stream. The output buffering schemes are discussed in section 21.6.1.

`putc()` is called by most higher level stream output functions to send individual characters to the stream. The `fputc()` function is a true function which serves the same purpose as the `putc()` macro. Like `fgetc()`, `fputc()` is provided for use where a true function is required, but is far less efficient than `putc()` due to the added overhead of the function calls.

Example:

It is just as important to know how *not* to use stream I/O as it is to know how. The example below demonstrates one common misuse of `getc()` and `putc()`.

This function implements a simple version of the `cp` command. While it serves to demonstrate the use of `getc()` and `putc()`, this is not an efficient way to copy a file. A much more efficient method is presented in section 25.2.6.

```
/*
 * Use getc() and putc() to copy source to dest.
 * Return error codes if either file cannot be opened.
```

```
        */

    int     copy(char *source,char *dest)

    {
        FILE    *infile, *outfile;
        int     ch;

        /* Attempt to open files */
        infile = fopen(source,"r");
        if ( infile == NULL )
        {
            fprintf(stderr,"Cannot open %s for reading.\n",
                    source);
            return EX_NOINPUT;
        }

        outfile = fopen(dest,"w");
        if ( outfile == NULL )
        {
            fprintf(stderr,"Cannot open %s for writing.\n",
                    dest);
            return EX_NOINPUT;
        }

        /* Copy files on character at a time */
        while ( (ch=getc(infile)) != EOF )
            putc(ch,outfile);

        fclose(infile);
        fclose(outfile);
        return EX_OK;            /* Success */
    }
```

Programming for Performance:

Stream I/O should be used only when there is a need to examine each individual character, such as if the program needs to look for a newline in the input, or convert input text to numeric values. The `copy` function presented in the previous example merely needs to blindly copy data from one file to the other, and would be much more efficient if implemented using `read()` and `write()` calls directly to copy large chunks of the file.

What makes this function so inefficient, is that it copies data from one buffer to another, one character at a time before writing it to the output file.

There is no efficient way to copy raw data using stream I/O functions. Since the higher level functions (discussed in subsequent sections) are based on `getc()` and `putc()`, using them only adds more CPU overhead to the program.

The efficient way to copy raw data is to simply read in blocks of characters using `read()` and output the data directly from the original buffer using `write()`. This method is demonstrated in chapter section 25.2.6.

21.3.5   Reading Lines: `fgets()`

Synopsis: *char *fgets(char *string,size_t maxlen,FILE *stream);*

Return value: The address of `string`, or NULL upon end of file or error.

    This function may perform a system call.

The `fgets()` function uses `getc()` to read one line of text from a stream, and place it in the array `string`, followed by a null terminator ('\0'). A line, as defined by `fgets()` is any number of characters up to and including a newline ('\n') character, but not to exceed `maxlen` characters.

If a newline is encountered, it is included in the string. Since this is not always desirable, and the removing the newline from the end of the string would require an extra loop, you may wish to write your own line input function to use in place of `fgets()` when you don't want a newline character in the string.

Programming for Performance:

The `fgets()` function is useful for reading single *lines* of text from a file (or from `stdin`) when the lines of input need to be separated. It is *not* an efficient way to read blocks of text quickly, since it uses `getc()` calls to grab one character at a time. If you are looking for an efficient way to grab a chunk of data, use `read()` directly, as discussed in chapter 25.

21.3.6 Writing Strings: `fputs()`

Synopsis: *int fputs(char *string,FILE *stream);*

Return value: 0 on success, EOF on error.

 This function may perform a system call.

The `fputs()` function prints a string to the specified stream. Unlike `puts()`, `fputs()` does not add a newline character following the string output. Hence, `fputs()` is not a *line* printing function, but can be used to print any string whether it ends the line or not.

21.3.7 Reading Numbers and Formatted Text: `fscanf()`

Synopsis: *int fscanf(FILE *stream,char *format,...);*

Return value: The number of items successfully read and converted.

 This function may perform a system call.

The `fscanf()` function is used to read numeric data, or a mixture of numeric, string, and single character data from a stream. The `fscanf()` function is the generalized form of `scanf()`. The only difference between them is that `fscanf()` takes a `FILE` pointer as an argument, while `scanf()` implicitly uses `stdin`. For a full description of `scanf()`, see chapter 7.

Programming for Performance:

>   Using `fscanf()` where `fgets()` or `fgetc()` would suffice wastes CPU time, since `fscanf()` expends a great deal of effort parsing the format string for place-holders. If you need to input a simple string, it's faster to use `fgets()` or a similar function.

21.3.8   Writing Numbers and Formatted Text: `fprintf()`

Synopsis: *int fprintf(FILE *stream,char *format,...);*

Return value: The number of *characters* printed.

   This function may perform a system call.

The `fprintf()` function writes formatted numeric data and text to a stream. The `fprintf()` function is the generalized form of `printf()`. For a full discussion of these functions, refer to chapter 7.

Programming for Performance:

>   Using `fprintf()` where `fputs()` or `fputc()` would suffice wastes CPU time, since `fprintf()` expends a great deal of effort parsing the format string for place-holders. If you need to print a simple string, `fputs()` will do the job faster.

21.3.9 Detecting End-of-file: `feof()` and EOF

The `feof()` macro checks the `flags` field of a `FILE` structure for the end of file indicator. `Feof()` only returns true (non-zero) *after* a read operation fails due to an end of file condition. Thus, it cannot be used to *predict* when the end of file is about to be encountered.

When using `getc()`, it is often easier to simply check the return value of `getc()` for the `EOF` flag, rather than introduce a second macro call. For example, consider the following code fragment:

```
while ( !feof(infile) )
{
    ch = getc(infile);
    ...
}
```

If `getc()` reaches the end of file, it will return `EOF`. Thus, a redundant check for the end of file condition is *required* immediately following the call to `getc()`, to prevent the use of the EOF flags as input. The same effect can be accomplished in a much cleaner and more efficient way:

```
while ( (ch=getc(infile) != EOF )
{
    ...
}
```

The return values of other I/O functions can often be used in a similar fashion. For example, `fgets()` will return `NULL`, and `fscanf()` will return EOF upon reaching the end of a file.

Note that `EOF` is not a character, but merely a cardinal `int` value which is returned by certain I/O functions to indicate end of file or error conditions.

21.3.10 Stream I/O Example

Example:

The program below demonstrates how to open an input file stream and
read a list of numbers from the file using `fscanf()`.

```c
#include <stdio.h>

#define NO_LIST -1
#define MAX_LIST_SIZE    1000

/* Flexible floating point type */
typedef double float_t;

/* Prototypes */
void    print_list(float_t list[],size_t list_size);
void    sort_list(float_t list[],size_t list_size);
size_t  read_list(char *pathname,float_t list[],
                  size_t list_size);

/*
 * Read numbers from a file, sort, and print the
 * sorted list to stdout.
 */

int     main(int argc,char *argv[])

{
    size_t  list_size;
    float_t  list[MAX_LIST_SIZE];

    list_size = read_list("input",list,MAX_LIST_SIZE);
    if ( list_size != NO_LIST )
    {
        sort_list(list,list_size);
        print_list(list,list_size);
    }
    return EX_OK;
```

```
}

/*
 * Open the specified file and read values until end
 * of file, placing each value in list.
 */

size_t  read_list(char *pathname,float_t list[],
                  size_t max_list_size)

{
    FILE    *infile;
    size_t  c = 0;

    /* Attempt to open file */
    infile = fopen(pathname,"r");
    if ( infile == NULL )
    {
        fprintf(stderr,
                "Cannot open \"%s\".\n",pathname);
        return NO_LIST;
    }

    /* Read until array is full or end od file */
    while ( (c < max_list_size) &&
            (fscanf(infile,"%lf",list+c) == 1) )
        ++c;

    fclose(infile);
    return c;
}
...
```

21.3.11 Binary I/O: fread() and fwrite()

Synopsis: *int fread(void *base,size_t size,size_t count,FILE *stream);*

Return value: The number of *items* read.

 This function may perform a system call.

Synopsis: *int fwrite(void *base,size_t size,size_t count,FILE *stream);*

Return value: The number of *items* written.

 This function may perform a system call.

The `fread()` and `fwrite()` functions read and write a fixed number of bytes to or from a `FILE` stream. Note that the number of bytes is specified by two arguments, namely `size` and `count`. Using two arguments helps prevent programmers from forgetting the size portion, as is a common mistake with `malloc()`. (See chapter 16) It actually doesn't matter if you inadvertently switch the `size` and `count` arguments, since `fwrite()` merely multiplies them to compute the number of bytes to read. The only ill effect will be the confusion you cause the next programmer who examines the code.

These functions *can* be used to read and write fixed length blocks of text, much like `read()` and `write()`. However, since they use the `FILE` stream interface, they are much less efficient than direct system calls. They are provided for convenience, in case you need to read or write fixed size text blocks or binary information and must use a `FILE` stream from some reason.

These functions can also be used to read (inhale) and write (dump) raw binary data, such as structures. This is often much faster and easier to program than using `fprintf()` and `fscanf()` to store the data in ASCII format. Moreover, the program won't require any changes if the structure is modified, although it will no longer be able to read the old binary data files. Also, storing data in binary format is not portable, since different machines may use different data sizes for `int` and `double`, and different structure alignment.

The following code fragment demonstrates how `fread()` can be used to quickly input a structure:

```
typedef struct
{
```

```
        int     rank;
        char    first_name[NAME_MAX+1];
        char    last_name[NAME_MAX+1];
    }   player_t;

int     main()

{
    player_t    players[MAX_PLAYERS];
    size_t      c;
    FILE        *infile;

    infile = fopen("player.data","r");
    if ( infile == NULL )
    {
        fputs("Cannot open player.data.\n",stderr);
        return -1;
    }
    for (c=0; fread(&players[c],sizeof(player_t),
                1,infile) == 1; ++c)

        ;
    ...
    return EX_OK;
}
```

21.4   Temporary files

Programs often need to store data temporarily, for use later during execution. Rather than store it in expensive memory, or try to invent a unique filename (which will inevitably collide with another file eventually), you can use one of the standard library functions to generate a temporary file.

21.4.1   Named Temp Files: tmpnam(), tempnam(), mkstemp()

Synopsis: *char *tmpnam(char *name);*

Return value: A pointer to the generated pathname, either `name`, or, if `name` is NULL, and internal `static` string.

This function performs a system call.

Synopsis: *char *tempnam(char *tempdir,*prefix);*

Return value: A pointer to the generated pathname, which is allocated with `malloc()`.

This function performs a system call.

Synopsis: *char *mktemp(char *template);*

Return value: A pointer to the generated pathname, which is a modified in place in the string `template`.

This function performs a system call.

The `tmpnam()` and `tempnam()` functions generate temporary pathnames that are guaranteed to be unique at the time they are generated. These pathnames can then be used to create files or directories using other functions such as `fopen()`.

The `tmpnam()` function generates a pathname for a file residing in the system's standard temp directory, usually */tmp* or */usr/tmp*. The actual temp directory used is defined in stdio.h. If the argument `name` is NULL, `tmpnam()` stores the name in it's own `static` local character array, and returns a pointer to it. Thus, the generated name may be overwritten on the next call to `tmpnam()`. If `name` is not NULL, `tmpnam()` places the pathname into `name`, and returns the address of `name`. The array `name` must be at least L_tmpnam characters in length. L_tmpnam is defined in *stdio.h*.

The `tempnam()` function also generates a pathname, but allows you to specify which directory the file should reside in, as well as a prefix for the pathname. For example, the following call will generate a name such as *./temp00453*. Each subsequent call will produce a different sequence of numbers and or letters following *./temp*.

```
char    *tempfile;

tempfile = tempnam(".","temp");
```

If `tempdir` is NULL, `tempnam()` will use one of the standard temp directories, such as that used by `tmpnam()`. If `prefix` is NULL, it is simply ignored.

The `tempname()` function allocates memory for the pathname using `malloc()`. This memory must be freed using `free()` when the pathname is no longer needed.

The `mktemp()` function generates a unique pathname based on the given template. The template string passed to `mktemp()` must have some number of trailing 'X' characters, which `mktemp()` replaces with a unique sequence of letters and or digits. For example, to create a temporary filename in */tmp*, use a template such as "/tmp/temp.XXXXX". Note that the string `template` is modified by the function, so multiple calls to `mktemp()` will require separate template variables.

21.4.2 Anonymous Temp Files: `tmpfile()`, `mkstemp()`

Synopsis: *FILE *tmpfile(void);*

Return value: A pointer to a temporary FILE stream.

 This function performs a system call.

Synopsis: *int mktemp(char *template);*

Return value: A file descriptor referring to the generated pathname, which is opened for reading and writing.

 This function performs a system call.

The `tmpfile()` function opens a temporary file and creates an associated FILE stream to reference the file. The name of the file is inaccessible to the program, and the file is automatically deleted when it is closed. Both read and write operations are allowed on the file, i.e. the open mode is equivalent to "w+" with `fopen()`.

The purpose of `tmpfile()` is to create a stream for dumping temporary data. The program can use `rewind()` at some later time to go back to the beginning of the data and reread it. This is useful for programs that process data in multiple passes, such as compilers, assemblers, and external sort programs.

The `mkstemp()` function uses `mktemp()` to generate a filename, and immediately opens the file, returning a low-level file descriptor.[3] Using `mkstemp()` eliminates the possibility of a name collision, which may occur using `mktemp()`. Collisions can occur if `mktemp()` is called twice before either file is created, since `mktemp()` guarantees uniqueness of a filename by checking for the file's existence. If a filename is generated, and the file is not immediately opened, then it does not yet exist, and `mktemp()` could generate the same name again.

21.5   Writing Filter Programs

Many Unix commands can be classified as **filter programs**, commands which can be used to process the output of another command, linked to it through a pipe, as described in section 4.8.3. To qualify as a filter command, a program merely needs the ability to read input from `stdin`, and send output to `stdout`. However, it is often useful for a program to be able to use *either* a specified filename *or* the standard streams. An example of such a command is `more`. The `more` command can take a filename on the command line to specify the input source, or, if no filename is given, can read from `stdin`. For example, the following two commands can be used to view the output of `ls` one screen at a time:

```
tcsh 1: ls > temp
tcsh 2: more temp
```

We can achieve the same effect by using `more` as a filter:

```
tcsh 1: ls | more
```

Writing Unix programs to function as filters is very simple. The following code fragment can be used as a template for a simple filter command:

---

[3]File descriptors are described in chapter 25.

```
#include <stdio.h>

int process(FILE *);

int     main(int argc,char *argv[])

{
    FILE    *infile;

    switch(argc)
    {
        /* No arguments - use stdin */
        case    1:
            infile = stdin;
            break;

        /* 1 argument - use as input file */
        case    2:
            infile = fopen(argv[1],"r");
            if ( infile == NULL )
            {
                fprintf(stderr,
                        "Cannot open %s for reading.\n",
                        argv[1]);
                return 2;
            }
            break

        /* Too many arguments - print help message */
        default:
            fprintf(stderr,
                    "Usage: %s [input-file]\n",argv[0]);
            return 1;
    }
    return process(infile);
}

int     process(FILE *infile)
```

```
    {
        ...
    }
```

21.6   Advanced: Controlling FILE streams

21.6.1   Controlling Output Buffering: setvbuf()

Synopsis: *int setvbuf(FILE *stream,char *buff,int mode,size_t size);*

Return value: 0 on success, EOF on error.

FILE streams are buffering mechanisms for I/O devices. Different types of I/O devices need different types of buffering to maximize performance. There are three types of output buffering used by FILE streams:

Block buffered I/O is used by disks, tapes, and other devices that transmit and receive data in fixed sized blocks. In this type of buffering, output buffers are flushed to the device only when they are full.

Line buffered I/O is most commonly used for terminals. In this type of buffering, characters are buffered until a newline is printed, the buffer is full, or input is requested from the same device (in order to ensure prompts are printed before input is expected from a user). For example, the stdout stream is normally line buffered, and is flushed when input is requested from stdin.

Unbuffered I/O is used when individual characters must be transferred immediately. The stderr stream is unbuffered, so that error messages are always displayed, even if the program crashes shortly after they are printed.

The setvbuf() function can be used to control the style of output stream buffering, as well as the size of the buffer.

Increasing the size of a buffer can improve performance when writing to disk files, since the standard buffer size (usually 1024 bytes) is often smaller than a disk block. If this is the case, several write system calls will end up updating the same disk block, which is an enormous waste of time. Table 25.2 (page 520) shows the effects of buffer size on I/O performance.

When using setvbuf(), you must provide a character array through the argument buff.

The size of the buffer is specified by the size argument.

If buff is NULL, *and* size is 0, then setvbuf() allocates an appropriately sized buffer for you, which will be automatically freed when the stream is closed with fclose().

The mode argument should be one of the following constants, which are defined in *stdio.h*:

_IONBUF for unbuffered I/O.

_IOLBUF for line buffered I/O.

_IOFBUF for block (fully) buffered I/O.

Pitfall: Empty Buffers Only

The setvbuf() function should only be used on a newly opened file stream, before the first write operation. Otherwise, any output in the buffer will be lost when the old buffer is replaced.

In addition to setvbuf(), several other buffering control functions, which are based on setvbuf(), are provided for convenience.

Synopsis: *void setbuf(FILE *stream,char *buff);*

Return value: None.

The setbuf() function sets the buffering mode to block buffered, provided buff is not NULL. The buffer size is assumed to be BUFSIZ, as defined in *stdio.h*. Thus, buff must be given an array of at least BUFSIZ characters. If buff is NULL, buffering is set to unbuffered mode.

Synopsis: *void setbuffer(FILE *stream,char *buff,size_t size);*

Return value: None.

The `setbuffer()` function is equivalent to `setbuf()`, except that you may specify your own buffer size.

Synopsis: *int setlinebuf(FILE *stream);*

Return value: 0 on success, EOF on error.

 This function performs a system call.

The `setlinebuf()` function puts the stream into line buffered mode, using a system allocated buffer.

Note that these functions only control *output* buffering. Control of input buffering is handled at a different level, as discussed in chapter 26.

21.6.2   Clearing an Output Buffer: `fflush()`

Synopsis: *int fflush(FILE *stream);*

Return value: 0 on success, EOF on error.

 This function performs a system call.

The `fflush()` function forces all data in a stream's output buffer to be transmitted to the operating system via an underlying `write()` system call.

```
fflush(stdout);
```

Note that `fflush()` only affects the *stream* buffer, which is controlled by the process. Further buffering may be performed by the kernel at the system level, buffering data submitted by `write()` calls. These buffers are not affected by stream functions such as `fflush()`, and must be flushed using `sync()` or `fsync()`, which block the calling process until the data is actually written to the device.

21.6.3   Moving Around in a File

Synopsis: *int fseek(FILE *stream,long offset,int whence);*

Return value: 0 on success, -1 on error.

 This function may perform a system call.

The `fseek()` function moves the file's positional pointer to the specified character position within the file. Note that we are referring to the operating system's internal pointer to the position with the *file*, not the member of the `FILE` structure that states the position within the *stream buffer*. The argument `offset` specifies the position in the file relative to the starting point given by `whence`. `Whence` must be one of the following constants, which are defined in *stdio.h*:

SEEK_SET specifies the beginning of the file. `Offset` must be positive.

SEEK_CUR specifies the current position in the file. `Offset` may be positive or negative.

SEEK_END specifies the end of the file. `Offset` may be positive or negative. If positive, the file is automatically extended with the character zero.

Note that `offset` must be a `long` value. If specified as a constant, it must have an 'L' suffix:

```
fseek(tempfile,-5L,SEEK_CUR);
```

Seeking is undefined for pipes and non storage devices such as terminals and network connections.

Programming for Performance:

> The performance of `fseek()` depends heavily on the underlying file structure. Systems such as Unix, which implements files as arrays of pointers to blocks, can move directly to any block within a file. Thus, seeks will complete seek requests in a small, constant time.

Table 21.1 shows the relative seek performance of several brands of *Unix* alongside *Windows* running a Win32 binary. The first four tests were run on the same machine, a 486 66Mhz PC with 32 megabytes of RAM, a *Quantum* SCSI disk, and *Adaptec* SCSI host adapter. The last two were run on a 486 66Mhz PC with a Western Digital Caviar (EIDE) disk, and 16 megabytes RAM. Linux runs are shown for both disks to allow comparison between the two machines.

The test involved an empty loop from 0 to 40,000,000 followed by creation of a 32 megabyte file using `write()` to write 1024 bytes at a time, 1000 random seeks uniformly distributed within the file, and a sequential read through the file, reading 1024 bytes at a time. The results shown are the average of three runs. The variance was no more than a few percent in all cases, except the write operation under Linux on the SCSI system, where the first run took about 15% longer than the other two.

Under Unix, the benchmark program was compiled with `cc -O bench.c`. Under *Windows*, it was compiled using *Borland C/C++* 4.52, with the optimizer set to maximize speed. The target CPU was i486, and the target platform was win32. Compiling for *Windows 3.1* and the 80286 CPU decreased the empty loop performance by 29%, and had no effect on disk performance.

Note that there is a wide variation in performance among all systems. In particular, *Windows* disk performance was much slower overall than Unix, because it uses the *FAT* (File Allocation Table) filesystem, whereas Unix uses an indexed filesystem. The *FAT* filesystem keeps track of disk blocks using a linked list of block pointers, while the indexed method uses an array of pointers, which allows for faster lookup. Modern Unix systems also keep files in more or less contiguous disk blocks, which minimizes the need for disk head movements.

Windows 95 improves performance by using better FAT **caching**. In essence, more data from the FAT is kept in RAM, which eliminates some disk operations at the expense of having less memory available for other purposes. As you may already know, *Windows 95* requires *a lot* more memory than *Windows 3.1*.

SCO Unix showed much slower write performance, because it uses a **journaling filesystem**, which writes all data directly to an area on disk known as the **journal**. Other systems use RAM buffers, which improves performance, at the risk of data loss in the event of a system

OS	Loop	Write	Random Seek	Sequential Read
FreeBSD	3.0	21.0	7.3	17.8
Linux	3.0	14.9	16.3	18.2
SCO	2.4	34.1	16.6	24.5
Windows 3.1	6.2	190.4	26.6	56.8
Linux	3.0	15.97	11.98	13.95
Windows 95	6.65	125.94	11.79	47.45

Table 21.1: Benchmark Results

crash. *FreeBSD* and *Linux* performed very similarly overall, except that *FreeBSD* sacrifices some write performance in exchange for better seek performance.

The `fseek()` function is the stream interface to the system call `lseek()`, which is discussed in chapter 25.

Synopsis: *long ftell(FILE *stream);*

Return value: The current position of the file pointer, or -1 on error.

The `ftell()` function returns the current character position within the file.

In addition to `fseek()` and `ftell()`, there are a few other functions provided for convenience.

Synopsis: *void rewind(FILE *stream);*

Return value: None.

 This function may perform a system call.

The `rewind()` is a synonym for `fseek(stream,0L,SEEK_SET);`

Synopsis: *int fsetpos(FILE *stream,fpos_t *position);*

Return value: 0 on success, -1 on error.

This function may perform a system call.

The `fsetpos()` function is roughly equivalent to `fseek()` with SEEK_SET passed to the **whence** argument. Note, however, that `fsetpos()` takes the *address* of the position argument. The type `fpos_t` may be a long integer or a structure, so you should avoid writing code that makes assumptions about it in order to maintain portability. A good practice would be to apply the concept of encapsulation, and create a macro or function to alter object of type `fpos_t`:

```
/* Macro for when fpos_t is a long int */
#define SET_FPOS(var,value) ((var) = (value))

int     main()
{
    fpos_t  position;
    FILE    *stream;

    ...

    SET_FPOS(position,1000L);
    fset_pos(stream,&position);
    ...
    return EX_OK;
}
```

If you then port the code to a system that defines `fpos_t` as a structure, then only the macro will need to be changed.

Synopsis: *int fgetpos(FILE *stream,fpos_t *position);*

Return value: 0 on success, -1 on error.

The `fgetpos()` function is roughly equivalent to `ftell()`. The only functional difference is it's use of the type `fpos_t` instead of `long`. Hence, any programs that use `fsetpos()` to move a stream pointer should use `fgetpos()` rather than `ftell()`.

21.7 File Error Handling

The C stream libraries provide extensive error feedback. Most of this feedback is (unfortunately) provided in the global variable **errno**, rather than as function return values or arguments. Most I/O functions at both the stream level and system level will affect the **errno** variable when I/O errors occur.

With stream I/O functions, some error information is also stored in the **FILE** structure directly. The following sections briefly describe how to make use of the information stored in the **FILE** structure and in **errno**.

21.7.1 Detecting Errors: ferror()

Synopsis: *int ferror(FILE *stream);*

Return value: Non zero to indicate an error.

The **ferror()** function simply indicates whether an error condition has occurred on a **FILE** stream. If so, the program should take corrective action, and then clear the error indicator using **clearerr()**.

```
if ( ferror(stream) )
{
    fprintf(stderr,...);
    ...
    clearerr(stream);
}
```

21.7.2 Printing Errors: perror() and strerror()

The system generates a wide variety of error conditions for I/O failures. To free the programmer from the task of interpreting these integer error codes, the system provides two functions which translate the integer codes into text messages.

Synopsis: *void perror(char *prefix);*

Return value: None.

This function may perform a system call.

Synopsis: *char *strerror(int err_code);*

Return value: A pointer to the error message text.

The `perror()` function prints the message corresponding to the current value of the global variable `errno`, on `stderr`. If `prefix` is not `NULL`, it is prepended to the system error message. `perror()` adds a ':' to separate the prefix and system message. The code fragment below demonstrates how to use `perror()` to print a message following a failed `fopen()`:

```
infile = fopen(filename,"r");
if ( infile == NULL )
{
    perror("Could not open file");
    exit(1);
}
```

If the open failed due to file permissions, the output would be:

```
Could not open file: Permission Denied.
```

The `strerror()` function simply returns the string associated with a given error code. This provides programs with more freedom than the `perror()` function allows. For example, you may wish to print error messages to a log file or a pop-up window, rather than just dumping them to *stderr*. You might also want to format the message with something more than just a prefix to the system error message.

```
infile = fopen(filename,"r");
if ( infile == NULL )
{
    sys_message = strerror(errno);
    fprintf(logfile,"Could not open \"%s\": %s\n",
```

```
                    filename,sys_message);
   }
```

The output would look something like the following:

```
    Could not open "animals.dat": Permission denied.
```

21.8 Manipulating Whole Files

21.8.1 Removing Files: remove() and unlink()

Synopsis: *remove(char *pathname);*

Return value: 0 for success, -1 on error.

 This function performs a system call.

Synopsis: *unlink(char *pathname);*

Return value: 0 for success, -1 on error

 This function performs a system call.

The remove() and unlink() functions are synonymous. Both remove a directory entry, officially called a **link** in Unix. The name remove() is provided as a convenience, since the name unlink() is somewhat cryptic for anyone unfamiliar with Unix filesystems and links. Also, using the unlink() function requires the header *unistd.h* to be included, which is otherwise superfluous for most programs using FILE streams. The remove() function, on the other hand, is prototyped in *stdio.h*, which is required for all stream I/O programs anyway.

Pitfall: No Turning Back

Both functions should be used with caution. There are no *"Are you sure?"* messages at this level, and it's probably a good idea to put one in your program before calling `remove()` or `unlink()`.

Also, removing a directory entry will break any hard links that exist to the file. For instance, if a user used `ln` to create a hard link to *foo.c* called *bar.c*, then the call `remove("foo.c");` will remove the directory entry for *foo.c*, while the file still exists as *bar.c*. If *foo.c* is then re-created, it will no longer be linked to *bar.c*.

If you would like to have the option of restoring the file, move it to a *trash can* directory instead of just deleting it.

21.8.2   Moving and Renaming Files: `rename()`

Synopsis: *int rename(const char *from,const char *to);*

Return value: 0 on success, -1 on error.

   This function performs a system call.

The `rename()` function changes the pathname of a file, by removing the *from* directory entry, and creating the *to* directory entry to take its place. Note that the file data is *not physically copied*: Only the directory entries associated with the old and new names are modified. The pathnames specified need not be in the same directory, but they must be on the same filesystem. To move a file to a different filesystem, it must be physically copied, using a function like the example presented in section 21.3.4, and the original file must be deleted.

21.8.3   Creating Links: `link()` and `symlink()`

Synopsis: *int link(const char *from,const char *to);*

Return value: 0 on success, -1 on error.

This function performs a system call.

Synopsis: *int symlink(const char *from,const char *to);*

Return value: 0 on success, -1 on error.

 This function performs a system call.

The `link()` function creates a duplicate directory entry, also known as a **hard link**, named by `to`, for the file named by `from`. Following the call, the two directory entries refer to the same data (i.e. the same **inode** and data blocks) on disk, and are equivalent in every way, except of course, that their names are different. The pathnames specified by `from` and `to` must reside in the same filesystem, or the call will fail. `link()` may not be used to create a link to a directory.

The `symlink()` function creates a **soft link**, or **symbolic link** to a file or directory. A symbolic link is a directory entry that points to another pathname, rather than pointing directly to the file. Unlike hard links, if the pathname pointed to by a symbolic link is deleted, the symbolic link becomes invalid. Symbolic links that point to non-existing pathnames are known as a **dangling links**. If the file is then recreated, the dangling link becomes valid again, so symbolic links are not broken when the file is removed and recreated.

Also unlike hard links, symbolic links can point to files on a different filesystem, and can point to directories.

21.8.4 Creating Files and Directories

Normal files are created by `fopen()`, as described in section 21.3.1, or by `open()`, as described in section 25.2.1.

Directories can be created using the `mkdir()` function:

Synopsis: *int mkdir(char *path,mode_t mode);*

Return value: 0 on success, -1 on error.

This function performs a system call.

This function creates the directory specified by `path`, which may be a full pathname or a relative pathname (relative to the current working directory for the calling process). The argument `mode` specifies the permissions for the directory. This mode is modified by the process' umask, as describe in section 4.3.3.

Note that a directory must be marked as *executable* in addition to *readable* in order to access it's contents. For example, the following call creates a new directory called *Samples* which is accessible to the owner and group, but not to the rest of the world.

```
if ( mkdir("Samples",0750) == -1 )
    fputs("Error creating directory.\n",stderr);
```

Creation of special files, such as pipes, is handled by `mknod()`. This function is covered in chapter 27.

Chapter 22

String and Character Functions

Before you begin...

You should be familiar with the material on arrays presented in chapter 15.

22.1 Basic String Manipulation

A **string** in C is simply an array of characters. The only support for strings offered by the language itself is the implementation of **string constants**, also called **string literals**. All string operations, such as copying, comparison, input, output, and so on, are handled by library functions.

Since arrays are generally fixed in size, strings use a **null terminator**, the character '\0', to mark the end of the actual data within the array. This should not be confused with the constant NULL, which is a pointer. When you use a string constant such as "Hello, world" in a program, the compiler automatically inserts a null byte at the end of the string.

Tip of the trade: Make Some Room

When defining an array to hold a string, it's a good idea to add 1 to

461

the dimension to make room for the null byte. If you don't add 1 in the definition, you'll have to subtract 1 from the size every time you manipulate the string, to leave room for the null byte.

The two programs below demonstrate the importance of extending the size of a string array by 1, to make room for the null byte.

```
#define MAX_NAME_LEN     20

int     main()

{
    char     first_name[MAX_NAME_LEN];

    ...
    /* Input a string using getchar() */
    for (c=0; ((ch = getchar()) != '\n') &&
            (c < MAX_NAME_LEN - 1); ++c)
        first_name[c] = ch;
    ...
    return EX_OK;
}
```

If you forget to subtract 1 from MAX_NAME_LEN in the loop above, the input may go beyond the end of the array, causing data corruption in other variables, or if you're lucky, a segmentation fault. By adding 1 in the definition, we can use MAX_NAME_LEN throughout the program instead of MAX_NAME_LEN-1.

```
#define MAX_NAME_LEN     20

int     main()

{
    char     first_name[MAX_NAME_LEN+1];

    /* Input a string using getchar() */
    for (c=0; ((ch = getchar()) != '\n') &&
```

```
                (c < MAX_NAME_LEN); ++c)
          first_name[c] = ch;

      ...

      return EX_OK;
  }
```

Null terminated strings are the most efficient string implementation for most operations, since we can terminate the loop after the minimum number of iterations, instead of processing the whole length of the array.

One negative consequence, however, is that *every* string operation requires a loop. An alternative to null terminated strings is to store the length of the string in the first byte or first few bytes. Using this approach, we could retrieve the length of the string very quickly, rather than search from the beginning for the null byte. The disadvantage is that the length of a string is limited by the number of bits used to store the size, and it requires slightly more storage space.

22.2 String Functions

22.2.1 Copying Strings: strlcpy()

Synopsis: *char *strcpy(char *dest,const char *source,size_t maxlen);*

Return value: dest.

The strlcpy() function copies characters from the array source to the array dest, stopping at the null terminator, or at maxlen-1 characters.

This is a replacement for the standard library function strcpy().

Dangerous Function: strcpy()

The strcpy() function is one of several dangerous functions in the standard C library, along with gets(), which is described in chapter 7. Like gets(), strcpy() blindly copies characters to the destination array without knowing the size of the array. It simply copies characters until a null byte is encountered in the source array. If the source string is larger than the destination array, the program will overwrite variables that follow the destination array in memory.

As if that wasn't enough, the alternative function provided by the standard C library is also flawed. The `strncpy()` function copies a string, but limits the number of characters copied using a third argument.

Synopsis: *char *strncpy(char *dest,const char *source,size_t len);*

Return value: `dest`.

The problem with `strncpy()` is that it *does not null terminate the string if the maximum number of characters is reached.* The next time this new string is used, it will most likely cause serious problems. Thus, using `strncpy()` is like planting a bomb in your program, that could go off at any time.

The best alternative is to write your own string copy function, and place it in your personal library.[1] The `strlcpy()` function below, which guarantees the copy is properly null terminated, is a safer equivalent to `strncpy()`.

```
int     strlcpy(dest, src, len)
char    *dest, *src;
int     len;

{
    char    *save_dest, *end;

    /* Copy as much of src as possible */
    save_dest = dest;
    end = src + len;
    while ((*src != '\0') && (src < end))
        *dest++ = *src++;

    /* Null terminate dest */
    *dest = '\0';
```

---

[1] Creating libraries is covered in chapter 20.

```
        /* Return indication if array full */
        if ( *src == '\0' )
            return SUCCESS;
        else
            return NOT_ALL_COPIED;
    }
```

Pitfall: Copying Strings: Data or Pointer?

A common mistake when using pointers to strings is to attempt to use the assignment operator, instead of the `strcpy()` function. While this is *valid* in C, it may not do exactly what you wanted. Consider the code fragment below:

```
char    name1[MAX_NAME_LEN+1],
        name2[MAX_NAME_LEN+1],
        *p1 = name1,
        *p2 = name2;

p2 = p1;
```

A novice C programmer might think that the statement `p2 = p1;` copies `name1` to `name2`. In reality, it only makes p2 point to `name1`. The contents of `name2` are unaffected. To actually copy the string using the pointer variables, use a function such as `strlcpy()`:

```
strlcpy(p2,p1,MAX_NAME_LEN);
```

This is not to say that such a pointer assignment should never be done. In fact, a simple pointer assignment is much more efficient than using `strlcpy()`, and *should* be used when it serves the purpose. However, you must be aware that it will not duplicate the string.

22.2.2   Duplicating Strings: strdup()

Synopsis: *char *strdup(const char *string);*

Return value: A pointer to a newly allocated copy of `string`.

The `strdup()` function uses `malloc()` to allocate `strlen(string)+1` bytes of memory, and copies `string` into it. This function is particularly useful in filling an array of pointers to strings, which will use the minimum amount of memory needed to contain all the text.

The memory allocated should be freed using `free()` as soon as the string is no longer needed.

22.2.3   Finding a String Length: strlen()

Synopsis: *size_t strlen(const char *string);*

Return value: The length of the string in bytes.

The `strlen()` function counts the characters in a string, searching from the address `string` to the null terminator.

Programming for Performance:

Use of `strlen()` should be avoided if possible, since it uses a loop to determine the string length. If the length of a string is known, it can be stored in a `size_t` variable to avoid the need for future `strlen()` calls.

22.2.4   Comparing Strings: strcmp() and strcasecmp()

Synopsis: *int strcmp(const char *str1,const char *str2);*

Return value: 0 if equal, a value less than 0 if `str1<str2`, a value greater than 0 if `str1>str2`.

The `strcmp()` function lexically compares two strings. Characters are compared starting at the first, and continuing until a null terminator is encountered in either string, or until two corresponding characters differ.

If two strings are equal to the end of one of the strings, the shorter string is considered the lesser. For example, "aardvark" is less than "aardvarks". This is actually a fortuitous property of null terminated strings: The null byte is lexically less than any other ASCII character, so when the end of the shorter string is reached, it is recognized as the lesser string by comparison of the null byte to any character in the longer string. Hence, the strcmp function can be coded in a very simple way:

```
int     strcmp(const char *s1,const char *s2)

{
    /* Advance until two different chars are found, one
       of which may be a null char. */
    while ( (*s1 != '\0') && (*s1++ == *s2++) )
        ;

    return s1 - s2;
}
```

The lexical comparison compares the ASCII values of corresponding characters. Thus, 'A' (65) is less than 'a' (97), and "Aardvark" is therefore less than "aardvark".

The `strcasecmp()`, also known as `stricmp()` on many systems, performs a case-insensitive comparison. It is essentially the same as `strcmp()`, except that upper and lower case letters are treated as equal. For example, "Aardvark" is considered equal to "aardvark".

22.2.5   Concatenation: `strlcat()`

Synopsis: *char *strcat(char *string,const char *append,size_t maxlen);*

Return value: string.

The `strlcat()` function appends the null terminated string contained in `append` to the string in `string`, ensuring that the resulting string is no more than `maxlen-1` characters long.

This is a replacement for the standard function `strcat()`.

Dangerous Function: `strcat()`

Like `gets()` and `strcpy()`, `strcat()` doesn't know the size of the array
it writes to, and can therefore overfill it, causing data corruption in
other variables. The alternative function `strncat()` is also flawed. The
`strncat()` function requires a third argument specifying the maximum
number of characters to copy. The third argument *does not specify the
size of the destination array*, so you need to know the length of the
original string and calculate the number of available spaces remaining.
A better alternative is to use a function like the one shown below, and
add it to your personal library, as outlined in chapter 20.

```
char    *strlcat(dest,src,maxlen)
char    *dest,*src;
int     maxlen;

{
    char    *dp,*sp;

    /* Find end of first string */
    /* Subtract this length from maxlen */
    for (dp=dest; (*dp != '\0') && --maxlen; ++dp)
        ;

    /* Concatenate second string */
    for (sp=src; (*sp != '\0') && --maxlen; )
        *dp++ = *sp++;

    /* Null terminate */
    *dp = '\0';
    return dest;
}
```

22.2.6 Searching Strings: strstr() and strchr()

Synopsis: *char *strstr(const char *string,const char *substring);*

Return value: A pointer to the first occurrence of substring within string, or NULL if it wasn't found.

Synopsis: *char *strchr(const char *string,int ch);*

Return value: A pointer to the first occurrence of ch within string, or NULL if it wasn't found.

The strstr() function looks for the first occurrence of substring within string.

The strchr() similarly searches for the first occurrence of the character ch within string.

Subsequent occurrences or strings or characters can be found by passing the return value from the previous call as follows:

```
char    string[STR_MAX+1],substr[STR_MAX+1],*p1, *p2;


...


/* Find first occurrence of substr */
p1 = strstr(string,substr);

/* Find second occurrence */
if ( p1 != NULL )
    p2 = strstr(p1,substr);
```

You can locate the *last* occurrence of a character within a string using strrchr(). This function is useful for finding extracting the extension from a filename, or separating the directory from the base filename. An example is shown below.

```
char    pathname[PATH_LEN+1] = "/usr/bin/ls",
        *basename, *extension;

/* Find last '/' in pathname */
```

```
basename = strrchr(pathname,'/');

/* Null terminate directory name, and advance pointer
   to first char in base filename */
if ( basename != NULL )
    *basename++ = '\0';

/* Find last '.' in base name */
extension = strrchr(basename,'.');
if ( extension != NULL )
    ...
```

22.2.7   Building Formatted Strings: `snprintf()`

Synopsis: *int sprintf(char *string,size_t maxlen,const char *format,...);*

Return value: The number of characters written to `string`.

The `snprintf()` function behaves exactly like `printf()` and `fprintf()`, except that it writes the formatted text to a character array instead of a `FILE` stream.

This is a replacement for the dangerous function `sprintf()`.

Dangerous Function: `sprintf()`

> The `sprintf()` function is another function that does not check the size of the array it writes data into, and is therefore dangerous to use. The `snprintf()` function, which does limit itself to the specified array size should be used instead.
>
> **Synopsis:** *int snprintf(char *str,size_t maxlen,const char *format,...);*
>
> **Return value:** The number of characters written.

The `snprintf()` function converts any type of data into ASCII text, which is stored as a null terminated string in `str`. It is the converse of all of the text-to-number conversion functions such as `atoi()` and `atof()`, which are described in chapter 23.

22.2.8   Tokenizing Strings: `strtok()`

Synopsis: *char *strtok(char *string,char *separators);*

Return value: A pointer to the next token within `string`.

The `strtok()` function is used by shells and other programs to break up a string into it's components, which are usually separated by white space or some form of punctuation. Each call to `strtok()` returns a pointer *within the string* to the next token, as defined by the separators you specify.

Calls to `strtok()` take two forms:

- The initial call takes the string to be tokenized as the first argument.

- All subsequent calls to tokenize the same string should be passed `NULL` in place of the string. The `NULL` value tells `strtok()` to continue tokenizing the same string used in previous calls, using a `static` internal pointer to the last location returned. This internal pointer is reset each time `strtok()` is passed a new string.

Pitfall: Ashes and Smoke from `strtok()`

The `strtok()` function anihilates the string passed to it, by inserting null bytes at the end of each token. If the original string will be needed for later purposes, you will need to make a copy of it, and send `strtok()` the copy instead.

Example:

The code fragment below demonstrates how a shell program would use `strtok()` to split Unix commands into separate arguments.

```
int    main()
```

```
    {
        char    command[LINE_LEN+1] = "",
                temp[LINE_LEN+1],
                *argv[MAX_ARGS];
        int     a;

        do
        {
            fgets(command,LINE_LEN,stdin);
            strlcpy(temp,command,LINE_LEN);

            /* Split command into args separated
               by white space */
            argv[0] = strtok(temp," \t\n");
            a = 1;
            while ((argv[a] = strtok(NULL," \t\n") != NULL)
                ++a;

            /* Execute the command */
            ...

        }   while ( strcmp(command,"exit") != 0 );
        return EX_OK;
    }
```

22.3   Classifying Characters: The *Ctype* Functions

The header file *ctype.h* contains prototypes for a set of functions used to determine the category a character belongs to. Table 22.1 lists the standard functions, which return true if the argument is in the specified category.

To check for a letter, for example, simply do the following:

```
if ( isalpha(ch) )
{
```

Function	Category
`isalnum()`	Letter or digit
`isalpha()`	Letter
`islower()`	Lower-case letter
`isupper()`	Upper-case letter
`ispunct()`	Punctuation
`isdigit()`	Decimal digit
`isxdigit()`	Hexadecimal digit
`iscntrl()`	Control character
`isspace()`	Whitespace (space, tab, nl)
`isprint()`	Printable
`isgraph()`	Graphic (printable and not whitespace)

Table 22.1: Standard Ctype Functions

```
    . . .
}
```

These functions use a table of bit masks, which is indexed by the ASCII value of the character. Each word in the table contains bits which are set to indicate that the character is a member of a particular category. For example, the `isalpha()` function is defined as follows:

```
unsigned long    _table[256];

int      isalpha(int ch)

{
    ch &= 0xff;  /* Trim ch to 255 or less */
    return table[ch] & _ALPHA_BIT;
}
```

This lookup table method, also presented in section 15.6, is far more flexible and efficient than checking ranges of characters. For example, we could also check for a letter using the following conditional:

```
if ( ((ch >= 'a') && (ch <= 'z')) ||
       (ch >= 'A') && (ch <= 'Z'))
{
    ...
}
```

However, this if statement is clumsy, slow, and does not work on EBCDIC systems, since the EBCDIC letters are not arranged contiguously. Furthermore, in today's international computing world, we cannot assume that 'a' and 'z' represent the first and last letters of every alphabet. Use of the `isalpha()` function is far simpler, more efficient, and reliable with any character set and locality. For example, many ISO character sets have special non-English characters, such as the German ö and the Spanish ñ, which are outside the normal range of 'a' to 'z' in the ASCII set.

In addition to the Boolean functions above, the functions `tolower()` and `toupper()` are provided to convert characters between upper and lower case.

Pitfall: Converting the Wrong Characters

Some older versions of `toupper()` and `tolower()` don't check to see that the argument is a letter before performing the conversion. Instead, they simply add or subtract the value ('A' - 'a') to the argument. Hence, it's a good idea to check the character using `isalpha()` before using these functions.

22.4   Pattern Matching Functions

In addition to simple string matching functions like `strcmp()` and `strstr()`, the Unix libraries provide several functions for matching *patterns*. There are two commonly used types of patterns:

Regular Expressions are a type of pattern used by programs like `grep`, `egrep`, and `awk` to locate specific items such as words or numbers within a file. Regular expressions are like strings, except that certain special symbols within them

Symbol	Matches
?	0 or 1 occurrences of the preceding token
*	0 or more occurrences of the preceding token
+	1 or more occurrences of the preceding token
.	Any single character
[list]	1 occurrence of any character in list
	list may include ranges of characters such as a-z
\c	1 occurrence of the character c (useful for matching special characters such as *, +, etc.)

Figure 22.1: Regular Expression Symbols

Symbol	Matches
*	Any string of characters
?	Any single character
[list]	Any single character in list
{s1,s2,...}	Any of the strings s1, s2, etc.

Figure 22.2: File Specification Symbols

can represent a wide range of character patterns. Figure 22.1 describes some of the most common special symbols.

For example, the pattern "`[0-9]*\.[0-9]+`" matches a floating point constant such as 54.61 or .9, and "`[a-zA-Z_][a-zA-Z0-9_]*`" matches a C identifier.

For more detailed information on regular expressions, consult the man page for `egrep`, `awk`, `regex`, or `re_format`.

File Specifications (filespecs) are a type of pattern used by shells such as Bourne shell and C shell to generate lists of filenames. Figure 22.2 lists the common special symbols used for filespecs.

For example, the pattern "`*.cc?`" represents all the files in the current directory ending in ".c" or ".cc". The pattern "`{Yac,Gn}[cu]`" matches all files beginning with "Yac" or "Gn", followed by 'c' or 'u', i.e. files named *Yacc*, *Gnu*, *Yacu* and *Gnc*.

The functions described below are not declared in *string.h*, but require their own header files. Consult the `man` page for each function on your system for details about which headers to include.

22.4.1   The Regex Functions

Regular expressions can be complex, and hence expensive to match. The standard libraries therefore use a system of *compiled* regular expressions to improve efficiency.

Pitfall: Duplicate Library Functions

Some systems may have more than one set of regular expression handling functions using the same names. The functions described here are the *POSIX* interface for regular expressions. These are described in the online manuals under `man regex`. Note that issuing a `man` command on specific functions, such as `man regcomp`, may display information on *an older, non-POSIX version of the function.*

The following four *POSIX* functions are used to handle regular expressions:

Synopsis: *int regcomp(regex_t *preg,const char *pattern,int options);*

Return value: 0 on success, defined error codes otherwise.

The `regcomp()` function is used to "compile" the regular expression `pattern`. This converts the character string pattern into an expanded binary form, stored in the `regex_t` structure `preg`. Individual strings can be matched against this structure much more efficiently than they could against a raw pattern. The `options` argument specifies which form of regular expression to use, whether or not to use case sensitive comparison, and so on. This generally consists of one of the following constants:

REG_EXTENDED: Use extended regular expressions as defined by the `egrep` command.

REG_BASIC: Use basic regular expressions.

REG_NOSPEC: Match only string literals, essentially making `regexec()` behave like `strcmp()`, and is provided for programs that determine the matching options on the fly.

Additional options may be combined with these three to control other options such as case sensitivity. These options are defined in *regex.h* and described in the `regex` man page.

Synopsis: *int regexec(regex_t *preg, char *str, size_t count,regmatch_t match[],int flags);*

Return value: 0 if `string` matches `preg`, a non-zero code otherwise.

The `regexec()` function "executes" the compiled regular expression in `preg` against `str`. If any occurrences of the regular expression `preg` are found within `str`, the match information is placed into the array `match`. The argument `count` specifies the size of the `match` array, and thus the maximum number of matches that will be returned. `Match[0]` describes the first substring that matched the entire regular expression `preg`. Other elements of `match` describe matches of parenthesized subexpressions.

Synopsis: *void regfree(regex_t *preg);*

Return value: None.

The `regfree()` function frees all memory allocated by `regcomp()` in constructing `preg`.

Synopsis: *size_t regerror(int errcode, regex_t *preg, char *err_str, size_t max_len);*

Return value: Length of the error message.

The `regerror()` function converts the integer error code produced by `regcomp()` or `regexec()` to a text error message, which is placed in `err_str`. `Max_len` specifies the size of the `err_str` array, so that `regerror()` can cut off the message rather than overfill the array. The `regerror()` function returns the length of the whole message, which may be greater than `max_len`. `Preg` may be `NULL`. Otherwise, it should contain the regular expression that caused the error so that an accurate error message can be generated.

Example:

The program below inputs a regular expression and a string, and then
uses the **regex** functions to search for the expression within the string.

```c
#include <stdio.h>
#include <regex.h>

#define MAX_RE_LEN      40
#define MAX_STRING_LEN  80
#define MAX_ERR_LEN     80

int     main(int argc,char *argv[])

{
    char    regex[MAX_RE_LEN+1],
            string[MAX_STRING_LEN+1],
            error[MAX_ERR_LEN+1];
    int     comp_code, exec_code;
    regex_t preg;
    regmatch_t  match[1];

    /* Get regular expression and string to test */
    fputs("Enter expression: ",stdout);
    fgets(regex,MAX_RE_LEN,stdin);
    fputs("Enter string: ",stdout);
    fgets(string,MAX_STRING_LEN,stdin);

    /* Compile regular expression */
    comp_code = regcomp(&preg,regex,
                        REG_EXTENDED|REG_ICASE);
    if ( comp_code != 0 )
    {
        regerror(comp_code, &preg, error, MAX_ERR_LEN);
        fprintf(stderr,"Error compiling RE: %s\n",
                error);
        return comp_code;
```

```
    }

    /* Search string for regular expression */
    exec_code = regexec(&preg,string,1,match,0);
    /* Match */
    if ( exec_code == 0 )
    {
        printf("Match found at character %u.\n",
                match[0].rm_so);
    }
    /* No match */
    else if ( exec_code == REG_NOMATCH )
    {
        printf("No match.\n");
    }
    /* Error in regexec */
    else
    {
        regerror(comp_code, &preg, error, MAX_ERR_LEN);
        fprintf(stderr,"Error executing RE: %s\n",
                error);
        return exec_code;
    }
    return EX_OK;
}
```

22.4.2   File Specification Matching: `fnmatch()` and `glob()`

Synopsis: *int fnmatch(const char *pattern,const char *string,int options);*

Return value: 0 if string matches pattern, otherwise FNM_NOMATCH.

The `fnmatch()` function compares `string` to the filespec `pattern`. This function can be used by commands such as `find` to check individual pathnames against a pattern.

The glob() function is an alternative which automatically reads the directory structure and generates a *list* of pathnames matching a given filespec.

typedef int (*func_t)(char *,int);

Synopsis: *int glob(char *pattern,int options, func_t errfunc,glob_t *pathlist);*

Return value: 0 on success, non-zero error codes on error.

Synopsis: *void globfree(glob_t *pathlist);*

Return value: None.

The glob() function generates a list of pathnames matching **pattern**. Note that glob() does not search directories in the manner of **find**, but simply matches each pathname accessible from the current directory directly against **pattern**. For example, a **pattern** of "*.c" matches only files in the current directory whose names end in ".c". To match those in subdirectory *Programs*, you must use the pattern "Programs/*.c".

The argument **pattern** specifies which filenames to match. **Options** contains optional bitwise flags to control the behavior of glob(). See the glob() man page on your system for a specific list of options. **Errfunc** is a pointer to a function which glob() calls if it cannot get the status of a file, open a subdirectory, or if any other error is encountered. This argument may be passed **NULL** if no error handling is desired. The **pathlist** argument is a structure which will contain a list of pathnames generated by glob(). Memory is allocated as needed to store the list in a pointer array. Thus, the globfree() function should be called as soon as the pathnames are no longer needed.

Example:

The program below demonstrates a simple use of glob().

```
#include <stdio.h>
#include <glob.h>

int     main(int argc,char *argv[])
```

```
{
    glob_t  paths;
    int     code;
    char    **p;

    code = glob("*.c",0,NULL,&paths);
    if (code == 0)
    {
        for (p=paths.gl_pathv; *p != NULL; ++p)
            puts(*p);
        globfree(&paths);
    }
    else
        fprintf(stderr,
                "Glob error.  Code = %d\n",code);
    return EX_OK;
}
```

22.5 Bulk Memory Manipulation

The string functions (those beginning with `str`), deal with null terminated strings. A similar set of functions exist for dealing with fixed length blocks of memory. Naming is similar to the string functions, but with `str` replaced by `mem`. A few of these functions are discussed below.

22.5.1 Copying Blocks: `memcpy()` and `memmove()`

Synopsis: *void *memcpy(void *dest,const void *src,size_t len);*

Return value: `dest`.

The `memcpy()` function copies `len` bytes from `src` to `dest`. If the blocks overlap, the copy is not reliable. In these cases, use `memmove()`.

Synopsis: *void *memmove(void *dest,const void *src,size_t len);*

Return value: `dest`.

The `memmove()` function copies a block of memory like `memcpy()`, but is guaranteed to work properly even if the blocks overlap. This requires a small amount of additional work, so `memcpy()` is somewhat faster for non-overlapping blocks.

22.5.2   Comparing Blocks: `memcmp()`

Synopsis: *int memcmp(const void *address1,const void *address2);*

Return value: Same as `strcmp()`.

The `memcmp()` function compares two blocks of memory in the same fashion as `strcmp()`, but the number of bytes compared is limited by the number of bytes specified by `len`, rather than by a null terminator.

Chapter 23

Odds and Ends

Before you begin...

You should be familiar with the material on arrays presented in chapter 15.

23.1   Math Functions

The math functions provided in the standard libraries are far too numerous to list here, so we'll focus on a few important points.

Because they are so numerous, and used by relatively few programmers, the math functions are not found in the main library, *libc*.a. Instead, they are stored in a separate library file called *libm*.a. Hence, to build a program that uses math functions, you must specify *libm*.a using "-lm" in the link command. For example, to compile a program in a single source called *calc.c*, use the following command:

```
gcc -Wall calc.c -lm
```

In a makefile, this option would appear in the link command only:

```
OBJS    = calc.o trig.o
CC      = gcc
CFLAGS  = -c -Wall

calc:   $(OBJS)
        $(CC) -o calc $(OBJS) -lm

calc.o: calc.c calc.h
        $(CC) $(CFLAGS) calc.c

trig.o: trig.c calc.h
        $(CC) $(CFLAGS) trig.c
```

There are two header files that are important to programs using math functions.

The *math.h* header contains prototypes for all the math functions, and definitions for many common mathematical constants, such as M_PI for π, M_E for the natural log base, and M_SQRT2 for the square root of 2 ($\sqrt{2}$).

Each type of computer hardware may use different floating point formats, as described in chapter 2. The header *float.h* provides named constants describing the limits and specific features of each machine's floating point system. The names of these constants are standardized, so that you can write portable code that works within the limitations of the underlying hardware.

The gcc math library contains more than 150 math functions to choose from, so if you're doing any math programming, it's a good idea to look here before you write your own functions. Odds are, you'll find what your looking for. For a list of functions, try apropos math, man math, or for a complete listing of the library, ar t /usr/lib/libm.a | more.

In addition to the standard math library, there are additional math libraries available on the internet, such as *CLAPACK*, the C Linear Algebra Package. *CLAPACK* is an extensive library of routines for performing linear algebraic computations, which was originally written in *FORTRAN* under the name *LINPACK*. *CLAPACK* is available on the World Wide Web from *http://www.netlib.org*.

23.2 Data Conversion Functions

23.2.1 General Conversion Functions

Synopsis: *long strtol(char *string,char **end,int base);*

Return value: The value converted, or LONG_MIN or LONG_MAX. Unreliable if an error occurred.

The strtol() function converts the ascii text beginning at the address string to a signed long value.

The second argument, end, should be the address of a char * variable, which will be filled with the address of the first character following the text that was converted. If you don't need to know where the number ended, you can pass this argument the value NULL. However, the only way to detect when a number could not be converted is to check the end value, which will contain the address string if no digits were found.

The argument base specifies the base to use in the conversion. The base may be any integer from 2 to 36.

Synopsis: *unsigned long strtoul(char *string,char **end,int base);*

Return value: The value converted, or ULONG_MAX. Unreliable if an error occurred.

The strtoul() function is equivalent to strtol(), except that it converts to an unsigned long. Hence, strtoul() cannot convert negative values (strings starting with the character '-'), but can convert positive values up to $2^{32} - 1$, whereas strtol() is limited to $+2^{31} - 1$.

Synopsis: *double strtod(char *string,char **end);*

Return value: The value converted. Unreliable if an error occurred.

The strtod() function converts ASCII text representing a real number to a double value, in the same manner that strtol() converts integers. Note that strtod() always uses base 10. The format of string may be any of the real number formats accepted by scanf().

Example:

The code fragment below extracts decimal numbers from a string containing mixed text. All intervening whitespace and other text is discarded.

```c
#define BASE            10
#define MAX_LINE_LEN    256
#define MAX_VALS        100

char    line[MAX_LINE_LEN+1],
        *p, *end;
long    vals[MAX_VALS];
int     v = 0;

for (p=line; *p != '\0'; ++p)
{
    if ( isdigit(*p) || (*p == '-') || (*p == '+') )
    {
        /* Attempt to convert text */
        vals[v] = strtol(p,&end,BASE);

        /* Was this really a number? */
        if ( end != p )
        {
            ++v;
            p = end;
        }
        /* False alarm - just a '-' or '+' */
        else
            ++p;
    }
    else    /* Ignore intervening text */
        ++p;
}
```

In addition to the conversion functions discussed above, several other functions are provided for convenience.

Synopsis: *int atoi(char *string);*

Return value: The value converted. Unreliable if an error occurred.

Equivalent to `(int)strtol(string,NULL,10);`

Synopsis: *long atol(char *string);*

Return value: The value converted. Unreliable if an error occurred.

Equivalent to `strtol(string,NULL,10);`

Synopsis: *double atof(char *string);*

Return value: The value converted. Unreliable if an error occurred.

Equivalent to `strtod(string,NULL);`

23.3   Random Numbers

Synopsis: *int rand(void);*

Return value: A pseudo-random value.

Synopsis: *void srand(unsigned seed);*

Return value: None.

Synopsis: *long random(void);*

Return value: A pseudo-random value.

Synopsis: *void srandom(unsigned seed);*

Return value: None.

The rand() and random() functions generate sequences of **pseudo-random** numbers. Pseudo-random numbers are not truly random, but are actually a predictable sequence generated by an algorithm. The quality of a pseudo-random sequence is, in part, determined by it's **period**, which is how many values are produced before the sequence repeats itself. The longer the period, the more difficult the sequence is to predict.

In addition to the period, random sequences can be made less predictable by altering the starting point of the sequence, a process know as **seeding the sequence**.

The srand() and srandom() functions cause rand() and random() functions to start at different points and thus generate different initial sequences.

The rand() and srand() functions are considered obsolete, and have been replaced by random() and srandom(), which produce much less predictable sequences.

23.4   Basic Process Control

23.4.1   Normal Termination: exit()

Synopsis: *void exit(int exit_code);*

Return value: Does not return.

 This function performs a system call.

The exit() function gracefully terminates the calling process. Any open files are first closed, and the program then terminates, returning the argument value exit_code to the parent process. Calling exit(code); from anywhere in the program is roughly equivalent to return code; in main().

A header file called *sysexits.h* is provided to maintain some consistency in exit codes among programs. This file contains manifest constants naming common reasons for a program to terminate. For example, if a program is run with incorrect command line arguments, it should use exit(EX_USAGE);. If the program must terminate because it can't open an input file, it should use exit(EX_NOINPUT);.

23.4.2   Last Requests: atexit()

Synopsis: *int atexit(void (*function)(void));*

Return value: 0 on success, -1 on error.

The `atexit()` function registers `function` to be called upon program exit, i.e. when `exit()` is called, or when the `return` statement is executed by `main()`. Before exit, the registered functions are executed *in reverse order*. Hence, the last function registered through `atexit()` is the first called before the program terminates.

The `atexit()` function is most useful for registering functions that restore environmental parameters such as the tty state, which is discussed in chapter 26.

23.4.3 Creating a Core File: `abort()`

Synopsis: *void abort(void);*

Return value: Does not return.

 This function performs a system call.

The `abort()` function causes the calling process to terminate abnormally and dump its **core**, by sending itself the `SIGABRT` signal. A core is a snapshot of the memory image of a program. It contains the contents of the CPU registers and all the program's in-memory data at the time of the core dump. The core file is very useful in debugging programs, since debuggers can utilize the information inside to determine where problems have occurred. Signals are discussed in chapter 27. Termination is not graceful; no files are flushed or closed before exit.

The `abort()` function is useful for forcibly generating a core image for examination by a debugger. Core images and debuggers are discussed in chapter 19.

23.5 Manipulating the Environment

23.5.1 Reading the Environment: `getenv()`

Synopsis: *char *getenv(char *name);*

Return value: A pointer to the *value* of the environment variable `name`, or `NULL` if `name` is not defined.

The `getenv()` function searches the process environment string for the variable
name. The environment is a string containing a sequence of definitions of the form
"name=value\0". The end of the environment is marked by two consecutive null
bytes.

The environment is inherited from the parent process. Thus, a program can extract
information set by the parent process it is running under, and can pass information
to it's children. Processes are covered in chapter 27.

Example:

> The code fragment below extracts the variable `TERM` from the environ-
> ment. This is a common operation for full-screen programs such as
> editors and mailers.

```
int     main()

{
    char    *term_type;

    if ( (term_type = getenv("TERM")) == NULL )
    {
        fputs("No TERM variable defined.\n",stderr);
        return EX_CONFIG;
    }
    ...
    return EX_OK;
}
```

The environment can also be accessed via **envp**, the third optional argument to
`main()`. See section 16.6 for details.

23.5.2   Writing to the Environment

Synopsis: *int putenv(char *string);*

Return value: 0 on success, -1 on failure.

The `putenv()` function adds `string` to the environment. String must have the form "name=value\0". This function is considered obsolete, and has been replaced by `setenv()`.

Synopsis: *int setenv(char *name,char *value,int overwrite);*

Return value: 0 on success, -1 on failure.

The `setenv()` function adds the string "name=value\0" to the environment. If the variable `name` is already defined, and `overwrite` is non-zero, then the value of `name` is replaced with the new value.

Synopsis: *void unsetenv(char *name);*

Return value: None.

The `unsetenv()` function removes the variable `name` from the environment, if it exists. If `name` is not defined, `unsetenv()` has no effect.

23.6 Sorting and Searching

23.6.1 Sorting: `qsort()`

typedef int (*cmp_t)(void *,void *);

Synopsis: *void qsort(void *base,size_t count,size_t size,cmp_t compare);*

Return value: None.

The `qsort()` function implements the quicksort algorithm on an array of objects pointed to by `base`. The arguments `count` and `size` represent the number and size of each element in the array. The last argument, `compare`, must point to a *function* which compares two elements, and returns a status value like that of `strcmp()`. See section 22.2.4 for a description of function pointers.

Example:

The code fragment below demonstrates how to sort an array of strings using `qsort()`.

The total amount of data moved by `qsort()` is the product of the second and third arguments.

```
int     main()
{
    char    name_list[MAX_NAMES][MAX_NAME_LEN+1];
    size_t  names;

    names = read_names(name_list);
    qsort(name_list,names,MAX_NAME_LEN+1,strcmp);
    ...
}
```

Programming for Performance:

The example above is inefficient, since it requires entire strings to be swapped in memory. Note that `qsort()` must move the entire row of `MAX_NAME_LEN+1` bytes, since it doesn't know that it is sorting null terminated strings. This is even more expensive than using `strlcpy()`, which would stop at the null byte. A better approach is demonstrated in the second code example below.

The example below uses an array of pointers rather than an array of strings. This will allow `qsort()` to simply swap the *addresses* of the strings, rather than move the entire strings. This requires a new compare function which takes pointers to the pointers in `name_list`:

Example:

```
int     strptrcmp(const char **s1,const char **s2)

{
    return strcmp(*s1,*s2);
}


int     main()
{
    char    *name_list[MAX_NAMES];
    size_t  names;

    names = read_names(name_list);
    qsort(name_list,names,sizeof(char *),
        strptrcmp);
    ...
}
```

If MAX_NAME_LEN is forty, and a pointer is four bytes, this program will move one tenth as much data as the first example.

Quicksort is an $O(NlogN)$ (Order N times log of N) algorithm, which means the time it takes to sort N elements is proportional to N times the log of N. The quicksort algorithm has shown the best average performance of any general sorting algorithm. However, it also shows a high variance in performance. In the worst case, when the data is already sorted, the basic quicksort algorithm behaves exactly like selection sort, and thus exhibits $O(N^2)$ performance. Most implementations of qsort() have safeguards against poor performance on a sorted list. However, there are still certain arrangements of values that can cause degraded performance.

In addition to qsort(), some libraries offer other $O(NlogN)$ sort functions such as mergesort() and heapsort(). These functions are more stable than quicksort, and guarantee $O(NlogN)$ performance in all cases. However, they tend to show a slightly slower average sort time due to the overhead costs they incur. In addition, the mergesort algorithm requires a duplicate array, and therefore twice as much memory as quicksort.

The **radix sort** algorithm is an $O(N)$ sorting algorithm. While faster than any other sort algorithm, the radix sort has limited applications, and may require vast amounts of memory to implement. For more information on sorting, consult a text on data structures and algorithms.

23.6.2   Searching: bsearch()

typedef int (*cmp_t)(void *,void *);

Synopsis: *void *bsearch(void *key,void *base,size_t count,size_t size, cmp_t compare);*

Return value: A pointer to the first match found, or NULL if no match was found.

The bsearch() function implements the **binary search** algorithm. This algorithm searches a *sorted* list much in the same way you would look up a name in the phone book. If the list is not sorted, you have no choice but to use a simple **linear search**, which checks every element in the list until the item is found, or the end of the list is reached.

Let's assume we have a list sorted in ascending order. The binary search begins searching in the middle of the list. If the value in the middle of the list is greater than the value sought, then the latter half of the list can be eliminated. If the value is less than the value sought, then the first half can be eliminated. We then recursively apply the binary search process to the remaining half of the list until the value is found, or the number of remaining elements is reduced to 1. Thus, the number of comparisons is limited by how many times we can divide the list in half, which is $log_2 N$. For example, to search a sorted list of 1,000,000 values will require no more than $log_2 1,000,000$, or 20 comparisons.

The first argument to bsearch(), key, is a pointer to the value you want to find. The argument base is a pointer to the first element in the array. The count and size arguments state the number and size of each element in the array. The last argument, compare, must point to a *function* which compares two elements in the array. Note that the compare function takes two *pointers* to array elements as its arguments.

Key and base must be of the same type, namely the type expected by the function pointed to by compare.

Example:

```
#include <stdio.h>
#include <stdlib.h>
#include <string.h>
#include "extra.h"

#define MAX_NAMES       100
#define MAX_NAME_LEN    40

/* Prototypes */
int     strptrcmp(char **s1,char **s2);
size_t  read_list(char *name_list[],size_t max_names);
void    print_names(char *name_list[],size_t names);
void    free_names(char *name_list[],size_t names);

int     main(int argc,char *argv[])

{
    char    *name_list[MAX_NAMES],
            key[MAX_NAME_LEN+1],
            *skey[1],
            **match;
    size_t  names;

    /* Read and sort name list */
    names = read_list(name_list,MAX_NAMES);
    qsort(name_list,names,sizeof(char *),strptrcmp);
    print_names(name_list,names);

    /* Get search criteria */
    fputs("Enter a name to search for: ",stdout);
    fgetline(stdin,key,MAX_NAME_LEN);
    skey[0] = key;

    /* Search list */
    match = bsearch(skey,name_list,names,
```

```
                        sizeof(char *),strptrcmp);
    if ( match != NULL )
        printf("Found: %s",*match);
    else
        puts("No match.");
    free_names(name_list,names);
    return 0;
}



/*
 * Compare strings at two locations in an array of
 * pointers to string.
 */

int     strptrcmp(char **s1,char **s2)

{
    return strcmp(*s1,*s2);
}



/*
 * Read list of names into a pointer array
 */

size_t  read_list(char *name_list[],size_t max_names)

{
    size_t  c = 0;
    char    temp[MAX_NAME_LEN+1] = "x";

    fputs("Enter names followed by a blank line.\n",
            stdout);
    while ( (c<max_names) &&
            (fgetline(stdin,temp,MAX_NAME_LEN) != 0) )
    {
        name_list[c++] = strdup(temp);
    }
```

```
        return c;
        fpurge(stdin);
    }



/*
 * Print list of names in a pointer array
 */

void    print_names(char *name_list[],size_t names)

{
    size_t  c;

    for (c=0; c<names; ++c)
        puts(name_list[c]);
}



/*
 * Free memory allocated by read_list()
 */

void    free_names(char *name_list[],size_t names)

{
    while ( --names > (size_t)-1 )
        free(name_list[names]);
}
```

23.7 Functions with Variable Argument Lists

Some functions, such as `printf()`, `scanf()` and `execlp()`, take a variable number of arguments. These functions require some special treatment from the compiler, as well as a bit of tricky coding.

The old K&R compilers, which ignored function argument lists, didn't have any trouble compiling these functions. These compilers would simple pass whatever arguments were present in a function call, and *assume* the function would know what to do with them.

ANSI compilers, however, check the argument lists in function calls to make sure the right number and types of arguments are passed to the function. Thus, a special type of prototype is needed to allow the argument list to vary. This format uses an elipsis to designate the variable arguments. For example, the prototype for `printf()` is shown below:

```
int     printf(const char *format,...);
```

This prototype specifies that `printf()` should receive a character string followed by zero or more other arguments.

Definitions for functions with variable argument lists are handled by one of two special macro packages, which are described in the next two sections.

23.7.1   ANSI Form: *stdarg.h*

The *stdarg* package is the more modern package for processing variable argument lists. This package requires at least one fixed argument to be defined. This package uses three special macros to process arguments, and a pointer of the type `va_list`, which is usually a simple `char *`. Note that these are merely macros, and are not supported by the compiler. The only knowledge the macros require is the orginization of the arguments in memory. Generally, when arguments are passed to a function, they are pushed onto the stack in either forward, or reverse order. For example, the call

```
printf("Runs: %d  Hits: %d  Errors: %d\n",runs,hits,errs);
```

will produce an argument list looking something like this:

Address	Contents
1000	Format-string address.
1004	A copy of `runs`.
1008	A copy of `hits`.
1012	A copy of `errs`.

The *stdarg* package simply uses the address of the format string as a starting point, and moves down the list from there.

va_start(argptr,last_fixed) locates the first non-fixed argument, using the address of the last *fixed* argument as a reference. This macro simply sets `argptr` to `&last_fixed + sizeof(last_fixed)` (assuming arguments are passed with the first at the lowest address).

va_arg(argptr,type) returns the next non-fixed argument in the argument list, and updates `argptr` by adding `sizeof(type)` to it.

va_end(argptr) gracefully closes down the *stdarg* system. On most systems, this macro actually does nothing, but it is present in case a particular system needs to free memory, or perform any other cleanup tasks.

Example:

```
#include <stdio.h>
#include <stdarg.h>

void    print_nums(int num,...);

int     main(int argc,char *argv[])

{
    print_nums(1,2,3,4,-1);
    print_nums(1,2,-1);
    return 0;
}


/*
 * Print one or more positive values.  The end of
 * the list is marked by a -1 value.
 */

void    print_nums(int num1,...)
```

```
    {
        va_list argptr;
        int     num;

        /* Print first value */
        printf("%d ",num1);

        /* Get pointer to argument list */
        va_start(argptr,num1);

        /* Print remaining arguments */
        while ( (num = va_arg(argptr,int)) != -1 )
            printf("%d ",num);

        /* Shut down */
        va_end(argptr);
    }
```

23.7.2   Unix Form: *varargs.h*

The *varargs* package is the older standard, and is generally considered obsolete. However, it does have one advantage, in that it allows the creation of functions with no fixed arguments.

The macros are generally the same as in *stdarg*, execpt that the **va_start**() macro takes only one argument, namely the **va_list** pointer to be initialized.

The definition of a *varargs* function *must* have a single argument named **va_alist**. This argument is defined K&R style using the **va_dcl** macro. Note that there is no semicolon after **va_dcl**. A semicolon is included in the macro definition.

Example:

```
        #include <stdio.h>
        #include <varargs.h>
```

```
void      print_nums();

int       main(int argc,char *argv[])

{
    print_nums(1,2,3,4,-1);
    print_nums(1,2,-1);
    return 0;
}


/*
 * Print one or more positive values.  The end of
 * the list is marked by a -1 value.
 */

void      print_nums(va_alist)
va_dcl

{
    int       num;
    va_list argptr;

    /* Get pointer to argument list */
    va_start(argptr);

    /* Print remaining arguments */
    while ( (num = va_arg(argptr,int)) != -1 )
        printf("%d ",num);

    /* Shut down */
    va_end(argptr);
}
```

Chapter 24

Working with the Unix Filesystem

Before you begin...

> You should be familiar with the material on Unix, arrays, and structures presented in chapters 4, 15 and 18.

24.1   File Information: `stat()` and `fstat()`

Synopsis: *int stat(const char *path,struct stat *st);*

Return value: 0 on success, -1 on error.

 This function performs a system call.

Synopsis: *int lstat(const char *path,struct stat *st);*

Return value: 0 on success, -1 on error.

This function performs a system call.

Synopsis: *int fstat(int fd,struct stat *st);*

Return value: 0 on success, -1 on error.

The `stat()`, `lstat()` and `fstat()` functions retrieve the information in a file's **inode**, and place it in the structure pointed to by `st`. Inodes are disk structures maintained by Unix which contain most of the information about a file, such as permissions, the file's owner, file type, file size, and so on. **There is exactly one inode per file.**

Inodes should not be confused with directory entries, known as **links** in Unix, which are discussed in section 24.3. There may be more than one link for the same file, and links contain very little information. The main purpose of a link is to give each file a pathname and to point to the file's inode.

The `stat()` and `fstat()` functions return exactly the same information. The only difference between them is that `stat()` identifies the file through a path name, while `fstat()` does so through a file descriptor. If a file is currently open, it's faster to get the inode information with `fstat()`. A call to `stat()` requires reading the directory and inode from disk, whereas `fstat()` can retrieve the information from memory, since the `open()` call that opened the descriptor has already read the directory entry and inode information.

The `lstat()` function only differs from `stat()` in that it returns information about a symbolic link, whereas `stat()` returns information about the file referenced by the link.

Pitfall: Pointing to Nowhere

A very common programmer error with `stat()`, `fstat()`, and many other functions that take pointers is giving it a garbage pointer. For example, consider the following code fragment:

```
char     path[PATH_LEN+1];
struct stat *st;
```

```
stat(path,st);
```

While this code will compile cleanly, it will most likely cause a segmentation fault or bus error, since the pointer `st` contains a garbage address, and doesn't point to a real structure object. In fact, no structure object is even defined here. The correct way to use stat is as follows:

```
char    path[PATH_LEN+1];
struct stat st;

stat(path,&st);
```

Errors like these stem from a lack of understanding of pointers. If you find yourself making these types of mistakes, you may want to review chapters 14, 15, and 16.

Section 24.3 and chapter 25 contain several examples of using `stat()` and `fstat()`.

24.2 Changing File Information

24.2.1 Changing Ownership: `chown()`

Synopsis: *int chown(char *path,uid_t uid,gid_t gid).*

Return value: 0 on success, -1 on failure.

 This function performs a system call.

The `chown()` function changes the user and group ownership of the file named by `path`. Note that the ownership information is stored in the *inode*, not the *directory*, so the change in ownership will be reflected in every link to the file.

The `uid` and `gid` arguments specify the user and group you wish to own the file.

Only the superuser, *root*, can change the individual ownership of a file. This prevents users from inadvertently changing the ownership of their files, and subsequently losing access to them. It also prevents malicious users from intentionally changing ownership of their files (so that another user will be accountable for the disk space, for example).

You may, as an ordinary user, change the *group* ownership of the file to any group that you belong to.

24.2.2   Changing Permissions: chmod()

Synopsis: *int chmod(char *path,mode_t mode);*

Return value: 0 on success, -1 on error.

 This function performs a system call.

The chmod() function changes the permissions on the file named by path to mode.

Only the lowest 12 bits of mode have meaning on most current systems. Modes may be specified as octal values (which must begin with a 0), or preferably as the bitwise *OR* of bit masks defined in *stat.h*. Octal values are convenient, because each group of three bits in mode share a common meaning. The name and meaning of each bit is described in figure 24.1.

The SUID, SGID, and sticky bits are described in section 4.3.3.

The remaining bits specify the read, write, and execute permissions on the file or directory named by path. For example, to make your *.login* file executable to everyone, readable to the group, and writable only to yourself, use the following call:

```
if ( chmod(".login",0751) != 0 )
    fputs("Unable to change permissions.\n",stderr);
```

Using the manifest constants, this would be:

```
if ( chmod(".login",S_IRWXU|S_IRGRP|S_IXGRP|S_IXOTH) != 0 )
    fputs("Unable to change permissions.\n",stderr);
```

Octal	Name	Meaning
04000	S_ISUID	Set user ID on execute.
02000	S_ISGID	Set group ID on execute.
01000	S_ISVTX	Sticky bit.
00400	S_IRUSR	User who owns the file can read.
00200	S_IWUSR	User can write.
00100	S_IXUSR	User can execute.
00040	S_IRGRP	Group who owns the file can read.
00020	S_IWGRP	Group can write.
00010	S_IXGRP	Group can execute.
00004	S_IROTH	Other users (i.e. anybody) can read.
00002	S_IWOTH	Others can write. (Bad idea)
00001	S_IXOTH	Others can execute.

Figure 24.1: Bit Values for `chmod()`

To mark the file *a.out* SUID, and make it executable to everyone, use the following:

```
if ( chmod("a.out",04711) != 0 )
    fputs("Unable to change permissions.\n",stderr);
```

or

```
if ( chmod("a.out",S_ISUID|S_RWXU|S_XGRP|S_IXOTH) != 0 )
    fputs("Unable to change permissions.\n",stderr);
```

24.3 Accessing Directories

A **directory** is a special type of file which lists the names and locations of other files in the filesystem. It is analogous in form to a building directory, the glass case usually found in the lobby of an office building which contains the names and locations of each building occupant.

Each Unix directory entry, called a **link**, contains the following items:

- The file's inode number, which uniquely identifies the file on the disk.

- The length of the directory entry in bytes.

- The length of the filename in bytes.

- The filename of this link. Note that Unix allows more than one link to the same inode. Put another way, a file may be referenced by multiple directory entries.

A Unix directory is a simple concatenation of such directory entries.

24.3.1   Reading Directories

Unix directories *can* be read using standard file functions such as **read()** or **fread()**, but this is not advisable. Instead, a separate set of routines are provided to make reading directories convenient and portable. These routines manage a **directory stream**, analogous to the file streams defined in *stdio.h*. These routines are prototyped in the header *dirent.h*.

Synopsis: *DIR *opendir(char *dirname);*

Return value: A pointer to the open directory, or **NULL** if the open failed.

 This function performs a system call.

The **opendir()** function opens a directory for *reading*. Note that writing to a directory is very risky, since any errors that occur could cause the destruction of the only link to a file. Such an error can only be fixed by an exhaustive filesystem and directory structure check. Hence, updating directories should be left to the operating system, and not done by user programs.

Synopsis: *struct dirent *readdir(DIR *dp);*

Return value: A pointer to an internal static structure containing the next directory entry, or **NULL** when the end of the directory is reached or an error occurs.

 This function performs a system call.

The `readdir()` function reads the next directory entry into a *local static structure*, and returns the address of the structure. In other words, `readdir()` does not allocate memory for each new entry, but simply overwrites the previous entry in its internal structure variable each time it is called.

Pitfall: Single Occupancy Only

Since `readdir()` returns a pointer to it's own local structure variable, the entry is overwritten by the next call to `readdir()`. Hence, if you need to keep the entry beyond the next `readdir()` call, you must copy the contents of the structure to a different location.

```
struct dirent    *entry, save;

entry = readdir(dp);
save = *entry;  /* Save the current entry since *entry
                   is overwritten by next readdir() */
```

Synopsis: *int closedir(DIR *dp);*

Return value: 0 on success, -1 on error.

 This function performs a system call.

The `closedir()` function closes the directory and frees all memory allocated for the `DIR` structure.

Example:

The program below implements a rudimentary `ls` command.

```
#include <stdio.h>
```

```
#include <dirent.h>

int     main(int argc,char *argv[])

{
    DIR     *dp;
    struct dirent   *entry;

    /* Open the current working directory */
    dp = opendir(".");
    if ( dp != NULL )
    {
        /* List each entry's inode and name */
        while ( (entry = readdir(dp)) != NULL )
            printf("%ld %s\n",entry->d_ino,
                    entry->d_name);
    }
    closedir(dp);
    return 0;
}
```

24.3.2   Creating Directories

Synopsis: *int mkdir(char *path,mode_t mode);*

Return value: 0 on success, -1 on error.

This function performs a system call.

The `mkdir()` function creates a new directory named `path`, with permissions specified by `mode`. This function is described fully in section 21.8.4.

Chapter 25

Low-Level I/O

Before you begin...

You should be familiar with the material on stream I/O presented in chapter 21.

25.1   Why Use Low-level I/O?

ALL Unix I/O is ultimately performed by a small set of low-level I/O functions, regardless of which I/O interface your program uses. The low-level functions `open()`, `read()`, `write()`, and `close()` represent the lowest layer of software used to control every I/O device.

`FILE` streams are a second layer of I/O software. Stream functions use low level I/O functions to communicate directly with devices. For example, `fopen()` calls the low-level `open()` function, `fclose()` calls the low-level `close()` function, and `putc()` indirectly calls `write()` when it's stream buffer is full.

Programming for Performance:

Using low-level I/O in place of streams directly eliminates an entire layer

of software from the application, leaving your programs smaller and often
much faster in terms of CPU use.

Equally important is the fact that a typical I/O operation to a disk or
terminal takes more time than the *total* CPU time used by the program.
Hence, reducing the total number of I/O operations is one of the major
goals in program optimization, since it eliminates many long delays in
program execution.

Programs that perform I/O in large blocks, rather than one or a few
characters at a time, should use low level I/O in order to maximize performance. This will save CPU time by avoiding unnecessary buffering,
and can also reduce the number of I/O operations. Stream I/O typically
uses a rather small 512 or 1024 byte buffer by default. Using low level
I/O directly allows you to specify a much larger buffer size, in order to
minimize the number of I/O system calls.

Note that using low level I/O can also *decrease* performance if your program requires many I/O operations that transfer small amounts of data.
In fact, this is why stream I/O was created. The buffering mechanisms of
streams greatly reduce the number of I/O system calls when performing
single character I/O operations.

Simple programs such as `cat` and `cp`, which blindly move data from one
place to another without even looking at it, are great candidates for low
level I/O.

On the other hand, programs such as `cpp, grep`, and `sed`, which must
examine every character in the stream, are much easier to implement
using stream I/O, and therefore would not benefit much from the use of
low level I/O.

25.1.1   Cat: A Bad Example

A common mistake among C programmers is using stream I/O when low level I/O
would be more efficient. Many programmers tend to make this mistake because they
are more accustomed to using stream I/O, and know little or nothing about the potential performance benefits of low level I/O. The following sections will demonstrate
this point.

Example:

Consider the following program, which implements the Unix `cat` command.

```
#include <stdio.h>
#include <sysexits.h>

int     main(int argc,char *argv[])

{
    switch(argc)
    {
        case    1:
            fpin = stdin;
            break;
        case    2:
            if ( (fpin = fopen(filename,"r")) == NULL )
            {
                fprintf("Could not open file: %s\n",
                        file_name);
                return EX_NOINPUT;
            }
            break;
        default:
            fprintf(stderr,"Usage: %s [file]\n",
                    argv[0]);
            return EX_USAGE;
    }
    while ( (ch=getc(fpin)) != EOF )
        putchar(ch);
    fclose(fp);
    return EX_OK;
}
```

The sequence of `getc()` and `putc()` calls maintains *two* stream buffers, one for `fpin` and one for `stdout`. Characters are copied *one at a time* from the `fpin` buffer to `ch`, and then to the `stdout` buffer, before they are eventually written to the output device. The `stdout` buffer, when full, has the *exact* same contents as the `fpin` buffer did when it was initially filled. It would be much more efficient for `cat` to simply read data into a buffer, and output it directly from the same buffer. The following sections will demonstrate how this can be done.

25.2 Basic Input and Output

25.2.1 Opening Files: `open()`

Synopsis: *int open(char *filename,int flags,mode_t mode);*

Return value: The *lowest available* file descriptor, or -1 if the file cannot be opened.

 This function performs a system call.

The `open()` function attempts to open the file named by `filename`. The `flags` argument contains individual bits that specify the open mode and other options for the file and for the device driver that controls it. Flags are specified by constants defined in *fcntl.h*, which may be combined using a bitwise OR. Some of the common values are described below.

O_RDONLY: Open the file for reading only. If the file does not exist, the open fails.

O_WRONLY: Open for writing only. If the file does not exist, the open will fail, unless the `O_CREAT` flag is also present. If it does exist, it will not be immediately erased, but will be overwritten by subsequent `write()` calls.

O_CREAT: Create the file if it does not exist, and is being opened for writing.

O_RDWR: Open the file for both reading and writing.

O_TRUNC: Specifies that if the file already exists, it should be truncated (erased) immediately upon being opened. This flags is commonly used with `O_WRONLY`.

O_APPEND: Open the file for writing, and cause `write()` calls to add to the end of the file, rather than overwrite it.

O_NONBLOCK: Causes `read()` operations to return immediately if no data is available, rather than wait for input. Most useful when the device being opened is an asynchronous device such as a terminal, network, or pipe. Usually a needless waste of CPU time. Other methods for watching descriptors, such as `select()`, should be considered first.

O_EXLOCK: Causes the process to obtain an exclusive lock on the file if `open()` is successful.

O_SHLOCK: Causes the process to obtain an shared lock on the file if `open()` is successful.

The `mode` argument specifies the permission mode to use when a file is created. This mode is modified by the process' `umask`, as describe in section 4.3.3. If a file is not being created, as with `O_RDONLY`, this argument is irrelevant, and is usually passed the value 0.

25.2.2 Reading Files: `read()`

Synopsis: *size_t read(int fd,char *buff,size_t count);*

Return value: The number of bytes read (0 at end of file), or -1 on error.

 This function performs a system call.

The `read()` function attempts to read `count` bytes from the file descriptor `fd`, and place them in the buffer `buff`. If reading from a file, and fewer than `count` bytes remain, `read()` will read the remaining bytes, and return the number of bytes read. If reading from an asynchronous device, such as a keyboard, `read()` will cause the process to block (wait) until input becomes available, unless the `O_NONBLOCK` flags has been set by `open()` or by `fcntl()`. Some device drivers, such as certain PC bus mouse drivers, may be non-blocking by default.

25.2.3 Writing Files: `write()`

Synopsis: *int write(int fd,const char *buff,size_t count);*

Return value: The number of bytes written, or -1 on error.

 This function performs a system call.

The write function attempts to write `count` bytes from `buff` to the file described by `fd`. Errors generally occur only if the file descriptor is invalid, or the device is full or not operating.

25.2.4   Closing Files: `close()`

Synopsis: *int close(int fd);*

Return value: 0 on success, -1 on failure.

 This function performs a system call.

The `close()` function closed the file descriptor specified by `fd`. Any output buffered by the device driver is first written to the device.

25.2.5   Moving Within a File: `lseek()`

Synopsis: *off_t lseek(int fd,off_t offset,int whence);*

Return value: The new position relative to the beginning of the file.

 This function performs a system call.

The `lseek()` function repositions the descriptor's pointer to the specified byte position in the file. This function is the low-level equivalent to `fseek()`. For a full description, refer to `fseek()` in section 21.6.3.

25.2.6   Cat: A Better Example

Example:

The program below is a more efficient version of the Unix `cat` command, using low-level I/O. It avoids the needless copying of characters from one stream buffer to another that was present in the previous example. Also, given the fairly large (64k) buffer, this program will read small files in a single `read()` call, and will therefore be in the system for a much shorter amount of time than the previous example.

Note that this program can be easily converted to a `cp` command by simply adding support for another command line argument which specifies the destination.

Since we are using low level file descriptors instead of streams, we need to use the `fileno()` function to get the descriptors associated with `stdin` and `stdout`. These descriptors is almost invariably 0 and 1, but programs should never assume this, since a process could inherit altered file descriptors from its parent.

```
#include <stdio.h>
#include <unistd.h>
#include <sys/types.h>
#include <fcntl.h>
#include <sysexits.h>

/* 64k buffer will mean few read and write calls */
#define BUFF_SIZE    65536

int     main(int argc,char *argv[])

{
    char    buff[BUFF_SIZE+1];
    int     infd;
    size_t  bytes;

    switch(argc)
    {
        case    1:  /* Used as filter */
            infd = fileno(stdin);
```

```
                    break;
            case    2:   /* Open the given filename */
                infd = open(argv[1],O_RDONLY);
                if ( infd == -1 )
                {
                    fprintf(stderr,
                            "Could not open file: %s\n",
                            argv[1]);
                    return EX_NOINPUT;
                }
                break;
            default:
                fprintf(stderr,"Usage: %s [file]\n",
                        argv[0]);
                return EX_USAGE;
        }

        /* Read and write 64k blocks */
        while ( (bytes=read(infd,buff,BUFF_SIZE)) != 0 )
            write(fileno(stdout),buff,bytes);
        close(infd);
        return EX_OK;
    }
```

To add a bit of perspective, consider the data in table 25.1. This table compares
two simple programs used to copy a 32 megabyte file. One program uses stream
I/O, as follows:

```
    while ( (ch=getc(infile)) != EOF )
        putc(ch,outfile);
```

The other uses low level I/O, with a 4096 byte buffer:

```
    while ( (bytes=read(infile,buff,BUFF_SIZE)) > 0 )
        write(outfile,buff,bytes);
```

I/O Method	User CPU	System CPU	Real Time	% of Total CPU
Stream	52.615	12.350	1:10.82	91.7
Low level	0.187	19.530	0:43.38	45.4

Table 25.1: Streams vs. Low Level I/O

As indicated in table 25.1, the low level I/O copy ran about 40% faster in real time, and used almost no user CPU time. Virtually all of the CPU time used by the process was **system time**, i.e. time spent executing kernel routines (system calls).

In contrast, the stream I/O copy used 52 seconds of user-level CPU time to manage the stream buffers with getc() and putc(). This should come as no surprise when you consider that the program had to perform 32 million getc() and putc() calls. Imagine the effects this code would have if incorporated into a software package used by dozens of people on the same system. Note also that the stream I/O version used up virtually *all* of the available CPU cycles, leaving none to spare for other processes. Obviously, this program would heavily impact the performance of other processes in the system.

25.2.7 Choosing the Right Buffer Size

When reading or writing disk files using low-level I/O, performance depends heavily on the number of bytes read or written with each call. This is because disks are divided into fixed sized **disk blocks**.[1] (See figure 3.1.)

The disk controller always reads or writes exactly one block at a time. If your program requests part of a block, the disk controller will read the whole block anyway, and the operating system will throw away the part your program didn't ask for. If you later want to read the rest of the block, the whole block must be read again.[2]

For example, imagine your disk has 1024 bytes in each block, and your program reads in a file sequentially 512 bytes at a time. When your program requests the

---

[1]A block is the amount of information that the operating system reads or writes at a time. A block is one or more **sectors**, where a sector is the unit of information used by the disk hardware. A block that consists of multiple sectors is also known as a **cluster**. A typical sector size is 512 bytes, and some typical block (cluster) sizes are 1, 2, 4 and 8 kilobytes.

[2]The remaining information may not really be discarded if your system performs disk caching, but it isn't safe to assume the data will still be in the memory buffer when you need it later.

BUFSIZ	User time	System time
1	5.30	41.63
2	2.58	20.80
4	1.43	10.27
8	0.70	5.30
16	0.42	2.60
32	0.13	1.40
64	0.07	0.70
128	0.03	0.37
256	0.03	0.18
512	0.02	0.10
1024	0.00	0.08
2048	0.00	0.05
4096	0.00	0.03
8192	0.00	0.03

Table 25.2: Time used reading a large file with `read()`

first 512 bytes, the disk controller actually reads 1024 bytes, and the operating system will discard the latter 512 bytes. When your program reads the next block of 512 bytes, the disk controller will have to read the *same block again*, and this time, throw away the *first* 512 bytes. This program will eventually read every block in the file *twice*, which will seriously reduce program performance. Performance will be further degraded if the program reads even smaller blocks. If your program reads 1024 bytes at a time instead, each block will be read only once, and the program will complete it's input operations in half the time. Table 25.2 shows the effects of different block sizes in `read()` calls. Note that the time required to read the file drops quickly as the block size is increased toward 4096 bytes. The time for 8192 bytes is the same as for 4096, suggesting that 4096 is the block size for this disk. Note also that reading an entire block at a time reduced system time by a factor of about three over reading 512 or 1024 bytes (the typical size of a stream buffer) at a time. The '0.00' entries under user time indicate that the user time used by the program was simply too small to measure.

A general rule of thumb is to always use a buffer size which is a *multiple* of the block size of the disk. It doesn't matter whether you read one block or two, as long as you never read or write a *fraction* of a block. Since different disks use different block sizes, and you can never predict what kind of hardware your program will be run on next, it is impossible to determine the best buffer size when you write a program. Instead, your program must determine the optimal buffer size at run time. This can be done using the `stat()` or `fstat()` library functions. The stat information returned by these functions includes a member which specifies the block size used by the device on which the file resides.

Example:

The function below determines the block size of the disk to be read from.

```
#include <sys/stat.h>

int     catfile(filename)
char    *filename;

{
    struct stat fileinfo;
    int         fd,bytes;
    long        buffsize;
    char        *buff;

    /* Open file */
    if ( (fd = open(filename,O_RDONLY)) == -1 )
    {
        fprintf(stderr,"Cannot open %s.\n",filename);
        return -1;
    }

    /* Determine block size and create buffer */
    fstat(fd,&fileinfo);
    buffsize = fileinfo.st_blksize;
    buff = alloca(buffsize);

    /* Display file */
    while ( (bytes = read(fd,buff,buffsize)) > 0 )
        write(fileno(stdout),buff,bytes);
    close(fd);
```

```
        return bytes;
    }
```

Unix systems commonly have more than one disk drive, and different disks may use different block sizes. If you write a program that reads from one file and writes to another, the read and write operations may be using different disks, and therefore have different optimal buffer sizes. So how does one choose a buffer size that suits both the read and write operations?

Fortunately, there is a simple solution. By using the *least common multiple* (LCM) of the two block sizes, you can ensure that both read and write operations will deal only with whole blocks. A function to compute the LCM of two values is given in the example below.

It is extremely unlikely, but nevertheless possible, that the LCM of two buffer sizes could be larger than you would want to allocate memory for. For example lcm(31k,16k) is 496k, almost 1/2 megabyte. Most disks don't have odd block sizes such as 31k, but just in case, it won't hurt to set a maximum buffer size. This can be easily done using the MIN() macro provided in the sample program below.

If your program chooses the maximum buffer size because it is smaller than the LCM, your program performance will be slightly decreased since it will occasionally read a fraction of a block. For example, if the buffer size is chosen as 64k, and one block size is 9k, your program will read $7\frac{1}{9}$ blocks at a time. The eighth block will have to be re-read, but the first seven will not. This is a small price to pay to avoid using a 1/2 megabyte buffer.

Example:

The function below copies a file using the optimal buffer size, up to a maximum of 64 kilobytes. The buffer is allocated using **alloca()**, so it is freed automatically when the function returns.

```
#include <unistd.h>
#include <fcntl.h>
#include <sys/types.h>
#include <sys/stat.h>
```

```
int     cp(char *src,char *dest)

{
    int         infile,outfile;
    struct stat instats,outstats;
    long        optimal, buff_size, bytes;
    char        *buff;

    /* Open source and destination files */
    if ( (infile = open(src,O_RDONLY)) == -1 )
        return -1;

    if ( (outfile = open(dest,O_WRONLY|O_CREAT|
                        O_TRUNC,0700)) == -1 )
        return -1;

    /* Compute optimal buffer size */
    fstat(infile,&instats);
    fstat(outfile,&outstats);
    optimal = LCM(instats.st_blksize,
                outstats.st_blksize);
    buff_size = MIN(optimal,65536);
    buff = (char *)alloca(buff_size);

    /* Copy file */
    while ( (bytes = read(infile,buff,buff_size)) > 0 )
        write(outfile,buff,bytes);
    close(infile);
    close(outfile);

    /* Return 0 for success */
    return bytes;
}
```

25.2.8   Handling Multiple Files: `select()`

Programs often need to act on input from more than one source. For example, a program may provide an interface for both the keyboard and a mouse. The problem this presents is how to detect input availability on one device while waiting for input on the other. For example, how would a program know when the mouse has moved if it is stuck waiting for keyboard input?

One (very poor) solution which is sometimes employed is to use non-blocking I/O. In this case, read calls return immediately if no input is available, rather than place the program into a blocked state until new input arrives. This approach is an enormous waste of CPU time, since the program has to sit in a loop issuing read calls on both descriptors until an input event occurs.

Another approach, which is more efficient, but cumbersome to program, is to use signals. A program can be set up to receive signals when an input event occurs on a given descriptor. This approach requires the use of signal handlers, which are difficult to integrate into modular code.

A third option, which is also inefficient, is to create multiple cooperating processes. Each process responds to events from one of file descriptors. This is undesirable, both because of the difficulty in programming it, and the added system load caused by creating extra processes.

Fortunately, Unix provides an interface for such **event-driven** programs. The `select()` function simply blocks the calling process until an event occurs on *any* one of the file descriptors given to `select()`.

Synopsis: *int select(int limit,fd_set *readfds, fd_set *writefds, fd_set *exceptfds, struct timeval *timer);*

Return value: The total number of ready descriptors, or -1 on error.

 This function performs a system call.

The `select()` function blocks the calling process until one of the named file descriptors becomes ready for service, or until `timer` expires. An event is defined as any of the following:

- Input has arrived on one of the read descriptors listed in `readfds`.

- A write operation has completed on one of the write descriptors listed in **writefds**, and the device is now ready for more output.

- An exception has occurred on one of the descriptors listed in **exceptfds**.

A timer value of **NULL** specifies that the **select()** call should wait indefinitely for an I/O event. Otherwise, when the specified amount of time has passed with no I/O events, **select()** returns 0, indicating no I/O events have occurred.

The **limit** argument specifies the highest numbered file descriptor to be watched, and must be one greater than the highest file descriptor in any of the lists.

The **fd_set** arguments are initialized using the following macros.

Synopsis: *FD_SET(int fd,fd_set *set);*

Return value: Undefined.

The **FD_SET()** macro adds the file descriptor **fd** to the specified set.

Synopsis: *FD_CLR(int fd,fd_set *set);*

Return value: Undefined.

The **FD_CLR()** macro removes the file descriptor **fd** from the specified set.

Synopsis: *FD_ISSET(int fd,fd_set *set);*

Return value: Non-zero if an event is pending on **fd**.

The **FD_ISSET()** macro can be used to determine whether or not a file descriptor is part of a set.

Synopsis: *FD_ZERO(int fd,fd_set *set);*

Return value: Undefined.

The **FD_ZERO()** macro initialized **set**, clearing any file descriptors included in it.

Each descriptor set is modified in place by the **select()** function, and therefore must be reinitialized before the next call to **select()**. The **timer** argument, if not **NULL**, also may be modified on some systems, so it must also be reset before the next **select()** call.

Example:

The code fragment below uses `select()` to wait for input from a keyboard and a mouse.

```
static struct timeval    *timeout = NULL;
fd_set           readfds;
int              fd_count, status, key_fd, mouse_fd;

key_fd = fileno(stdin);
mouse_fd = open("/dev/mouse",O_RDONLY,0);
if ( mouse_fd == -1 )
{
    fputs("Unable to open mouse.\n",stderr);
    exit(EX_NOINPUT);
}

do
{
    /* Initialize fd set for select() */
    FD_ZERO(&readfds);
    FD_SET(key_fd,&readfds);
    FD_SET(mouse_fd,&readfds);
    fd_count = MAX(key_fd,mouse_fd) + 1;

    /* Get new event */
    if ( (status = select(fd_count,&readfds,
                     NULL,NULL,timeout) != 0) )
    {
        /* Keyboard event? */
        if ( FD_ISSET(key_fd,&readfds) )
            get_key_event(terminal,&temp_event);

        /* Mouse event? */
        if ( FD_ISSET(mouse_fd,&readfds) )
            tget_mouse_event(terminal,&temp_event);
        ...
```

```
        }
    }   while (...);
```

25.2.9 Controlling File Descriptors: `fcntl()`

Synopsis: *int fcntl(int fd,int command,int arg);*

Return value: Depends on `command`.

 This function performs a system call.

The `fcntl()` system call is used to control the parameters of a file descriptor. `fcntl()` is actually the interface to a variety of different kernel services for file descriptors. `Fd` specifies an open file descriptor on which to operate. `Command` is one of several constants defined in *fcntl.h*, including the operations listed below. The meaning of `arg` depends on `command`.

F_DUPFD: Duplicates the file descriptor. This operation is more conveniently handled by the `dup()` or `dup2()` functions, which issue the `fcntl()` calls for you. These functions are discussed in section 27.2.

Given this command, `fcntl()` returns the new duplicate file descriptor.

F_GETFL: Retrieves the current flags for the file descriptor `fd`, as set by `open()` or previous `fcntl()` calls.

Given this command, `fcntl()` returns the value of the flags.

F_SETFL: Set the current flags for `fd` to `arg`. This command is usually used after retrieving the flags using **F_GETFL**, and setting or clearing bits in the flags variable.

Given this command, `fcntl()` returns -1 on error, or any value on success.

F_SETOWN: Set the process or process group to receive `SIGIO` signals when `fd` becomes ready.

F_GETOWN: Return the process ID or process group currently receiving SIGIO signals for fd.

F_SETFD: Set the *close-on-exec* flag for fd to the low-order bit of arg. If this flag is set, then the file descriptor *will not* be inherited by a child process. Instead, it will be closed when the parent calls execve(). (See chapter 27 for details.)

F_GETFD: Return the *close-on-exec* flag for fd.

F_SETLK: Sets or clears a file lock on fd. This operation is more conveniently handled by the flock() interface.

F_GETLK: Returns the current lock status of fd.

Example:

The code fragment below uses fcntl() to set the non-blocking read() attribute for fd.

```
int     main()

{
    int     infd, flags;

    /* Open file */
    infd = open(filename,O_RDONLY,0);
    ...

    /* Set non-blocking operation */
    flags = fcntl(infd,F_GETFL,0);
    flags |= O_NONBLOCK;
    if ( fcntl(infd,F_SETFL,flags) == -1 )
    {
        fputs("Can't set non-blocking I/O.\n",
              stderr);
        return EX_OSERR;
    }
    ...
```

```
        return EX_OK;
    }
```

Chapter 26

Controlling I/O Device Drivers

Before you begin...

You should be familiar with the material on low-level I/O presented in chapter 25.

Device drivers often can operate in more than one mode. For example, terminal drivers normally operate in **line-buffered mode**, also known as **cooked mode** or **canonical mode**, in order to reduce the number of **read()** system calls necessary to process keystrokes. Programs running in this mode wait in an I/O queue until an entire line of input is types, i.e. until the user presses *enter*. At that point, the program is placed back in the ready queue to await service from the CPU, so that it can process the line of input characters it just received.

This chapter discusses ways to manipulate the mode of a device driver. The techniques discussed here can apply to almost any device in the */dev* directory, but are most commonly used to control **tty** (terminal) modes.

Device driver control is performed using the **ioctl()** (I/O control) system call, which uses a wide variety of *commands* to manipulate the driver in different ways. In addition, some methods provide higher level functions for convenience, which perform the necessary **ioctl()** calls for you. These methods are discussed in the following sections.

26.1   Termios

There are several different interfaces for controlling device drivers. The most modern is the **termios** package, which is an extension of the *System V* **termio** package, discussed in section 26.1.8.

The termios package consists of various `ioctl()` commands, plus several higher level functions and macros which issue `ioctl()` calls for you. Termios stores all the terminal driver parameters in a `termios` structure, which is defined as follows:

```
#define NCCS     20

typedef unsigned long    tcflag_t;
typedef unsigned char    cc_t;
typedef long             speed_t;

struct termios
{
    tcflag_t        c_iflag;        /* input flags */
    tcflag_t        c_oflag;        /* output flags */
    tcflag_t        c_cflag;        /* control flags */
    tcflag_t        c_lflag;        /* local flags */
    cc_t            c_cc[NCCS];     /* control chars */
    speed_t         c_ispeed;       /* input speed */
    speed_t         c_ospeed;       /* output speed */
};
```

The structure consists of four sets of Boolean flags, a list of control characters, and the input and output speeds. Many of these fields apply only to serial port (e.g. RS232) devices. The RS232 interface is the standard used by many modems, printers, mice, and other devices. Figure 26.1 describes the standard pins of an RS232 serial connection.

The following sections describe the most commonly used flags and functions. For more details on advanced functionality, try `man termios`.

Information is loaded into the structure using `tcgetattr()`. For example,

```
struct termios  term;
```

Pin	Name	Description
2	TD	Transmit data line output
3	RD	Receive data line input
4	RTS	Request to send output
5	CTS	Clear to send input
6	DSR	Data Set read input
7	GND	Ground
8	DCD	Data carrier detect input
20	DTR	Data terminal ready output
22	RNG	Ring indicator input

Figure 26.1: The RS232 Serial Interface for a DB-25 connector

```
int             fd;

tcgetattr(fd,&term);
```

The flags in the structure are then modified, and the updated structure sent back to the device driver using `tcsetattr()`. A complete example is presented in section 26.1.6.

26.1.1 Input Flags

The `c_iflag` field contains Boolean flags that control the processing of input on the file descriptor. The most commonly used flags are:

INPCK: Enable parity checking.

INLCR: Convert incoming newlines to carriage returns.

IGNCR: Ignore carriage return characters. This is useful when uploading a text file from *DOS* or *Windows* to Unix through a serial connection. These files contain NL-CR pairs marking the end of each line, while Unix files use only the NL character. By setting the `IGNCR` flags, you eliminate the need for the file transfer program to strip the CR characters manually.

ICRNL: Convert incoming carriage returns to newlines.

IXON: Enable output flow control. This causes the driver to stop sending output when a stop character (usually ctrl+S) is received.

IXOFF: Enable input flow control. Causes the driver to send a stop character when the input buffer is full.

26.1.2   Output Flags

The `c_oflag` field contains flags that control output processing. The most common flags are described below.

OPOST: Enable output processing. If 0, all other output processing flags are disabled. This provides a simple method for switching output processing on and off without having to keep track of individual flags.

ONLCR: Add a carriage return character following each newline character in the output. This allows Unix files, which contain only a newline at the end of each line, to be copied directly to a terminal for viewing. Most terminals only move the cursor down when a newline is received, so a carriage return is also necessary to move it back to column 1. With `ONLCR` set, programs such as `cat` and `more` have no need to manually insert carriage returns.

OXTABS: Expand tabs to spaces before output. This option is useful for terminals that don't support tab characters well.

26.1.3   Control Flags

The `c_cflags` field contain the control flags. These flags control features implemented in the device's hardware. Most of these flags apply only to RS232 and similar serial ports. The following are the most commonly used flags.

CSIZE: Mask for the two bit flags specifying the number of data bits in each character transmitted. These bits should be set to `CS5`, `CS6`, `CS7` or `CS8`.

CSTOPB: Configures the device to use two stop bits instead of one.

PARENB: Enables parity checking and generation by the serial port *hardware*. This differs from the `INPCK` flag, which enables parity checking in the driver. Both of these flags must be set to utilize parity checking.

PARODD: Enables odd parity, if `PARENB` is set. If `PARENB` is set, and `PARODD` is 0, even parity is used.

HUPCL: Causes a hang up signal to be sent when the last file descriptor on the line is closed.

CLOCAL: Local line flag. Tells the driver that this line is *not* connected to a modem, so modem control wires such as carrier detect should be ignored.

CRTSCTS: Enables hardware flow control. This causes the RTS (ready to send) and CTS (clear to send) lines of an RS232 or similar port to be utilized, if present. Some terminal connections, particularly those using RJ-11 phone wire, don't have RTS and CTS wires. In these cases, CRTSCTS must be disabled.

26.1.4 Local Flags

The `c_lflags` field contains various other control flags which are generally handled locally by the driver.

ECHOE: Echo erase (backspace) characters. If not set, some terminals will merely move the cursor left when a backspace is typed, without erasing the character.

ECHO: Enable automatic echoing of input characters. This flag is usually set when the input is being line buffered, so that users will see the characters they type even though they are not being processed by the program.

ECHOCTL: Causes any control characters typed to be echoed back as a '^' followed by the corresponding letter. For example, typing ctrl+L will cause the string '^L' to be sent back by the driver.

ISIG: Enable signal keys such as INTR (normally ctrl+C) and STOP (normally ctrl+Z). When ISIG is disabled, it is not possible to kill a program using ctrl+C.

ICANON: Enables input line buffering (canonical processing). Programs that need to process keystrokes immediately, such as editors, should disable `ICANON`.

TOSTOP: Blocks background processes from sending output to this descriptor. Any output process that attempts to do so is sent a STOP signal.

26.1.5   Control Characters

The c_cc field contains a list of special characters used by the driver, as well as some additional control information.

c_cc[VEOF]: The end-of-file character. Simulates the end-of-file condition on the keyboard.

c_cc[VSUSP]: Suspend character. When typed, causes a SIGTSTP signal to be sent to the current foreground process. Normally ctrl+Z.

c_cc[VINTR]: Interrupt character. When typed, causes the SIGINT signal to be sent to the current foreground process. Normally ctrl+C.

c_cc[VSTOP]: Stop character. (Software flow control) When typed, causes the foreground process to be blocked upon further output to the terminal. The process will wait in the I/O queue until the terminal is unblocked by a VSTART. Also sent by some terminal emulators and file transfer programs to prevent buffer overflow. Normally ctrl+S.

c_cc[VSTART]: Unblocks the terminal for output. Normally ctrl+q, unless IXANY is set, in which case any character typed will serve as a VSTART.

c_cc[VMIN]: If canonical processing is *disabled*, this specifies the minimum number of characters needed before a read() returns successfully. Setting c_cc[VMIN] to a value greater than 1 will reduce the number of system calls executed by your program, and thus improve efficiency. If 0, read() will return immediately with no data if no input was waiting when the read() call was issued. Some applications, such as editors, must set c_cc[VMIN] to 1, since they must act immediately on every keystroke. The default value varies from system to system.

c_cc[VTIM]: If canonical processing is disabled, this specifies the maximum amount of time (in tenths of a second) a read() call will wait for the number of characters specified by c_cc[VMIN]. If c_cc[VTIM] is 0, read() will wait indefinitely.

26.1.6   The Termios Functions

The normal procedure for manipulating the driver state using termios is calling tcgetattr() to read the current state into a structure, modifying the structure using various functions and bit operations, and then setting the new state using `tcsetattr()`.

Synopsis: *int tcgetattr(int fd,struct termios *p);*

Return value: 0 on success, -1 on error.

 This function performs a system call.

The `tcgetattr()` function reads the current state of the driver underlying the file descriptor `fd`, and places it into the termios structure pointed to by `p`.

Synopsis: *int tcsetattr(int fd,int when,struct termios *p);*

Return value: 0 on success, -1 on error.

 This function performs a system call.

The `tcsetattr()` function sets the state of the driver behind file descriptor `fd` to the state specified by `p`. The second argument determines when the change should take place, and must be one of the following values:

TCSANOW: Set the new state immediately. Any previous output still in the output buffer will be transmitted under the new state.

TCSADRAIN: Delay setting the new state until after all pending output has been transmitted to the terminal. This is usually desirable, since any output written prior to the `tcsetattr()` call is probably expected to be transmitted under the old state.

TCSAFLUSH: Same as `TCSADRAIN`, except that any pending input is also discarded.

Example:

The following function demonstrates how to shut off canonical processing, so that a program can respond immediately to key commands.

```
void     traw_mode(int fd)

{
    struct termios  term;

    /* Get current state */
    tcgetattr(fd,&term);

    /* Force read() to wait for exactly 1 char */
    term.c_cc[VMIN] = 1;
    term.c_cc[VTIME] = 0;

    /* Disable output processing */
    term.c_oflag &= ~OPOST;

    /* Disable canonical mode, echo, etc. */
    term.c_lflag &= ~(IEXTEN|ICANON|ISIG|ECHO);

    /* Disable flow control and CR-NL conversions */
    term.c_iflag &= ~(IXON|IXOFF|ICRNL);

    /* Set new state */
    tcsetattr(fd, TCSADRAIN, &term);
}
```

26.1.7 Alternatives to the Termios Interface

26.1.8 Other Low Level Methods

The **termio** method is the old *System V* standard interface. The **sgtty** method is the old *BSD standard*. Both of these methods rely on direct calls to the `ioctl()` function. In addition, the *BSD standard* includes the `stty()` and `gtty()` functions which predate the `ioctl()` interface.

As mentioned earlier, the termios interface is the most modern method for controlling terminal devices. Although this method evolved out of the *System V* standard, it is also used by most recent *BSD* compatible systems, so new code should be written using termios. The other interfaces are only mentioned here only for completeness.

26.1.9 High Level Libraries

In addition to the low-level interfaces mentioned above, there are many high-level libraries available for controlling terminals. These libraries generally contain a rich set of functions for manipulating text windows within a terminal screen, as well as some high-level functions for controlling the driver mode.

Curses

The *Curses* library is a standard component of most Unix systems. There are several free versions of the Curses package available. The most recent and popular is the *Ncurses* packages, which is available at your favorite GNU site.

Curses uses a set of image manipulation routines to build a *picture* of each window, and of the entire terminal screen. The programmer must insert `refresh()` calls at each point in the program where the physical screen needs to be updated. This method minimizes the number of I/O operations required to draw and update windows on the screen.

The down side comes to light when using Curses for highly interactive programs, which need to update the screen after each keystroke. The `refresh()` calls are expensive in terms of CPU use, and somewhat of a nuisance for the programmer. Each call examines the entire screen image to determine which characters need to be redrawn. Hence, calling refresh for each new character received on input is very expensive. For this reason, you may want to consider using one of the commercial alternatives to curses.

Commercial Libraries

There are several commercial libraries available as alternatives to curses. Two of the most popular are *Vermont Views* and *Vitamin C/CE*. Both of these libraries are extremely rich in features that allow programmers to quickly create highly interactive programs with pop-down menus, dialog boxes, and so on. They are also available for multiple operating systems including many versions of *Unix*, *DOS*, *OS/2*, and *Windows*. Hence, they make it easy to create highly portable applications, with attractive, intuitive interfaces.

Chapter 27

Unix Processes

Before you begin...

You should be familiar with the material on Unix, arrays, and pointer arrays presented in chapters 4, 15, and 16. Some knowledge of structures, as presented in chapter 18, is also helpful.

A process is, as described in chapter 4, the execution of a program. All operating systems must provide a mechanism for creating new **processes** or **jobs**.[1] For example, each time you type a command on the Unix command line, the shell process creates a new **child process** to run the command. Consider the following command:

```
tcsh 1: ls
```

The shell process, which is running `tcsh`, creates a child process to run the `ls` command. The the `ls` program is finished, the process **terminates**, or dies.

The shell process normally waits for each child process to complete before it continues. It then prints the next command prompt, and waits for the next command to be entered.

---

[1]The term *process* refers specifically to a job in a preemptive multitasking operating system such as Unix. Batch (non-interactive) systems use the term **job** to refer to a running program.

Since Unix is a multitasking operating system, it is possible to run more than one process at a time. For example, placing a '&' character at the end of any Unix command causes it to be run as a **background process**. (See section 4.9) This simply means that the parent process, namely the shell, doesn't wait for the command to finish, but instead continues running *in parallel*, at the same time as the child. This is often useful when a child process takes a long time to run, since it allows you to continue using the shell while the background process runs.

The following sections discuss how programs such as shells can create and manipulate other processes.

27.1   Creating Processes

27.1.1   Creating Processes: `fork()`

All Unix processes are created with the `fork()` system call.

Synopsis: *pid_t fork(void);*

Return value: 0 to the child, the process ID of the child to the parent.

 This function performs a system call.

The way `fork()` works will probably seem a little strange at first, but will make sense once you begin to understand the intricacies of processes in a multitasking environment.

The `fork()` function creates an *exact duplicate* of the calling process, and returns the **process ID**, or **PID** of the new child process to the parent. The name *fork* comes from the fact that this system call causes the calling process to split into two identical processes, much like an amoeba. This creates a fork in the execution path of the parent process. The `fork()` function is the only function that can be called by *one* process, and return to *two* of them!

The new process created is *exactly the same* as the parent in every aspect, except that it has a different PID, and receives a return value of 0 from `fork()`. In other words, the child process runs the same program as the parent, and begins its execution *following the* `fork()` *call*, just like the parent process, rather than starting over at the beginning of `main()`. The *only* way to distinguish between the parent and child is by the PID, or the return value from `fork()`.

You may be wondering why you would want to create an exact duplicate of a process. The reason for this design comes from experience with the many operating systems that preceded Unix. It was discovered that there were some severe limitations imposed by systems that started a new program from scratch for every new process. In particular, it is difficult to pass vital information contained in the parent process to the child. If, on the other hand, the child is an exact duplicate of the parent, it inherently has all the same knowledge that the parent process has. The information inherited by a child process includes the contents of all the parent process' variables, and all open file descriptors. The child process can utilize and alter this information *before* it transforms itself into a new program. For example, consider the following command:

```
tcsh 1: ls > files.list
```

The first step the shell takes in running `ls` is to call `fork()`. This action creates an identical shell process. This child shell then redirects the standard output file descriptor so that it refers to the file *files.list* instead of the terminal screen. After taking care of this housekeeping chore, the child shell transforms itself into the `ls` command, which inherits the new file descriptor, and as a result, unwittingly sends all of its output to *files.list*.

Now, let's consider what would have to happen if the `ls` command were run directly, instead of duplicating the shell first. Somehow, the `ls` command would need to be instructed to send it's output to the file *files.list* instead of the screen. This would require two additional features:

1. A special communication interface between the shell and any program that it could run.

2. *Every* program would have to be equipped with the ability to perform redirection.

By using the `fork()` system to duplicate the parent process, *only* the shell needs to contain the code to perform redirection. This code is executed by the child shell immediately after the fork, and before the process loads and runs `ls` or any other program. A code example is shown in section 27.2.

27.1.2   Transforming Processes: execve()

After a process forks, it generally continues to execute the parent code for only a short time, enough to perform redirection or other housekeeping chores. The child process then transforms itself by loading and running a new program, replacing the current program image, but keeping the same PID. In essence, Unix processes are changelings. They can alter their form at will, but retain their identity until they die. This is done by the execve() system call.

Synopsis: *int execve(char *path,char *argv[],char *envp[]);*

Return value: Does not return if successful. -1 on error.

 This function performs a system call.

The execve() system call replaces the current program image with a new program, which will run under the same PID. Since the calling program is replaced, execve() cannot return if it is successful.

The path argument must specify either the full or relative pathname of the executable. The argv argument must be constructed exactly as described in section 16.6, with argv[0] being the program name, and the remaining elements being the arguments. The envp argument is a list of environment variables, as described in section 16.7.

There are several higher level exec functions provided for convenience, which call execve() after performing some other service for the programmer. The execve() function is rather inconvenient in many situations. For example, the path argument must contain the full pathname of the command, which your program must determine in advance. Also, the envp argument is often not available in functions other than main(), unless it is passed down as an argument.

Synopsis: *int execvp(char *progname,char *argv[]);*

Return value: The return value of the underlying execve() call.

 This function performs a system call.

The execvp() function (the 'p' is for "path") is somewhat more convenient, since it automatically searches the PATH environment variable, and thus doesn't require the full pathname of the command. It also eliminates the envp argument entirely from the programmer's view, and takes care of it behind the scenes.

Synopsis: *int execlp(char *prog,char *arg0,...);*

Return value: The return value of the underlying execve() call.

 This function performs a system call.

Like execvp(), execlp() function searches the PATH, but it also builds the argv array for you. This function is convenient for executing a specific command which is hard coded into your program. Each argument to the program is taken as a separate argument to execlp(). Thus, execlp() takes a variable number of arguments. The last argument must be NULL, so that execlp() will know where the end of the argument list is.[2]

The prog and arg0 arguments are often identical, although prog may specify a pathname, while arg0 should be only the base filename.

The following code fragment produces a long listing of the files in */etc*, using execlp():

```
if ( fork() == 0 )
{
    /* In child */
    execlp("ls","ls","-als","/etc",NULL);
    perror("ls");
    exit(errno);
}
else
{
    /* In parent */
    ...
}
```

---

[2]The execlp() function uses the variable argument macros discussed in section 23.7.

If `execve()` fails, it returns -1 and sets `errno` to indicate the cause of the failure. Note that the return value is really irrelevant, since the mere fact that `execve()` returned indicates that it failed. Hence, the first statement following any `execve()` call can begin processing the error. Also, there should usually be an `exit()` call following each exec, so that the child process doesn't linger in the system.

27.1.3   Waiting for Godot: `wait()`

Synopsis: *pid_t wait(wait_t *status);*

Return value: The PID of the child.

  This function performs a system call.

The `wait()` function causes the calling process to block until one of its children terminates. The PID of the child that terminated is returned, and the exit status of the child process is stored in `status`.

The `status` argument is defined as a structure on some systems, and as an integer on others. In either case, the status contains at least two parts:

1. One part contains information on *how* the child process terminated or stopped. For instance, it may have exited normally, using `exit()`, or a `return` from `main()`, or it may have been terminated by a signal such as a segmentation fault or interrupt.

2. The other part contains the exit status (from `exit()` or return) of the child process if it terminated normally.

Several macros are defined for processing the `status` argument.

- `WIFEXITED(status)` is true (non-zero) if the child process exited voluntarily, using `exit()` or `return`.

- `WIFSIGNALLED(status)` is true is the child process was killed by a signal.

- `WIFSTOPPED(status)` is true if the child process was stopped and may be continued.

If the child process terminated normally, you can use `WEXITSTATUS(status)` to extract the exit status from the `status` argument.

If the child was killed by a signal, `WTERMSIG(status)` will produce the signal value that caused the termination, and `WCOREDUMP(status)` will be true if the termination produced a core file.

If the child was stopped, `WSTOPSIG(status)` will provide the signal value that stopped it.

In some cases, a parent may produce several child processes, and may wish to wait for a particular child process to terminate. This can be done using the `waitpid()` or `wait4()` functions.

Synopsis: *pid_t waitpid(pid_t pid,wait_t *status,int options);*

Return value: The PID of the child.

 This function performs a system call.

The `options` argument may be 0, or a combination of the the options defined in *sys/wait.h*. These options are somewhat advanced, so we'll skip the explanation here.

Synopsis: *pid_t wait4(pid_t pid,wait_t *status,int options,struct rusage *usage);*

Return value: The PID of the child.

 This function performs a system call.

The `wait4()` function is the most general of all the wait functions. In addition to the information returned by `waitpid()`, `wait4()` sends back the child process' resource usage statistics. This information is used by programs such as `time` and and `gdb`, which monitor and report on other processes.

27.1.4   A Complete Example

Example:

The program below implements a rudimentary, yet fully usable Unix shell.

```c
#include <stdio.h>
#include <stdlib.h>
#include <string.h>
#include <unistd.h>
#include <sys/wait.h>

#define COMMAND_LEN 255
#define MAX_ARGS    1024
#define STAT_MAX    20

enum {FALSE, TRUE};

int     main(int argc,char *argv[], char *envp[])

{
    char    cmd[COMMAND_LEN+1],
            *new_argv[MAX_ARGS],
            *path,
            stat_str[STAT_MAX+1];
    int     c,
            status;

    /* Input commands until "exit" is entered */
    do
    {
        fputs("Skel-shell: ",stdout);
        fgets(cmd,COMMAND_LEN,stdin);

        /* Set up argv array for execvp */
        path = new_argv[0] = strtok(cmd," \t\n");
        for (c=1; (new_argv[c] = strtok(NULL," \t\n"))
                    != NULL; ++c)
```

```
                        ;

            /* If it's an external command, fork */
            if ( strcmp(path,"exit") != 0 )
            {
                /* Create child process */
                if ( fork() == 0 )
                {
                    /* If child, run command */
                    execvp(path,new_argv);

                    /* Error: kill child */
                    perror(cmd);
                    exit(1);
                }
                else
                {
                    /* If parent, wait for child */
                    wait(&status);

                    /* Set ''status'' environment variable,
                       like C-shell does. */
                    snprintf(stat_str,
                            STAT_MAX,"%d",status);
                    setenv("status",stat_str,TRUE);
                }
            }
        } while ( strcmp(cmd,"exit") != 0 );
        return 0;
}
```

27.2 Redirection

Redirection is the act of changing the source or destination of a process' file descriptors, often *without any action by the process itself*. Redirection allows the output of

any program to be sent to a file, or the input read from a file, even if the program
lacks the ability to open files. For example, consider the following command:

```
tcsh 1: ls > files
```

This command *redirects* the output of the `ls` command to the file *files*. The `ls`
command itself does not open the file, and is actually unaware that it's output
is being sent there. The redirection here is performed by the shell, before `ls` is
executed.

Redirection is an extremely powerful shell feature, which allows many programs to
read and write files without being coded to do so on their own. The alternative is to
code each and every program with file management capability, and command line
options to specify the input and output files. Adding the same features to hundreds
or thousands of Unix commands would greatly increase the coding and maintenance
effort for the system. Much of this effort would be redundant, since all the programs
would be using essentially the same code to manipulate the files, a problem known
as **creeping feature syndrome**. Since the shell can open files for each program
before it is executed, these file manipulation features need only be present in the
shell, instead of in every program in the system.

Performing redirection in Unix is quite simple, due to the system of fork and exec
calls used to run programs. The sequence of events is as follows:

1. Call `fork()` to create a child process.

2. Alter the file descriptors you want redirected.

3. Call an exec function to run the new program.

Since a program run by an exec call inherits the file descriptors of the program it
replaces, the new program will receive input from, and send output to the same files
used by the caller.[3]

Performing redirection on a given file descriptor is simple. The simplest method
depends on the fact that the `open()` function always uses the *lowest* available (i.e.
not already open) file descriptor. Closing a file descriptor makes it available for

---

[3]You can prevent individual file descriptors from being inherited by setting the *close-on-exec*
flag, using `open()` or `fcntl()`.

use by the next `open()` call. Assuming that no lower-numbered descriptors are available, this will cause `open()` to choose the descriptor that was just closed. For example, consider the following code fragment:

```
close(0);
open(filename,O_RDONLY,0);
```

The `open()` call will choose file descriptor 0, since it must use the lowest available descriptor. Since descriptor 0 underlies `stdin`, these two statements redirect the standard input to *filename*. We can similarly redirect `stdout` by closing descriptor 1, and `stderr` by closing descriptor 2.

Example:

The program below is an extension to the shell example in section 27.1. This example includes the ability to perform redirection on `stdin` and `stdout`.

```
#include <stdio.h>
#include <stdlib.h>
#include <string.h>
#include <unistd.h>
#include <fcntl.h>
#include <sys/wait.h>

#define COMMAND_LEN 255
#define MAX_ARGS    1024
#define STAT_MAX    20

enum {FALSE, TRUE};

/* Prototypes */
int     parse_cmd(char *cmd,char *argv[],char **infile,
                  char **outfile,char **errfile);
int     redirect(char *infile,char *outfile,
                  char *errfile);
```

```
/*
 * The Skel-shell, a skeletal Unix command interpreter
 * with redirection.
 */

int     main(int argc,char *argv[], char *envp[])

{
    char    cmd[COMMAND_LEN+1],
            *new_argv[MAX_ARGS],
            *path,
            stat_str[STAT_MAX+1],
            *infile,
            *outfile,
            *errfile;
    int     status;

    /* Input commands until "exit" is entered */
    do
    {
        fputs("Skel-shell: ",stdout);
        fgets(cmd,COMMAND_LEN,stdin);

        /* Set up argv array for execvp */
        parse_cmd(cmd,new_argv,
                &infile,&outfile,&errfile);
        path = new_argv[0];

        /* If it's an external command, fork */
        if ( strcmp(path,"exit") != 0 )
        {
            /* Create child process */
            if ( fork() == 0 )
            {
                /* Perform redirection */
                redirect(infile,outfile,errfile);

                /* If child, run command */
                execvp(path,new_argv);
```

```
                /* Error: kill child */
                perror(cmd);
                exit(1);
            }
            else
            {
                /* If parent, wait for child */
                wait(&status);
                snprintf(stat_str,STAT_MAX,
                        "%d",status);
                setenv("status",stat_str,TRUE);
            }
        }
    } while ( strcmp(cmd,"exit") != 0 );
    return 0;
}



/*
 * Break a command into a list of arguments,
 * and separate * out redirection filenames.
 * The redirection operators * '<', '>', and '>&'
 * all must be surrounded by whitespace.
 */

int     parse_cmd(char *cmd,char *argv[],char **infile,
                char **outfile,char **errfile)

{
    int    c;

    /* Initialize redirection filenames */
    *infile = *outfile = *errfile = NULL;

    /* Tokenize command */
    argv[0] = strtok(cmd," \t\n");
    for (c=1; (argv[c] = strtok(NULL," \t\n"))
            != NULL; ++c)
```

```
        {
            if ( strcmp(argv[c],"<") == 0 )
            {
                *infile = strtok(NULL," \t\n");
                --c;
            }
            else if ( strcmp(argv[c],">") == 0 )
            {
                *outfile = strtok(NULL," \t\n");
                --c;
            }
            else if ( strcmp(argv[c],">&") == 0 )
            {
                *errfile = strtok(NULL," \t\n");
                --c;
            }
        }
        return 0;
}


/*
 * Perform redirection on default stdin,
 * stdout, and stderr * file * descriptors.
 */

int     redirect(char *infile,char *outfile,
                 char *errfile)

{
    if ( infile != NULL )
    {
        close(0);
        open(infile,O_RDONLY,0);
    }
    if ( outfile != NULL )
    {
        close(1);
        open(outfile,O_WRONLY|O_TRUNC|O_CREAT,0644);
```

```
        }
        if ( errfile != NULL )
        {
            close(2);
            open(errfile,O_WRONLY|O_TRUNC|O_CREAT,0644);
        }
        return 0;
    }
```

27.2.1 Redirection and Restoration

The example above *permanently* redirects certain file descriptors. In some cases, you may wish to redirect a descriptor *temporarily*, and later restore it to it's original file or device. In order to accomplish this, you will need to save the current device name or descriptor before you call `close()`.

The filename associated with a descriptor can only be determined if it refers to a **tty**, a terminal device. Plain files can be renamed at any time, even while processes have them open, so attempting to determine the filename associated with an open descriptor is difficult. Also, there may be many links to a plain file, which further complicates matters. This can be easily determined using the `isatty()` function. The name of the tty can then be determined using `ttyname()`.

```
    char    *old_ttyname,
            *new_filename;

    ...
    if ( isatty(fd) && ((old_ttyname=ttyname(fd)) != NULL) )
    {
        /* Redirect stdin */
        close(0);
        open(new_filename,O_RDONLY,0);
        ...

        /* Restore stdin to old tty */
        close(0);
```

```
        open(old_ttyname,O_RDONLY,0);
}
```

For other files, we must save the file descriptor itself, using the dup() function, which creates an exact duplicate of a file descriptor. Since a file descriptor refers to a specific file (inode), this will allow the redirected descriptor to be re-attached later with a second dup() call. Note that dup(), like open(), always selects the lowest available file descriptor.

```
int     save_fd;

/* Save current descriptor for stdin */
save_fd = dup(0);

/* Redirect stdin */
close(0);
open(new_filename,O_RDONLY,0);
...

/* Restore old descriptor */
close(0);
dup(save_fd);
```

Chapter 28

Interprocess Communication (IPC)

Before you begin...

> You should be familiar with the material on processes presented in chapter 27.

There are many methods for passing information from one Unix process to another. Some methods are inherently simple, but limited. Others are more powerful, and at the same time, more complex to use.

Pitfall: Doing Things the Hard Way

> Like all other programming situations, it is important to consider the *simplest* method first, and graduate to more complex methods *only* as needed. There may be a temptation to challenge yourself or, use a particular project to learn more about a new IPC method, or even impress your colleagues. However, choosing an over-complicated method will drive up the cost of the project, in terms of both your time, and resource usage. Avoid the temptation to use the most *interesting* method, and instead, always use the *easiest* and/or *fastest*.

557

The following sections describe the major IPC methods, in order of increasing intimacy and complexity.

28.1   The Environment

The **environment**, discussed in sections 4.10 and 23.5, is a list of string variables possessed by every Unix process. Each process inherits a copy of its parent's environment, which it is then free to modify and pass on to its children, much like a folk tale. Hence, the environment provides a simple mechanism for processes to communicate with their children.

This mechanism is used for many purposes by the shell. For example, the TERM environment variable is set by the shell, and used by its child processes such as editors, mailers, and other full-screen programs.

Note however, that the environment provides a one-way (parent to child) interface. At least in this environment, children are not able to talk back to their parents.

28.2   Signals

Signals are special messages that a process can receive either from another process, or directly from the kernel. Signals are **asynchronous**, that is, a signal may arrive at any moment without warning. All processes may potentially receive signals at any moment, and therefore must be properly set up to handle them. There are many different types of signals, some sent by the operating system, and some by other processes. Each process must know what to do for each type of signal that arrives. Therefore, each Unix process is initially assigned certain **default actions** for each type of signal. These default actions can be overridden by setting up a **signal handler** function in your program. Table 28.1 lists some of the common signals used in Unix systems, and their default actions. For a more complete listing of signals on your system, check the man page on *signal*, or view the header *signal.h*.

To set up a signal handler, use the `sigaction()` function. The `signal()` function provides a simpler interface, but behaves differently across systems, and is generally considered obsolete.

Synopsis: *int sigaction(int sig,struct sigaction *new, struct sigaction *old);*

Name	Default action	Description
SIGHUP	Terminate	Sent by OS when terminal connection lost.
SIGINT	Terminate	Interrupt generated by ctrl+C.
SIGILL	Core dump	Sent by OS following illegal instruction.
SIGABORT	Core dump	Process sends to itself using `abort()`.
SIGFPE	Core dump	Sent by OS following a floating point error.
SIGTERM	Terminate	Default signal sent by `kill` command.
SIGKILL	Terminate	Sent by `kill -9`.
SIGBUS	Core dump	Sent by OS following BUS error.
SIGSEGV	Core dump	Sent by OS following segmentation fault.
SIGTSTP	Suspend	Sent by suspend key (usually ctrl+Z).
SIGCONT	Ignore	Sent by `fg` command.

Table 28.1: Common signal types.

Return value: 0 on success, -1 on failure.

If `new` is not NULL, `sigaction()` installs a new action in response to subsequent signals of type `sig`.

If `old` is not NULL, it receives a copy of the old action installed for `sig`. This can be used to find out what the current action for a signal is, or to save the current action to be restored later.

The `sigaction` structure is defined as follows:

```
struct sigaction{
{
    sig_t       sa_handler;
    sigset_t    sa_mask;
    int         sa_flags;
}
```

The `sig_t` type is a pointer to a `void` function, which can be defined as follows:

```
typedef void (*sig_t)();
```

The `sa_handler` field specifies the action to take upon receipt of a signal. This is the address of the handler function, or one of the following constants, which are defined in signal.h.

SIG_IGN causes the signal to be ignored.

SIG_DFL specifies the default action. This is only needed when restoring a signal to its default state after it has been caught by a handler.

When a signal is received, that signal is **blocked** during the execution of the handler function. When a signal is blocked, the operating system will hold it in a pending state until it is unblocked. Hence, a process will not receive the same signal again until the handler finishes processing the first one.

The `sa_mask` field specifies a set of additional signals which will be blocked during execution of the handler. For example, you may wish to block `SIGINT` signals during the execution of a handler, so that it may complete important processing before the process is terminated by the user.

The `sa_flags` field, if non-zero, specifies some additional options for processing signals. These options include `SA_NOCLDSTOP`, which specifies that the `SIGCHLD` signal will only be delivered to a parent process in the event that a child process terminates, and not when it is merely stopped.

Example:

The program below demonstrates how to catch the `SIGINT` signal sent by ctrl+C, and prevent the process from being terminated.

```
#include <stdio.h>
#include <signal.h>

void    catch_sigint(void);

int     main(int argc,char *argv[])

{
    struct sigaction new, old;
    int     ch;
```

```
        /* Install new signal handler */
        new.sa_handler = catch_sigint;
        new.sa_mask = 0;
        new.sa_flags = 0;
        sigaction(SIGINT,&new,&old);
        while ( (ch = getchar()) != 'q' )
            printf("%d\n",ch);

        /* Restore old action, just for demonstration */
        sigaction(SIGINT,&old,NULL);
        return 0;
}


void    catch_sigint()

{
    puts("Caught a SIGINT signal!");
}
```

28.3 Pipes

A **pipe** is a unidirectional communication link between two or more processes, which resembles an ordinary file from the process' perspective. Processes can write data into one end of a pipe for others to read. Pipes are most often implemented as sockets (discussed in section 28.4), but some systems implement them using filesystem buffers.

Pipes are accessed by reading and writing to file descriptors, just like ordinary files. There are important differences, however.

- Data written to a pipe is stored in a fixed-sized (bounded) memory buffer. Once this buffer is full, any further attempts to write will cause the process to block until some data is removed from the pipe.

- A read operation on a pipe is known as a **destructive read**, i.e. the data read from a pipe is removed from the pipe, unlike reading from ordinary files. Read operations on an empty pipe will cause the process to block until a process writes data into the pipe. There is no true end of file on a pipe, since processes could potentially write data to it forever. However, the end of file flag is set on a pipe when the last process with write access closes its write descriptor.

Pitfall: First come, first served

An individual process can have both read and write access to the same pipe. Therefore, care must be taken to ensure that a process doesn't read back its own output. If more than one process has read access to a pipe, the first process that issues a read call will get the data. In most Unix systems, there is no way of knowing which process will be executed next, so it is difficult to ensure that the right process will get the data.

For bidirectional communication, it is usually easiest to create two separate pipes; one for each direction.

There are two types of pipes, which are created and opened in different ways:

Unnamed pipes are created with the `pipe()` and `popen()` functions.

Synopsis: *int pipe(int fd[2]);*

Return value: 0 on success, -1 on failure.

 This function performs a system call.

This function creates a pipe, and two associated file descriptors. The first descriptor, `fd[0]` is used for reading from the pipe, and `fd[1]` is used for writing. The pipe is automatically destroyed when the last file descriptor referring to it is closed.

This type of pipe is typically used to set up a link between a parent and child process. The `pipe()` function is called *before* the `fork()`, so that the child process will inherit copies of the read and write descriptors. Normally, one process is designated as the reader and the other only writes to the pipe. Hence, each process would close one of the descriptors immediately *after* the `fork()`.

Example:

This program demonstrates how pipes can be used to pass data from a parent to a child, or vice versa. Since children don't like to listen to their parents, the child process immediately closes `fd[0]` shortly after birth. It then sends a message to its parent through the pipe via `fd[1]`, which the parent reads through its `fd[0]` descriptor, and then prints for everyone to see. (Which may cause the child to blush.)

```c
#include <stdio.h>
#include <unistd.h>

#define BUFF_SIZE    40

int     main(int argc,char *argv[])

{
    int     fd[2];
    char    buff[BUFF_SIZE+1];

    if ( pipe(fd) == 0 )
    {
        if ( fork() != 0 )
        {
            /* Parent: reader */
            close(fd[1]);

            /* Read message from parent */
            read(fd[0],buff,BUFF_SIZE);
            printf("Got the message: %s.",buff);
            close(fd[0]);
        }
        else
        {
            /* Child: writer */
            close(fd[0]);
```

```
                  /* Get a message to send */
                  fputs("Enter a message to send: ",stdout);
                  fgets(buff,BUFF_SIZE,stdin);

                  /* Send message, including nul */
                  write(fd[1],buff,strlen(buff));
                  close(fd[1]);
              }
          }
          return 0;
      }
```

Synopsis: *FILE *popen(char *command,char *mode);*

Return value: A pointer to the opened stream. `NULL` on error.

    This function performs a system call.

The `popen()` function executes the specified `command`, and establishes a pipe connection to either its standard input (if mode is `"r"`) or its standard output (if mode is `"w"`).

The command is passed to the **Bourne shell**, as with `system()`. This function provides a very simple way to send data to, or receive data from a child process.

Example:

The program below demonstrates how to use `popen()` to input a list of files from the current directory. Note that this can be done more efficiently using the directory access functions described in section 24.3.1, since this would avoid creating two extra processes (namely, `sh` and `ls`). Use of `popen()` should be reserved for situations where a more direct approach would be very difficult to code.

```
#include <stdio.h>
#include <string.h>

#define MAX_LIST_SIZE        1000
#define MAX_FILENAME_LEN     128

int     main()

{
    FILE    *infile;
    char    *list[MAX_LIST_SIZE],
            file[MAX_FILENAME_LEN+1];
    size_t  list_size = 0;

    infile = popen("ls","r");
    if ( infile != NULL )
    {
        while ( (list_size < MAX_LIST_SIZE) &&
                (fscanf(infile,"%s",file) == 1) )
        {
            list[list_size++] = strdup(file);
            puts(file);
        }
    }
    pclose(infile);
    return 0;
}
```

FILE streams opened with **popen()** must be closed with **pclose()**, rather than **fclose()**, in order to properly shut down the pipe.

A **named pipe** is referenced as a special file, which can be opened by name just like an ordinary file. Named pipes can be used to easily set up communication links between unrelated processes. Named pipes are created with the **mknod()** system call, which creates special files.

Synopsis: *int mknod(char *path,mode_t mode,int dev);*

Return value: 0 on success, -1 on failure.

     This function performs a system call.

The `mode` argument specifies the type of special file, such as a pipe, character special, or block special file, as well as the file permissions. The `dev` argument applies only to certain types of files, and is ignored for pipes.

```
tmpnam(pipe_name);
mknod(pipe_name,S_IFIFO|S_IRWXU,0);
```

The `mkfifo()` function provides a more convenient interface, and issues the appropriate `mknod()` call for you.

Synopsis: *int mkfifo(char *path,mode_t mode);*

Return value: 0 on success, -1 on error.

     This function performs a system call.

The `mode` argument in `mkfifo()` specifies only the file permissions, since the file type is always a pipe. As always, be sure to specify the mode using the named constants in *stat.h*, or use an *octal* value, which must begin with a 0 digit.

```
tmpnam(pipe_name);
mkfifo(pipe_name,S_IRWXU);
```

Once a named pipe file is created, it can be opened using `open()` or `fopen()`, just like a normal file. It must also be explicitly closed, and *will not* be removed upon the last close operation. To remove a named pipe file, use `remove()` or `unlink()`.

28.4   Sockets

A **socket** is a special file descriptor used to send messages to, or receive messages from another process.

Sockets are one of the most powerful communication facilities available. Pipes, which are discussed in section 28.3, are usually implemented using sockets behind the scenes. Thus, sockets provide the means by which two processes on the same machine can talk to each other. The `pipe()` function generally creates a pair of connected sockets using the `socketpair()` function. For example, consider the code fragment below:

```
int      fd[2];

if ( pipe(fd) != -1 )
{
}
```

The code above is functionally equivalent to the following:

```
int      fd[2];

if ( socketpair(AF_UNIX,SOCK_STREAM,0,fd) != -1 )
{
}
```

In fact, the `pipe()` function issues a `socketpair()` call on many systems. The `pipe()` function is merely a convenience for programmers who don't want to deal with the complexity of sockets.

The real power in sockets is that they provide a mechanism for communication between *any* two processes, whether they are running on the same machine or not. Sockets can be used to establish a communication link between any two processes on the same network. In fact, virtually all of the data transferred over the Internet (and hence the World Wide Web) is transmitted through sockets.

The interface for using sockets is somewhat complex, due mainly to the flexibility necessary to support the many different forms of communication. Socket libraries must support both local communication between two processes on the same machine, and remote communication across many different kinds of networks.

The general procedure for creating a socket connection is as follows:

1. Create two sockets, A and B

2. Connect the sockets

    (a) Set socket A to listen for connection requests

    (b) Send a connection request from socket B to socket A

    (c) Have socket A accept the connection request

This procedure is designed to provide the mechanism for establishing a communication link across a network. Generally, a process on one machine creates and manages socket A, while a process on a different machine creates and manages socket B. This procedure is much more complicated than necessary for setting up a local communication link, especially when the two sockets are being set up by the same process, as is often the case. This is why functions like `socketpair()` and `pipe()`, which hide the unnecessary details, are provided in the standard libraries.

To demonstrate the procedure for setting up a socket connection, we'll begin with local communication.

Example:

> The program below is a replica of the example presented in section 28.3. This example, however, includes an implementation of the `pipe()` function using low-level socket calls.

```
#include <stdio.h>
#include <unistd.h>
#include <sys/types.h>
#include <sys/socket.h>

#define BUFF_SIZE    40

int     home_made_pipe(int fd[]);
```

```
int     main(int argc,char *argv[])

{
    int     fd[2];
    char    buff[BUFF_SIZE+1];

    if ( home_made_pipe(fd) == 0 )
    {
        if ( fork() != 0 )
        {
            /* Parent: reader */
            close(fd[1]);

            /* Read message from parent */
            read(fd[0],buff,BUFF_SIZE);
            printf("Got the message: %s",buff);
            close(fd[0]);
        }
        else
        {
            /* Child: writer */
            close(fd[0]);

            /* Get a message to send */
            fputs("Enter a message to send: ",stdout);
            fgets(buff,BUFF_SIZE,stdin);

            /* Send message, including nul byte */
            write(fd[1],buff,strlen(buff)+1);
            close(fd[1]);
        }
    }
    else
        perror("socketpair() failed");

    return 0;
}
```

```c
/*
 * Home-made pipe function with informative output.
 * This function creates a pair of connected sockets
 * for local interprocess communication.
 */


int    home_made_pipe(int fd[2])

{
    struct sockaddr name0 = {4, AF_UNIX, "Barny"};
    struct sockaddr name1 = {4, AF_UNIX, "Fred"};
    struct sockaddr name3 = {7, AF_UNIX, "Nobody"};
    int    s0, s1, s2, namelen1 = 14, namelen3 = 14;

    /* Create a pair of sockets */
    s0 = socket(AF_UNIX,SOCK_STREAM,0);
    if ( s0 == -1 )
        return -1;

    s1 = socket(AF_UNIX,SOCK_STREAM,0);
    if ( s1 == -1 )
        return -1;

    /* Name the sockets */
    bind(s0,&name0,namelen1);
    bind(s1,&name1,namelen1);
    getsockname(s1,&name3,&namelen3);
    printf("Socket name = %s (%d).\n",
            name3.sa_data,name3.sa_len);

    /* Set socket s1 to listen for connect requests */
    if ( listen(s1,1) == -1 )
    {
        perror("listen() failed");
        return -1;
    }

    /* Send connection request from s0 to s1 */
    if ( connect(s0,&name1,namelen1) == -1 )
```

```
    {
        perror("connect() failed");
        return -1;
    }

    /* Accept first connection request sent to s1 */
    if ( (s2=accept(s1,&name3,&namelen3)) == -1 )
    {
        perror("accept() failed.");
        return -1;
    }
    else
    {
        printf("Accepted connection from %s.\n",
                name3.sa_data);
        close(s1);
    }

    /* Return socket pair through fd[] argument */
    fd[0] = s0;
    fd[1] = s2;

    /* Must remove names before next listen() */
    unlink("Barny");
    unlink("Fred");
    return 0;
}
```

Example:

This example demonstrates how two separate processes create and connect a pair of sockets. One process must listen for and accept the connection requested by the other.

The first program creates a socket, binds the name "Fred" to it, and then listens for a connection request.

```
/*
 * listen.c
 */

#include <stdio.h>
#include <unistd.h>
#include <fcntl.h>
#include <sys/types.h>
#include <sys/socket.h>

#define BUFF_SIZE    40

int     main(int argc,char *argv[])

{
    char     buff[BUFF_SIZE+1];

    /* Reader */
    int     s, s2, namelen = 14, peernamelen = 14;
    struct sockaddr name = {4,AF_UNIX,"Fred"},
                    peername = {14,AF_UNIX,""};

    /* Create socket */
    s = socket(AF_UNIX,SOCK_STREAM,0);
    if ( s == -1 )
        perror("socket() failed");

    /* Name the new socket so others can connect */
    if ( bind(s,&name,namelen) == -1 )
        perror("bind() failed in parent");

    /* Listen and accept a connection request */
    if ( listen(s,1) == -1 )
        perror("listen() failed");
    s2 = accept(s,&peername,&peernamelen);
    if ( s2 == -1 )
        perror("accept() failed");
    else
        printf("listen: Accepted connect from %s.\n",
```

```
                    peername.sa_data);

    /* Read message from socket */
    printf("listen: Read %d bytes.\n",
            read(s2,buff,BUFF_SIZE));
    printf("listen: Got a message from %s: %s\n",
            peername.sa_data,buff);

    /* Clean up */
    close(s);
    close(s2);
    unlink("Fred");
    return 0;
}
```

The second program creates a socket, and then attempts to connect it to the socket named "Fred", which was created by the first program.

```
/*
 * connect.c
 */

#include <stdio.h>
#include <unistd.h>
#include <fcntl.h>
#include <sys/types.h>
#include <sys/socket.h>

#define BUFF_SIZE    40

int     main(int argc,char *argv[])

{
    /* Writer */
    int     s, namelen=14;
    struct sockaddr myname = {4, AF_UNIX, "Barny"},
                    name = {4, AF_UNIX, "Fred"};
```

```
/* Create socket */
s = socket(AF_UNIX,SOCK_STREAM,0);
if ( s == -1 )
    perror("socket() failed.");

/* Name socket so Fred knows who's calling */
if ( bind(s,&myname,namelen) == -1 )
    perror("bind() failed in child");

/* Connect to socket "Fred" in other process */
if ( (connect(s,&name,namelen)) == -1 )
    perror("connect() failed");

/* Send message, including nul terminator */
printf("connect: Wrote %d bytes.\n",
        write(s,"Hello!",7));
close(s);
unlink("Barny");
return 0;
}
```

To test these two programs, compile the first to an executable called *listen*, and the second to *connect*. Then run `listen` in the background first, so it will be ready to accept the connection, and run connect in the foreground.

```
tcsh 1: cc -Wall listen.c -o listen
tcsh 2: cc -Wall connect.c -o connect
tcsh 3: ./listen &
tcsh 4: ./connect
```

Making connections over a network is somewhat different. Rather than a *name*, network connections specify a **port number**. Choosing a port number can be somewhat tricky, since you must know which port numbers are available on each host. Generally, all port numbers under 100 are reserved for widely used applications

such as `ftp` (port 21), and World Wide WEB servers (port 80). If you are going
to experiment, you'll have better luck avoiding collisions if you use very large port
numbers, such as 2000 or higher. There must be a process on the receiving end
of the connection listening for connections on the port number specified, much like
local processes listen for connections on a named socket. The listening process is
often referred to as a network **daemon**.

The `listen()` and `connect()` functions use a structure called `struct sockaddr_in`,
for Internet connections, rather than the `struct sockaddr` used for local connections. This structure contains a port number and Internet address instead of the
name field on `struct sockaddr`.

Example:

Network programming is somewhat involved, and requires that you be
able to run programs on two different machines with a network connection. Since this will not be the case for many readers, we'll examine
an example that only requires you to have access to one Internet host.
We'll use existing network daemons to accept the connections from your
program.

This program demonstrates how to make a connection to an `ftp` server
using direct socket calls. Ftp servers listen for connections on port 21,
so this program will try to connect to port 21 on the specified host.

All you need to do is compile this program on an Internet machine, run it,
and enter the name of your favorite `ftp` server. The program will state
whether or not the connection was successful, and then immediately
terminate.

```
#include <stdio.h>
#include <sys/socket.h>
#include <netinet/in.h>
#include <arpa/inet.h>
#include <netdb.h>

#define NAME_LEN    80

int     main(int argc,char *argv[])
```

```
{
    /* Internet socket address */
    struct sockaddr_in  sin;

    /* Host information structure */
    struct hostent       *host_ent;

    /* File descriptor for socket */
    int     s;
    char    hostname[NAME_LEN+1];

    /* Specify Internet address */
    sin.sin_family = AF_INET;

    /* Get ftp hostname */
    fputs("Enter the host name of the ftp server: ",
          stdout);
    gets(hostname);

    /* Get host address from name */
    host_ent = gethostbyname(hostname);

    /* Copy address to sockaddr_in structure */
    memcpy(&sin.sin_addr,host_ent->h_addr,
           host_ent->h_length);
    printf("Name: %s Address type: %d Length: %d",
           host_ent->h_name,host_ent->h_addrtype,
           host_ent->h_length);
    printf("Address: %lX\nAlias: %s\n",
           sin.sin_addr.s_addr,
           host_ent->h_aliases[0]);

    /* Alternatively, get address from numeric
       address string If you know the numeric
       equivalent of your server's host name,
       type it in place of the address below.

       sin.sin_addr.s_addr = inet_addr("0.0.0.0");
       printf("s_addr = %lX\n",sin.sin_addr.s_addr);*/
```

```
/* Port 21 is for ftp server, which should be
   listening.  This host may be big-endian or
   little-endian, and all communication over the
   network must use the same standard.  htons()
   will make sure the port number is transmitted
   in the right byte order for the Internet. */
sin.sin_port = htons(21);

/* Create socket */
if ( (s = socket(AF_INET,SOCK_STREAM,0)) == -1 )
    perror("socket() failed");

/* Connect to ftp server */
if ( connect(s,(struct sockaddr *)&sin,
             sizeof(sin)) == -1 )
    perror("connect() failed");
else
    printf("Connection established!\n");

/* Perform ftp transactions ... */

return 0;
}
```

Once the connection is established, the two processes can communicate through their socket file descriptors using ordinay **read()** and **write()** calls. The communication may involve the use of system protocols, and higher level protocols specific to applications like **ftp**. If you are interested in finding out more about **ftp** protocols, the **ftp** source code is freely available as part of any *FreeBSD* or *Linux* distribution. On *FreeBSD* systems, you'll find it in */usr/src/lib/ftpio*.

Example:

If you have access to two Unix hosts, you can run both the client *and*
server programs below to see how network connections are established.
The first program, *client.c*, is similar to the `ftp` client above. It attempts
to contact a server on the specified IP address and port. The second program, *client.c*, is a network server, which waits for a connection request
from a client such as *client.c*.

The server should be run first, so that the client has something to connect
to. The server takes a single command line argument, which specifies the
port number to listen to. The client takes two command line arguments,
namely the numeric IP address of the host that the server is running on,
and the port number that the server is expected to be listening to.

When you run these programs, use high port numbers such as 2000, since
lower port numbers are reserved for specific uses such as `ftp`, `http`, `nfs`,
and so on.

The server program:

```
/* server.c */
#include <stdio.h>
#include <sysexits.h>
#include <string.h>
#include <stdlib.h>
#include <unistd.h>
#include <sys/socket.h>
#include <netinet/in.h>
#include <arpa/inet.h>

#define MAX_QUEUE    10
#define BUFF_SIZE    256

int     main (int argc, char *argv[])
{
    int     fd, fd;
    struct sockaddr_in server_address;
    short   tcp_port;   /* Need short for htons() */
```

```
int     address_len = sizeof (struct sockaddr_in);
char    buff[BUFF_SIZE + 1];

if (argc != 2)
{
    fprintf (stderr, "Usage: %s <port>\n", argv[0]);
    return EX_USAGE;
}

/* Get port number from command line */
tcp_port = atoi (argv[1]);
if ((fd = socket (AF_INET, SOCK_STREAM, 0)) < 0)
{
    fprintf (stderr, "Error open socket \n");
    exit (1);
}

server_address.sin_family = AF_INET;
server_address.sin_addr.s_addr = htonl (INADDR_ANY);
server_address.sin_port = htons (tcp_port);

/* Bind socket to server address */
if (bind (fd, (struct sockaddr *) &server_address,
        sizeof (server_address)) < 0)
{
    perror ("bind() failed");
    return 1;
}

/* Listen for connection requests */
if (listen (fd, MAX_QUEUE) != 0)
{
    fputs ("listen() failed.\n", stderr);
    return 1;
}

/* Accept a connection request */
if ((fd = accept(fd, (struct sockaddr *)&server_address,
        &address_len)) == -1)
```

```
        {
            fputs ("accept() failed.\n", stderr);
            return 1;
        }
        printf ("Accepted connection. fd = %d\n", fd);

        /* Read a message through the socket */
        read (fd, buff, 100);
        puts (buff);

        close (fd);
        close (fd);
        return EX_OK;
    }
```

The client program:

```
    /* client.c */
    #include <stdio.h>
    #include <sysexits.h>
    #include <string.h>
    #include <stdlib.h>
    #include <unistd.h>
    #include <sys/socket.h>
    #include <netinet/in.h>
    #include <arpa/inet.h>

    int     main (int argc, char *argv[])
    {
        short   tcp_port;   /* Need short for htons() */
        int     fd;
        struct sockaddr_in server_address;
        char    *machine_address, *message;

        if (argc != 3)
        {
            fprintf (stderr,
                    "Usage: %s <machine address> <port>\n",
```

```
                    argv[0]);
        return EX_USAGE;
    }

    /* Get IP address and port from command line */
    machine_address = argv[1];
    tcp_port = atoi (argv[2]);

    /* Set up socket structure */
    server_address.sin_family = AF_INET;
    server_address.sin_addr.s_addr =
            inet_addr (machine_address);
    server_address.sin_port = htons (tcp_port);

    /* Create a socket */
    if ((fd = socket (AF_INET, SOCK_STREAM, 0)) < 0)
    {
        fprintf (stderr, "Error open socket of client\n");
        exit (0);
    }

    /* Attempt to connect to server */
    if (connect (fd, (struct sockaddr *)&server_address,
                sizeof (server_address)) < 0)
    {
        fprintf (stderr, "Error connect of client\n");
        exit (0);
    }

    /* Send a message to the server */
    message = "Hello, TCP world!\n";
    write (fd, message, strlen (message) + 1);

    close (fd);
    return EX_OK;
}
```

28.5   Shared Memory

An alternative form of interprocess communication that does not involve file descriptors is **shared memory**. Shared memory objects are memory blocks which can be accessed directly by more than one process.

For related processes, creating a shared memory object is simply a matter of allocating it and mapping it into the process *before* calling `fork()`. Access to the object will be inherited by the child process, much like access to an unnamed pipe (See section 28.3).

Shared memory objects are requested and created by `shmget()` (Shared memory get).

Synopsis: *int shmget(key_t key,int size,int flags);*

Return value: A positive integer ID on success, or -1 on error.

 This function performs a system call.

The argument `key` is a tag that can be used by unrelated processes to gain access to the shared memory object. For related processes, use the value `IPC_PRIVATE`.

The `size` argument specifies the number of bytes of shared memory to allocate.

The `flags` argument specifies the permissions for the shared memory, and optionally the `IPC_CREAT` flag, which states that the semaphore should be created if it doesn't exist. If key is `IPC_PRIVATE`, the `IPC_CREAT` bit is not necessary. `SHM_R` and `SHM_W` specify read and write permission for the owner. To give read or write permissions to the group, use (`SHM_R >> 3`) and (`SHM_W>>3`), and for world use (`SHM_R>>6`) and (`SHM_W>>6`).

After the shared memory object is created, it must be mapped into the process' address space using `shmat()` (Shared memory attach).

Synopsis: *void *shmat(int id,void *address,int flags);*

Return value: The address mapped to if successful, or -1 on error.

 This function performs a system call.

The argument `id` is the ID returned by `shmget()`. Address specifies the address you want the memory mapped to. The address is usually `NULL`, which requests that `shmat()` choose an appropriate address for you.

When the process is finished with the shared memory, it must be detached from the process' address space using `shmdt()` (Shared memory detach).

Synopsis: *int shmdt(void *buff);*

Return value: 0 on success, -1 on error.

 This function performs a system call.

When the shared memory object is no longer needed, it *must* be deleted. Shared memory object **are not owned by any process, and therefore not deleted when any process terminates.** Shared memory objects can be deleted from within the program using `shmctl()` (Shared memory control).

Synopsis: *int shmctl(int id,int cmd,struct shmid_ds *buf);*

Return value: 0 on success, -1 on error.

 This function performs a system call.

The `id` argument is the ID returned by `shmget()`. The `cmd` argument specifies the operation to perform on the shared object. To delete the object, use `IPC_RMID`. The `buf` argument is relevant only to commands that retrieve or alter information about the semaphore. For more information on commands, see the documentation on your system.

Shared objects can also be deleted using the Unix command `ipcrm`. A list of existing objects can be obtained using `ipcs`.

Example:

> The program below demonstrates how to create a shared memory object and pass a message from one process to another. The process that

reads the message uses `sleep()` to allow the writer time to place the
message into the shared buffer. Otherwise, it cannot be predicted which
process will execute first, and the reader may access the buffer before
the writer has had a chance to put anything there. Using `sleep()` is
not the preferred method for synchronizing processes, since it does not
absolutely guarantee the proper order of execution, and it blocks the
process longer than necessary for synchronization. A better example is
provided in section 28.5.1.

```c
#include <stdio.h>
#include <string.h>
#include <unistd.h>
#include <sys/types.h>
#include <sys/ipc.h>
#include <sys/shm.h>

#define BLOCK_SIZE  40

int     main(int argc,char *argv[])

{
    static char    *buff;
    int     shmid,
            mode = SHM_R|SHM_W;

    /* Create shared memory object */
    if ( (shmid=shmget(IPC_PRIVATE,
                    BLOCK_SIZE,mode)) == -1 )
        perror("shmget() failed");

    /* Map object into this process' memory space */
    if ( (buff = shmat(shmid,0,0)) == (void *)-1 )
        perror("shmat() failed");

    /* Create second process to share memory with */
    if ( fork() != 0 )
    {
        /* Write message to shared memory */
        strcpy(buff,"Hello, clone!");
```

```
        printf("Writer has: %s\n",buff);

        /* Detach shared memory from process */
        shmdt(buff);
    }
    else
    {
        /* Allow writer time to write message */
        sleep(1);

        /* Print message stored in shared memory */
        printf("Reader has: %s\n",buff);

        /* Detach shared memory from process */
        shmdt(buff);

        /* Delete shared memory object from system */
        shmctl(shmid,IPC_RMID,NULL);
    }
    return 0;
}
```

For unrelated processes, the shared object must be given a **key**, analogous to a name, which both processes agree upon. Each process can then refer to the shared object by its key in order to gain access to it. The `ftok()` function can be used to generate a key from a filename if a mnemonic name is desired.

28.5.1 Process Synchronization: Semaphores

The example above uses the `sleep()` function to buy time for the writer to put something in the shared memory buffer. While this is good enough for such a simple program, it causes unnecessary program delays, and will not work well for long running programs. In order to keep two processes synchronized, we need some further communication. This communication can be provided by another type of shared object, called a **semaphore**.

A semaphore is a shared integer variable whose value can be increased and decreased by two or more cooperating processes. The system strictly limits access to the semaphore to one process at a time, to ensure that any change to its value occurs as an **atomic operation**. That is, a program cannot be interrupted while it is updating the semaphore, so no other process' updates can overlap. This type of limited access is called **mutual exclusion**, since each process excludes the other from accessing the object.

Semaphores are created by the `semget()` function:

Synopsis: *int semget(key_t key,int count,int flags);*

Return value: A positive semaphore ID on success, or -1 on error.

 This function performs a system call.

The `key` argument is the same as for `shmget()`.

The `count` argument specifies how many semaphores are to be allocated. Hence, the `semget()` function can allocate an entire array of semaphores at once.

The flags argument is the same as for `shmget()`.

Once the semaphore has been created, it can be updated using `semop()`.

Synopsis: *int semop(int semid,struct sembuf ops[],unsigned count);*

Return value: 0 on success, -1 on error.

 This function performs a system call.

The `ops` array specifies a list of semaphore operations to perform on the semaphore set specified by `semid`.

```
struct sembuf
{
    unsigned short   sem_num;
    short            sem_op;
    short            sem_flg;
};
```

Each element in ops may specify a different semaphore within the set, and a different operation. The semaphore numbers specified by sem_num range from 0 to count-1.

The sem_op field may be positive, negative, or 0. If positive, the semaphore specified by sem_num is increased by the value of sem_op.

If zero, the process is blocked until another process causes the semaphore's value to become 0.

If negative, semop() will do one of the following:

- If the semaphore's current value is greater than or equal to the absolute value of sem_op, the semaphore is decremented.

- If the semaphore's current value is less than the absolute value of sem_op, semop() either blocks the process until another process makes the semaphore large enough to be decremented, or, if the semaphore has been set to non-blocking mode, returns an error code.

Like shared memory objects, semaphores *must* be deleted when they are no longer needed. This can be accomplished within the program using semctl(), or on the command line using ipcrm.

Example:

> The program below demonstrates how to use a semaphore to synchronize access to a shared memory buffer. The semaphore initially has a value of 0. Hence, if the reader issues a decrement operation, it will be blocked until the semaphore is incremented to a positive value. The writer thus increments the semaphore *after* writing a message into the buffer, which signals that the reader may proceed.

```
#include <stdio.h>
#include <string.h>
#include <unistd.h>
#include <sys/types.h>
#include <sys/ipc.h>
#include <sys/shm.h>
#include <sys/sem.h>
```

```
#define BLOCK_SIZE   40

int     main(int argc,char *argv[])

{
    static char     *buff;
    int     shmid, semid,
            mode = SHM_R|SHM_W;

    /* Create shared memory object */
    if ( (shmid=shmget(IPC_PRIVATE,
                        BLOCK_SIZE,mode)) == -1 )
        perror("shmget() failed");

    /* Map object into this process' memory space */
    if ( (buff = shmat(shmid,0,0)) == (void *)-1 )
        perror("shmat() failed");

    /* Create semaphore for locking shared memory */
    if ( (semid=semget(IPC_PRIVATE,1,mode)) == -1 )
        perror("semget() failed");

    /* Create second process to share memory with */
    if ( fork() != 0 )
    {
        /* Options to increment semaphore */
        struct sembuf   ops[1] = {{0,1,0}};

        /* Write message to shared memory */
        strcpy(buff,"Hello, clone!");
        printf("Writer has: %s\n",buff);

        /* Detach shared memory from process */
        shmdt(buff);

        /* Increment semaphore to signal release of
           shared memory to reader */
        semop(semid,ops,1);
    }
```

```
        else
        {
            /* Options to decrement semaphore */
            struct sembuf   ops[1] = {{0,-1,0}};

            /* Semaphore decrement operation will block
               the process until the semaphore is
               incremented to something > 0 by writer */
            semop(semid,ops,1);

            /* Print message stored in shared memory */
            printf("Reader has: %s\n",buff);

            /* Detach shared memory from process */
            shmdt(buff);

            /* Delete shared memory object from system */
            shmctl(shmid,IPC_RMID,NULL);

            /* Delete semaphore from system */
            semctl(semid,0,IPC_RMID,0);
        }
        return 0;
}
```

28.6 Threads

Programming often presents situations that are difficult to handle using a single process. For example, consider a WEB server handling requests for WEB pages from many different places at once. This can be accomplished using a single **daemon** process, which takes requests from a queue. (Daemon is a common term applied to any process that lurks in the system waiting to service requests from some sort of client. For instance, when you send mail to another user, the mail daemon takes the message and either writes it into the recipient's mail box, or sends it over the network to a daemon on another host.) If a WEB server uses a single daemon process to service all the requests, it is possible that many new requests may come in while the daemon is waiting for disk or other resources, and service could become rather slow.

One of the advantages of multitasking systems is the fact that it is possible for multiple hardware components to be utilized simultaneously by different processes. For example, while one process is waiting for disk data, another can be transmitting a network packet, while still another is using the CPU. In the case of a WEB server, if we run 3 or more identical daemons, then it is possible for the CPU, network, and disk to be utilized at the same time by different daemons, and the overall performance of the server can be improved.

There are some problems with this approach however. For one thing, running redundant processes consumes a lot of memory and other system resources in a rather wasteful fashion. Another problem is that the daemons must be designed to cooperate with each other since they all service requests from the same queue.

Threads, also know as **lightweight processes**, are an alternative to traditional processes which are well suited to situations like this one. Although they have limited applications, threads are ideal for situations where many similar processes need to cooperate in a **tightly coupled** fashion. Each thread in a system belongs to a group of processes, which are usually identical to each other. Threads differ from traditional, or **heavyweight processes**, in that all the threads in a group inherently share the same memory space. Unlike heavyweight processes, threads don't need to make explicit system calls to create and connect to shared memory buffers: They are simply born that way.

Each thread has its own system stack and register set, so that each thread can be executing at a different part of the program at a given time. All the threads share the same code and data space, however. As a result, multiple threads use less memory than the same number of heavyweight processes,[1] and most importantly, they can easily communicate with each other through their shared memory.

Threads can be implemented in one of two ways. **Kernel-supported threads** have the advantage that they can be independently scheduled, so that multiple threads can actually utilize different hardware components simultaneously. Hence, kernel threads provide the full benefits that threads have to offer in terms of maximizing system performance, and are well suited to I/O-intensive applications. Kernel support for threads is a standard feature of many modern Unix systems, and will likely be offered by virtually all Unix systems in the near future.

---

[1] In most Unix systems, heavyweight processes also share code space in order to save memory, so the memory savings of threads is generally limited to the size of the data space

User-level threads execute as part of a single heavyweight process. As such, they cannot be scheduled independently: If one user-level thread is waiting for disk data, for example, then the entire heavyweight process is blocked, and the rest of the threads will have to wait. The main advantage of user level threads is that they can be implemented on *any* system, even single-tasking systems such as *DOS*. User-level threads also have somewhat less overhead than kernel supported threads, and therefore are well suited to situations requiring a large number of CPU-intensive threads, such as parallel processing simulations.

POSIX defines a standard interface for threads, known as *pthreads*. If you would like to experiment with threads on your system, there is a free user-level implementation of the *pthreads* standard available via `ftp` from *sipb.mit.edu:/pub/pthreads*.

Chapter 29

Unix Graphics: X Windows

Before you begin...

> You should be familiar with the material on Unix, arrays, and structures, presented in chapters 4, 15, and 18.

Unix is known for its adherence to open standards and the generality of its interfaces. The primary Unix graphics subsystem, called the *X Window system*, or just *X Windows*, is no exception. The designers of the *X Window* system went to great lengths to ensure it would useful across platforms, and even across the planet.

The goal of this chapter is to introduce X Window programming, and provide a basic understanding of how X works. X Window programming is a topic worthy of several textbooks in itself, so it is not possible to provide a comprehensive overview here. If you intend to take up X Window programming, there are many textbooks available on the subject, including those listed in the bibliography.

29.1   How X Windows Works

Unix programs do not directly manipulate a graphics screen. The X Window system is a **client-server** based program interface, which is designed to allow the use of graphics across a network.

The X Window system is often mistakenly referred to as a **GUI**, or **Graphical User Interface**. Unlike some other graphics systems, however, X Windows does not provide or define any specific user interface. The designers of X Windows were careful to provide only the *mechanism* for creating GUI applications, and *not* to enforce any particular policy.

The task of displaying output on and receiving input from an X Window display is split into two separate processes, called a **client** and a **server**. These two processes may run on the same machine, or on different machines connected by a network. Hence, users can run X Window *client* programs on a machine on the other side of the planet, while viewing its graphical output on the *display server* sitting on their desk. Of course, it's pretty rare for users to run client programs this far away. More often, the client programs are run on a machine in the same building, or even the same machine as the X display server.

Regardless of the distance between the CPU and the display, the interface used by X Window client programs is the same. The client and server communicate with each other using a **byte stream protocol**, called the **X protocol**, which consists of special byte sequences that represent each request a client may send to the server, or informative data passed in either direction.

Once you build a client program on a particular machine, it can display it's output on any X server, regardless of the type of hardware or operating system the server runs on. There is no need to rewrite or recompile X clients for different servers, since all the servers use the same protocol. For example, once a client program is compiled on a *Sun Sparc* workstation, users can run the program from their *Windows* PC, *MacIntosh*, or *Unix* workstation, provided they have an X server installed on it, and it is connected by a network to the *Sun Sparc* machine running the client.

29.1.1   The X Server

The role of the X server is to maintain the **display**. The display in X terminology refers to the server process, and all the input and output devices it controls, such as the screen, keyboard, and mouse. The server process runs on a machine which is directly connected to the screen and other devices, so that the *enormously expensive* task of maintaining a graphical screen can be handled through a high-bandwidth connection such as the computer's system bus.

The server receives relatively brief, high-level commands from client programs either on the same computer, or across a network, using a protocol such as the **X11** protocol. The protocol defines the structure of each command such as *Draw a* *line from 10,10 to 100,150.* The server receives these commands as relatively short strings of characters, and then performs the (usually extensive) work necessary to update the display. The server also receives keyboard input on the display, and dispatches it (possibly across a network) to the appropriate client program.

The X server is capable of serving any number of clients, running simultaneously on many different computers of different types. For example, an X server running on your PC can simultaneously display graphical results from client programs on the PC itself, and from a Cray supercomputer located in another state. The server must keep close track of the requests from each client, to ensure all the output is displayed in the correct window. Furthermore, the server must keep track of which client should receive any input from the keyboard and mouse.

29.1.2 X Clients

X Window clients receive user input from the X server, and also must ask the server to display their output in a **window** on the appropriate display. Most X clients follow the same general pattern:

1. Request a connection to the server.

2. Create one or more windows on the server's display.

3. Process input and output through its windows.

X Windows clients are almost always highly interactive programs. After all, why would anyone go to the trouble of creating a graphical interface for a batch program? As such, they are usually designed to respond to user input and other **events** of various types. Since there are so many different types of events that X Window programs can process, X client programs are often referred to as **event-driven**. The following sections contain a few examples of X Window programs which demonstrate how to get connected with the server, and how to process events.

29.2 Programming with Xlib

The basic interface to X in C programs is the *Xlib* library. This library contains an extensive and powerful set of primitive functions for manipulating **X resources**. A resource in X Windows is any piece of data that a client works with, such as a window or bitmap.

Using Xlib directly is the most flexible, most efficient, and most difficult way to create X client applications. Typical user applications are often more easily written using a higher level library, such as the **X Toolkit**, commonly called **Xt**.

All Xlib programs must perform certain routine steps before they can begin using the display.

1. Connect to the server using `XOpenDisplay()`

2. Get the screen ID and screen attributes

3. Create windows

4. Create a graphics context for each window

5. Map each window to the display

The graphics context is all the information regarding the appearance of a window, such as foreground and background color, fonts, line style, and so on. This is kept separate from the window in order to save space, since the programmer may want to use the same graphics context for more than one window.

In order to process events, the client program must first tell the X server which events should be reported. Because the server may be running on a different machine from the client, the server by default only reports a minimal set of events. This keeps network traffic within reason, and improves performance. For example, mouse motion is almost never reported to a client, since few applications need to respond every time the mouse is moved, and reporting motion events would flood the network with unnecessary information. For example, a *Microsoft* serial mouse reports motion 120 times each second while it is moving. This is enough to create a noticeable impact on a network. It is more typical for client programs to respond only to key or mouse button press events.

Finally, to improve output performance, server requests are buffered at the client's side of the connection until Xlib determines that the display needs updating. Each packet of data transmitted over a network requires a **header**, which identifies and describes the destination and contents of the packet. For example, a **TCP/IP** packet consists of about 20 bytes of data. (The structure can be viewed in the header */usr/include/tcp.h*.) If many small packets are sent, the header in each packet will greatly increase the amount of data to be transmitted, so it's better to save up a large amount of data, and transmit it in a single packet, to minimize the number of headers transmitted. In addition, there are system call delays involved with each packet sent. Hence, both time and space can be saved by buffering network output.

If you need to display updated earlier, you'll need to *flush* the X output using XFlush().

Example:

The program below demonstrates the basics of using Xlib to connect to the X server, create a window, and display graphic output in it.

```c
#include <X11/Xlib.h>
#include <X11/Xutil.h>
#include <stdio.h>
#include <time.h>
#include <unistd.h>

#define WIDTH              620
#define HEIGHT             460
#define SPACING            10
#define DRAWINGS           10
#define LINES_PER_DRAWING  300
#define MSG       "Press any mouse button to continue"

long    random(void);
void    srandom(long);
void    draw_lines(Display *disp,Window win,GC gc);

int     main()

{
    /* Display */
    Display                 *disp;
    int                     screen,depth,borderwidth;

    /* Window stuff */
    int                     win_x,win_y;
    XSetWindowAttributes    winat;
    unsigned long           atmask;
```

```
Window                    win,root;

/* Graphics context */
XGCValues                 gcvalues;
GC                        gc;
unsigned long             gcmask;

/* Get server connection */
if ( (disp = XOpenDisplay(NULL)) == NULL )
{
    fprintf(stderr,"Cannot open display.\n");
    exit(1);
}

/* Get screen ID */
screen = DefaultScreen(disp);

/* Get color capabilities */
depth = DefaultDepth(disp,screen);

/* Print information retrieved from server */
printf("Server: %s version %d X%d R%d\n",
    ServerVendor(disp),
    VendorRelease(disp),
    ProtocolVersion(disp),
    ProtocolRevision(disp));
printf("Color plane depth = %d\n",depth);
printf("Display: %s dimensions: %d x %d\n",
    XDisplayName(NULL),
    DisplayWidth(disp,screen),
    DisplayHeight(disp,screen));

/* Set up information for a new window */
winat.border_pixel = BlackPixel(disp,screen);
winat.background_pixel = WhitePixel(disp,screen);
winat.override_redirect = True;
atmask = CWBackPixel|CWBorderPixel|
        CWOverrideRedirect;
```

```
        /* Get root window pointer */
        root = RootWindow(disp,screen);

        /* Create new window under root */
        win_x=10;
        win_y=10;
        borderwidth=2;
        win = XCreateWindow(disp,root,win_x,win_y,
                            WIDTH,HEIGHT,
                            borderwidth,depth,
                            InputOutput,CopyFromParent,
                            atmask,&winat);

        /* Display new window */
        XMapWindow(disp,win);

        /* Create graphics context for color, etc. */
        gcmask = 0L;
        gc = XCreateGC(disp,win,gcmask,&gcvalues);

        /* Draw funky line patterns */
        draw_lines(disp,win,gc);

        /* Remove window and shut down */
        XDestroyWindow(disp,win);
        XCloseDisplay(disp);
        return(0);
}

void    draw_lines(Display *disp,Window win,GC gc)

{
    /* Line drawing vars */
    int                 x1,y1,x2,y2,
                        dx1,dx2,dy1,dy2,
                        line,drawing;
    time_t              cur_time;
    XEvent              event;
```

```
/* Ask server to send button press events */
XSelectInput(disp,win,ButtonPressMask);

/* Draw funky line patterns */
time(&cur_time);
srandom((long)cur_time);
for (drawing=0; drawing<DRAWINGS; ++drawing)
{
    /* Generate random spacing and endpoints */
    x1 = random() % WIDTH;
    x2 = random() % WIDTH;
    y1 = random() % HEIGHT;
    y2 = random() % HEIGHT;
    dx1 = random() % SPACING;
    dx2 = random() % SPACING;
    dy1 = random() % SPACING;
    dy2 = random() % SPACING;

    XClearWindow(disp,win);
    XFlush(disp);

    /* Draw lines */
    for (line=0; line<LINES_PER_DRAWING; ++line)
    {
        XDrawLine(disp,win,gc,x1,y1,x2,y2);

        /* "Bounce" endpoints off window edges */
        if (((x1+dx1) > WIDTH) || ((x1+dx1) < 0))
            dx1 = -dx1;
        if (((x2+dx2) > WIDTH) || ((x2+dx2) < 0))
            dx2 = -dx2;
        if (((y1+dy1) > HEIGHT) || ((y1+dy1) < 0))
            dy1 = -dy1;
        if (((y2+dy2) > HEIGHT) || ((y2+dy2) < 0))
            dy2 = -dy2;

        /* Move endpoints for next line */
        x1 += dx1;
        x2 += dx2;
```

```
                        y1 += dy1;
                        y2 += dy2;
                }
                XDrawString(disp,win,gc,10,10,MSG,strlen(MSG));
                XFlush(disp);

                /* Wait for user to press a mouse button */
                XNextEvent(disp,&event);
        }
}
```

29.3   Programming with the Xt toolkit

In order to alleviate some of the pain involved in programming with *Xlib*, several higher level libraries, known as **toolkits** have evolved.

It is important to realize that most toolkits are designed to *augment Xlib*, not replace it. While toolkits provide a generally higher level interface to X Windows, most programs will still need to use *Xlib* calls to perform primitive operations such as drawing lines and text, changing colors, and so on. Hence, it is important to be familiar with *Xlib*, even if you plan to do all of your X programming with toolkits.

One of the first, and most common toolkits is the **X Toolkit**, or **Xt** for short. Xt provides a set of **intrinsics**, the basic functions that define how the toolkit works, as well as some additional functions useful for creating graphical user interfaces.

Rather than dealing with displays, screens, and windows directly, Xt programs manage higher level objects called **widgets**. A widget usually contains a window, along with a set of operations that apply to the widget according to the **widget class** it belongs to. For example, the **Xt** library provides different widget classes for scroll bars, dialog boxes, and so on. Obviously, a scroll bar requires different operations than a dialog box. Hence, these two widget classes each offer a different set of functions for manipulating them.

Once you become familiar with the Xt intrinsics and the standard widget classes, Xt programming becomes a matter of discovering other widget classes, and defining some of your own. There is a large body of widget classes available from many sources, including your favorite GNU site.

Xt programs generally follow a conventional format, which differs somewhat from
the Xlib tradition. Like Xlib programs, Xt programs are usually **event-driven**,
meaning that they wait for events such as key presses, button presses and pointer
movements to occur, and then respond. However, rather than waiting for events,
checking the event type, and then explicitly processing the event, Xt programs use
event handler functions, which are *registered* before the main program loop begins.
The program then enters a loop something like the following:

```
/* Register event handlers */
XtAddEventHandler(widget,event_mask1,non_maskable,
                  function1,client_data);
XtAddEventHandler(widget,event_mask2,non_maskable,
                  function2,client_data);

...

/* Process events */
while (condition)
{
    XtNextEvent(&event);
    XtDispatchEvent(&event);
}
```

The `XtDispatchEvent()` function calls the event handler function that has been registered for the given event type. Xt maintains a function pointer table (See chapter
17) which is used by `XtDispatchEvent()` to call the appropriate handler when an
event occurs. This method of handling events has two significant consequences:

- The program does not need to explicitly check the event type using `if` or
  `switch` statements in order to process the event.

- All event handlers must conform to the same standard interface, so that
  `XtDispatchEvent()` can correctly pass information to any one of them.

Each event handler must therefore fit the following template:

Synopsis: *void handler(Widget w,caddr_t client_data,Event *event);*

Return value: None.

Once a handler function is registered, it will be automatically called each time an event in the event_mask occurs in a window associated with widget.[1] The handler receives the widget instance, a pointer to the event information, and the address of an additional variable through caddr_t. This address may point to *any* data, and must be passed to XtAddEventHandler().

The general pattern followed by an Xt program is:

1. Initialize.

2. Create Widgets.

3. Register event handlers.

4. Realize Widgets (Create and map their windows).

5. Begin the event loop.

Example:

The program below is an Xt version of the *Xlib* example in the previous section.

```
#include <stdio.h>
#include <stdlib.h>
#include <time.h>
#include <unistd.h>
#include <X11/Intrinsic.h>
#include <X11/StringDefs.h>
#include <X11/Xaw/Text.h>

#define WIDTH          620
#define HEIGHT         460
#define SPACING        10
#define DRAWINGS       10
```

---

[1]This interface resembles the use if signal handlers covered in section 28.2.

```
#define LINES_PER_DRAWING   300
#define MSG     "Press any mouse button to continue"

/* Prototypes */
void    draw_line(Widget canvas,caddr_t client_data,
                  XEvent *event);

int     main(int argc,char *argv[])

{
    /* Widget stuff */
    Widget      toplevel, canvas;
    static Arg  wargs[] =
                {
                    { XtNwidth, WIDTH },
                    { XtNheight, HEIGHT }
                };

    /* Graphics context */
    XGCValues       gcvalues;
    GC              gc;
    unsigned long   gcmask;

    XEvent      event;      /* For XtNextEvent() */
    int         drawing;    /* Drawing counter */
    time_t      cur_time;   /* Random number seed */

    /* Initialize intrinsics; connect to X server */
    toplevel = XtInitialize("xdemo","Xdemo",NULL,0,
                            &argc,argv);

    /* Create generic widget for drawing on */
    canvas = XtCreateManagedWidget("lines",widgetClass,
            toplevel,wargs,XtNumber(wargs));

    /* Register event handler for button press */
    XtAddEventHandler(canvas,ButtonPressMask,FALSE,
                    (void (*)())draw_line,&gc);
```

```
    /* Create window for widget */
    XtRealizeWidget(toplevel);

    /* Create graphics context for color, etc. */
    gcmask = 0L;
    gc = XCreateGC(XtDisplay(canvas),XtWindow(canvas),
                    gcmask,&gcvalues);

    /* Seed random number generator */
    time(&cur_time);
    srandom((long)cur_time);

    /* Do 10 line drawings */
    drawing = 0;
    while (drawing < DRAWINGS)
    {
        /* Wait for next event */
        XtNextEvent(&event);

        /* If button press, do a drawing */
        if ( event.type == ButtonPress )
        {
            XtDispatchEvent(&event);
            ++drawing;
        }
    }
    return EX_OK;
}


/*
 * Do a funky line drawing
 */

void    draw_line(Widget canvas,caddr_t client_data,
                XEvent *event)

{
    /* Line drawing vars */
```

```
int     x1,y1,x2,y2,
        dx1,dx2,dy1,dy2,
        line;

/* Get display and window for Xlib calls */
Display *disp = XtDisplay(canvas);
Window  win = XtWindow(canvas);

/* Get graphics context from extra client data */
GC      *gc = (GC *)client_data;

/* Generate random spacing and endpoints */
x1 = random() % WIDTH;
x2 = random() % WIDTH;
y1 = random() % HEIGHT;
y2 = random() % HEIGHT;
dx1 = random() % SPACING;
dx2 = random() % SPACING;
dy1 = random() % SPACING;
dy2 = random() % SPACING;

XClearWindow(disp,win);
XFlush(disp);

/* Draw lines */
for (line=0; line<LINES_PER_DRAWING; ++line)
{
    XDrawLine(disp,win,*gc,x1,y1,x2,y2);

    /* "Bounce" endpoints off window edges */
    if (((x1+dx1) > WIDTH) || ((x1+dx1) < 0))
        dx1 = -dx1;
    if (((x2+dx2) > WIDTH) || ((x2+dx2) < 0))
        dx2 = -dx2;
    if (((y1+dy1) > HEIGHT) || ((y1+dy1) < 0))
        dy1 = -dy1;
    if (((y2+dy2) > HEIGHT) || ((y2+dy2) < 0))
        dy2 = -dy2;
```

```
        /* Move endpoints for next line */
        x1 += dx1;
        x2 += dx2;
        y1 += dy1;
        y2 += dy2;
    }
    XDrawString(disp,win,*gc,10,10,MSG,strlen(MSG));
    XFlush(disp);
}
```

Part IV

The C++ Programming Language

Chapter 30

Introduction to C++

Before you begin...

You should be familiar with the material on structures presented in chapter 18.

30.1   Object Oriented Programming

Object oriented programming (OOP), which is discussed throughout this text, has gained a great deal of popularity in recent years. Many languages have arisen with special features to support object-oriented design. Among the most popular are *C++*, *SmallTalk*, and *JAVA*. SmallTalk and JAVA are examples of **interpreted** languages. Programs written in these languages are run by another program, called an **interpreter**, rather than being translated to machine language and executed by the CPU directly. Some interpreted languages, such as JAVA are **crunched** to a special **byte code**, which is simpler for the interpreter to process than the strings contained in raw source code. The JAVA marketing team prefers the term **Virtual Machine** over "interpreter", which may cause some confusion. In reality the JAVA virtual machine is simply a JAVA byte code interpreter, which runs on the underlying CPU. The main advantage of an interpreted language is ease of use. There is no need to wait for programs to compile before they can be executed. The

611

main disadvantages are much slower performance than compiled languages, greater CPU and memory requirements because each running program must also have an interpreter running behind it, and the need for every user to have an interpreter installed on their system. End users of a compiled program don't need a compiler, since the pre-compiled program can run directly on the CPU.

C++ is by far the most popular compiled language with object oriented support. The popularity of C++ is due largely to the fact that it is a *superset* of C. This fact has allowed many organizations to utilize existing C code while making the transition to object oriented programming. However, this also means that C++ cannot *enforce* object oriented design practices.

Objective C (See [11, 12]) is another compiled OO language, which is available free from the GNU project as part of the `gcc` package. While not as popular as C++, it offers an alternative for those who want the performance and other features of a compiled language, combined with object oriented programming support.

It is important to understand that choosing an OO language doesn't make you an OO programmer. A great deal of C++ code has been and is being written that doesn't follow object oriented design at all. Object oriented design is a discipline that *you* must choose to follow. If you understand the methodology, you can write OO programs in any language. This generally means applying the concepts of encapsulation and reusability, i.e. limiting access to the data members in object to designated member functions, and writing code that is generalized enough to serve different types of data. Object oriented languages provide special features to *help* you follow this approach, but most don't force you to do so.

As noted earlier, C++ is a superset of C. Hence, all the features of C are also part of C++. If you've already read the chapters in this text on C, you already know most of the syntax of C++. The following sections discuss the major features of C++ that aid in OO design and programming. While the features added by C++ are relatively few, they are very powerful and offer a wealth of new possibilities in your approach to programming. This chapter provides an overview. To fully explore the various techniques possible with C++ programming, you'll need to consult a textbook dedicated to C++ programming.

30.2   Basic Terminology

Object oriented programming has its own jargon, which is essential to any discussion of the subject. Some of the fundamental terms used in C++ are defined below.

Class: A data structure combined with all the operations that can be performed on it. Conceptually, this is similar to the mathematical concept of a **group**. For example, the *integer* group is defined as all whole numbers, and the operations of addition, subtraction, multiplication, etc.

In C++ programming, classes are an extension to structures. Both classes and structures may define any number and type of data members. Classes, however, also define the *functions* that operate on the data type as members of the class, and generally allow only member functions to access the data members.

Object: An object is any piece of information. This usually refers to data in memory, and is used to distinguish between actual data and pointers or references to it.

Instance: A particular variable or function, i.e. any object named by an identifier in a program.

Polymorphic: (*Poly-*: many, *morph*: form) Having more than one form and meaning, depending on context. For example, the / operator in C, C++, and most languages is polymorphic, since it works for both integer and real division, which are distinct operations. The `printf()` function is also polymorphic, since it can take any number and type of arguments. C++ provides facilities for easily creating polymorphic functions and operators.

Overloading: The act of defining multiple instances of the same function or operator. The meaning for a given situation must be clear from the context the operator or function is used in. For example, an operator can have only one meaning for a given set of operand types, and a function can have only one meaning for a given set of argument types.

30.3 Fundamental Syntactic Differences

30.3.1 Comments

In addition to the /* */ syntax used by C, C++ supports another style of comment. This second style begins with // and ends at the end of the current line.

```
/* This is a C comment, also acceptable in C++ */
```

```
// This is the preferred style of a C++ comment
```

30.3.2   Basic I/O

One of the most visible differences between C and C++ programs is the method used for stream I/O. The various C library functions such as `putchar()`, `puts()`, and `printf()` have been replaced by C++ **class objects** called `cin`, `cout`, and `cerr`. These objects are used with the `<<` (output) and `>>` (input) operators to perform I/O on `stdin, stdout` and `stderr`. It is easy to confuse these operators with each other, but there is also an easy way to keep them straight: Just remember that the "arrow" always points to where the data is going.

Like C, C++ also has no built-in I/O capabilities, so the `cin` and `cout` objects require the inclusion of specific header files and libraries, such as *iostream.h*.

Example:

```
#include <iostream.h>

int     main()

{
    cout << "Hello, world!\n";
    return 0;
}
```

Cin, cout and `cerr` are **instances** (variables) of the `istream` and `ostream` classes, which represent stream I/O buffers, along with the operations that may be performed on them. The `<<` and `>>` operators actually perform the I/O operations, while the instances they are used with merely specify which stream to use. For example, `cin` is roughly equivalent to `stdin`, except that `cin` is an instance of a C++ class, whereas `stdin` is an instance of a `FILE` pointer. The details of classes are covered in section 30.4. For now, we'll focus on introducing basic I/O operations.

The `<<` and `>>` operators are an example of **overloaded operators**, the details of which are covered in section 30.7.3. The normal purpose of `<<` and `>>` in C and

C++ is to shift the bits of an integer variable. However, the `istream` and `ostream` classes *overload* them, that is, give them additional meaning and purpose in new contexts. When used for bit shifting, both the left and right operands to `<<` and `>>` must be integers. For example, the following code shifts the bits of `mask` 3 positions to the left, and places the result in `newmask`:

```
int     mask, newmask;

newmask = mask << 3;
```

In C++ programs that use the `ostream` class, the `<<` operator takes on a new meaning when the left operand is an instance of `ostream`. In this context, the `<<` operator becomes the **output operator**. The right operand can be any data type for which `<<` is overloaded. The standard C++ libraries contain many instances of this operator, including one for each of the basic data types. The `ostream` class itself allows the `<<` operator to be used with all of the standard C++ data types. For example, to output an integer value to `stdout`, you would use the following:

```
int     age;

cout << age;
```

You can also create new instances of the `<<` operator, to output data from your own classes, by defining new overloading functions. This process is described in section 30.7.3.

One important feature of the `<<` operator is that the value of the expression is the same as the `ostream` instance used within it. For example, the value of the expression (`cout << age`) is `cout`, and the value of (`cerr << "Unable to open file.\n"`) is `cerr`. This feature allows multiple values of any type to be strung together in a single output statement. For example,

```
cerr << "The square of " << num << " is " <<
        num*num << ".\n";
```

The `>>` operator can similarly be used to input several values at once:

```
char     name[MAX_NAME+1];
int      age;

cout << "Enter your name and age: ";
cin >> name >> age;
```

Programming for Performance:

Much of C++ is built *on top* of C. As an example, some implementations of << and >> simply call `printf()` and `scanf()`. This is not the most efficient method for performing simple I/O operations of strings and characters, but it is the simplest to implement.

In addition, the >> operator doesn't check the size of a character array, so like `gets()`, it is dangerous to use for string input.

To improve performance and safety, you can use the `get()` and `put()` member functions. For example, to input a string, you could use the following:

```
char     name[MAX_NAME+1];

cin.get(name,MAX_NAME,'\n');
```

30.4   Classes and Encapsulation

The heart of C++ programming is the definition and use of **classes**. A class defines both the structure of a data type and all the operations that may be performed on it. For example, the `int` class consists of a single whole number, and a limited set of operations such as addition, subtraction, multiplication, input, output, and so on.

In normal procedural programming, a data type and its operations are defined and used separately. A complex data type is defined by a *structure*, and the operations that go with it are defined by separate external *functions*.

In object oriented programming, the structure and functions of a data type are bound together, or **encapsulated**, and viewed as being part of a single object. This improves the overall organization and modularity of a program, and aids in the production of *reusable* code. While object oriented programming can be done in any language, some languages, such as C++, provide special facilities for defining classes. These facilities greatly reduce the amount of self-discipline necessary to modularize a program into classes.

30.4.1 Class Definitions

In C++, a class is an extension to the familiar *structures* used in C. The general form of a class definition is as follows:

```
class name
{
    private:
        Data members
    public:
        Member function prototypes
};
```

The `private` and `public` keywords determine which members of the class are visible to non-member functions. Generally, *all* data members are defined as private, and *most* member functions are public. The definition below defines a simple class consisting of some information about a customer.

```
class customer
{
    private:
        char    name[MAX_NAME+1];
        int     age;
    public:
        void    print(void);
        void    read(void);
}
```

Since **name** and **age** are defined as **private** members, they can only be referenced directly by the **read()** and **print()** member functions. For example, consider the following code fragment:

```
int     main()

{

    customer   customer1;

    cin >> customer1.age;      // Illegal
    ...
}
```

This code will cause a compile error, since the statement **cin >> customer1.age** attempts to access a private member of the **customer** class, and **main()** is not a **customer** member function. Unrestricted references to an object's data members is exactly what OOP is designed to eliminate, since all such references may require changes when the data structure is changed. By restricting references to the member functions, we can greatly reduce the number of functions that have to be modified when the data structure is modified.

Functions may be either *defined* or merely *declared* within the class definition. The general rule is to only declare them, unless the definition is especially short. This allows member functions to be separated and placed into a library. Member function definitions are almost identical to ordinary function definitions, except that an additional tag is added to specify that the function belongs to a class. The general form is:

```
<type> <class> :: <name> ( <arguments> )
{
    <body>
}
```

For example, the **print()** member function for the **customer** class could be defined as follows:

```
void customer :: print(void)
```

```
{
    cout << "Name: " << name << "\nAge: " << age;
}
```

Similarly, the **read()** member function might be defined as follows:

```
void customer :: read(void)

{
    cout << "Name? ";
    cin.get(name,MAX_NAME,'\n');

    cout << "Age? ";
    cin >> age;
}
```

Note the direct use of the variables **name** and **age** in the member functions. Since these variables are not defined locally within the function, the C++ compiler assumes they refer to the members of the **customer** instance of which the function is a member.

The instance is specified in the call to the member function as follows:

```
int     main()

{
    customer   customer1;

    customer1.read();
    ...
    return 0;
}
```

Given the call **customer1.read()**, the variable **name** inside the read function refers to **customer1.name**, and **age** refers to **customer1.age**. Although this may seem a

little confusing, it is actually no different than C, except for the syntactic arrangement. The equivalent code using a structure and ordinary function would appear
as follows:

```
typedef struct
{
    char    name[MAX_NAME+1];
    int     age;
}   customer;

int     main()

{
    customer  customer1;

    read(&customer1);
    ...
    return 0;
}



void    read(customer *cl)

{
    cout << "Name? ";
    cin.get(cl->name,MAX_NAME,'\n');
    cout << "Age: ";
    cin >> cl->age;
}
```

The only way to explicitly refer to the object `customer1` in the `read()` function is
by using the `this` pointer. The `this` pointer is a seldom-used feature of the C++
language, which exists only inside a member function, and always points to the
object the function belongs to. For example, the `read()` function could have been
defined as follows:

```
void customer :: read(void)
```

```
    {
        cout << "Name? ";
        cin.get(this->name,MAX_NAME,'\n');
        cout << "Age? ";
        cin >> this->age;
    }
```

This example is provided only to clarify the implicit nature of objects in member functions. The `this` pointer is almost never needed, and is considered bad style by many C++ programmers.

Example:

Putting it all together, we now have our first complete C++ program:

```
#include <iostream.h>
#include <sysexits.h>

#define MAX_NAME    40

// Information about a customer
class customer
{
    private:
        char    name[MAX_NAME+1];
        int     age;
    public:
        void    print(void);
        void    read(void);
};


// Print customer data
void    customer :: print(void)

    {
```

```
        cout << "Name: " << name << "\nAge: " << age;
    }


    // Input customer data
    void    customer :: read(void)

    {
        cout << "Name? ";
        cin.get(name,MAX_NAME,'\n');
        cout << "Age? ";
        cin >> age;
    }


    // Simple test program for customer class
    int     main(int argc,char *argv[])

    {
        customer  customer1;

        // Read data into customer1
        customer1.read();

        // Print data in customer1
        customer1.print();

        return EX_OK;
    }
```

Pitfall: C vs. C++ Function Declarations

In C++, every function declaration is considered a prototype. There is no analog to the K&R *allusions* discussed in chapter 11. Hence, in C++, a declaration such as

```
void      print();
```

is exactly the same as

```
void      print(void);
```

If, while using C++, you get into the habit of omitting the `void` argument in the declaration, this may cause problems when you write C code later, since a declaration such as `void print()` instructs the *C* compiler *not* to check the argument list in each call to `print()`. Generally, it's a good idea to always specify a `void` argument list explicitly, even though the C++ compiler doesn't require it.

The whole point of using a class instead of a structure is to define a clear set of operations for the data type, as well as a standardized *interface* to the data. By encapsulating, and keeping the data members private, we force all non-member functions to use the member functions as an interface to the class. This is very similar in concept to the Unix kernel. Recall that application programs under Unix cannot directly access any hardware in the system, but must ask the kernel to do it for them. This allows the kernel to *hide* the hardware from the application, so that different hardware can be substituted without requiring any changes to the application programs that run on it.

Similarly, classes can hide data from the outside world, a concept known simply as **data hiding**. Like the Unix kernel, this allows the class to provide a standard interface, which is stable over long periods of time. The definition of the data members can often be drastically altered *without changing the interface as defined by the member functions*. As a result, code that uses the class will seldom need to be modified, even if the internal structure of the class is altered dramatically.

Pitfall: Why Bother?

The fact that C++ even allows public data members to be defined in somewhat unfortunate. There may be a temptation to be lazy, and define certain data members as public, to avoid the need to call member functions to access them. Doing so, however, defeats the purpose of using a class. If you want to use public data members, just use a structure, or don't use C++ at all. There is no point dealing with the added complexities of an object oriented language, if you don't take advantage of its features.

Tip of the trade: Get and Set Functions

If access to a particular data member is needed by a non-member function, you can define two simple member functions to handle it, rather than make the data members public. The convention is to use the data member's name preceded by "get_" and "set_". For example, the get and set functions for the `name` member in the `customer` class would look something like this:

```
class customer
{
    private:
        char    name[MAX_NAME+1];
        int     age;
    public:
        char    *get_name(void)
        {
            return name;
        }
        void    set_name(char *str)
        {
            strlcpy(name,str,MAX_NAME);
        }
};
```

Programming for Performance:

Because C++ classes tend to contain many small functions, C++ can make especially good use of `inline` functions. As you may recall from chapter 11, inlining a function eliminates the overhead of calling and returning from a function by inserting the function's code in place of each call, rather than placing it at one point in the program, and inserting code to branch to it. Inlining is especially useful for simple functions such as constructors, destructors, and get and set functions.

Note that the compiler must have access to the *source code* of an inlined function in order to inline it. Thus, inlined member functions are usually *defined* directly in the class definition. Inlined functions generally cannot be linked into other object files without sacrificing their `inline` status. (At least not with today's compilers and linkers.) Furthermore, inlining is only a request. The compiler may choose not to inline a particular function for optimization reasons, and may choose to inline small functions even if it hasn't been requested.

Inlining a function is as simple as adding the `inline` keyword to the definition:

```
class customer
{
    private:
        char    name[MAX_NAME+1];
        int     age;
    public:
        inline char    *get_name(void)
        {
            return name;
        }
        inline void    set_name(char *str)
        {
            strlcpy(name,str,MAX_NAME);
        }
};
```

30.4.2   Constructors and Destructors

Each C++ class has two special member functions, called the **constructor** and **destructor**. The constructor is automatically invoked when a variable is **instantiated**, i.e. when its memory allocated. The purpose of a constructor is to initialize the new object.

Programming for Performance:

> Since the constructor is called for *every* variable in a C++ program, special attention must be given to making constructors as small and fast as possible. Even short constructors add overhead to a C++ program that isn't present in other languages, so C++ programs will generally be a little slower than an equivalent C program. If, however, you do a good job optimizing constructors, you can keep the difference in performance marginal. In general, a constructor should do no more than is necessary to make the new object *safe*, such as initializing pointer members to NULL, rather than allowing garbage addresses to be used by other functions. Avoid wasteful practices like initializing entire arrays. A few *scalar* initializations are usually all it takes to make a program safe.

The destructor is called when a variable is destroyed, such as at the end of the function or block in which it is defined. Destructors are only necessary for certain types of class objects, such as those that use dynamically allocated memory or open files.

Since constructors and destructors are not explicitly called in a program, they have no return type. The name of the constructor is the same as the name of the class. The destructor uses the same name, preceded by a '~' (tilde) character.

A simple constructor and destructor for the `customer` class might look like this:

```
class customer
{
    private:
        char    name[MAX_NAME+1];
        int     age;
    public:
```

```
            customer(void);
            ~customer(void);
};

// Constructor
inline customer :: customer(void)
{
    *name = '\0';
    age = -1;
}

// Destructor
inline customer :: ~customer(void)

{
}
```

Note that the destructor does nothing here, and could be omitted entirely to save time and space. An example of a useful destructor is presented in section 30.6.

Most C++ compilers automatically inline constructor and destructor functions, although you may still explicitly request inlining just to be safe.

30.5 References

Although C++ is an extension of C, the two languages have somewhat different personalities. C is small, simple, and concrete, with only the absolutely essential features, and no redundancy. In essence, C is the ultimate minimalist language. C++ on the other hand, is more verbose, abstract, and complex, and contains some redundancy, mainly due to its backward compatibility with C.

One such redundant feature is **references**. A reference serves the same purpose as a pointer, but is more abstract. A reference variable contains an address, just like a pointer. The main difference is that references don't have to be explicitly *dereferenced*, using the '*' operator, and don't require the use of '&' when assigned the address of a variable. In other words, reference variables are used just like ordinary data variables in a program. The designers of C++ found references to be a more convenient way to handle addresses than the explicit use of pointers chosen by the designers of C. References are not a new concept, however. Many older languages such as Pascal and PL/1 use references instead of C style pointers.

Consider the following code fragment:

```
int     x,          // A data variable
        &r = x,     // A reference
        *p = &x;    // A pointer

cout << x << '\n';
cout << r << '\n';
cout << *p << '\n';
```

The three cout statements all have exactly the same effect, since x, y and *p all refer to the value of x.

All reference variables *must* be initialized to the address of another variable. After that, the two variables refer to the same address, and can be used interchangeably. This is one of the advantage of references over pointers: A reference *always* points to a legitimate object. Note that this is not an inherent property of references, but rather, it is a feature of the C++ language. We could just as easily design a language that requires all *pointers* to be initialized, but doing so in C++ would have broken its compatibility with C, which has no such requirement.

Pitfall: Dangers of Abstraction

While references are a convenient way to handle addresses, there is some danger in their use. When using references, you must be aware that they are really pointers in disguise. For example, try to predict the output of following code:

```
int     x = 1, y = 2, &r = x;

r = y;
cout << r << ' ' << x << '\n';
```

The actual output is

2 2

The assignment `r = y;` is *exactly the same* as `x = y;`, since they `r` and `x` both refer to the same address. It is easy to think of `r` as a separate variable from `x`, since it is used as such in the code. This is one reason the designers of C chose to use explicit pointers to handle addresses. Although explicit pointers are a bit more cumbersome, there is no possibility of confusing a pointer with the data it points to, since the pointer always requires a dereference operator in front of it to access the object that it points to.

While the code above illustrates the use of references in a simple setting, it is *not* the way references are most commonly used in C++ programming. More often, references are used to pass information to and from functions.[1] As an example, consider the `swap()` function defined in section 14.5. Using pointers, it would be written as follows:

```
void    swap(int *a,int *b)

{
    int     temp;

    temp = *a;
    *a = *b;
    *b = temp;
}
```

The same effect could be achieved using references:

```
void    swap(int &a,int &b)

{
    int     temp;
```

---

[1]This is also how they are typically used in Pascal and many other languages.

```
        temp = a;
        a = b;
        b = temp;
    }
```

Similarly, references can be used in place of pointers for function return values. Doing so has the same performance benefits as returning a pointer. In fact, many of the `istream` and `ostream` functions return a reference to the stream object. For example, the `operator<<` function, which defines the `<<` operator, returns a reference to the `ostream` object used as its left operand. This is why it is possible to string several `<<` operations together, as in:

```
    cout << "Name: " << name << "Age: " << age << '\n';
```

Pitfall: No Privacy

Note that you must be very careful not to modify the contents of reference argument variables, unless they are meant to be modified, since they refer to addresses outside the function. Doing so will cause unexpected side effects on other functions, which create *extremely* difficult debugging problems.

It's a good idea to use the **const** keyword with any reference argument that isn't meant to be modified. This is usually the case for arrays or structures which are passed by reference simply to save time, rather than to have their contents updated by the function.

The simple set function below demonstrates:

```
    void    customer :: set_age(const int & new_age)

    {
        age = new_age;
    }
```

Any attempt to modify `new_age` in this function would result in a compiler error, so by having the `const` keyword in the argument definition, it is impossible for the programmer to cause any side effects from this function.

30.6 Dynamic Memory Allocation in C++

Memory allocation in C++ involves the same system call as `malloc()`, but uses a different interface, and maintains a separate free store. In C++, memory is allocated with the `new` operator, and freed using the `delete` operator. The general form of a `new` operation is:

```
<pointer> = new <type>[count];
```

The `[count]` argument is optional. If omitted, `new` allocates enough memory for a single object of type `<type>`. Note that it is not necessary to multiply `count` by the size of the object, as it is with `malloc()`.

The general form for `delete` is simply

```
delete [] <pointer>;
```

The `[]` is only needed if a count was used when the array was allocated with `new`.

Pitfall: Memory Mix Ups

You should *never* intermix the use of `malloc()` and `new`, because these two allocation methods maintain separate tables keeping track of used and available memory. All memory allocated with `malloc()` *must* be freed with `free()`, and all memory allocated with `new` *must* be freed with `delete`.

Note that many C library functions, such as `strdup()` and `tempnam()` use `malloc()` to allocate memory. Any memory blocks allocated by these functions must therefore be freed using `free()`, not `delete`.

It isn't a good idea to mix C and C++ methods in general. There are many subtle differences, besides memory allocation, that can sneak up and bite you when you least expect it. If you plan to use C++ for a particular project, it's best to commit yourself to writing the purest code possible, to avoid exposing yourself to any more pitfalls than necessary.

Pitfall: Memory Leaks with `delete`

Unfortunately, the `delete` operator doesn't know if the object pointed to is a scalar or an array. It is up to you as the programmer to tell `delete` if the object is an array, by placing [] before the variable name. For example, the following code fragment illustrates how to allocate and free a single `double` object.

```
double  *p;

p = new double;
...
delete p;
```

The following code allocates and frees an array of `doubles`.

```
double  *list;

list = new double[LIST_SIZE];
...
delete [] list;
```

If you omit the [] for an array of class objects, it may cause the destructor to be called only for the first element of the list, rather than all of them. The remaining elements are no longer accessible to the program, and cannot be freed. This is known as a **memory leak**. The brackets are not strictly necessary for all arrays, but it is a good practice to use them anyway. They won't hurt anything if they weren't needed, and they help document the program a little by showing the reader that it is an array that is being freed.

Example:

The program below allocates an array just big enough for a list of numbers, and then inputs the list into the array. This program is equivalent to the example presented in section 16.1.

The input consists of the number of values, followed by the values themselves.

```
5
2.3 0.9 8.7 4.6 -1.5
```

The program...

```
#include <iostream.h>
#include <sysexits.h>

size_t  read_list(double **list);

int     main()

{
    size_t  listsize;
    double  *list, *p;

    // Read list of real numbers into array
    listsize = read_list(&list);
```

```
    // Print the list
    for (p=list; p < list+listsize; ++p)
        cout << *p << '\n';

    // Free memory allocated for the list
    delete [] list;
    return 0;
}



//
// Allocate memory for a list and read in the values
//

size_t  read_list(double **list)

{
    size_t  listsize;
    double  *temp, *p;   // Use temp in place of
                         // *list to simplify code

    // Get size of list
    cin >> listsize;
    temp = new double[listsize];
    if (temp == NULL)
    {
        cerr << "Out of memory.\n";
        exit(EX_OSERR);
    }

    // Read until EOF encountered or array is full
    for (p=temp; p<temp+listsize; ++p)
        cin >> *p;

    *list = temp;        // Return pointer to list
    return listsize;     // Return list size
}
```

30.7 Overloading and Templates

Overloading is the act of defining multiple versions of the same function or operator. This feature eliminates the need to define and remember many similar names for functions with essentially the same purpose. For example, the `strcpy()` function is unsafe to use, since it writes into an array without knowing its size. To avoid this problem, new functions such as `strncpy()` (also dangerous) and `strlcpy()` were created. Similar sets of functions exist, such as `dup()` and `dup2()`, `strcat()` and `strlcat()`, and `sprintf()` and `snprintf()`.

30.7.1 Function Overloading

Rather than come up with new function names for each variant of a function, C++ allows the same name to be used for multiple functions, as long as each function has a different **signature** (i.e. a different argument list). As long as the interface to each function is unique, the C++ compiler can easily distinguish them from each other, just as if they had different names.

For example, consider the problem of defining an absolute value function. The C library defines a separate function for each data type, including `abs()` for `int`, `labs()` for `long`, `fabs()` for `double`, and `fabsf()` for `float`.

The alternative in C is to use a macro, such as the following:

```
#define ABS(x)   ((x) < 0 ? -(x) : (x))
```

This macro works well, and is type-independent, but it still has one problem. If the argument has any side-effects, they are executed *twice*. For example, the statement

```
a = ABS(b++);
```

translates to

```
a = ((b++) < 0 ? -(b++) : (b++));
```

which cause **b** to be incremented twice.

Function overloading solves this problem by allowing us to define multiple functions with the same name, as follows:

```
int     abs(int x)

{
    return x < 0 ? -x : x;
}

long    abs(long x)

{
    return x < 0 ? -x : x;
}

double  abs(double x)

{
    return x < 0 ? -x : x;
}
```

Since each function takes a different type of argument, the C++ compiler can determine which one to call by looking at the argument list. For example, the statement

```
y = abs(2.0);
```

will call the **double** version, while

```
y = abs(2);
```

will call the **int** version.

30.7.2 Constructor Overloading

One very useful type of overloading involves constructors. The default constructor has no arguments, and simply initializes the data members using fixed values.

However, it is often useful to create additional constructors which allow the programmer to initialize a new object in different ways. For example, the `customer` class could be defined with an extra constructor which allows the programmer to specify a name and age:

```
class customer
{
    private:
        char     name[MAX_NAME+1];
        int      age;
    public:
        customer(void);         // Default constructor
        customer(char *,int); // Constructor with initializer
    ...
};


customer :: customer(void)
{
    *name = '\0';
    age = -1;
}

customer :: customer(char *iname,int iage)
{
    strlcpy(name,iname,MAX_NAME);
    age = iage;
}
```

Definitions of class instances can then take arguments to specify the initialization data.

```
customer  customer1("Bob",45);
```

30.7.3   Operator Overloading

In addition to defining normal functions, C++ allows us to define **operator functions**, which give C operators new meaning in new contexts.

The general syntax for defining an operator is

```
<type> operator <op> ( arguments )

{
    body
}
```

For example, to overload the '=' operator, you would define a function as follows:

```
class   & operator +(class arg1,class arg2)

{
    ...
}
```

Example:

> Consider the example in section 30.4, where we used member functions
> called `read()` and `print()` to input and print customer data. While
> fairly convenient, these functions don't quite fit into the C++ scheme
> for input and output. It would be nice if we could instead use the `<<`
> and `>>` operators to input and output `customer` objects directly. The
> program below demonstrates how to do this using overloaded `<<` and `>>`
> operators.
>
> ```
> #include <iostream.h>
> #include <sysexits.h>
>
> #define MAX_NAME    40
> ```

```
// Information about a customer
class customer
{
    private:
        char    name[MAX_NAME+1];
        int     age;
    public:
        customer(void);
        char    *get_name(void) { return name; }
        void    set_name(char *str)
                { strcpy(name,str); }
        int     get_age(void)   { return age; }
        void    set_age(int a) { age = a; }
};


// constructor
inline customer :: customer(void)

{
    *name = '\0';
    age = -1;
}


// Print customer data
ostream &operator <<(ostream &stream,customer &cl)

{
    stream << "Name: " << cl.get_name() <<
            "\nAge: " << cl.get_age() << '\n';
    return stream;
}


// Input customer data
istream &operator >>(istream &stream,customer &cl)
```

```
    {
        char      name[MAX_NAME+1];
        int       age;

        cout << "Name? ";
        stream.get(name,MAX_NAME,'\n');
        cl.set_name(name);
        cout << "Age? ";
        stream >> age;
        cl.set_age(age);
        return stream;
    }


    // Simple test program for customer class
    int      main(int argc,char *argv[])

    {

        customer  customer1;

        // Read data into customer1
        cin >> customer1;

        // Print data in customer1
        cout << customer1;

        return EX_OK;
    }
```

Operator functions take one or two arguments, which represent the operands to the operator. In the case of member functions, the object to which the function belongs serves as the left operand, and the single argument serves as the right operand.

Example:

The class definition below demonstrates how to define an overloaded

'+=' operator for complex numbers.

```
#include <iostream.h>

class complex
{
    private:
        double  real_part;
        double  imaginary_part;
    public:
        void print(void)
        {
            cout << '(' << real_part << ','
                 << imaginary_part << ')';
        }
        complex(double real,double imaginary)
        {
            real_part = real;
            imaginary_part = imaginary;
        }
        complex & operator +=(const complex & num2)
        {
            real_part += num2.real_part;
            imaginary_part += num2.imaginary_part;
            return *this;
        }
};


int     main(int argc,char *argv[])

{
    complex n1(4.0,5.0), n2(1.0,2.0);

    // Print raw numbers
    n1.print();
    n2.print();

    // Add numbers using overloaded += operator
```

```
        n1 += n2;

        // Print result
        n1.print();
        return 0;
    }
```

30.7.4 Template Functions

In addition to overloading, C++ offers one more feature to handle cases where a similar function must be defined for more than one type.

Consider again, the problem of defining an `abs()` function. In most languages, including C, we need a different function name for each type, such as `abs()` for `int`, `labs()` for `long`, and so on. C++ allows us to *overload* the `abs()` function, i.e. define multiple functions called `abs()`, each with a different type of formal argument. The compiler then uses the argument type to determine the appropriate instance of the function to call. While this solution is an improvement over using different function names, it still requires multiple versions of the function to be defined. These versions are highly redundant, only differing in their formal argument and return types.

A **template function** is a truly **polymorphic** function, whose formal arguments and/or return type are unspecified in the definition. Each template function definition and declaration must be preceded by a `template` statement, which defines an indeterminate type name to be used in the template function.

```
    template <class Generic_type>
```

This type name can then be used to define the arguments and return type of the function:

```
    Generic_type    abs(Generic_type a)

    {
```

```
        return a < 0 ? -a : a;
    }
```

When the function is called, the program automatically instantiates a version of the template function by substituting the type of the argument for the template type.

Example:

```
        #include <iostream.h>

        template <class Generic_type>
        Generic_type    abs(Generic_type a)
        {
            return a < 0 ? -a : a;
        }



        int     main(int argc,char *argv[])

        {
            cout << abs(2) << '\n';
            cout << abs(-2.5) << '\n';
            return 0;
        }
```

30.8   File I/O

The C++ file I/O facilities are based on the `istream` and `ostream` classes, which are themselves based on the `FILE` type.

Each C++ program begins life with three stream instances, namely `cin`, `cout` and `cerr`. Additional streams can be created using either the `open()` member function, or using one of the stream class' constructor functions. In order to use the file functions, programs must first include the file *fstream.h*. The program may then define variables of type `ifstream` for input streams, `ofstream` for output streams, and `fstream` for read/write streams. These stream variables can be used exactly like `cin`, `cout` and `cerr`. In fact, `cin` is simply an instance of the `istream` class, which is very similar to `ifstream`. Likewise, `cout` and `cerr` are instances of `ostream`, which resembles `ofstream`.

The stream classes have many member functions, each with potentially many overloaded forms. It would be rather pointless to try to cover them all in this introduction. Instead, a simple example is provided to illustrate the basics. For further information, consult your online documentation.

Example:

The program below is a simple implementation of the Unix `cat` command, which simply copies the contents of a file to the standard output.

Be reminded that using streams for this is unnecessary and inefficient. For a better solution, see the low-level I/O example presented in section 25.2.6.

```
#include <iostream.h>
#include <fstream.h>
#include <sysexits.h>

int     main(int argc,char *argv[])

{
    ifstream    infile;
    char        ch;

    // Check usage
    switch(argc)
    {
        case    2:
            // Open file given on command line
            infile.open(argv[1]);
            if ( !infile )
            {
```

```
                        cerr << "Unable to open file.\n";
                        return(EX_IOERR);
                    }
                    break;
                default:
                    cerr << "Usage: " << argv[0] <<
                            " <filename>\n";
                    return(EX_USAGE);
            }

            // Read characters from file and print
            // Can't use infile >> ch; it skips whitespace
            while ( infile.get(ch) )
                cout << ch;

            // Close infile
            infile.close();
            return 0;
        }
```

30.9 Inheritance

Inheritance allows one class to inherit much of the functionality of another class. This if often useful when defining one class which is similar to another, but has some extended capabilities. When two classes have much in common, defining and maintaining each class separately would involve a potentially large amount of redundant effort. Inheritance eliminates this redundancy, thus reducing code size and maintenance effort. Whenever the inherited class is updated, the inheriting class can absorb the changes without being modified itself.

Inheritance involves defining a **subtype**, or **subclass**, and one or more **derived classes**.

The subtype describes a generic type, which contains all the features common to each derived class. The subtype may or may not be useful in and of itself. Often, subtypes are defined for no other reason than to consolidate the common features of two or more derived classes.

Each derived class inherits the members of the subtype, and also has some unique members of its own.

Using inheritance in C++ is similar to using sub-structures in C. For example, consider the following two structures:

```
typedef struct
{
    char    first_name[MAX_NAME_LEN+1];
    char    first_name[MAX_NAME_LEN+1];
    int     age;
    double  salary;
}   faculty_t

typedef struct
{
    char    first_name[MAX_NAME_LEN+1];
    char    first_name[MAX_NAME_LEN+1];
    int     age;
    double  tuition;
}   student_t

int     main()

{
    student_t   student;
    faculty_t   professor;

    student.age = 20;
    faculty.age = 40;
    ...
    return EX_OK;
}
```

These two structures are identical, save the fact that the student is paying tuition, and the professor is being paid a salary. Any changes made to the types of first_name, last_name, or age must be made *identically* to *both* structures. It's easy to accidentally introduce slight variations when updating redundant sections of code, and the run-time errors that arise are often rather tricky to track down.

The redundancy can be eliminated by using a sub-structure:

```
typedef struct
{
    char    first_name[MAX_NAME_LEN+1];
    char    first_name[MAX_NAME_LEN+1];
    int     age;
} person_t;

typedef struct
{
    person_t    personal_info;
    double      salary;
} faculty_t;

typedef struct
{
    person_t    personal_info;
    double      tuition;
} student_t;

int     main()

{
    student_t   student;
    faculty_t   professor;

    student.personal_info.age = 20;
    faculty.personal_info.age = 40;
    ...
    return EX_OK;
}
```

Now, if any changes need to be made to the personal info of both faculty and students, only one change is necessary to the program, namely in the person_t

structure. The only disadvantage is the need for the added structure identifier
`personal_info` in each reference, as seen in `main()` above.

If you are following strict object oriented design, you would need to use `get()`
and `set()` functions to reference the fields of `person_t`, since a statement such
as `student.personal_info.age = 20` accesses the data members of two different
structures. Technically, this violates the idea of encapsulation, since each function
should only access the data members of one class. As noted in section 18.3, encapsulation is important in minimizing the number of functions impacted by changes
to the structure. A `set_age()` function or macro would provide a simple cure for
this problem:

```
#define SET_AGE(person,age) ((person).age = (age))
...

SET_AGE(student.person,20);
```

Inheritance in C++ classes serves the same purpose, but provides a slightly more
convenient way to access the shared members. Member functions of derived classes
can *directly* access the data members of the subclass, without the need for extra
identifiers.

In order to make this possible, the data members to be inherited must be defined as
`protected`, rather than `private`. The `protected` members of a class are similar to
`private` members. The only difference is that `protected` members can be accessed
by member functions of a derived class.

Example:

> The program below demonstrates the use of inheritance, while at the
> same time, proving that professors really are people. In addition to the
> professor and student classes, you could also define a TA class, using
> `char` for salary to save space.

```
#include <iostream.h>
#include <sysexits.h>
#include <String.h>
```

```
#define MAX_STUDS    20

// Generic person class for use as a subtype
class person
{
    public:

        // Fields in person should be initialized here
        // not redundantly in derived classes
        person(void)
        {
            first_name = last_name = "";
        }

    // Data members inherited by derived classes
    protected:
        String  first_name;
        String  last_name;
        int     age;
};


// Professor class derived from generic person
class faculty : public person
{
    public:
        void    input(void);
        void    output(void);

    private:    // Info unique to faculty
        double  salary;
        double  research_grants;
};


// Input faculty information from standard input

void faculty :: input(void)
```

```
{
    cout << "First name? ";
    cin >> first_name;
    cout << "Last name? ";
    cin >> last_name;
    cout << "Salary? ";
    cin >> salary;
    cout << "Grant money? ";
    cin >> research_grants;
}


// Print faculty info to standard output

void faculty :: output(void)

{
    cout << "First name: " << first_name << endl;
    cout << "Last name: " << last_name << endl;
    cout << "Salary: " << salary << endl;
    cout << "Grant money: " << research_grants << endl;
}


// Student class derived from generic person

class student : public person
{
    public:
        void    input(void);
        void    output(void);

    private:    // Info unique to students
        double  tuition;
};


int     main(int argc,char *argv[])
```

```
    {
        faculty professor;
        student studs[MAX_STUDS];

        // Input and output info on a professor
        professor.input();
        professor.output();
        return EX_OK;
    }
```

30.10 Friend Classes

Friend Classes are a facility which allow one class to directly access the data members of another. While fairly simple to use, friend classes reduce the modularity of a program in the same way as public data members or global variables would. Friend classes offer an alternative to using `get()` and `set()` functions.

While they may save some tedium during coding, using friend classes directly violates the principle of data hiding. This, in turn, reduces the modularity and modifiability of your code. The potential loss of modifiability in the code is a good argument for not using friend classes at all.

Contrary to what you may hear elsewhere, the use of friend classes is *never* necessary. Avoiding friend classes in favor of data hiding, much like avoiding `gotos` in favor of structured code, may require adapting your ideas a little, but won't prove difficult. There is *always* a workable approach to be found that won't require you to sacrifice data hiding. Usually, creating a *get* or *set* function, or an overloaded operator, will prove simple enough.

30.11 Conclusion

Beyond the individual capabilities of the C++ features described here, is a wealth of possibilities as they are used in combination. These topics are best handled by a text dedicated to C++ programming and all of its nuances. Several references are listed in the bibliography for interested readers.

Appendix A

GNU Sites

The primary site for *GNU* software is *http://www.gnu.org*. This site is heavily loaded, however, so users are strongly encouraged to use one of the *mirror* sites instead. These sites are updated frequently to ensure that their content matches the primary site. The following is a list of GNU mirror sites as of Feb 15, 1999. For the latest list of mirrors, visit *www.gnu.org*.

Country	Mirror Site
Australia	http://gnu.cs.ntu.edu.au
Austria	http://gd.tuwien.ac.at/gnu.www.gnu.org/
Brazil	http://gnu.mirrors.com.br
France	http://gnu.april.org
	http://gnu.via.ecp.fr
Germany	http://agnes.dida.physik.uni-essen.de/˜gnu
Greece	http://www.auth.gr/gnu
Indonesia	http://gnu.indoglobal.com
Italy	http://it.gnu.org/
Norway	http://classic.csc.no/˜jonr/www.gnu.org/
Poland	http://pl.gnu.org
Russia	http://www.gnu.org.ru
Sweden	http://gnu.archive.sunet.se
	http://gnu.nocrew.org
Turkey	http://gnu.bilkent.edu.tr
United Kingdom	http://www.gnu.nelefa.org
United States	http://gnu.internexus.net
Yugoslavia	http://gnu.fon.bg.ac.yu

Appendix B

News Groups

The following is a snapshot of existing Unix news groups as of Feb 15, 1999. For a current listing, run the command `newsgroups unix`.

alt.unix.interix
alt.unix.wizards
alt.unix.wizards.free
ca.unix
comp.infosystems.www.servers.unix
comp.security.unix
comp.sources.unix
comp.std.unix
comp.unix.admin
comp.unix.advocacy
comp.unix.aix]
comp.unix.amiga
comp.unix.aux
comp.unix.bsd.386bsd.announce
comp.unix.bsd.386bsd.misc
comp.unix.bsd.bsdi.announce
comp.unix.bsd.bsdi.misc
comp.unix.bsd.freebsd.announce
comp.unix.bsd.freebsd.misc
comp.unix.bsd.misc
comp.unix.bsd.netbsd.announce
comp.unix.bsd.netbsd.misc

comp.unix.bsd.openbsd.announce
comp.unix.bsd.openbsd.misc
comp.unix.cde
comp.unix.cray
comp.unix.dos-under-unix
comp.unix.internals
comp.unix.large
comp.unix.machten
comp.unix.misc
comp.unix.osf.misc
comp.unix.osf.osf1
comp.unix.pc-clone.16bit
comp.unix.pc-clone.32bit
comp.unix.programmer
comp.unix.questions
comp.unix.sco.announce
comp.unix.sco.misc
comp.unix.sco.programmer
comp.unix.shell
comp.unix.solaris
comp.unix.sys3
comp.unix.sys5.misc
comp.unix.sys5.r3
comp.unix.sys5.r4
comp.unix.ultrix
comp.unix.unixware.announce
comp.unix.unixware.misc
comp.unix.user-friendly
comp.unix.xenix.misc
comp.unix.xenix.sco
comp.windows.x.i386unix
de.comp.os.unix.apps
de.comp.os.unix.bsd
de.comp.os.unix.discussion
de.comp.os.unix.linux.hardware
de.comp.os.unix.linux.misc
de.comp.os.unix.linux.newusers
de.comp.os.unix.misc
de.comp.os.unix.networking

de.comp.os.unix.programming
de.comp.os.unix.sinix
de.comp.os.unix.x11
de.comp.sources.unix
de.comp.sys.amiga.unix
es.foro.unix
fj.questions.unix
fj.unix
fj.unix.wizards
fr.comp.os.unix
it.comp.unix
milw.unix
no.unix
relcom.fido.ru.unix
tw.comp.unix
uiuc.org.acm.sigunix
umich.caen.support.unix
umich.unix
umich.unix.admin
umn.comp.os.unix
umn.cs.systems.unix
umn.itlab.systems.unix
umn.local-lists.tc-unix
umn.local-lists.techc-unix
uwisc.unixpc
winternet.help.unix
z-netz.alt.rechner.unix.diskussion
z-netz.alt.rechner.unix.quellen
z-netz.rechner.unix
za.unix.misc
za.unix.sco

Index

Bibliography

[1] Alfred V. Aho, Ravi Sethi, and Jeffrey Ullman. *Compilers — Principles, Techniques, and Tools.* Addison-Wesley, Reading, Massachusetts, 1986.

[2] Fred Butzen. *COHERENT^{tm} User's Manual.* 1994.

[3] Curtis F. Gerald and Patrick O. Wheatley. *Applied Numerical Analysis.* Addison-Wesley, Reading, Massachusetts, 1989.

[4] Eric F. Johnson and Kevin Reichard. *X Window Applications Programming.* MIS Press, Portland, Oregon, 1989.

[5] Brian Kernighan and Dennis Ritchie. *The C Programming Language.* Prentice-Hall Software Series, Englewood Cliffs, New Jersey 07632, 1978.

[6] Richard J. Larson and Morris L. Marx. *An Introduction to Mathematical Statistics and Its Applications.* Prentice-Hall, Englewood Cliffs, New Jersey, 1986.

[7] H.T. Lau. *A numerical Library in C for Scientists and Engineers.* CRC Press, 1995.

[8] Stanley B. Lippman. *C++ Primer.* Addison-Wesley, Reading, Massachusetts, 1991.

[9] M. Morris Mano. *Digital Design.* Prentice-Hall, Englewood Cliffs, New Jersey, second edition, 1991.

[10] M. Morris Mano. *Computer System Architecture.* Prentice-Hall, Englewood Cliffs, New Jersey, third edition, 1992.

[11] Lewis J. Pinson and Richard S. Wiener. *Objective-C: Object-Oriented Programming Techniques.*

[12] Lewis J. Pinson and Richard S. Wiener. *Applications of Object Oriented Programming; C++, SmallTalk, Actor, Objective-C, Object PASCAL.* Addison Wesley, Reading, Massachusetts, 1990.

[13] William H. Press, Saul A. Teukolsky, William T. Vetterling, and Brian P. Flannery. *Numerical Recipes in C.* Cambridge University Press, second edition, 1993.

[14] Abraham Siblerschatz and James L. Peterson. *Operating System Concepts.* Addison Wesley, Reading, Massachusetts, 1988.

[15] Thomas P. Skinner. *Assembly Language Programming for the 8086 Family.* Wiley Press, New York, 1985.

[16] Mark G. Sobell. *A Practical Guide to the Unix System.* Benjamin Cummings, Reading, Massachusetts, 1989.

[17] Jean-Paul Tremblay and Paul G. Sorenson. *The Theory and Practice of Compiler Writing.* McGraw-Hill, New York, 1985.

[18] Douglas A. Young. *X Window Systems Programming and Applications with Xt.* Prentice-Hall Software Series, Englewood Cliffs, New Jersey 07632, 1989.